COPING WITH THE FUTURE

Coping with the Future has been written in response to widespread international awareness that the future is not predictable. In political and economic terms, we are in unknown territory, with daily developments around Brexit and the Trump Presidency, and "Kodak moments" in business. On the other hand, business leaders demand certainty, which is not available.

This book redefines the nature of modern business. In contrast to recent trends, it has a focus on human-centred manufacturing and on decision-making that goes beyond a focus on short-term profit. The liberal capitalism of the USA and the UK is not the only current variety of capitalism. Business is not just about managers, but also requires participation and engagement by workers.

Since the financial crash of 2008, there has been much talk about the need for fresh approaches to business, but little has changed. This book pulls together current research and practice and poses new questions based on case studies. There is no one simple best way, but an uncertain future can be addressed, drawing on diverse past experience and cases.

The book addresses an intended audience in business and universities, including business schools, around the world. The debate takes a broader approach, involving research in the social sciences and approaches from philosophy. The world has always been unpredictable, but we have allowed ourselves to be comforted by convenient myths. It is time to wake up.

Hans Christian Garmann Johnsen is a Professor at the University of Agder, Norway.

Halvor Holtskog is a Professor at the Norwegian University of Science and Technology (NTNU), Norway.

Richard Ennals is a Professor at the University of Agder, Norway and Linnaeus University, Sweden.

COPING WITH THE FUTURE

Rethinking Assumptions for Society, Business and Work

Edited by Hans Christian Garmann Johnsen, Halvor Holtskog and Richard Ennals

LONDON AND NEW YORK

First published 2018
by Routledge
2 Park Square, Milton Park, Abingdon, Oxon OX14 4RN

and by Routledge
711 Third Avenue, New York, NY 10017

Routledge is an imprint of the Taylor & Francis Group, an informa business

© 2018 selection and editorial matter, Hans Christian Garmann Johnsen, Halvor Holtskog and Richard Ennals; individual chapters, the contributors

The right of Hans Christian Garmann Johnsen, Halvor Holtskog and Richard Ennals to be identified as the authors of the editorial material, and of the authors for their individual chapters, has been asserted in accordance with sections 77 and 78 of the Copyright, Designs and Patents Act 1988.

All rights reserved. No part of this book may be reprinted or reproduced or utilised in any form or by any electronic, mechanical, or other means, now known or hereafter invented, including photocopying and recording, or in any information storage or retrieval system, without permission in writing from the publishers.

Trademark notice: Product or corporate names may be trademarks or registered trademarks, and are used only for identification and explanation without intent to infringe.

British Library Cataloguing-in-Publication Data
A catalogue record for this book is available from the British Library

Library of Congress Cataloging-in-Publication Data
Names: Johnsen, Hans Chr. Garmann, 1955- editor. | Holtskog, Halvor, 1963- editor. | Ennals, J. R. (John Richard), 1951- editor.
Title: Coping with the future: rethinking assumptions for society, business and work / [edited by] Hans Christian Garmann Johnsen, Halvor Holtskog and Richard Ennals.
Description: Abingdon, Oxon; New York, NY: Routledge, 2018. | Includes bibliographical references.
Identifiers: LCCN 2017055031| ISBN 9781138559318 (hardback) | ISBN 9781138559325 (pbk.)
Subjects: LCSH: Economic history–21st century. | Forecasting. | Future, The. | Social change. | Organizational change.
Classification: LCC HC59.3 .C67 2018 | DDC 303.49–dc23
LC record available at https://lccn.loc.gov/2017055031

ISBN: 978-1-138-55931-8 (hbk)
ISBN: 978-1-138-55932-5 (pbk)
ISBN: 978-0-203-71289-4 (ebk)

Typeset in Bembo
by Deanta Global Publishing Services, Chennai, India

CONTENTS

List of illustrations   x
List of boxes   xi
List of contributors   xiii
Preface   xviii

Introduction: A disruptive world and ways of knowing   1
Hans Christian Garmann Johnsen, Halvor Holtskog and Richard Ennals

   Coping with a disruptive world   2
   Facing change   3
   Are we facing systemic change?   6
   The social construction of social science   9
   Understand the past, make sense of the present and prepare for the future   11

PART I
Future political, social and institutional landscape   15

1   Coping with politics: From post-nationalism to re-nationalism   17
Hans Christian Garmann Johnsen and Jon P. Knudsen

   The re-emergence of the nation-state   18
   Historical traits   19
   Nationalism, universalism and enlightenment   30

2 Coping with structural change: Understanding
   framework conditions   34
   *Jon P. Knudsen, Hans Christian Garmann Johnsen
   and Aris Kaloudis*

   The importance of institutional structures 35
   Systems and institutions 35
   The shaping of competitive advantage and institutions 38
   Resilience of the Nordic model? 42
   The Norwegian collaborative system 44
   Forms of modernity 48

3 Coping with globalisation: Local knowledge and
   multinational companies   51
   Mariann Berge, Anne Grethe Syversen and Halvor Holtskog

   Globalisation and multinational companies (MNCs) 52
   The local economy 54
   MNCs and local strategies 56
   Knowledge sharing 62
   The two cases 63
   MNCs and local economies 66

4 Coping with economic policy: Innovation policy in
   times of disruption   69
   *Hans Christian Garmann Johnsen, Jan Ole Rypestøl and
   Ann Camilla Schulze-Krogh*

   Coping with the market 70
   Innovation policy 71
   Specialisation and diversification 77
   How can we cope with the market in times of disruption? 79

PART II
Knowing the future   85

5 Coping with ways of knowing: A pluralist perspective
   on knowledge   87
   Hans Christian Garmann Johnsen and Olav Eikeland

   Ways of knowing: Knowledge forms 90
   From individual knowledge to social knowledge 95

6 Coping with decisions: First I imagine, then I know 99
   Carla Susana A. Assuad and Hans Grelland

   The art of imagining 100
   The relation between knowledge and rational thinking 101
   Looking forward: Short and long-term perspective 103
   Imagination: A source of knowledge 105
   Science fiction that shapes the future 107
   Selective rationality: Predictions that never happened 108
   What do we imagine about artificial intelligence and
      genetic engineering? 109
   The role of imagination 110

7 Coping with sustainability: The need for
   non-instrumental thinking 114
   Karen Landmark, Hans Grelland and Christian Johnsen

   The sustainability challenge 115
   Corporate sustainability efforts today 116
   From nature to environment: The instrumentalisation
      of the world 118
   What can we learn from philosophy? 121
   Notes 125

8 Coping with methodology: Validity and knowledge
   about the future 126
   *Hans Christian Garmann Johnsen, Jan Ole Rypestøl
   and Mariann Berge*

   Rethinking methodology 127
   Social science in the post-positivist age 128
   Historical traits 131
   The one-dimensional concept of knowledge 135
   The two-dimensional concept of knowledge 138
   Comparison of the two concepts 140
   Actor and system 143
   Methodology for coping with the future 145

PART III
Future technology, organisation and work 149

9 Coping with technology: A future of robots? 151
   Halvor Holtskog, Lars Harald Lied and Geir Ringen

viii Contents

    What is technology? 152
    Absorption models of technology change 153
    Implications for policy and social organisation 162
    Note 165

10 Coping with Humanism: A Posthuman future?   166
   Evi D. Sampanikou and Hans Christian Garmann Johnsen

    What does it mean to be human? 167
    Our methodological approach 168
    Coping with Humanism or Humanism re-invented 170
    Posthumanism in times of Transhumanism 182
    Notes 185

11 Coping with social learning: Social and economic change
   through engagement   187
   *Richard Ennals, Björn Nelson, Anders Ingwald, Viktoria Johansson
   and Victor Lagercrantz*

    Learning and innovation through dialogue 188
    The importance of dialogue 190
    Collaborative advantage and development 192
    Taking forward sustainable regional development 194
    Learning to cope with local challenges 197

12 Coping with organisations: Socio-technical, dialogical
   and beyond   201
   *Hans Christian Garmann Johnsen, Ida Lervik Midtbø
   and Richard Ennals*

    The role of organisations 202
    Organisations as technical systems 207
    Organisations as human systems 208
    Beyond the divide 211

13 Coping with leadership: The role of judgement   214
   *Lars Harald Lied, Charles Barthold and
   Hans Christian Garmann Johnsen*

    Leadership in a disruptive world 215
    Decomposing leadership 217
    Leadership in a dialogical organisation 221
    The future leader must show good judgement 228
    Judgement is based on reflection 231

14 Coping with work: Redefining relations between work life
and society 234
Thomas Owren and Migle Helmersen

    The future of work 235
    Development of the "normal model" of work 236
    The new redundancies: The unhealthy worker and
        unhealthy youth effects 241
    The call for inclusion: Building down disabling
        barriers in organisations 245
    Redefining work? 255

Conclusion 258
*Hans Christian Garmann Johnsen, Halvor Holtskog
and Richard Ennals*

    The challenge 259
    Past, present and future 260
    Rethinking assumptions for society, business and work 260

References *265*
Author index *280*
Subject index *282*

LIST OF ILLUSTRATIONS

Figures

4.1	The relationship between politics and market	76
4.2	Innovation policies and change	82

Tables

I.1	The scope of the book	12
1.1	Contrasting the four traditions	25
2.1	The evolution of industrial capitalism	39
3.1	Local economy response to globalisation	67
5.1	Knowledge and time	89
5.2	Ways of knowing	90
8.1	Knowledge and mind	133
8.2	Knowledge and levels of analysis	134
8.3	How social science can influence society as a knowledge system	136
10.1	Transhumanism and Posthumanism in cartoons	183
13.1	Leader strategies related to the time and scope dimensions	230

BOXES

I.1	The Kodak moment	4
I.2	Creative destruction	6
I.3	The integrated nature of change	7
1.1	UK and Brexit	18
1.2	The future of Europe	22
1.3	Kinds of nationalism	26
1.4	Danish, Norwegian and Swedish states	27
1.5	Inaugural address by President Barack Obama	30
1.6	The Kodak moment of politics	32
2.1	The evolution of industrial structure	37
2.2	Structural social challenges	40
2.3	Development of the Norwegian Tripartite Collaboration	45
2.4	The Kodak moment of structural change	49
3.1	The Eyde cluster	53
3.2	Agglomeration	54
3.3	Case A: Norwegian oil service company	57
3.4	Case B: Norwegian manufacturing company	59
3.5	The Kodak moment of globalisation	66
4.1	Silicon Valley	71
4.2	The Digital Norway initiative	80
4.3	The Kodak moment of economic policy	82
5.1	The Kodak moment of knowing	98
6.1	Electric cars	100
6.2	The Kodak moment of rationality	112
7.1	Climate change	116
7.2	The Kodak moment of sustainability	124

8.1	The Kodak moment of methodology	146
9.1	The car industry	156
9.2	Different pathways required by a transition to a state of Industry 4.0	160
9.3	The Kodak moment of technology	164
10.1	*Watchmen*	171
10.2	*The Killing Joke*	171
10.3	*Judge Dredd*	172
10.4	Druuna	173
10.5	*The Black Incal*	174
10.6	*Metabarons*	175
10.7	Euromanga	176
10.8	*The City that Never Existed*	177
10.9	*The Sarcophagus*	178
10.10	*The Japanese*	178
10.11	*Deuteronomion*	180
10.12	Cashhan	182
10.13	The Kodak moment of Posthumanism	184
11.1	Sustainable Regional Development	189
11.2	The Kodak moment of social learning	199
12.1	The Norwegian workplace discourses	204
12.2	The Kodak moment of organisations	213
13.1	Diesel-gate	222
13.2	The Lean leader	223
13.3	The Kodak moment of leadership	233
14.1	Global challenges to the "normal model" of work	238
14.2	Sissel	242
14.3	Anne	244
14.4	Trygve	247
14.5	Frank	249
14.6	Scandic hotels are creating jobs for people with intellectual disability	253
14.7	The Kodak moment of work	256
C.1	Rethinking assumptions	261

CONTRIBUTORS

Carla Susana A. Assuad is a PhD Fellow at the Department of Manufacturing and Civil Engineering in the Norwegian University of Science and Technology. Her work focuses on using experimental research and computer simulation to identify decision-making patterns in social systems with long delays, feedback and nonlinearities. She is also interested in environmental issues and the dynamics of social institutions, humans and nature. She has worked with climate change and sustainable development topics both at the country and organisational level. Her PhD project focuses on understanding the rationality behind short-term and long-term decision making in the organisation in the context of sustainable development.

Charles Barthold is a Lecturer in People Management at the Open University (UK). Charles is interested in the intersection of financialisation and political and ethical responses to it. Similarly, he is interested in poststructuralism, critical management studies and precarity.

Mariann Berge is a PhD student at the School of Business and Law – University of Agder, Department of Working Life and Innovation. Her research interests focus on multinational companies (MNCs) and the role of regional innovation policy.

Olav Eikeland gained his PhD in ancient philosophy in 1993. He is Professor of Educational and Work Life Research at the University College of Oslo and Akershus (HiOA). From 1985 to 2008 he worked at the Work Research Institute (WRI) in Oslo. Besides ancient philosophy, his research centres on general theories of knowledge, philosophical and methodological aspects of social science and research and learning in modern organisations.

Richard Ennals is a Professor of Working Life and Innovation at the University of Agder, Norway; Professor of Skill and Technology, Linnaeus University, Sweden; editor-in-chief of the *European Journal of Workplace Innovation*; co-editor of the *International Journal of Action Research*; and review editor of *AI and Society: Knowledge, Culture and Communication*.

Hans Grelland is a Professor of Quantum Chemistry and Lecturer in Philosophy at the University of Agder, Norway. His background is in science and philosophy studies at the University of Oslo and Norwegian University of Science and Technology in Trondheim. He has an MSc and PhD in quantum chemistry, and an MA in philosophy. His research interests are phenomenology and existentialism, the philosophy of quantum and relativity physics and the mathematical structure of quantum mechanics.

Migle Helmersen has a PhD from the University of Oslo. Her thesis discussed health and work environment among women in unskilled occupations. Her research work is within the field of work-related health and work ability, health services and work environment, sickness absence, migration, vocational training, mastery, organisational well-being, social support and work ability.

Halvor Holtskog is a Professor at the Norwegian University of Science and Technology (NTNU), department of Manufacturing and Civil Engineering. The subject of his PhD was organizational learning and knowledge creation. His research interests lie in the field of studying socio-technical concerns, ranging from organizational to technology-based studies.

Anders Ingwald leads the Skill and Technology group in the Faculty of Technology at Linnaeus University and is director of the Master's programme in Skill and Technology. He has extensive experience as an engineer and lectures on Quality and Project Management. His research is on management issues in industry and higher education.

Viktoria Johansson is a Senior Lecturer in Skill and Technology at Linnaeus University. She is an experienced teacher and leads the Vocational Teacher Education programme and the Vocational Teacher Network at Linnaeus University, as well as co-operating on frequent projects with the National Agency of Education. Her research is on Dialogue Seminars in Vocational Teacher Education.

Hans Christian Garmann Johnsen is a Professor of Work Life Research at the Department of Work Life and Innovation, University of Agder, Norway. He has a background in economics and political theory and is currently teaching philosophy of science. He has published articles and books about the knowledge economy and the role of university in society. His latest book is *The New Natural Resource* (Routledge, 2015), and his latest edited books are *Higher Education in a Sustainable*

Society (2014) and *Applied Social Science Research in a Regional Knowledge System* (Routledge, 2017).

Aris Kaloudis has been a Professor of Sustainable Economics at the Norwegian University of Science and Technology (NTNU) since 2014 and is head of unit of the Department of Industrial Economics and Technology Management, section Economics and Management at NTNU Gjøvik. A considerable part of Kaloudis's research activities are dedicated to studies of structural change and specialisation trends in national, sectoral and regional innovation systems. He is teaching, among other topics, Norwegian Work Law for Business students and Scientific Methodology – Quantitative methods. He has more than seven years' experience as practitioner of economic and research policy making at the Central Bank of Norway and the Norwegian Ministry of Education and Research, as well as wide expertise in evaluations of research and innovation programmes, analysis of researcher mobility and employment trends and assessments of research policies in Norway, Scandinavia and the European Union.

Jon P. Knudsen holds a PhD in Cultural Geography from Lund University (Sweden) and is currently working as an Associate Professor at the University of Agder. His main research interests are within comparative cultural geography. He has mainly written on the variation in and interdependency between economic, political and religious rationales as they characterise European regions.

Victor Lagercrantz is a former chef and student of political science at Linnaeus University. After a year as president of Linnaeus University Student Union, he now chairs a new project in which Linnaeus University Student Union is addressing sustainable regional development, funded by the Kalmar region.

Karen Landmark is a PhD candidate at Agder University and the Norwegian University of Science and Technology (NTNU) in the field of Business Studies and Sustainability. She also works as an advisor for the process industry on sustainable transition, development of holistic organisational culture and change management.

Lars Harald Lied has a background in military and business life and has experience in leadership and industrial improvement processes. He is currently employed in a Norwegian industrial company (Nammo Raufoss AS), where he is working on an industrial PhD degree closely linked to the company's improvement processes focusing on Lean Management and work-life innovation. Academically, he is affiliated with the University of Agder.

Ida Lervik Midtbø is a PhD student at the Mohn Centre of Innovation and Regional Development at Western Norway University of Applied Sciences, studying innovation processes and professionalism within the context of education.

Björn Nelson is an Associate Professor in Skill and Technology at Linnaeus University. He is a forest owner and leads courses on Forest and Wood; Sustainable Enterprise; Dialogue, Reflection and Mentoring; and Sustainable Regional Development, working with local villages. His research is on the skill of product developers in a major international company based in the region.

Geir Ringen is a Professor at the Norwegian University of Science and Technology (NTNU) Department of Mechanical and Industrial Engineering and Department of Manufacturing and Civil Engineering. He completed his PhD at NTNU in 2010 on organisational learning and knowledge creation. His research interests lie in the field of studying socio-technical concerns, ranging from organisational to more technology-based studies.

Jan Ole Rypestøl is a PhD Research Fellow at the University of Agder and a researcher at Agder Research, Norway. His research focuses mainly on innovation, entrepreneurship and regional development. Rypestøl is a former serial entrepreneur with substantial international experience and also a highly appreciated facilitator of entrepreneurship training programmes.

Evi (Evangelia) D. Sampanikou is a Professor of Art History and Visual Culture in the Department of Cultural Technology and Communication at the University of the Aegean, Greece (esampa@ct.aegean.gr). Her research interests include art history and theory, the history of photography, comics and graphic-arts studies, pop culture, Postmodernism and Posthumanism, as well as new media art. Her earlier studies also include archaeology, English literature and c. sixteenth- and seventeenth-century Post-Byzantine art focusing on Renaissance influences. She has published several books and articles on the topics of art history, photography and visual culture.

Ann Camilla Schulze-Krogh is a PhD student at University of Agder, School of Business and Law, Department of Working Life and Innovation. Her major areas of interest are regional industrial development, regional innovation policy and regional policy learning.

Antonis Nikolopoulos Soloup is a caricaturist and comic-book artist who collaborates with newspapers and magazines in Greece. He studied Political Sciences at the Panteion University and obtained a PhD (Cultural Technology and Communication/University of the Aegean). He has published 14 books with cartoons and comics and his PhD on the History of Comics in Greece. His graphic novel *Aivali* received the prize for best comic and best scenario at 2015 Comicdom Athens and the "Coup de Coeur 2016" in the 17th Rendez-vous du Carnet De Voyage (Clermont Ferrand, France). It has also been translated into French and Turkish. To date it has been presented in Brussels, Paris, Clermont-Ferrand, Istanbul, Ayvalik, Oxford and Kiev. Original works and archives from *Ayvali* have been exhibited at the Benaki Museum, the Athens Concert Hall and many other galleries across Greece.

Thomas Owren is a PhD student at University of Agder and has a stipend position at the Mohn Centre of Innovation and Regional Development, Western Norway University of Applied Science. He has a BA in Social Education and an MA in Community Work, and he is currently researching innovation in working life, specifically exploring job creation for persons with intellectual disability in ordinary workplaces.

Anne Grethe Syversen is an Assistant Professor in the Department of Industrial Economics and Technology Management, Norwegian University of Science and Technology. She is a PhD candidate, and her main research interests are strategy and knowledge management.

PREFACE

Coping with the Future has been written in response to widespread international awareness that the future is not predictable. The book combines three lines of thought: (a) the changes that we see and that are likely to come and that will influence society, business and work; (b) different ways of building knowledge about social and economic change; and (c) the special role of social science in providing valid knowledge for the future.

The core things about the changes we describe are the assumptions that

1. they are disruptive, which means that they are to some extent unforeseeable;
2. we are in a transformation, that is, a change at a more basic system level;
3. there is an integrated and parallel change in different subsystems at the same time.

The point with these kinds of changes is that we cannot extrapolate from the past into the future, and we cannot isolate one factor and look at what influences it. Thus, some of the key preconditions in traditional scientific thinking – that the world consists of atomic facts, and that we can isolate a factor we would like to explain – do not apply.

Our team of contributors pulls together current research and practice and poses new questions based on case studies. Most of the contributors are Norwegian, but the perspective is international. There is no one simple best way, but an uncertain future can be addressed, drawing on diverse experience and cases. The book is a result of constructive discussions at seminars held in Copenhagen, Denmark and in Lesvos, Greece.

The book addresses an intended audience in business and universities, including business schools, around the world. The debate takes a broader approach, involving research in the social sciences and approaches from philosophy. The world has always been unpredictable, but we can no longer allow ourselves to be comforted by convenient myths. It is time to wake up.

Hans Christian Garmann Johnsen,
Halvor Holtskog and Richard Ennals
Kristiansand, Gjøvik, London

INTRODUCTION

A disruptive world and ways of knowing

*Hans Christian Garmann Johnsen,
Halvor Holtskog and Richard Ennals*

Coping with a disruptive world

How should we think as we prepare for the future, and how does that impact on the way we do social science? These are important questions at a time when there is a call for change in the trajectory that has produced modern society. Modern society is a result of social and economic development as well as science. Rethinking assumptions in modern society does not imply abandoning all aspects of modernisation but adjusting aspects of modern society that are less sustainable. What should be adjusted? If we cannot predict the future, how can we choose between strategies? In this book, we try to address this issue by pointing out some likely ways of adjusting the present trajectory in modern society, business and work towards more sustainable solutions; and by discussing ways of thinking that help us reflect on a sustainable future.

"We are entering upon an age of reconstruction, in religion, in science, and in political thought. Such ages, if they are to avoid mere ignorant oscillation between extremes, must seek truth in its ultimate depths", the British analytical philosopher Alfred North Whitehead wrote in 1925 (Whitehead 1967, p. 34). He sensed the social instability of the mid 1920s; we now know that the instability would become even worse in the following years. Whitehead believed in mathematical logic and its scientific counterpart, logical positivism. His main point was that the whole enlightenment project was under threat. Modern society, which started with the American and French revolutions and brought democracy to the Western world, had been interpreted by Nazism, Fascists and Communists in ways that created an inhuman society.

This was also the argument in Karl Polanyi's 1944 book *The Great Transformation: The Political and Economic Origins of Our Time*. Polanyi argued that the industrial era had seen a break-up of the former social and economic order: the rural and farmer society. The new industrial order developed in parallel with urbanisation, social structuration and a transformation from a relational into a transaction based society. In the twentieth century, he observed how this same order had escalated into mass production society and created a big class divide with an increasing working class with decreasing influence in society. This, he argued, was a situation that could not prevail.

In the reconstruction of society after World War II, Enlightenment principles of universal human rights and democracy had to be rediscovered. What followed was gradually expanding optimism in science and technology, leading to more material wealth and more people living in democratic countries and taking part in a globalised world. Martin Ford, in his award-winning book *The Rise of the Robots*, wrote:

> This "golden age" for the West was characterised by a seemingly perfect symbiosis between rapid technological progress and the welfare of the workforce. As the machines used in production improved, the productivity of the works operating those machines likewise increased, making them more valuable and allowing them to demand higher wages. Throughout the post-war period,

advancing technology deposited money directly into the pockets of average workers, as their welfare rose in tandem with soaring productivity. Those workers, in turn, went out and spent their ever-increasing incomes, further driving demand for the products and services they were producing.

(Ford 2015, p. x)

The post-war golden age was perhaps the culmination of the industrial area that Polanyi had described and that started in the nineteenth century. Instead of the gloomy vision that Polanyi portrayed, in the second half of the twentieth century, we see how industrialisation developed into a more computer-driven kind of flexible mass production and increased welfare for the mass of people beyond historical comparisons. This post-war order was enhanced by global development: Post-nationalism and the European internal market of the 1980s and the increased liberalisation of global trade in the 1990s after the end of the Cold War were followed by more countries becoming democratic. That made the first years of the twenty-first century into a decade of globalisation. This is now under threat.

There are several reasons for the contraction we now see in the form of hostility towards openness, re-nationalisation and anti-globalisation. Over several decades, there has been growing economic inequality, inequitable distribution of economic growth and unevenly distributed economic and social progress. This comes in addition to technological changes, the need to think more sustainable and changes in markets, in products and in technology, which are challenging regions, companies and organisations and have implications for social structure and work. What is the direction of the road ahead? Are we in a "normal" situation where these challenges are merely ordinary problems that can be handled within the "existing order", or are we facing a change of order, a *reconstruction*, as Whitehead talked about, or a *transformation*, the word used by Polanyi?

In this book, we discuss some of these changes from a social science perspective, and point to systemic changes that are happening as we write, but we are not trying to answer the question above. We do not claim a similarity between the situation today and in the mid-war period. However, what we argue is that in any period of systemic change one has to choose direction, and some choices turn out to be better than others. *The book points out important choices of directions in a wide range of areas that will define our common future and that will retain core enlightenment ideals.* We also argue that there is a big difference between coping with a future within an existing order, compared with a future facing systemic change. Our main focus is on discussing *how social science can be relevant to supporting social development within a situation of systemic change.*

Facing change

When we say "coping with", usually what follows is "the past". When we are coping with the past, we normally have lots of information and knowledge about what happened, but there is little we can do about it. We can learn from the past, and we can try to make remedies for what happened, or we can interpret that past in different ways, but we cannot act in the past. What has happened has happened. When we say "coping with the future", the challenge is different. We have limited knowledge about the future, but we can act in the future, and we can shape the future. None of us knows for sure what the future will look like, and yet much of what we do pre-supposes the future. There is an *asymmetric epistemology* between the past and the future that we deal with, specifically in the first part of this book, and we return to this throughout the book.

Box I.1 The Kodak moment

Consider the following case: The Eastman Kodak Company, founded in 1888, pioneered modern photography. In 1900, it introduced the Brownie camera, which created a new mass market for photography, and following that, advertisements like "This Kodak moment can't wait for Dad to get home" appeared. The term "Kodak moment" became the phrase for taking pictures and a symbol and manifestation of how dominant Kodak was within photography. Increasingly after World War II, one could find sign posts at picturesque places reading "Kodak moment". In January 2012, Eastman Kodak Company filed for bankruptcy. The company's market had been taken over by new digital cameras and smartphones. A first irony was that it was the Eastman Kodak Company that had invented the digital camera back in 1975. A second irony was that the shock created by the bankruptcy was described as a Kodak moment. A third irony of the Kodak moment, beyond the Kodak company itself, is that it illustrates how we as human society now have more knowledge, more technology and more power to identify and solve problems than ever before, but we seem to be unable to fully use that ability. The phrase "Kodak moment" was therefore transformed to describe how well-run companies can suddenly disappear from the market or, more generally, how things we take for granted are more vulnerable to change and less resilient than we would like to think. There might be a fourth irony in the story; Kodak is currently trying to relaunch its brand and get back into the market. A "Kodak moment" might again mean a unique, special and memorable moment captured on film.

We can and should prepare for the future, even though it is uncertain and disruptive. We point to strategies that will help us towards a more sustainable future for business and work. However thoroughly we think that we understand the past and the present, this does not provide a sound foundation for coping with the future. Currently, a "Kodak moment" means a sudden, surprising and unwanted change. What can the Kodak moment teach us? We see four relevant aspects of the story:

a. the disruptiveness of economic change;
b. the fact that one had knowledge but failed to use it;
c. the organisational challenge to be able to adjust to future changes;
d. that in any change there is an opportunity.

Kodak moments can be extrapolated into larger challenges than those facing single companies.

We do not argue against change. An alternative to the myth of stability has been innovation, and innovation has been celebrated for decades. The current innovation discourse is cast in a positive perspective, seen as changes in products, processes, services and social organisation; and bringing new products and services to the market, organised in ways that create a better future. Some changes are wanted; the status quo is not always wanted. Most people would like to see changes that represent progress but not changes that create fear or conflict or reduce welfare and peaceful social interaction. The first part of this book focuses on how structure and institutions are under pressure to change and reflects on meaningful responses to these changes.

Fast and disruptive changes are not a new phenomenon. In *Theorie der Wirtschaftlichen Entwicklung* from 1911, translated later as *The Theory of Economic Development: An inquiry into Profits, Capital, Credit, Interest and the Business Cycle* – regarded as a key classical work in evolutionary economics and a key reference for modern theory of entrepreneurship and the current innovation paradigm – the Austrian economist Joseph Schumpeter writes:

> But no therapy can permanently obscure the great economic and social processes by which businesses, individual positions, forms of life, cultural values and ideals, sink in the social scale and finally disappear. In a society with private property and competition, this process is a necessary complement to the continual emergence of new economic and social forms and of continual rising real incomes of all social strata.
>
> *(Schumpeter [1911] 2008, p. 255)*

Later, in *Capitalism, Socialism and Democracy*, first published in 1942, Schumpeter coined the term *creative destruction*, meaning that some changes are necessary, even though they are hurtful when they happen. However, in the same book, Schumpeter talked about the *crumbling walls* of capitalism. His argument was that in the ongoing development in the capitalist, mass-production society, markets would be increasingly monopolised and bureaucratised, with the effect that entrepreneurial activity would vanish and capitalist creativity and development would disappear, leading to the collapse of the whole capitalist system.

> **Box I.2 Creative destruction**
>
> Creative destruction can be celebrated. The landscape of organisations and events can be fragmented, leaving the future unpredictable. Schumpeter's gloomy vision is a more accurate description of what we experience than we would like to think. We are not predicting the future; that would be unsound and unreliable. The "simple truth" is that we have been given a series of myths to help us cope with an untidy future. We do not expect perfection. We like to sleep at night. Nursery rhymes are more comforting than horror stories. We are then obliged to fall back on our philosophical foundations, which may enable us to make sense of apparent chaos. Otherwise, our intellectual and institutional structures can be swept away by an economic tsunami. The Fukushima disaster, with an earthquake, tsunami and catastrophic damage to a nuclear power plant, had not been predicted and is hard to explain. Was it an example of a market failure or a government failure? Could it have been prevented? The market can be a powerful source for directing energy and resources into new fields. In his book *The Climate Casino: Risk, Uncertainty, and Economics for a Warming World*, W. D. Nordhaus discusses how to deal with the climate change problem (Nordhaus 2013). His remedy is a market-based approach, wherein the price mechanism is used for resource allocation and choices of technological solutions. As an illustration of this mechanism, the *New York Times* (April 4, 2017) reports that Tesla (the electric car maker) is worth more than Ford, indicating a historic shift in the belief in technology. They say that investment capital is *betting on the future*.

Most people do not want to wake up to disruptive changes. We prefer to see change as a rational, natural and deliberate process, by which we have been able to consider different choices, and then make the most reasonable decision. Coping with the future is therefore about the ability to anticipate, prepare for, and handle disruptive changes. We must process ever increasing amounts of knowledge, and organise our decision processes so that we make sustainable decisions, and build resilient institutions and societies.

Are we facing systemic change?

In this book, we focus our discussion on society, business and work. Our discussion goes beyond the current innovation paradigm and can be seen as a call for more sustainable perspectives on social and economic change. The innovation paradigm is too narrow in its scope, ignoring the comprehensiveness and inter-relatedness of change processes. Much innovation literature presupposes a relatively stable institutional landscape – at least that the founding structure in society is relatively stable. We have seen in recent years that radical innovation often changes "the rules of the game". If this adds to political and social change, the context for innovation becomes rather complex. Parallel to the innovation discourse is the sustainability discourse. There is a growing awareness that not just any balance, but a certain type of change, is needed in the long run in order to avoid the collapse of social and environmental change in the world. We present perspectives in sustainability, where we take a broad view, and include Enlightenment ideals. The innovation paradigm, we argue, has not paid enough attention to this comprehensive perspective. It also fails to address and analyse changes that are destructive in relation to social and economic values, even though this dual side of innovation was pointed out by Schumpeter.

These changes are part of the larger picture of change, such as technological, societal or political change. We make references to these changes. However, we concentrate our discussion on the relationship between society, business and working life and how they can cope with the future. We do not speculate on what the future will bring, but we reflect on perspectives on the future. This is the focus in part three of the book. *The core of this book is how we can work today in order to prepare for a sustainable future.* What we have learned is not that disruption happens, which it always has, but how *integrated* society now is, and how quickly changes in one place can create unexpected changes in a totally different place. It is this *integrated* nature of change that is hard to comprehend, but it poses a challenge to how we approach future change. The *comprehensiveness* of change challenges how we analyse change and how we propose strategies for coping with change. Solving one "problem" at a time will not work if the problem is integrated into a whole set of other relations. We need to see *the whole picture* in order to choose a strategy.

Box I.3 The integrated nature of change

An example is the fall of the Berlin Wall in 1989 and the change in the world economy and politics that followed. Even if (as few people or nobody did) one had foreseen the fall of the wall, one could not have foreseen its consequences. The same is the case with China's openness and engagement in the world economy after the World Trade Organization (WTO) agreement in 1992. The speed and scale of changes that this created was unforeseen. These two events gave us globalisation beyond anyone's imagination. The tremendous growth in money supply (and thus enormous consumption growth between 1995 and 2008), without inflation, was probably due to the enormous flow of inexpensive goods from China. It was also this paradox that fooled many into believing that the money supply had no negative effect; the financial crisis in 2008 came as a shock. Similarly, the type and extent of globalisation and its effect on institutions and culture, along with the restructuring of the industrial sector around the world, is the likely source of the political upheaval we saw in 2016. Maybe 2016 marks the end of the globalisation area, and renationalisation now is on the agenda on a scale that nobody foresaw a short time ago.

Another example is Apple's introduction of the iPhone (smartphone) in 2007, followed by Google's Android system in 2008. The new interactive patterns that this has created, not least the possibility of unlimited access to social media and media in general, has had a tremendous impact. It has influenced the whole structure of news distribution. It has given new channels to form social groups and distribute messages and thereby influenced the political landscape. It has also opened up new ways of working. A senior operator in one of the big production companies in Agder, Norway, explained that when he is on weekend duty, with responsibility for a huge production facility that operates 24/7, he can sit at home in his chair and manage the whole operation through his smartphone. A less obvious, but relevant, theme can be illustrated by an article in the *New York Times* (March 13, 2017). The article reflects on the Trump administration's effect on social and public institutions, referring to tendencies around the world in well-established countries to undermine institutions. Populist movements accuse institutions of playing political games, and complying with the ruling elite. One example is academia. Scientists may become environmental activists. Many see the debate over climate change as normative rather than scientific. The article argues that academic institutions and scientists, by taking that role, have undermined their long-time influence in the environment debate.

Are we facing systemic change, and if so, of what kind? We referred in the beginning of this chapter the development in the early years of the twentieth century. Whitehead, Polanyi and Schumpeter made sharp reflections on the development, talking about reconstruction, transformation and crumbling walls. They observed the Western world's deterioration in the midst of wars and the destructive forces that haunted society. Their pessimism was understandable, and their analyses are still read. However, in most of their predictions, they were simply wrong. Industrial, capitalist Western societies have not collapsed; the unskilled, oppressed working class has not expanded; entrepreneurial activity has not vanished; and logical positivism has not been the only way of establishing reason. So why should we be interested in their theories? Before addressing that, let us briefly argue why they were wrong.

Seen from today's perspective, we will in this book subscribe to the understanding that capitalism and industrialisation have developed through three main stages up till today. The first stage was the early industrialisation that happened in the Western world from the beginning of the nineteenth century and up till the late 1800s. In the late nineteenth century, this industrialisation entered a new stage. Electricity and the combustion engine, to mention two factors, paved the way for a whole new industrial area with mass production, strong urbanisation and a new consumer society as its result. Another aspect of this development was the sharp increase in low-skilled work that created an alienated labour class and, following that, political instability. In the period that follows, there was class conflict, two world wars and ideological struggle beyond any historical comparison. It is amidst this development that Whitehead, Polanyi and Schumpeter wrote.

What neither Whitehead, Polanyi nor Schumpeter could know when they wrote was that this industrial/capitalised structure partly transcended the two world wars, and that it also would develop into a new stage. It happened gradually, but from around 1960–1970, as Daniel Bell observed in his 1973 book *The Coming of Post-Industrial Society: A Venture in Social Forecasting*, industrial capitalism in the Western world developed a new face. The enormous increase in education levels, together with general wage increases and increased investment in research, and along with a tremendous flow of new technologies and the subsequent turn towards more knowledge intensive production, changed the face of industrial capitalism in the Western world. We could call it the *computer age*, or the *knowledge society*. Part of the explanation of the change was the fact that the USA had pioneered mass higher education, partly as a response to the political movement for civil rights. Globalisation was also part of the picture, and related to that the fact that the Western world had exported a lot of its stage-2 industrial activity to the developing world. The fact is that this changed the view on industrial capitalism from its gloomy description in the mid-war period to the positive description referred to by Martin Ford. What had emerged was what Richard Florida has described as the *creative class*. According to Florida (2002), this is a class that today covers something like 40% of the labour force in the Western world. They have outnumbered the earlier labour class. However, as we will discuss later, amidst this development, new class divides have emerged.

The reason why we are discussing a new system change is not the same as what concerned Whitehead, Polanyi and Schumpeter. The reason is related both to new technologies that might even make the computer age just an episode in the capitalist industrial development, but also the perspective that stage two and three of industrial development was based on a use of resources that is no longer regarded as sustainable. We probably need to reconsider the way we work, and this will have big consequences for society, business and work alike. However, as these short reflections on history tells us, the challenge of making right claims about the future is beyond the reach of even extremely knowledgeable people.

The social construction of social science

Why should we be concerned with theories on social change that turned out to be wrong, or believe that we can look into the future with better precision than great social scientists? The answer is that the question is wrong. We do not believe that we can predict the future, and the theories we have referred to are not redundant, even if they got the future wrong. The point is that the purpose of social science is not to predict the future. Rather, we argue, the purpose is to understand the past, make sense of the present and prepare for the future. One way of regarding the thinking of Whitehead, Polanyi and Schumpeter and others is that they painted a dramatic picture in order to influence the actions at the time they wrote. The purpose might not have been to argue what the future might be or to speculate about the consequences, but to show what consequences a certain development would have if it did not change course.

Social science is concerned with studying the society we live in, and it is part of this society and reality. Science in general, and social science especially, is in a double position when it is seen as part of social development. On the one hand, science is expected to deliver valid knowledge; on the other hand, science works within the context of our society. Habermas (1964, p. 166) wrote:

> Within a life-reference fixed by everyday language and stamped out in social norms, we experience and judge things as human beings with regard to specific meaning, in which the un-separated, descriptive and normative content states just as much about the human subjects who live in it as it does about the objects experienced themselves.

Science cannot avoid this relation to society. It can never be a purely outside spectator of society; it will always see society from within. Social science is thereby both part of the social discourse and often a place for critical reflection. At the same time, science is expected to deliver objective, valid knowledge. How can it balance these demands?

Stephen Toulmin (2001) argued for a "return to reason" by rethinking what he described as the "myth of stability"; for centuries, we fooled ourselves into thinking that the future would be like the past. Inductive thinking, which lies behind a large part of social science research, takes what has happened as a proof of what is. However, there is no necessary linearity between what was, what is and what will be. Systemic changes go beyond this linearity. Chaos had long been recognised by Poincare, but it was more comfortable to talk of stability in science and politics, making key issues predictable. Toulmin identified key myths of twentieth-century economics, and in his last book, *Return to Reason*, he provided the key explanation for the financial crash that came in 2008. Mechanistic rationality allows us to build artificial market structures and, in the words of the Red Queen in Lewis Carroll's *Alice's Adventures in Wonderland*, to "believe six impossible things before breakfast". Belief in systems can be ideological.

One interpretation of "Kodak moments" and unpredictability is that the myths of rationality are being exposed through startling examples. Stability and equilibrium are myths, so even if we would like them to be reliably true, and even if they are useful tools for thinking, we must accept that they are illusions. The implications are considerable. Once we have recognised the prevalence of chaos, we cannot cope with the future by simply reverting to previous ways of thinking and working. Some Kodak moments arise because we do not understand the situation. Toulmin would talk of rationality being culturally situated. Toulmin had some great vignettes, which enabled us to understand cultural differences and to re-frame rational explanations. The logic of induction depends on the assumption that experience is a reliable guide to the future. Most people will happily assume that "the sun will rise tomorrow" as it has done every day. If we can no longer make such routine assumptions, then normal life will become very difficult.

Michael Polanyi (the younger brother of Karl cited earlier) argued with reference to Toulmin in the forward to his book *Science, Faith and Society*, written during WWII as a response to how Communism was curbing scientific freedom in eastern Europe:

> Reality is that which is expected to reveal itself indeterminately in the future. Hence an explicit statement can bear on reality only by virtue of the tacit coefficient associated with it. This conception of reality and of tacit knowing of reality underlies all my writing. If explicit rules can operate only by virtue of a tacit coefficient, the ideal of exactitude has to be abandoned. What power of knowing can take its place? The power which we exercise in the act of perception. The capacity of scientists to perceive the presence of lasting shapes as token of reality in nature differs from the capacity of our ordinary perception only by the fact that it can integrate shapes presented to it in terms which the perception of ordinary people cannot readily handle. *Scientific knowing consists in discovering Gestalten that are aspects of reality.*
>
> (Polanyi 1964, p. 10)

Our book attempts to meet this ideal. Our chapters try to point at *Gestalts* that are important to consider. The nature of Gestalts is different in social science compared to natural science. The underlining structures of nature are relatively fixed phenomena. It is in line with our ambition on behalf of social science to understand the past, make sense of the present and prepare for the future. Social phenomena are not fixed, and assumptions are central to the working of society. Our chapters aim to *discover assumptions that are important aspects of a reality that supports a sustainable future.* The second part of the book is therefore concerned with two questions: what is knowledge, and how does social science make knowledge about the future?

Understand the past, make sense of the present and prepare for the future

The book asks how social science can provide relevant knowledge for preparing for the future. Science normally researches what has happened. In natural science, knowledge about how elements behave will often tell us what may happen in the future. In society, this is different. One has to apply different kinds of knowledge in order to see a comprehensive picture of where we are going. In the end, our long-term perspectives will be based on our assumptions. We see three levels in coping with developing rational and reasonable knowledge for the future: practical, methodological and philosophical. We try to explain what we perceive as the main practical and organisational aspects of this issue, and what they imply in terms of methodology and philosophy. We look at businesses and business environments and the landscape of organisations that are concerned with the future; this means that economic policy and implications for work and organisation are central to our discussion, as well as how society and business interact. We have an ambition to bridge the more fundamental theoretical discussion with more practical examples. In the interaction between the practical, the methodological and the philosophical,

TABLE I.1 The scope of the book

	Society	Business	Work
Practical, organisational	How well is the social and political order handling the challenges we face today?	What innovation creates institutional instability? How will the global order challenge local resilience?	How can we balance technology change and meaningful work: Developing learning at work?
Methodological	How to analyse and change the social and political order? What is the role of social science?	How can we redefine innovation policy and help leadership to redefine its generic core and business to rethink its role in the economy?	How can we promote pluralism in organisational thinking, creating human-centred systems and acknowledging the importance of local learning processes?
Philosophical	What is a sustainable political and social order?	How is sustainability related to how we think, acknowledging the limits to rationality and the need for a more comprehensive way of thinking?	How can we redefine work and more generally understand the impact on how we conceptualise things?

we believe we can sort out some of the fundamental assumptions and insights into gestalts or constituting structures and institutions that are important for a sustainable future. Table I.1 gives an overview of the issues we try to address.

In our co-authored chapters from a team of researchers, we exemplify the post-"Kodak moment" discourse, with some shared approaches to argumentation. The chapters discuss what changes we see coming, both social and technological; how society and policies should relate to these changes; how businesses should organise and manage; and what the implications are for work. It is not a matter of futurology and speculation but of recognising that we cannot know the future even though we can prepare for it. This has always been the case; it was thought to be more comfortable to pretend to live in a predictable world. It is clearer than before that too little knowledge can be a dangerous thing. Perhaps what we are offering is a return to some kind of "common sense". We consider unpredictability and uncertainty. There are fundamental challenges for social science, regarding evidence and explanation in relation to globalisation, technological change, sustainability, migration, demographic change and inequality, as they impact on business and work. There may be implications such as changes in business education, work organisation and management and challenges to conventional models. Labour markets could be transformed.

As our focus is on society, business and work, the book offers different viewpoints and critical views on innovation, work and business. In this introduction, we used the phrase "Kodak moment" to describe the disruptive changes that we experience in the economy and society; society now has more knowledge, more technology and power to identify and solve problems than ever before, but as in the case of Kodak, we seem unable to use that ability fully. As a diagnosis for society, this tells us that more knowledge is not the same as making wise judgements. Under disruptive conditions, we cannot copy the past or extrapolate from things that have happened. Coping with the future is about building a capacity to be able to prepare for the future, which has to do with the assumptions and directions we choose to follow. The purpose is to identify some of the fundamental elements needed in order to develop a liberal and sustainable society, democracy and economy.

The first part of the book: Future political, social and institutional landscape, sets the scene. The chapters discuss the driving forces for change. They present perspectives on change, mainly at a "system" level and reflect on some of the macro tendencies that we see around us. The kind of changes we see in society at present do not only create changes at an activity level in the sense of changes within the market or within society, there are also changes to some of the rules and institutions in the market and in society. In a sustainable strategy, one must address these changes, as well as day to day changes in the market and society.

The second part of the book: Knowing the future, we address the epistemological challenge of forming knowledge about the future. The chapters discuss the concept of knowledge. As was addressed in the introduction, the future poses a knowledge challenge. We argue for a social understanding of knowledge, which has implications for our perspective on the social challenges society is facing. We also discuss the relation between knowledge and truth. On the one hand, we want knowledge that is true, documented, factual, and not false and manipulating. On the other hand, we need knowledge that can guide us into the future, and we want this to be solid, science-based knowledge. How do we handle this dilemma? We investigate the asymmetric epistemology in terms of the problem of knowledge of the past versus the future, and the foundation of our thinking about a sustainable future.

The third part of the book: Future technology, organisation and work, we discuss the challenge of leading and organising for the future that have direct effects on business, organisation and work. We discuss strategies for coping with change. Will new organisational forms and ICT technologies develop new forms of global collaboration? Technology is changing the workplace and the way we work. What are the drivers behind implementation of new technology implementations? We argue that technology is transforming the context and work of organisations, changing assumptions regarding geographical location of work, and the balance between man and machine. Furthermore, work and social divide is addressed.

PART I
Future political, social and institutional landscape

1
COPING WITH POLITICS

From post-nationalism to re-nationalism

Hans Christian Garmann Johnsen and Jon P. Knudsen

The re-emergence of the nation-state

Is the nation state on its way out, and are we moving gradually towards an international order? There are many arguments for a post-national future. Foremost among these, perhaps, is the need to address issues wider than the border of a nation, such as pollution and environmental change, and peace. The ambition to have closer collaborations, and more open borders between nations, has increased over a long period, hence the term *post-nationalism*. Lately we have seen a revival of nationalist ideas and a reduced willingness to go into deeper collaborations across borders. The clearest example is perhaps Brexit.

Box 1.1 UK and Brexit

The UK electorate, in a referendum in June 2016, voted to leave the European Union (EU), which the UK had joined in 1973. This had not been expected by social scientists or by any of the leading protagonists. The implications of "Brexit" will be important and far-reaching. Detailed negotiations have begun, but the UK government is divided on many key issues. The Prime Minister called a General Election, seeking a strong majority and a personal mandate. Instead, she leads a minority government and faces the prospect of an imminent further General Election. The EU can be forgiven for not understanding what the UK wants.

Business decision-makers had not expected the majority for Brexit. They now call for certainty on key issues, but the negotiations will run until March 2019. There is now controversy over what will change in 2019: Will there be a cliff-edge, or a prolonged period of transition? Could the referendum decision be reversed?

Banks and financial services based in the City of London are making contingency plans to relocate their operations, typically to Dublin, Paris or Frankfurt. European agencies based in London are to be relocated. The value of the pound sterling has fallen, with implications for imports, exports and foreign travel. UK employers who have come to depend on EU migrant workers, such as hospitals, restaurants, hotels and fruit pickers, are considering how they can respond if there are new tight restrictions on immigration with the end of the free movement of labour.

International businesses are reconsidering where they should invest if tariffs are to be charged on exports from the UK to the EU, for example with automobiles and aerospace. UK withdrawal from the EU is to be followed by complex and lengthy trade agreements with countries around the world, such as the USA and India. There is likely to be a substantial period of uncertainty.

There is discussion as to whether the UK should follow the model of Norway, which remains in the Single European Market but is not a member of the EU. However, Norway pays a substantial financial contribution, complies with EU directives and respects freedom of movement. Trade unions are concerned with the future of working conditions and workers' rights, which have been protected through the UK's membership of the EU.

Those who voted in the June 2016 referendum had to choose between "Leave" and "Remain." Typically, voters understood few of the detailed issues, and they were subject to pressure from politicians, with misleading claims being made. The UK government had made no preparations for a decision to leave.

Issues at present include:

- There will be vigorous debate in all political parties.
- EU migrants will consider whether to return home.
- Currency values will fluctuate.
- UK universities worry that they will lose EU students and research funding.
- Productivity is likely to fall, together with real wages, while inflation rises.
- Ford, Nissan and Toyota plan to launch new models of cars, for the European market. Should these be made in UK factories, facing tariffs on exports and restrictions on recruiting overseas skilled workers?
- How should UK universities plan for the future, as they lose EU research and exchange links and risk losing EU students?
- To what extent do companies need to change their legal status and business strategies to maintain an active presence in the EU?

It is premature to declare that the nation state is a phenomenon of the past only. We exist in a political landscape where different entities of identity and decision are present. This complexity of political entities and identities is something we need to comply with, to avoid further disruptive political changes.

Historical traits

The tension between universalist and ethnically based states has played a major role in the political landscape of the Western world for centuries, dating back to ancient times. A well-known historical example is the trial of Jesus, in which Pontius Pilate, the fifth prefect of the Roman province of Judaea from AD 26–36, declined to interfere, as he thought it was an internal Jewish matter. Greek city states in antiquity and Italian city states in the Renaissance are early examples of political organisation based on local entities and identities. The modern nation-state was not fully established until around 1800. The Peace of Westphalia in 1648 established a landscape of proto-nations in continental Europe, but the Vienna Peace Congress after the Napoleonic wars is perhaps the modern manifestation of a Europe predominantly based on nation-states.

The Scandinavian countries offer important insights into the development of the nation states. They have a shared ethnic, linguistic and religious history based on a patchwork of Germanic tribes, which, in the medieval age, evolved into three distinct states fighting for hegemony in wider parts of northern Europe. Between 1397 and 1523, these states, as a function of dynastic mechanisms, merged into the unstable Kalmar Union. When it dissolved, Norway, with its subsidiaries in the North Atlantic, remained a part of Denmark. The modern frontier between Denmark and Sweden was fought over in the mid-seventeenth century and then again in the Great Nordic Wars between 1700 and 1721. During the Napoleonic wars, Sweden and Denmark were on different sides, and after the wars, Sweden forced Norway to join it in a union. This union lasted until 1905, when Norway again became an independent state. The wider Nordic nation-building processes followed suit. Finland gained its independence in 1917 and Iceland in 1944, while the Faroe Islands and Greenland are on their way to loosening their bonds with Denmark. Following lasting tension between Sweden and Russia, the entirely Swedish-speaking Åland Islands were never accorded a return to Swedish supremacy after the downfall of the Russian empire in 1917. Instead, these islands gained a semi-independent status under Finnish rule, which a large part of the population would like to see developed into full independence. Today, Denmark, Finland and Sweden have joined the EU, while Iceland and Norway are not members.

The modern nation-state tried to identify consistency between ethnicity, language, religion and territory. It succeeded in some places, but not in all. The Nordic case is instructive, in that the subsequent shifting of territories between Denmark, Norway and Sweden has resulted in reorienting national identifications with the different conquered populations, as far as these were Scandinavian-speaking in the first place. As such, Nordic nationalities display a high degree of plasticity. The Åland case illustrates this constructionist point from another angle. Under the right institutional circumstances, a small archipelago, otherwise doomed to become yet another periphery under a strong nation state, is reinventing its own nationality before our eyes.

Non-territorial states were also tested, and in some sense, were successful. The Hanseatic League, between the fourteenth and the seventeenth century, was such a construction; it established juridical links between cities, and its activity did not refer to a particular territory, but rather to a network of geographically linked entities. The Spanish throne at one point in time consisted of dots of territory scattered around Europe as a result of inheritance. However, it was a fragile construction, and this fact led to the War of the Spanish Succession (1702–1715).

After the Vienna Congress in 1815, the German question remained "unsolved," creating later enormous conflicts in Europe. In later years, the Balkans was the scene of a brutal war, re-establishing national boundaries. Ireland's independence from Britain in the early twentieth century, the struggle over Northern Ireland in the post-war period and the recent Scottish independence movement, further encouraged by Brexit, as well as the call for independence for the provinces of Catalonia and the Basque country in Spain, are reminders of the fact that the nation-state idea is not only history. Some of these processes point to the blurred line between nationalism and regionalism. In a continent with as many identities as Europe, and with these identities undergoing as many processes of heterogenisation as of homogenisation, the potential for nation states seems to be legion.

Parallel to this line of nation-state constructions, universalism represents a strong strand in European political thinking. The Roman Empire was based on an idea of a universal order. This order was largely inherited by the Roman Catholic Church, which established a universal cultural order in Western Europe in the middle ages. This order was challenged by the Reformation, which was used in mobilising the independence of nation-states. The Code Napoleon was an attempt to re-establish a Roman Empire kind of order in Europe. It failed, and the modern European order was founded on the idea of the nation-state. European wars, which escalated into two world wars, kept the dream of an international and universal order alive.

The League of Nations was founded in 1920, following the Versailles peace conference after World War I (WWI). In 1935, it had 58 members. The United Nations was established in 1945, with World War II (WWII) as its background. Still, these international orders, even though they tried to establish some universal principles, were mostly based on nation-states. Even the Universal Declaration of Human Rights, which was adopted by the United Nations General Assembly in Paris in 1948 and starts by declaring "All human beings are born free and equal in dignity and rights. They are endowed with reason and conscience and should act towards one another in a spirit of brotherhood," is based on the nation-state. In article 2, it says:

> Everyone is entitled to all the rights and freedoms set forth in this Declaration, without distinction of any kind, such as race, colour, sex, language, religion, political or other opinion, national or social origin, property, birth or other status. Furthermore, no distinction shall be made on the basis of the political, jurisdictional or international status of the country or territory to which a person belongs, whether it be independent, trust, non-self-governing or under any other limitation of sovereignty.
>
> *(UN 1948, art. 2)*

The key phrase here is "*the country or territory to which a person belongs*," although the following examples attenuate the ideal-typical role of the national state as its sole possible form.

Over the last generation, we have seen attempts to play down the role of the nation-state. The European Union, the fall of the Iron Curtain and globalisation in general have paved the way for an international order where the nation plays a lesser role. *Post-nationalism* has been used by some as a term for this development. Others point to the fact that the strengthening of the European Commission in the 1980s and 1990s came with the help of an alliance between Brussels and what was declared a "Europe of regions." Supra-nationalism depended on the embryonic forms of nationalism found in regionalism to be able to prevail. Parallel to this, Porter's (1990) reformulation of the economic world order as a global economy is built on a recognition that the real engines of economic growth and innovation are regional and not national in nature, though Porter ignores the political potential of his insights. However, these developments have been challenged, with Brexit being the most recent and strongest manifestation. We therefore need to revisit the issues of the foundations of the present political discourse. Along which dimensions should this discourse be constituted, the local/regional/national or the general/universal? This is a key tension that confronts us as we try to find our way to the future.

We argue that the modern idea of the political is historically founded in the nation state. This nation state has been challenged on several occasions, and is challenged again in the post-national area by globalisation, by migration and international cooperation and by regionalisation. An important back-drop to this challenge can be found in the roots of modern political thinking, that is, in the Enlightenment, which involves an inherent contradiction. This contradiction is exposed in the concept of modernity. By *modernity* we understand the socio-temporal category that is brought about by the merger of the modern and its contradiction. By *modernism* we understand the deliberate theming of modernity as it appears in symbolic forms, mostly in art, thinking and in cultural sciences. The future of the political is dependent on our ability to live with this contradiction, that is, to live with modernity in its various forms and to embrace it. The alternative could be the threat that the political degenerates and retreats to archaic, pre-modern forms. We reject the notion of "post-modernity" as a useful concept; we prefer the term "late modernity" to depict our present and future condition. Post-nationalism can then be seen as a pressing political concern, ready to be examined in the era of late modernity. As argued by Habermas (2001), one way ahead could be to re-establish polity and its related discourses in a post-national context that could draw on the historical virtues and past experiences of geographically secluded polities, while at the same time opening adequate arenas for discourses involving international actors and relations. This transformation from a national to a post-national political order has shown to be much more complicated than was perceived only a decade ago.

Box 1.2 The future of Europe

The European Commission has published a White Paper wherein it presents five scenarios for Europe's future. The five are:

Carry on: This scenario implies an incremental development along the path that is already in place, making different policy areas work better, expanding the euro zone and moving towards a more unified foreign policy.

Nothing but the single market: This scenario rolls back the EU to the economic aspects of the union, leaving the other political areas more or less up to the nation states.

Those who want more do more: This will open the door for a two-speed Europe, increasing and deepening co-operating between some states, while leaving others with a less integrated relation with the union.

> *Doing less more efficiently*: In this scenario, EU policy is reduced to a more limited set of areas but has a higher commitment to common policies in these areas, for example, common border control and a common currency.
>
> *Doing much more together*: This scenario both expands the areas of collaboration and tightens decision making and mutual commitments among the member states.
>
> Source: EU (2017) *White Paper on the future of Europe*, European Commission, March 2017.

The issues in this discussion are at the core of what *Politics* is. Politics is about making legitimate decisions that are binding for the whole of society. The fundamental question in politics is about how this legitimacy is founded. This chapter argues that seemingly contradictory ideas about the foundation of this legitimacy have much of the same source. A starting point could be the discussion between Paine and Burke on revolution or evolution, related to the French revolution. The discussion came to compare the British revolution in 1688 and the French in 1789 in terms of causes of the revolutions and ideas and content of the revolutions. The political philosophy of Burke and Paine can be seen from the perspective of the four traditions of democratic thinking that are presented: the libertarian idea of democracy, the republican idea of democracy, the communitarian idea of democracy and, finally, the deliberative idea of democracy (Johnsen 2014).

The four ideas of the political are founded in four different traditions of thought. The naturalist tradition has as its starting point that everything is nature; even the human mind is nature, and we can never escape nature. So, our reasoning must understand nature, as we are inside nature ourselves. What this means is that nature puts boundaries to our thinking. We may try to escape nature, to go beyond pure mechanical laws, but in vain. The best we can do is to understand nature, and even this understanding is limited. The naturalist is concerned with natural order and is sceptical of any artificial order imposed on society. The market order is logically in line with naturalist views on society. The libertarian idea of the political order grew out of this idea.

Epistemologically, the rationalist tradition takes as a starting point that thinking and reasoning is a category that exists independent of nature. There is a dualism between thinking and nature: We can think about nature, but we can also think about other things, like things that do not exist. Descartes and Kant are representatives of this tradition, and it is from Kant that we have some of the modern conceptions of the rule of law and a democratic state. For him, the rule of law is beyond democracy and anchored in universal principles that every rational and reasonable human being will accept. Constitutional democracy can be seen as a concept that combines these two arguments. The republican idea of political order is based on this dualist thinking.

The humanist tradition takes as a starting point human existence, seen from the individual perspective. It builds on the acknowledgement that how we see the world is as humans and from the perspective of being human. The human being is more important than nature, but the human being has to comply with and understand his or her relation to nature. The starting point for human thought is human existence. Existence is something much wider than thought. It includes the body and the whole self. We are, in our existence, embodied and embedded in the world. The world is seen from our existence, and we can choose to see the world in different ways. A key concept is the human will; we can construct the world. These ideas are strongly represented in the thoughts of both Rousseau and of Hegel, and they were the underlying drivers of the Romantic movement. This tradition has a strong influence on the modern concept of local, direct democracy, what we have chosen to call the *communitarian* idea of democracy.

The dialectical/discursive tradition builds on the idea that human life implies unresolved and unresolvable tensions and contradictions. There is not one simple solution to things. Life is not an equation that adds up or can be optimised. Some things are either too complex, or they meet conflicting assumptions, so that simple solutions are not available. We want to live peacefully, but also to improve our wealth. We want to live sustainably, but also consume goods. We enjoy like-minded people, but are also dependent on pluralism. These and similar examples face us both in everyday life and in reaction to more principled decisions. As humans, we live in this dialectic. As a society, we must accept that there is no single right solution to things, so criticism, dialogue and peaceful (democratic) decision making is the relevant way forward. At any one time, knowledge in society is never true, but it is the best that reasonable humans can agree on at that given moment. Based on this way of thinking, representative democracy is a reasonable way of handling the compromises that society at any time has to deal with and to live with, which is the idea of deliberate democracy.

The naturalist, the rationalist, the humanist and the dialectic tradition can be seen as inspirations for four models of political organisation: The market model (the naturalist tradition); the rule of law model, or constitutional democracy (the rationalist tradition); the direct democracy model (the humanist tradition); and the representative democracy (the dialectical tradition). How does one tradition contrast with or criticise the others? In Table 1.1, we try to illustrate this. Each cell in a row contains a criticism of the related column's heading.

We have already pointed to modernity as a historically rooted phenomenon, one characterised by the empirical ability to set out general positions and values, in contrast to what would be understood as essentialist or pre-modern positions. For matters of relevance, we have established some thresholds for where we can find this modern impulse in political thinking on the European scene. Others would argue differently. Theologians will state that an important root of modernity is to be found in the books of Genesis in the Bible, while the political scientist Francis Fukuyama will maintain that an early case of modernity is presented by the way political and administrative cultures evolved in ancient China (Fukuyama, 2011). Our point is that modernity empirically does not appear as one or as uniform; it appears as varieties. These varieties can either be seen as parallel and culturally coloured adaptations of the basic modernity theme or as unsynchronised patterns of

TABLE 1.1 Contrasting the four traditions

	Naturalist (market solution)	*Rationalist* (rule of law)	*Humanist* (direct democracy)	*Dialectic* (representative democracy)
Naturalist	**Libertarian democracy**	Naturalism will lead to a brutal order without the rule of law.	We understand nature through our perception on nature; we cannot ignore perception and meaning.	We do not know things for sure, so they can only be decided in a democratic process.
Rationalist	Rationalism is speculative. Ruling must be based on factual reality.	**Constitutional democracy**	Rational thought should be bounded by human values, and it is human thinking and interpretation that gives meaning to abstract principles.	There is a limit to human thinking; some democratic processes do not necessarily come up with absolute solutions but choose pragmatically the best alternative available.
Humanist	Humanism lacks a logical foundation. In the market solution, each individual can choose how to participate.	Humanism is normative and often appeals to emotions rather than reason.	**Communitarian democracy**	Even our ideas of human existence are developing and need to be supported by a (democratic) political system.
Dialectic	There is a reality of nature that is exposed in the transactions of society.	Dialectics is relativism and can endanger human beings if universal principles are not acknowledged.	Human values are absolute and cannot be overrun by representative democracy.	**Deliberate democracy**

modernity, meaning that some sectors appear permeated by modern ideas, while others do not.

The first position is often referred to by a prism metaphor of social change and thinking. A classical quote from Marc Bloch on the medieval interlude between antiquity and Renaissance illustrates this way of reasoning: "it imparted its own colouring to what it received from the past, as if passing through a prism, and transmitted it to succeeding ages" (Bloch 1993, p.279). The prism metaphor is often referred to by comparatively oriented historians as a way of singling out the way modernity manifested itself in European practice and thought. Todd (1990) hence distinguishes between three main strands of modernity paths: the political, the romantic and the utilitarian (paralleling the rational, humanist and naturalist positions described here), identified with the French, the German and the British ways to modernity respectively. We should, however, with Hirschman (1976), admit that they all borrowed much of their intellectual content from each other as well as from other sources, not least from Italian ideas of law and economics, where in fact the link back to Roman law was never completely broken (Bloch 1993).

Box 1.3 Kinds of nationalism

Nationalism, we argue, comes in two basic varieties, a liberal and a non-liberal version. Today, we see several examples of the latter. Nationalist arguments are put up against liberal and universalist arguments. The political consequence is increased pressure on liberal institutional systems, most visible in countries like Hungary, Poland and Turkey, but recently also affecting countries otherwise spearheading economic liberalism, such as the United Kingdom and the United States. The latter examples accentuate the actuality of understanding modernity as increasingly unsynchronised. We often forget that nationalism was at its Renaissance outset and during its Enlightenment processing and its widespread propagation in the second half of the nineteenth century, basically a liberal undertaking. The freeing of national sentiments by according ethnic groups linguistic, religious and constitutional self-determination runs alongside the enfranchisement of new social groups to political rights in Europe as in other continents. A proliferation of nation states characterises the international scene globally and, since the downfall of the iron curtain, also the European continent. In this liberal tradition, the formation of nation states merges with the prism-perspective on modernity.

One important problem with the continued tendency to state formation today is that there seems to be no obvious end to the list of candidates opting for recognition as nation states. There has, parallel to the proliferation of nation states in Europe, also been a rise in the cases of states adopting federal or semi-federal political systems. As our Åland case illustrates, in a given situation, almost any regional entity can invent a national identity. At the same time, nationalism generally seems to have taken an anti-liberal turn. In the four biggest Nordic states, the most fervent nationalist positions are all taken by political parties presenting themselves in this vein: the Progress Party and Danish People's Party in Denmark, the True Finns in Finland, the Progress Party in Norway and the Swedish Democrats in Sweden. In this tradition, nationalism is basically understood in essentialist terms, and the idea of the modern is subsequently decoupled from vital sectors of society.

The unsynchronised appearance of modernity is already explained by a reference to the writings of Fukuyama (2011). The uneven presence of modernity is becoming one of the striking features of the contemporary societal condition. While the economy in many advanced countries, despite signs of neo-protectionism, seems to presuppose a continued allegiance to the principles of modern economic reasoning, this is not the case within the realms of culture and politics. While modernity in the forms of modernism, universalism and cultural radicalism fought its way as far as through the 1960s, the following decades have witnessed a regression towards pre- or proto-modern forms in political, cultural and religious thinking in many European countries and North America. Within social philosophy, this phenomenon has caused an epistemological crisis as how to understand the modern and two of its main underpinnings, the notion of historical linearity and the idea that modernity contaminates across sectors, a debate in which the late Peter Berger (2014) engaged by promising more complex notions of the modern than those previously being employed.

The relationship between nationalism and universalism has had a dialectic nature through history. Developments at the national and universal level follow each other, not necessarily in a harmonious way. Nationalism and universalism, furthermore, appear in two capacities as ideas and as institutions.

Box 1.4 Danish, Norwegian and Swedish states

We can develop this analysis of the modern and of nationalism, together with a new take on our Scandinavian and further Nordic cases mentioned in the introduction, by drafting the following scheme on the dialectics between nationalism (N) and universalism (U):

A-(N). From a prehistoric common future, three political entities evolved into what was later to become a Danish, Norwegian and Swedish state.

A-(U). The early discourse arena was defined by tribes framed in a pan-Germanic framework of interchange. Thus, King Alfred in England could be visited and consulted without translators being needed. The period ended with an attempted Scandinavian union.

B-(N). With the end of the middle ages, the breaking up of the Kalmar union left Denmark and Sweden to reorganise themselves as the strong and remaining political forces of the region. Norway ceased to exist as a distinct political entity. A subsequent collapse of the Norse language paved the way for a plethora of dialects supporting local and regional identities, especially in Norway, and laid a foundation for later Faroese and Icelandic cultural identity.

B-(U). Lutheranism was adopted top-down and became the new Pan-Nordic creed attached to political authority.

C-(N). National liberal awakenings manifested themselves from the nineteenth century onwards, presenting a more heterogenous national Nordic realm.

Norway (1814–1905), Finland (1917) and Iceland (1944) achieved full independence, while Åland, the Faroe Islands and Greenland were accorded a semi-independent status.

C-(U). Pan-Scandinavianism flourished as a cultural and political movement towards the second half of the nineteenth century, especially among artists and intellectuals. Thus, a Scandinavian and wider Nordic discourse arena may be said to have existed. The inter-war period witnessed a strong Nordic engagement with the League of Nations.

D-(N). The economic and political crisis in the inter-war period spurred strong systemic changes in the Nordic countries, rebuilding them as welfare states with a dominant social-democratic imprint. After WWII, the state as a planned system challenged the state as a liberal construct.

D-(U). The Nordic countries joined the UN, the European Council and most international economic organisational co-operation. They joined the European Free Trade Association (EFTA). Later, three of them, Denmark, Finland and Sweden, join the EU. Three of them, Denmark, Iceland and Norway, joined the North Atlantic Treaty Organization (NATO), while Finland and Sweden remained neutral.

E-(N). The end of the 20th century witnessed a surge of anti-liberal nationalism, tapping into the liberal national legacy. This period also saw the establishment of new political parties opting for power.

E-(U). Universalist ideas and institutions were plunged into crisis by the retraction of national support from important players such as the United Kingdom and the United States.

What we try to illustrate with the Nordic example is that there is nationalism that goes hand in hand with universalism, but also that there are aspects or visions of nationalism that do not do so. In post-war, Western democracies, the foundation of democracy has been increasingly taken for granted. European politicians have assumed that the institutional development from national politics to international co-operation could continue to expand. Norway, which is not a member of the EU, has, as part of access to EU's internal market, had to comply with EU laws. With Brexit, the EU's second biggest country, the United Kingdom, is reversing this process. Is it a temporary setback for the bigger idea of a universal international order, or is it a return to the nation-state?

Is the post-national state the way forward, or is rather the way ahead to re-liberalise the nation state? What constitutes a modern, national, democratic state? Habermas argues:

> The list of problems that confront anybody who reads a newspaper these days can, of course, only change into a political agenda for a public which maintains

a degree of trust in the possibility of conscious transformation of society – and which can in turn be entrusted with it. The diagnosis of social conflicts transforms itself into a list of just as many political challenges only if we attach a further premise to the egalitarian institutions of rational law: the assumption that the unified citizens of a democratic community are able to shape their own social environment and can develop the capacity for action necessary for such intervention to succeed. The legal concept of self-legislation has to acquire the concept of a society capable of democratic mode of self-direction and self-intervention.

(Habermas 2001, p. 60)

Habermas continues:

The concept of a "democratic" self-control of society implies rational laws conception of a determinate number of persons, united by the decision to grant one another precisely those rights that are necessary for the legitimate ordering of their collective existence through the means of positive law.

(Habermas 2001, p. 63)

Habermas argues that democratic decisions are embedded in a political community that is regulated by law but also based in engagement and will. Expressed differently, for democratic deliberation to take place and be legitimate, there are some pre-conditions, both structural and cultural, founded in both the willingness to engage and find reasonable solutions to challenges and within a framework of rules and laws that are generally fair and accepted. However, Immanuel Kant in 1783 praised Frederick II (later called "The Great") for having paved the way for an open, free society, with extensive individual freedom and the rule of law. The paradox is that this happened in a pre-democratic period. It was inspired by natural-law thinking. This reminds us that the idea of a rule of law is prior to the idea of democracy, not its result. The rule of law is not based on the idea of what people decide, or what preferences they have. It is based on the idea that we (philosophically) can define some abstract rules that penetrate time, space and case. It is a non-contextual principle. In Kant's mind, it is an *a priori*; it even goes beyond our reflection. It is something of a universal kind that simply exists and that we, as rational individuals, recognise. Merged with the idea of democracy, the rule of law is inherent in the term *constitutional democracy*. A constitutional democracy thus represents a balance between the concrete and the abstract, the contextual and the universal, the deliberate and the accepted. There are, therefore, many possible responsive strategies to meet today's political challenges (see Box 1.5):

- return to liberal nationalism;
- deeper pan-European integration;
- deeper global integration;
- more regionally based identify formation, return of the city state?

We do not argue that we can point out the right way forward; rather, we contend that these issues should be debated. One can rethink the constitution of the nation state or our perception of democracy. Liberal nationalism is a different kind of nationalism than what we see many places today. Cities or local economies can in the future play a more important role. From the polis in antiquity, and partly so in the middle ages city state, to the present situation of poly-polises, cities have played a major role in political development, but they have limited political autonomy today. This can change. Discourse arenas have become integrated or/and conflicting: The various agoras should be able to comment on and contrast with each other. This, again, could form the basis for a new international order. There are possibilities in constituting the global discourses in new ways.

Nationalism, universalism and enlightenment

The Enlightenment era in Europe paved the way for the modern, democratic society. In fact, it contained a rich reservoir of thinking that supported the creativeness of the Western world that we have seen over the last two centuries, even if we regard the four traditions of thought we have presented here as some of the main ones. At the same time, it is important to acknowledge that Enlightenment thinking also included a complexity of thought that, taken alone, can be rather destructive: It promoted universal rights, but also the importance of the local context and reality; it supported rationalism, but also acknowledged that knowledge is more complex than rational thought alone; it promoted new, innovative thinking, but also acknowledged the importance of history. In fact, what the Enlightenment was about was for the first time in human history to allow plurality of thinking without some authoritarian structure defining what is right and what is wrong. This has been a source of its creativity but also shows why enlightenment is difficult. To live in an enlightened society is to acknowledge that there is this complexity, that there is not totalitarianism. Rather, it is to live in modernity in the sense of a society full of contradictions. These contradictions, for a society to work, must create some sort of balance. One person's right to expression, for instance, should be countered by accepting that others express themselves as well. Finding this balance, in the midst of contradiction, is the big challenge of modernism and of enlightenment.

Box 1.5 Inaugural address by President Barack Obama

Obama said:

What makes us exceptional, what makes us American, is our allegiance to an idea articulated in a declaration made more than two centuries ago:

> "We hold these truths to be self-evident, that all men are created equal; that they are endowed by their Creator with certain unalienable rights; that among these are life, liberty, and the pursuit of happiness."

> Today we continue a never-ending journey to bridge the meaning of those words with the realities of our time. For history tells us that while these truths may be self-evident, they've never been self-executing; that while freedom is a gift from God, it must be secured by His people here on Earth. (Applause.) The patriots of 1776 did not fight to replace the tyranny of a king with the privileges of a few or the rule of a mob. They gave to us a republic, a government of, and by, and for the people, entrusting each generation to keep safe our founding creed.
> January 21, 2013 (US Gov. 2013)

This contradiction can be exemplified by President Barack Obama's second inauguration speech in 2013. Here he praised the founding fathers, not because they allowed slavery, but because they stated some principles that made it possible to develop society in the right direction. However, as these are not fixed solutions for future challenges, they are principles for an ongoing debate but also some that give direction. In line with this, we argue that the four enlightenment positions we have presented represent such principles, which should be part of any discussion and a reservoir of thoughts for discussions about the future of politics.

Applying these general reflections to our discussion about the framework for the political dialogue implies that liberal nations are building blocks. Our position derives from the complexity in which politics is situated. Shifting political agendas and a growing amount of agoras, geographical as well as sectoral, have brought us far from the traditional polis as a frame for political action. Instead, we may justly speak of a world of interlinked poly-polises, in which the need for common codes and mutually respectful conduct is crucial to our future. In this, we join Habermas in his analysis, as in his worries. Whether this requires the reframing of a post-national citizenship and consciousness or not is another question. Since Habermas wrote his analysis, the global situation has altered. Nationalism has increasingly become illiberal, while supranational institutions, with the EU as the prime case, have met with problems of legitimating their authority. These different poles in the political dialectics clearly need the well-functioning of each other in other to secure a safe and progressing world, not least to accord sufficient authority to supra-national institutions in their co-ordinating efforts.

The multi-level constellation of polises engages in a form of meta-polis, where they can comment on and correct each other. Supra-national bodies such as the UN, the EU and the European Council in the present political climate clearly operate as checks on further illiberal tendencies in some of the nation-states. At the same time, sub-national political entities such as states in a federation, counties and cities may act to correct illiberal decisions and legislation in their nation states. This is happening in the United States, where local and regional politicians and the judicial system are acting to counter some of the initiatives by the Trump administration. A milder version may be found in Europe, where cities engage to host persecuted authors, artists and intellectuals. Regionalism could in this regard also be analysed as a way of voicing between loyalty and, ultimately, exit, with the Belgian, Italian, Scottish and Spanish exemplifying the various stages an ideological colouring being employed. In taking such steps, the classic polis could be said to mobilise its potential for acting as a counterweight to ongoing national political discourses. As we are used to talking of multi-level governance as nexuses for creating and executing policies, we may also talk of multi-level discourses as nexuses for forming politics as the input to policies.

Box 1.6 The Kodak moment of politics

***The disruptiveness of change*:**

The process towards internationalisation and global agreements and openness is countered by re-nationalism.

***The knowledge one failed to use*:**

We present criticism of the assumption that there is a choice between nationalism and internationalism/universalism. The danger is now that experts in closed rooms sit down and issue reports and "solutions," or that politicians make decisions as part of an internal power play instead of engaging in real, democratic deliberation, engaging people in discussions about the foundation of democracy and perspectives on international order.

***Ability to adjust to future changes*:**

Politicians often have past positions to defend: The EU has built a huge organisation, mainly in Brussels. Willingness to consider solutions that questions ideological positions or institutionalised power may be limited.

***The opportunity in the changes*:**

We should be rethinking assumptions in the current debate, like our conception of democracy, the nation state, local economies and international co-operation. We should look for new ways forward that balance localism, nationalism and internationalism.

There is a need to reargue the case for the nation state in its liberal traditions. The fact that modernism is an unfinished project wherein variations in interpretation and politics are striking; between geographical and cultural areas, calls for processes and structures where this plurality can be embedded and moderated in a civilised democratic deliberation. Our analysis of the Nordic countries has demonstrated how heterogenous forces over the centuries seem to have been more important in fostering identity than is often recognised. This also goes for contemporary processes of fostering political identity. Successful universalist strategies must take this into consideration and must not undervalue the need for local, regional and national building blocks. We agree with Habermas in his quest for more post-national political consciousness, but, in accordance with our understanding of the path of modernity as a historical evolution involving universalism and liberal nation states, we point to the need for well-functioning national and sub-national political entities to be in place for that to happen.

2

COPING WITH STRUCTURAL CHANGE

Understanding framework conditions

Jon P. Knudsen, Hans Christian Garmann Johnsen and Aris Kaloudis

The importance of institutional structures

We assert in this chapter that, in the future, we must pay more attention to the structural and institutional aspects and implications of innovations. This, to some extent, challenges the current innovation discourse, with its limited and limiting focus on product, processes, organisation and markets. There is a large body of literature investigating how institutional and cultural frameworks shape, and are shaped by, modes of innovation and entrepreneurship in the economic system. North (1990) provides the definition that institutions are the rules of the game in a society. Institutions may be formal (i.e. laws) or informal (beliefs or cultural practices). Institutions thus represent, by definition, not only a factor of societal stability, transparency and order but also a factor of societal inertia that could take the form of a hindrance to necessary structural changes and adaptations.

The crucial question we ask in this chapter is what kind of resilient institutions we need in order to handle economic and social structural changes of the future. As a case study for this discussion, we use the Nordic societies. In 2011, Francis Fukuyama published his book *The Origins of Political Order* wherein he used the term *Getting to Denmark*. By this he meant that the ideal for any political system would be to develop into a democracy with peaceful transformation of power, a rather solidary or equal population that can engage in a common discourse and a high level of cultural, political and social deliberation. In 2013, *The Economist* had its front page dedicated to *Northern Lights*. A longer article, *The Nordic countries are reinventing their model of capitalism* (*The Economist*, 2013) argued that the Nordic model had found ways to deal with the financial crisis of 2008 that did not imply the type of austerity policy, and subsequently unemployment, that we saw in other European countries. Anu Partanen's 2016 book contrasts the Nordic and the US model, and has also been referred to in the present US debate on health reforms. The wider international relevance is that we tap into present institutional challenges and coping strategies in some of the most advanced economies in the global economy, likely to be discussed by business, political and academic communities in the years to come. We see the Nordic model as a special variety of modernity and assume that it can be analysed in the context of modernity in general.

Systems and institutions

At the global level, "innovation" has come to be so widely discussed that its analytical precision is becoming diluted. To steer away from this trap, we should revise our discussion of the concept. We should distinguish between innovation studies as pertaining to

- technological changes in the economy in general and to the business community practices and markets more specifically;

- conditioning formal institutions, i.e. democratic (or not) political regimes, legal systems and their efficiency, property laws, work laws and the organisations of work life, and so on;
- conditioning informal institutions, i.e. social and cultural practices at regional and national levels.

The main body of literature dominating the current discussions on innovation falls into the first category, theming it as a concept with strong relevance to economic change. The forms in which new ideas, innovation possibilities and entrepreneurial endeavours work in an economic system depend on different kinds of diversity creation and selection mechanisms, conditioned by the economic, political and cultural spaces within which they take place. An ironic paradox appears, as the insistence of newness depends on geographical and historical patterns of institutional conditioning. We must therefore integrate a discussion of the main institutional characteristics of the countries in question, fusing literature with a broad take on institutional framing, with literature that concentrates more on the economic aspect of innovation following the "innovation system" tradition.

As such, place and tradition act as the gate-keepers to the future. We become what we inherit. Here, our system perspective makes a geographical leap, closing in on the national and regional as frames for coping with the future. This is one of the themes of the line of thought within institutional economics. When innovation refers to systems and systemic mechanisms, it argues that there are systemic effects beyond the individual actor or unit (like firms or agencies) that define how innovation happens and evolve. Clusters, learning networks and regional and national innovation systems are examples of concepts that are employed and that connect to systemic arguments in various innovation theories. What are the underlying systemic theories on which these concepts rely?

Social systems can be discussed from different perspectives, and the variety of forms that are referred to as *systems* in social science is vast. An important breakthrough in understanding systems came with the discussion on the relevance of biological systems in social science. While there are clear limits to comparing biological and social systems, notably for the role of meaning and intentionality, there is a common denominator between the two in the (semi-) openness of both. One way to see systems is as alternatives to hierarchy. Systems are networks with boundaries and relations. When a concept like cluster is applied, it often indicates relations, closeness and social capital. Normally, we would argue that we either must be able to identify mutual connectedness, in which elements impact each other; or be able to draw a border around the elements that impact each other.

The literature of national (and regional) innovation systems (NIS and RIS) constitutes a subgroup of the vast plurality of theories of social systems. This strand of literature emphasises technological change within and between national and regional boundaries. OECD (1997) argues that NIS is a network of institutions in the public and private sectors for the diffusion of technology. Freeman (1987) and other scholars from this tradition read systemic changes from the angle of historical development. The developed part of the world has gone through fundamental stages in terms of social and technological development. Changes in the social/ institutional and technological spheres have, according to Carlota Perez (2002), been fundamentally interlinked with each other since the beginning of the nineteenth century. Perez emphasises, in particular, the interconnections between the various phases in the development of a technological revolution and the subsequent responses of financial markets. Her study furnishes a clear proposition of how institutions can be shaped by major disruptive technological innovations at a systemic level. Perez claims that for each technological revolution, financial markets "[e]nded with the most virulent crashes, recessions and depressions, later to give way, through the establishment of appropriate institutions, to a period of widespread prosperity, based on the potential of that particular set of technologies" (Perez 2002, p. xvii). Having said that, a fundamental claim in the theoretical perspective of Perez is that technology and the institutions of capitalism have *co*-evolved over time in complex and interlinked modes. This co-evolution has not been smooth; on the contrary, "societies are profoundly shaken and shaped by each technological revolution and, in turn, the technological potential is shaped and steered as a result of intense social, political and ideological confrontations and compromises" (Perez 2002, p. 22).

So the emerging deeper research question of this chapter is how to equip our societies with resilient institutions that may accommodate the structural economic and societal changes that we know will come, and concurrently avoiding their breakdown and the enormous social costs this might imply.

Box 2.1 The evolution of industrial structure

The corporate system and business structure could be discussed in terms of the way it has evolved historically. A current debate is about how to define the stages of development and, through that, seeing what might be the next stage. This development is, according to Drath and Horch (2014, p. 56), divided into four stages:

- The first stage of industrial development came more than 200 years ago, with mechanisation and the steam engines.
- The second stage started around 1900 with mass production and the development of continuous production lines based on the division of labour and conveyor belts. This period is often referred to as the period of *electrification*.
- The third stage of industrial development enabled digital programming of automation systems (1969). This era is still governing our industrial production in a major way, and it is referred to as the period of *digitalisation*.

- Industry 4.0 is the fourth era. The expression is German in origin, used for the first time at the Hanover Fair in 2011. It is understood as "the application of the generic concept of cyber-physical systems to industrial production systems." Industry 4.0 is occasionally called the *internet of things*, and it addresses an active interaction between man and machine. This new human–machine interface (HMI) brings us into unknown territory.

Perez (2000) also provides a similar time-line of shifts in techno-economic paradigms in the period 1770–2000. As argued in the introduction to this book, most of the arguments in the chapters subscribe to these meta-phases of industrial and economic development, as presented in Table 2.1.

The shaping of competitive advantage and institutions

The spatial perspective of Nordic varieties is as important to our argument on temporal change. The complexity interweaving the three components of innovation, systemic/structural change and institutional change poses problems beyond the reach of mainstream policy creation. Still, we would like to think that institutions are instruments in our hands, allowing us to play the tunes of the future. This is not merely a theoretical discussion. We use the example of the Nordic countries as a doorway to understanding some of the dynamics in operation. By doing this, we point to the embedded nature of institutions, meaning that institutions, be they formal or informal, often develop through social processes that take endemic forms, even though their backdrop is global in nature. Hence, the transferability of institutions is mostly overvalued by policy makers who optimistically think of them as tools in a kit for a copy-and-paste modernisation, about which we are sceptical, as argued in Chapter 1.

We take the view that well-functioning institutions enhance our ability to cope with change. Institutional reforms are a common phenomenon in the democratic and developed world. Such reforms are initiated on the basis of democratic processes and perceived national or regional challenges, opportunities and threats. Yet, they are not always implemented in an efficient and effective manner, and this is where nations differ considerably and consistently. For example, the Global Competitiveness report (2016–2017) ranks countries based on their relative performance in a number of key institutional arrangements that are believed to shape national competitive advantages (World Economic Forum 2016). Among the listed measures we find indicators on health and primary education, higher education and training, goods markets (including taxation) and labour markets (of which co-operation in labour–employer relations is a specific indicator). These institutional areas represent not simply a background of real economic processes, but are also perceived by the present economic and policy elites as the backbone of national economic performance.

TABLE 2.1 The evolution of industrial capitalism

Period/production, social and work forms	Production form	Social form	Work form	Societal structure
Before 1800: Pre-industrial society	Craft, manual labour	Peasant society	Master/apprentice	Communities/local engagement
1800–1880: Early industrialisation	From workshop and work to standardisation and division of labour: Workshop, specialisation	Rise of the working class	Specialised skills, skilled labour	Industrial towns, early legal framework, alienation, labour class
1880–1950: Mass production	From division of labour to specialisation and routinisation. Production halls, specialisation	Bourgeois class, the rise of the middle class. Consumer society	Specialised non-skilled work	Urbanisation, strong engagement between politics and marked labour laws, regulations, tripartite collaboration
1950–2010: Globalisation, flexible production	From standardisation to customising and increased production of services. Knowledge workers, lean production, teamwork.	Diversity, multicultural society. The rise of the precariat.	Team work, skills and cross disciplinary co-operation. Creative work.	A new kind of multicultural urban areas arises. Focus on social security, health and safety and education.
2010–future: Knowledge economy, digitalisation	From labour-based production to intelligent factories	?	?	?

On the other hand, every nation is immersed in deeper social institutional structures – informal institutions like creeds, mores, languages and other means of social communication and regulation – that are equally important in understanding how societies and economies are conditioned to react to major endogenous or exogenous factors of change. Changes in these informal institutions tend to occur incrementally and only seldom as systemic earthquakes of the revolutionary kind. Even political changes mediating between the informal and formal institutional realm mostly tend to present old institutions in new disguises (Todd 1990).

Box 2.2 Structural social challenges

Demographic change: Age and migration

Across the world there is scope to adjust demographic factors:

- retention of older workers in order to keep out migrants;
- recognition of challenges of an aging society;
- pressure to reduce pensions and increase retirement age;
- strain put on traditional family structures;
- intergenerational tensions;
- the fact that politicians face choices or priorities;
- whether it is necessary to monitor political activities of international students and migrants.

Social inequality

Inequality threatens social cohesion, economic development and political stability:

- awareness of widening gap between rich and poor;
- awareness of implications for education, housing, health;
- urban riots.

Multicultural society

Following migration, societies are differently made up:

- unrest linked to refugees and asylum seekers;
- problems of adjustment in formerly mono-cultural countries;
- diversity as a positive resource;
- race riots in high immigration areas.

Hall and Soskice (2011) argue that institutional economic thinking has gone through different periods since World War II (WWII). In its first period, up to the 1970s, there was what they call the *modernisation* period. During this period, there was a strong belief in national industrial policy, technology, capital-driven investments and heavy state planning. The second period came in the 1970s under the inflation period; they call it the *neo-corporatist* period. A key theme in this period was how large organisations like labour unions were brought into economic and industrial policy. Their role offered them the possibility of influencing development, but it also implied that they disciplined their members and had a stabilising role in the economy. The third period, called *social systems of production*, came in the 1980s and 1990s. In this period, the social and sociological characteristics of organisations and networks were highlighted. Production regimes were understood, as in Piore and Sabel's 1984 famous analysis of the Third Italy, as social systems of interaction, learning and trust relations.

In this thinking on the institutional economy, Hall and Soskice (2011) call for an approach that is more linked up with strategic perspectives by companies manoeuvring in ideal-typical sociological and political environments. Thus, institutional economics and economics of space have reappeared as an area of general interest and importance. The new focus starts from what given regions and space are, what they can be, how they can develop and how they can retain and develop factors of production. This leads Krugman to ask if the new institutional economics and economics of space are not about comparative advantages but about developing absolute advantages (Krugman 1991). This leads to the provocative position that regional and spatial differences in economic structures can probably be explained by traditional factor terms like agglomeration, comparative advantage, monopolistic competition and economics of scale. Collaboration can also be seen along these dimensions as functional organising of local activity. Contrary to this, Porter (1990), Jacobs (1985) and Piore and Sable (1984) argue that there are local and regional forms of development that cannot be explained with these theoretical concepts but should be analysed by looking at the historical development of cities and regions and their specific informal institutions. In this, informal institutions are increasingly being considered as influential determinants of socio-economic development.

The basic varieties of capitalism (VoC) scheme displaying the bifurcated categories of the liberal market economy (LME) and the co-ordinated market economy (CME) exemplified by the almost typical cases of UK/US (LME) and Germany/Japan/Sweden (CME) is well elaborated in the literature (Hall & Soskice 2001; Gertler 2004; Hancké, Rhodes & Tatcher, 2007). In the VoC tradition, the Nordic countries are normally classified as co-ordinated market economies. However, subsequent analyses of their positioning have pointed to their being swayed in a more liberalist direction over recent decades, with Denmark being driven furthest in this direction and Sweden positioning itself as the last man standing, closest to the archetypical image of the Nordic model. Moreover, these countries are also analysed as being much more internally heterogenous than generally referred to, this heterogeneity showing in regional varieties in economic profile, demographic patterns, class structure and cultural traditions. We can exemplify this by pointing at the varieties of capitalist practices categorised in a study by Wicken (2005) on the modernisation of the Norwegian society. Of special interest is a form of economic integration and innovation practices found in some sub-regions in western Norway where industrialisation took place as a socially non-hierarchical practice based on rural communities with an extreme degree of lateral solidarity following community and lineage.

Hall and Soskice (2011), in their discussion of the Nordic institutional systems, broadly label them as reflecting the existence of co-ordinated market economies. Todd, on the other hand, points to splits in the Nordic institutional realm between a liberalist Denmark and a co-ordinated, or rather organicist, Finland and Sweden, with Norway as a hybrid case. Schneider and Paunescu (2012) point to an apparent drift over the years, bringing more liberalist traits to the models as well as a more heterogenous status to the Nordic regions in general. These observations should lead us to take a closer look at the underlying regional institutional patterns at operation. In fact, Todd (1990, p. 420–432) claims that Norway is regionally split between two types of institutionalised cultures, a liberalist culture in the southeast and an organicist one in the rest of the country. Norway is a sparsely populated country with a large territory consisting of fjords and mountains, making internal communications difficult. A geographically diverse resource base and a small internal market have historically disposed the country to modernise as a handful of regionally separated, but globally coupled, economies rather than as one nationally integrated economy. Despite the development of a strong national economic transfer and welfare system, the continued uneven geographical distribution of new industries such as fish-farming and oil and gas and the closure of some sun-set industries coupled to land-locked resources, such as arable land and forests, has confirmed this picture. Institutionally, this feature of regional diversity and conflicting interests is being reinforced by strong cultural and political interests vested in regional struggle over the historical nation building processes (Rokkan 1967; Todd 1990, p. 420–432). Thus, following Todd, the ambiguous status accorded to the national VoC position should be interpreted as a compromise between conflicting regional varieties rather than as a national consensus.

Resilience of the Nordic model?

There has in recent years been a notable interest in the Nordic Model and the Nordic way of life in many corners of the world. Much of this interest derives from the impression that these countries have been able to tackle social and economic crises that otherwise have shaken presumably robust economies. The model is further believed to be resilient, as it still offers a comparatively generous welfare system to its citizens. Finally, these countries continue to top rankings of countries indexed for well-being and for quality of life (Helliwell, Layard & Sachs 2017). As such, many argue that the Nordic model offers a case for learning, as we argued in the introduction to this chapter. The Nordic countries have done considerably better than other Western countries in terms of economic growth, employment, a high degree of welfare and more equal income distribution, as well as scoring high on democratic dimensions like high participation and involvement of workers in company decisions.

Thus, the Nordic countries are often perceived as rather homogeneous countries, offering cases of wealthy, socially robust and innovative societies that have fared comparatively well through recent economic crises. However, a closer look at the countries in question reveals important national and regional variation regarding business structures, organisational behaviour and entrepreneurial/business culture (Fellmann, Iversen, Sjögren & Thue 2008; Mjøset & Cappelen 2011; Wicken 2005).

To start with, all Nordic countries have had their experience of Kodak moments. In Finland, it came with the sudden weakening of Nokia, which for several years had been the main economic locomotive of the country. In Sweden, the troubles that hit Ericsson had some of the same effects, though milder in their consequences. The bankruptcy of SAAB and the sale of Volvo are other examples. Iceland, famous for its economic volatility and historic track record of high inflation, presented a spectacular bank crisis that resonated through the financial world, while Norway in recent years has been digesting the effects of lower prices for its main export items, oil and gas. The Kodak moments could also have been the fish-farming industry being denied access to important markets such as Russia, China and the EU, and the Norwegian automotive industry struggling with oversaturation just before the financial crisis. Only Denmark, with its more diverse and consumer market oriented exports, seems to have avoided the roller-coaster experience, on which it had it rides in the 1970s. Still, Lego was on the brink of bankruptcy and made a remarkable recovery. And the liberal–conservative government that took office after the 2001 general election presented a policy on public employment reshuffling until then unseen in this part of the world.

The Nordic countries have demonstrated a remarkable degree of resilience over the course of the last three or four decades, while they have adapted successfully to major shifts in how the world of work, business models and social interactions are organised. Still, there are reasons to believe that Nordic institutional frameworks will be seriously challenged in the future. The glossy face-value starting point is that the macroeconomic collaboration framework involving unions, capital owners and government; the generous and, by and large, effective public education system; the strict and efficient work law system; and the advanced welfare state all contributed to the establishment of the Nordic model, though blended differently in each country. This complex and rich institutional framework is generally understood to have induced responsible and inclusive participation of workers at the micro level, combined with democratic management styles and a basic feeling of trust that, in turn, have unleashed the creativity and innovation potential of the societies.

The first severe attacks on this institutionally balanced system came with the cultural, economic and political turmoil that characterised the late 1960s and early

1970s in the Western world. Following this crisis, the modifications made to the model in recent decades have been described as "flexicurity," to better describe the model with its adaptive as well as safe-guarding capacities. This stereotype disguises important national variations. The term *flexicurity* originally covered the adaptation of the Danish welfare system to the internal strains brought on it by the late-twentieth-century exposure to increased international competition and economic hardship (Tangian 2007). Its double message of flexibility and security immediately spurs a critical examination of the balance between its components, within each country and between the countries. Signalling an ideologically and politically disputed concession to flexibility, this tendency is most clearly spotted in Denmark, and in the two countries with the shortest history of welfare state arrangement and the most turbulent experiences with global economic integration, Finland and Iceland (Andersen 2011; Ólafsson 2011; Vartiainen 2011). Norway and Sweden could be said to have retained comparatively more institutional security than the three others. For Norway, this is largely explainable by the revenues of its important oil and gas sectors, which have stimulated the national economy and secured the further development of transfers and welfare through the establishment of a huge sovereign wealth fund (Mjøset & Cappelen 2011). For Sweden, the successive devaluations of the national currency in 1982 and 1992 seem to have offered a sufficient systemic concession to the need for economic reorientation and the retaining of most of the original welfare institutions in place, though at lower absolute levels than in the previous two decades (Erixon 2011).

On the other hand, we believe that the Nordic model as a theoretical concept is overly simplified and fails to acknowledge important differences within the Nordic area, differences that are both historical and spatial. Furthermore, the Nordic countries struggle more to retain and modernise their increasingly more heterogenous societal models than recognised by the foreign observer, and their *modi operandi* are hard to transfer to other social contexts, as they happen to be more institutionally embedded and historically path dependent than policy makers would like them to be. These issues crucially define the area of possibility relating to a future of sustainable development, and not least the forms of sustainable development at hand in a given context within each one of the Nordic countries. In the next section, we examine more closely the case of the Norwegian tripartite collaborative scheme as an example of a challenged formal national and Nordic institution.

The Norwegian collaborative system

The Norwegian organisation of the labour market offers an example of regional system variations within a country that was otherwise thought to offer a homogenous institutional set-up. Box 2.3 describes the historical development of tripartite collaboration in Norwegian work life. The exposé in Box 1.2 reflects the discussion of the evolution of industrial revolutions encountered earlier in this chapter in Box 2.1 and also draws from the discussion of Industry 4.0 in Chapter 14 of this book.

Box 2.3 Development of the Norwegian Tripartite Collaboration

Norway can be used as a case for this development. In the eighteenth century, Norway was a rural society, where farming, fisheries and the export of timber and iron as well as shipping were the main trades and sources of income. Norway did not have a large bourgeois class, as it was part of the Danish kingdom and was ruled from Copenhagen. In 1814, Norway got its independence but was soon forced to accept a union with Sweden and to have the Swedish king as its head of state. This lasted until 1905, when Norway gained sovereignty as an independent state. However, even during the nineteenth century, Norway developed as if it was an independent society, and urbanisation and industrialisation started to make its impact on society. With an abundance of natural resources like wood, fish and minerals, and with the possibility of developing hydroelectric power, industrialisation accelerated around 1900.

Industrialisation had started to develop already in the early 1800s, and Norway got its first Factory Act in 1833 (Fabrikkloven). It was a law that mainly regulated who could start factories. In the last part of the nineteenth century, that political debate made it more and more obvious that industrial development needed more attention as tension grew between capital and work. The parliament initiated a commission in 1885 to look into the condition in work life (Arbeidekommisjonen). Their work, together with events like the Match workers' strike (Fyrstikkarbeiderstreiken) in Kristiania (Oslo) in October 1889, led to the first comprehensive law on industrial activity, the Factory Supervision Act (Fabrikktilsynsloven) in 1892.

The National Congress of Labour Unions (Arbeidernes Faglige Landsorganisasjon) was established in 1899, and the first voluntary agreement between employers' organisations and unions, the Workshop Agreement (Verksted overenskomsten), came in 1907. In spite of this, there were tensions in work life, and in order to try to regulate this, a labour law was passed in 1915. This law initiated a labour court to handle disputes (arbeidsretten), and also a national mediator (Riksmeglingsmann) for labour disputes. The first ruling came in 1916. However, tensions grew in the relations between the labour movement and employers in the 1920s and culminated in a battle in which the military were used against workers (Menstadslaget) on 8 June 1931. This became a turning point in industrial relations in Norway.

A Social Peace Committee (Arbeidsfredskomiteen) was initiated by parliament and work in the period 1931–1935. It led to the General Agreement (Hovedavtalen) of 1935, which became, and still is, the cornerstone in the tripartite collaboration in Norwegian work life. It was followed up in 1936 with the Work Protection Act (Lov om arbeidervern), which had a more detailed specification of minimum conditions at work. This agreement and the legal arrangements that had been developed made it possible to mobilise general support for a strong investment in industrial development after WWII. This development, based on Norway's natural resources and made possible by foreign direct investment (FDI) and with strong government engagement, became the role model for development when Norway discovered oil resources along its coasts in the 1960s.

The General Agreement between the social partners was reaffirmed in 1966 (Samarbeidsavtalen: Hovedavtalens del B). It had a unique element, namely that unions and employers should co-operate not only on working conditions, but also on business development. This came parallel to a common research project that had been initiated in order to look into work conditions and efficiency. The collaborative studies (Samarbeidsforsøkene), as it was named, was led by Einar Thorsrud and Fred Emery. Their work was cross-disciplinary and close to practice. Interactive research approaches integrated human and productivity aspects in enterprise development. It had its roots in the human relations tradition, but moved beyond that in terms of democratic and broad direct participation at all levels in the organisation.

The broad, tripartite collaboration got its most comprehensive manifestation in the Work Condition Act (Arbeidsmiljøloven) in 1977. This law stated the participatory structure of work life, where employers and employees have mutual responsibility for developing healthy workplaces. This collaborative structure works at different levels in companies and relates not only to the specific work conditions, but also to more strategic issues. Recently, this collaborative thinking has been reconfirmed in the concept of employee-driven innovation (EDI). EDI has come into focus, extending effective engagement. "Employees typically acquire exclusive and in-depth and highly context-dependent knowledge that managers often do not possess," Kesting and Ulhøi (2010). High technology creates exclusive and in-depth context-dependent knowledge. Only employees can hold this kind of knowledge embedded in the context of the work.

Parallel to this development, work has become a key denominator in the modern welfare state. Work gives access to benefits and is decisive for certain services. Even citizenship is, to some extent, related to work. The case of Norway illustrated how work life is regulated, but it is integrated into the social and administrative structure of society. It had its parallel in Sweden and Denmark. This has created the Nordic kind of welfare state, which is highly structured but also very vulnerable; it cannot allow for high levels of unemployment, as so much in society is dependent on employment. This was clearly seen in the 1970s when industrial production, not least shipbuilding, was facing a severe crisis. That created lots of social unrest. In recent decades, the Norwegian oil-driven economy has had a high level of activity and has induced high rates of employment. However, it is generally believed that we are now facing a new transformation, and that this will pose challenges for work life.

The historical development of the Norwegian Tripartite Collaboration illustrates how institutions co-evolve and adapt over time with the broader techno-economic systemic trends in modern capitalism. New production forms interrelate with and partly shape social forms, work forms and societal structures. The industrial towns in the early nineteenth century in Norway emerged in the immediate vicinity of new factories with the subsequent alienation of the working class, a threat that became apparent in the second stage of industrial development. Despite alienation and social unrest, Norway managed to develop an institutional framework to respond to the changes of the first three industrial revolutions, both through the parties in work life and through political intervention. This framework shaped also the current generous and responsive welfare model. As mentioned earlier, this did not happen as a planned process. It was a development fuelled by political struggle and class conflict, though it should be pointed out that the level and the intensity of work conflicts in Norway was far lower compared to many other Western countries.

The Norwegian tripartite collaboration is very similar to that in Sweden. In fact, this institutional arrangement alone, taken together with common strict provisions in the national work laws protecting safety and job security at the work place, explain to a great extent why the Nordic countries have welfare policies that are so remarkably similar. As we discuss in Chapter 14, on work, the structures of fixed contract employment are still, by far, the norm in current Nordic labour markets. On the other hand, work life in Nordic countries is exceedingly regulated compared to other countries (e.g. the US), while it is better integrated into the social and administrative structure of society as a whole. Hence, the Nordic work life cannot allow for high levels of unemployment, as so much in society depends on having people at work. Table 2.1 connects the historical cycles in the evolution of industrial capitalism to the analysis provided in this section, specifying differences in production forms, social classes, work organisation and dominant societal structures across time.

We will return to Table 2.1 in Chapter 14. Here, we briefly comment on the argument that can be read from it. What Table 2.1 illustrates is that seeing work life from a systemic perspective implies considering different factors like production forms, social forms, types of work form and broader societal structure as integrated phenomena that change in parallel over time, forming a certain continuity. We will return to the question of whether or not we are facing disruptive system changes today, and thus we leave the last column with question marks.

One important consequence of the integration processes connecting capital, modes of work life and societal forms has been the passing of laws stating the participatory structure of work life, where employers and employees have a mutual responsibility to collaborate in developing healthy workplaces. This collaborative structure works at different organisational levels and relates not only to the specific work conditions in a firm, but also to more strategic issues. Recently, this collaborative thinking has been reconfirmed in the concept of employee-driven innovation (EDI). EDI has come into focus, extending effective engagement (Kesting & Ulhøi 2010). The argument supporting EDI is that the adoption of high technology creates exclusive and in-depth context-dependent knowledge in the entire economy.

Only employees can hold this kind of knowledge embedded in the context of their work. In this respect, work life legislation and work life culture not only interfere with, but are also a precondition for, innovations taking place as a joint interest between the management and the workers within organisations.

However, few are able to predict the future of the tripartite collaboration in the Nordic area. We shall briefly mention three challenges that may threaten it; these are not exclusively challenges for the Nordics, but they may be particularly demanding for the Nordic institutional arrangement. First, one of the thorniest changes in the modern work life is the fragmentation of the notions of employment and work, and the adversities this could imply in setting boundaries for the scope of labour law in the future. The "personal work" model, where the idea is to increase flexibility by contracting and not employing, is by no means dominant yet, neither in the Nordic area nor in the EU. Yet, as non-fixed work employment modes win in terms of popularity, especially among the younger generations, the meaning of security, precariousness and autonomy in work life changes. The sheer number of work hubs and flexible co-working spaces in all major metropolitan areas, including Stockholm and Oslo, is an indication of what might be coming. If these modes of work gain momentum, what will be the implications for the Nordic institutions of work life?

Second, robots may very well replace more jobs than they create. It is not only in manufacturing where this is about to happen; in the service sector especially, a massive raid of robots may raise unemployment levels, induce social unrest and spread a general sentiment of discontent, insecurity and alienation in the general public

Third, social dumping is illegal in all advanced countries, yet these laws are not always effectively enforced. Businesses in many sectors in Norway and other Nordic countries complain about unfair competition due to clear violations of labour law by national or foreign competitors. Such unethical practices erode the level of trust in the social fabric. Trust is widely held to be an asset in any society. A person coming from a country with a high level of trust to a country with a low level of trust for business will not be rewarded. He will most likely be cheated. Any institutional quality has its contextual aspects.

As long as we live in a world where modernity appears as parallel forms of diverse practices and important sectors of society continue to exist in, or even revert to, pre-modernity, as argued in Chapter 1, there will be no best institutional practice that will apply globally. Instead, the best answer to coping with change in a disruptive world will be to cope with diversity while celebrating universalism. In this, the Nordic example still makes sense.

Forms of modernity

The crucial question behind this chapter is how to handle the triangle of structural change, institutional preconditions and innovation in coping with the future. What kind of resilient institutions are available? Our answer has been to present theories on systems, institutions and innovation, using as an example the Nordic countries.

Understanding how institutional arrangements co-evolve with economic structures is of paramount importance.

The forces of globalisation, which are often seen as factors causing global homogenisation by their reaction with specific societies in space and time, often create varieties of social realities beyond our imagination, like light passing through a prism. Most institutional forms have their merits and their shortcomings in meeting specific challenges in the future. They are constantly shaped by complex and collective practices in an effort to tackle endogenous and exogenous impulses.

Box 2.4 The Kodak moment of structural change

The disruptiveness of change: There are indications of large systemic changes, driven by technology, political sentiments and changes in international relations.

The knowledge one failed to use:

To understand effects on changes in the future, one must acknowledge and understand both structural differences in time and changes over time. This implies that any change will materialise differently in different social contexts. This is a criticism of assumptions that there are changes that work the same way in all societies.

Ability to adjust to future changes:

Any political or social system will respond to a change on the basis of its own situation. Some systems are more rigid than others.

The opportunity in the changes:

One has to acknowledge that structures differ in time and that changes over time will look differently in different contexts, and subsequently, any social system has to discuss their own way of responding to change.

This chapter criticises innovation theories that, by and large, have ignored the issue of how innovation, both incremental and disruptive, depends on *institutional stability as well as flexibility*. The recent economic crisis, gloomy predictions of forthcoming climate change and its impacts and the general shift in public sentiments due, to a large extent, to the impoverishment of the middle classes and jobs combined with the conspicuous changes in the status of modes of employment in the labour markets may be an indication of something more fundamental: a new techno-economic paradigm that breeds new relations of power and economic order. Green growth will not come alone. There will be fundamental changes in how we perceive politics, work and growth and prosperity in the future.

Another important point derived from scrutinising the Nordic cases is the need to respect informal institutions and cultural embeddedness. Societal formations and their institutional solutions have been arrived at as dialectical processes in space and time. One often forgets how profound and traumatising these processes have been and hence also tends to overlook whether ahistorical or aspatial shortcuts devoid of experience and context may produce the same results. This we will refer to as a contemporary fallacy, that is, forgetting that *policies* require a basis in *politics* to be legitimate. Being too instrumental on this entails unjustified optimism guiding policy adoption. Our position will be that learning is always possible, but that transfer of models hardly is. Every society has to compose its own institutional blend to cope with its own challenges. This means acknowledging and coming to terms with one's own prerequisites and shortcomings in future institutional development.

3

COPING WITH GLOBALISATION

Local knowledge and multinational companies

*Mariann Berge, Anne Grethe Syversen
and Halvor Holtskog*

Globalisation and multinational companies (MNCs)

How can regional and local strategies cope with globalisation? Multinational corporations (MNC) are agents of globalisation. We look at how they think about knowledge, not least local knowledge. They can shift resources between markets and thereby create local imbalance. For local economies, it is a task to both utilise the flow of competence and knowledge that MNCs represent, and at the same time to protect against sudden, disruptive changes due to strategic decisions in MNCs. This chapter discusses how local knowledge represents an important value to MNCs and has an impact on strategic decisions on where and how they build and develop their business units. These discussions are also seen from the perspective of the implications for the local economy. MNCs take globalisation as the business strategy, and knowledge management turns out to be increasingly important in the globalised process. Knowledge is progressively exchanged across geographically dispersed individuals and subsidiaries of MNCs, implying knowledge transfer across organisational and national borders. MNCs infer knowledge exchange across hierarchical and national outskirts. At the same time, local knowledge is an essential resource in the local economy. How can this divide be moderated? This chapter zooms in on some of the issues we have already addressed in the two first chapters; that regions represent an important building brick in the political process of identity formation, and the argument that local, resilient institutions are an important precondition for social balance.

A major argument in the globalisation discourse has been that the region will prosper if it manages to utilise its unique characteristics. Such unique characteristics can be the local competencies and tacit knowing (Amin & Cohendet 2004; Rodrigues 2002; Nonaka & Takeuchi 1995) as well as its unique institutional configuration and collaboration (Etzkowitz & Leydesdorff 2000; Nowotny, Scott & Gibbons 2001). In theory, comparative advantage should support the development of regional characteristics, like local knowledge. However, in practice, this is not necessarily the case. Using MNCs as cases, this chapter reflects on how knowledge can be transferred across territories, questioning the local/global divide.

Globalisation is a term used to describe the fact that national boundaries are reduced and that people, capital and goods can move quite easily between nations. Europe's internal market was an initiative to open up movements across nations in Europe in this way. It came parallel to the wider openness of global order. One operational definition of globalisation is whether international trade grows at a higher rate than domestic economies. In the period from the 1990s until recently, that has been the case. Another indicator of globalisation has been international agreements. The General Agreement on Tariffs and Trade (GATT) has been central in the post-war area to reduce tariffs and taxes on international trade. Its successor, the World Trade Organisation (WTO), continued this work. The American journalist Thomas L. Friedman captures this development in his 2005 book with the metaphorical title *The World Is Flat*.

Box 3.1 The Eyde cluster

The Eyde cluster was established in 2007 as a co-operation between ten companies in the process industry in the Agder region of Norway. However, these companies represent over 100 years of technological development in the Agder region and have for generations been the community's supportive beams. The cluster takes its name from Sam Eyde, a foresighted and innovative entrepreneur born in Arendal in 1866, who took the initiative to establish what are today some of Norway's largest corporations within the process industry. The purpose of the cluster today is to develop sustainable solutions that will benefit future generations. In order to achieve this, the cluster takes constant steps to strengthen the process industry and ensure sustainable jobs in southern Norway.

One such initiative was the Eyde Environmental Programme, launched in 2012. The idea was for the industry to take a proactive initiative to promote a more environmentally friendly future. It was inspired by the World Business Council for Sustainable Development and its Vision 2050. The cluster started several projects and initiatives, such as Eyde 0 Waste (involving the cost efficient treatment of by-products), Eyde bicarbon (aiming to replace fossil carbon with bicarbon) and Eyde Waste Heat (aiming to minimise and utilise waste heat so as to lower total energy consumption). In addition, the Eyde Innovation Centre was established, which was to put the focus on circular economy. The Eyde Cluster initiative was the first to establish a regional strategy for a more environmental friendly future, thus inspiring other public and private institutions at Agder to follow (Torjesen, Rodvelt & Landmark 2015).

MNCs play a key role in economic globalisation by co-ordinating and internalising economic activity across nations, by exploiting locally created knowledge worldwide and by sharing their knowledge across inter-organisational boundaries. MNCs help flatten the world. At the same time, the competitive advantage of multinational corporations relies upon their ability to activate knowledge inside their multiple locations by recognising, distilling and diffusing knowledge within their multiple host locations. Although the main reasons for MNCs' existence can be explained by their ability to transfer and exploit knowledge more effectively in the intra-unit context rather than through the market, most MNCs have significant problems with efficient knowledge sharing. Part of this problem can be explained by the fact that subsidiaries are simultaneously expected to co-operate and share their knowledge with other unit parts of the same corporation, and they are also often forced to compete with each other for internal resources as well as external market share. In this manner, this paradox has turned into a major challenge for knowledge management in MNCs. Another problem associated with knowledge sharing within MNCs is related to their different knowledge structures.

While scientific knowledge is developed from reflection-on-action, presented in codified form as theory, and may easily be transmitted and stored, local knowing is related to practical skills and experience and may be difficult to share within MNCs. Subsequently, there might be an inherent conflict of interest between local economies and MNCs: Local economies want to utilise competitive advantage for their local knowledge, whereas MNCs want to be able to transfer knowledge to the economically preferable location.

The local economy

The argument that globalisation would be counteracted by regionalisation because of important local knowledge and networks, favoured facilitating strong regions with broad supportive networks and specialised local competence. If we look at what brings competitive advantage to a firm, the literature on the resource-based perspective sees knowledge as a crucial element in survival. This means that both general, explicit knowledge and implicit local knowledge are seen as important for building competitive advantage. Subsequently, different kinds of industries settle and develop their business units in areas where such important knowledge is available. The local knowledge argument also means that when a company has developed its own local knowledge over the years, this gives the firm a reason to stay in the region, to uphold and build even stronger competitive advantage.

Bringing these two angles together, we find that in spite of different interests in utilising knowledge, both regions and companies seem to have a common interest in building a local knowledge base. The chapter takes this assumption as a starting point. Still, we think it is time to ask whether changes in organisations and technology may challenge our understanding when it comes to the importance of local knowledge: Can we rest in this common understanding, or will ongoing changes force us to think differently?

Box 3.2 Agglomeration

That local economies can be drivers in economic development is not a new idea. For example, the British economist Alfred Marshall (1842–1924) wrote at the beginning of 1890:

> When an industry has thus chosen a locality for itself, it is likely to stay there long: so great are the advantages which people following the same skilled trade get from near neighbourhood to one another. The mysteries of the trade become no mysteries; but are as it were in the air, and children learn many of them unconsciously. Good work is rightly appreciated, inventions and improvements in machinery, in processes and the general organisation of the business have their merits promptly discussed: if one man starts a new idea, it is taken up by others and combined

with suggestions of their own; and thus it becomes the source of further new ideas. And presently subsidiary trades grow up in the neighbourhood, supplying it with implements and materials, organising its traffic, and in many ways conducing to the economy of its material. [...] The advantages of variety of employment are combined with those of localised industries in some of our manufacturing towns, and this is a chief cause of their continued growth. But on the other hand, the value which the central sites of a large town have for trading purposes, enables them to command much higher ground-rents than the situations are worth for factories, even when account is taken of this combination of advantages: and there is a similar competition for dwelling space between the employees of the trading houses and the factory workers. The result is that factories now congregate in the outskirts of large towns and in manufacturing districts in their neighbourhood, rather than in the towns themselves.

Marshall thus distinguishes between internal and external (to the company) economic forces that determine development and competitiveness (economics of scale). According to Marshall, the further agglomeration process (concentration of an industry in a geographical location) is defined by the skills that develop in that location, supporting industry and personal skills in the labour force.

Local economic development and the economic differences of spaces can easily be explained by functional processes like agglomeration, economics of scale and monopolistic competition. This was also the argument made by Paul Krugman when he "reinvented" the economics of space (Krugman 1991). If we look at this historically, general neoclassical economics in the mid-war period disregarded the economics of space. It has been argued that in the globalised economy, local aspects achieve new significance. This has inspired efforts to develop collaboration between companies at a local and regional level as well as regional innovation systems. This has also led to changing roles of institutions as regions are forced to become more active in developing economic strategies and supporting business development, as discussed in Chapter 2. This challenges the traditional role of public administration and universities. Michael Porter argues that

> A cluster is a geographically proximate group of interconnected companies and associated institutions in a particular field, linked by commonalities and complementarities. The geographic scope of a cluster can range from a single city or state to a country or even a network of neighbouring countries.
>
> *(Porter 1998)*

Richard Florida argues, about the new production of knowledge and creativity, that

> The shift to knowledge-based capitalism represents an epochal transition in the nature of advanced economies and societies. Ever since the transition from

feudalism to capitalism, the basic source of productivity, value and economic growth has been physical labour and manual skill. In the knowledge-intensive organisation, intelligence and intellectual labour replaces physical labour as the fundamental source of value and profit.

(Florida 1995)

However, as argued in Chapter 2, these arguments to a large extent ignore the specific regional institutional setup. Phillip Cooke (2002) argues that there is a new type of growth dynamics in the new knowledge-based economy. It develops in ways that are different from the more traditional economy, such as soft institutional infrastructure and un-traded interdependencies, institutional thickness, learning, networking, reduced transaction costs, associated economy, stability and risk reduction, participation, trust and social stability. In normative terms, this signifies new ways of organising knowledge development processes between universities and businesses. In descriptive terms, we can see the emergence of new governance structures, new organisational forms between university and business and new practice-based ways of organising education. This implies overcoming traditional dilemmas related to roles (like role of the researcher) and institutional understanding (like the role of the university, or new arenas for university/business collaboration) in the regional context. The question this raises is how these qualities can countervail the globalisation forces in specific, local contexts? In order to address this and to exemplify it, we need to look into how specific MNCs think about knowledge as a resource in a specific context: Is knowledge locally embedded, or is it tradeable, seen from the MNC's perspective; and how does the MNC interact with this knowledge?

MNCs and local strategies

The governance of knowledge production and use is central to the theory of MNCs. Vernon's (1979) product life cycle hypothesis proposes that MNCs' capacity to apply locally established learning abroad is critical to understanding their strategies. While information created and exemplified inside a firm is a critical wellspring of upper hand (Barney 1991; Grant 1996), research in systems demonstrates that learning from outside a company's limits additionally adds to its prosperity. MNCs thereby play a key role in economic globalisation by co-ordinating and internalising economic activity across national borders. Competing in a rapidly changing, global environment calls for management and organisations with the ability to integrate, build and even reconfigure internal and external resources (Teece, Pisano & Shuen 1997). Thus, with strategically important knowledge dispersed across their different units, MNCs' competitive advantage depends on their ability to mobilise knowledge by identifying, extracting and diffusing knowledge within their multiple host locations. Some of these challenges are related to their technology-specific, local tacit knowing, which is developed over time in the local environment. At the same time, the ability of a local economy to maintain its competitive attractiveness is dependent on retaining a specific institutional structure and knowledge-developing ability.

Box 3.3 Case A: Norwegian oil service company

The company in question is a leading global provider of drilling solutions and services. It has units in 20 different countries, with the largest subsidiary situated in Kristiansand, Norway. In Kristiansand, the company has built up their local tacit knowing, while the global knowledge is more scientifically codified. The local, tacit knowing in Kristiansand has been largely built up through experience acquired over many years and is mostly technology-specific.

Recently, the company conducted a major restructuring, where they changed their organisational structure from a traditional to a matrix structure and decided to close down their research and development (R&D) department in Kristiansand. Previously they had a strong innovation milieu located in Kristiansand, where up to 100 people worked only with R&D. They found it too costly to maintain and wanted to channel these resources into different kinds of delivery projects. However, the subsidiary in Kristiansand has still a global function and co-ordinates all of the innovation work. Most of the innovation projects take place in Kristiansand, while other innovation projects are carried out in two other national places and in Houston. When the corporate function initiates an innovation project, key personnel will be extracted from the matrix, based on the necessary expertise they possess in relation to the product to be developed. Subject-specific teams follow the development to put these projects together during the whole process. One common challenge is to implement the necessary specific expertise during this process. However, they do not have any strategy on how to use the experience of previous projects for new projects, but they have lately become more aware of the importance of their different project managers, their unique knowledge and the unique experience they possess.

The company is a dynamic and flexible organisation that tailor-makes its products to its customer's specifications and requirements. The customers often take part in the whole innovation process, from the idea phase to testing out the product. Often, the customers have certain preferences – certain criteria they have to fulfil. These changes will most often lead to incremental changes but may also lead to significant changes. By involving their customers in these innovation projects, the company's management gets access to their expertise and an understanding of their customer's needs as well as financing for new projects, but it also provides an opportunity to test out the products. Apart from their customers, the company's external knowledge sharing with the other actors in the Agder region, of which Kristiansand is the main city, such as business networks and R&D institutions, has been limited but has become more relevant in recent years.

The management have tried several times to move the unique knowledge they have built up in Kristiansand abroad, especially to Houston in the

United States, but with varying success. The main idea has been to build up their expertise in the United States and provide an entrance to the American market. One example was three years ago and involved engineering-intensive equipment, which required much in-depth knowledge. A group was built up in the United States from the local area, who were responsible for the development of a machine. After the first delivery, they realised that it did not work. One year later, they tried again to build a specific machine, with a milieu in Houston being responsible for the development of the machine. It was a mechanically complex machine but still considered a simple machine. In this case, they brought in experts who had previously been working in other industries with manufacturing tractors and helicopters. The machine got good engineering support from the employee from Kristiansand, Norway, with knowledge on how the machine would be used. They seem to realise quickly how to design a machine, but when it comes to know-how – how to use the machine over time and in operation – it is less clear if they have succeeded.

Based on their experience, the local management in Kristiansand argued that in some of the cases, there has not been any active transferring of knowledge, and they explain this by the fact that people involved in the subsidiary in Norway and people from Houston have their own cultures, and have their own way of doing things. They also argue that there is a misunderstanding of tacit knowing, as it takes time to transfer tacit knowing. Thus, when employees have been assisting during these processes, the people involved have only stayed abroad for a short period of time before returning home. Finally, in Kristiansand they have succeeded in building up more expertise over time. The expertise in the same area is smaller in Houston; it is difficult to replicate the same expertise abroad, and it takes time. The management has also tried to implement new software in order for the employees to share their knowledge with other parts of the same company, but how effective this software is for sharing their knowledge is unclear.

The production also takes place in countries outside Norway, like Taiwan, South Korea and Poland. In recent times, more of the production has been moved to Poland. This is primarily because Poland is a low-cost country, and it just involves actual production. This does not involve any appreciable in-depth knowledge, but Case A has done much work in advance by proving detailed – specifically engineering – backing in order to create the best equipment. They have also lately been moving some of the production back to Norway. Although Poland is a low-cost country, it requires expensive apparatus, which facilitates and supports production. In Norway, they have a more flat, more flexible and more effective organisation with an already established production process, and sometimes it is more profitable to move some of the production back.

What gives industries from certain nations a competitive advantage in their segments compared to their rivals? This main question was the background when Michael Porter (1990) developed his theory on the competitive advantage of nations. Porter makes a distinction between multi-domestic industries and global industries. The term *multi-domestic* refers to companies with rather autonomous subsidiaries like finance, insurance and retail that we find almost worldwide. These companies meet rivalry on a country-to-country basis, have a low level of international trade and can therefore hardly claim to have competitive advantages depending on location. At the other end of the scale, we find the global industries, such as automobiles, watches and commercial aircraft, which have to cope with global rivalry on a daily basis. In addition to economy of scale, these companies build strategies based on a co-ordinated structure, drawing on competitive advantages from their home country as well as from company units in other nations, and thereby have an impact on national and regional economies. To be attractive destinations for MNCs subsidiaries, nations or regions have to offer relevant resources and structures that meet the needs of the MNC's global strategy. These attributes are relevant factor conditions (skilled work force, physical and financial resources, infrastructure and knowledge resources), an appropriate structure for establishing new companies and attractive domestic rivalry, demanding customers and related and supporting industries. These four characteristics are mutually reinforcing and are the foundation for the development of industry clusters.

Box 3.4 Case B: Norwegian manufacturing company

The company has a strong connection to the regional perspective of developing local knowledge and skills. It all started in Raufoss, a small Norwegian town in the middle of Norway, when the case company in an early phase started producing wooden matches way back in the 1870s. Through the years, production changed from matches to ammunition for the Norwegian defence ministry, and later to civil products for the automobile industry, starting in the 1950s. Parallel to the changes and progress of the production, the factory grew into an important cornerstone for regional development, largely depending on local competence and entrepreneurial skills developed over a long period, and working closely together with regional and national facilitators and later even with international network relations. Because of the increased focus on climate change that has evolved over the last few decades, the market for cars built from lightweight materials grew very fast. Another main issue at the end of the last century was the strategic restructuring of a big company into four specialised companies. This was a real kick-off for building further expert competence on how to develop and produce aluminium products for the automotive industry, with three manufacturing companies and one joint-venture company with common competence-building and internal and external relations as a mission. The Raufoss area hosted an industrial cluster, both producing for the private sector and continuing to produce for the Norwegian Defence ministry. The technology and competence on the production of lightweight materials in the region are now world-class. Additionally, the industries in the cluster have kept developing important organisational structures at a local, national and international level.

In 1999, our case company signed a big contract for building aluminium wheel suspensions for General Motors' (GM) European platform. This production is rather complicated and requires a deep insight into the whole process, as well as very precise assembling. Due to broad experience, internal and external knowledge and the fact that the local milieu had developed the relevant technology, the company was able to establish a fully automated assembly line for aluminium wheel suspensions ready for use at the end of 2001. At that time, the company had signed another contract with General Motors for the North American platform. This contract implied that our company had to build a new assembly line somewhere in North America, and for several reasons the decision turned out to be Boisbriand, a small town in the Montreal area. There was already an industrial milieu in Boisbriand, and moreover, labour and rental were supposed to be available at a lower cost than in a bigger city like, for instance, Detroit, which one could see as a more obvious location due to industry. Maybe even more important for the final choice was the access to a well-qualified workforce, because of the location close to Montreal with a high level of R&D competence. An important success criterion for the new factory was the transfer of both technology and knowledge from Raufoss to Montreal. The Raufoss company held broad experience in building up new factories and therefore put a lot of effort into this transfer. The main strategy was to move people between the plants. When the Canadian representatives visited Raufoss, they got involved in the local production and the knowledge bases at Raufoss, and this was supposed to enhance the learning processes. Because of long experience from developing technology and competence on this type of production, people from the Raufoss milieu had the overall responsibility for developing the Canadian company. Still, it was a strategic choice that local competence from Montreal should carry daily operational responsibility for the North American production and send reports to Raufoss. The Canadians worked with recruitment for the management at the same time as they built the factory, and the Raufoss representatives worked closely together with them in these processes. Additionally, the Raufoss company was well aware of the importance of local networks and support. Therefore, they started building relations with the Société Générale de Financement du Québec (SFC) at a very early stage. SFC was a publicly owned organisation with a mission to attract and buy shares in new companies that wanted to create business in the Montreal region. The organisation held an important local competence in addition to a broad private and public network, and they made a direct investment in the new factory with 20% ownership. Given the fact

> that the Raufoss company had very good experience in developing factories and network, they still faced challenges in the new environment. Being able to develop important internal and external relations is of great importance, and both rational and cultural competence take time to build. Our company met difficulties when it came to building cultural competence in the interlink between norms, language, knowledge, habits and values, which, together with technology, often form the core competence in a company. On the other hand, transferring structures for routines, reporting and organisational design went well.

Local knowledge is a part of the factor conditions that include a workforce with certain distinct skills, as well as the relation and closeness to universities and other R&D institutions (Porter 1990); and global clustering has a significant effect on innovations outputs from R&D activities (Audretsch & Feldman 1996; Feldman 1994). Therefore, technology-intensive industries, where the companies depend on both scientific and tacit knowing in their innovation processes, will choose to establish units in knowledge-intensive areas. This allows MNCs to gain competitive advantage by sharing and utilising tacit knowing from one knowledge-intensive region to other markets with less competition. Even though this shows the importance of clusters for MNCs and their access to local knowledge, MNCs can also be vital for clusters through their knowledge diffusion (Mudambi & Swift 2010).

A company can develop a long-term competitive advantage, focusing on the internal resources that are valuable, rare, inimitable and well organised (Barney 1991). Still, for MNCs that operate within a global competition and in many different environments, focusing on a company's internal resources alone will not be enough. We can recognise a firm's dynamic capabilities through a high level of leadership and management skills to lead and adjust firm processes, resources and a strategy that utilises the firm's assets to meet future market demand and win over their rivals. Unlike ordinary capabilities, which allow the firm to produce and deliver goods in today's market conditions, dynamic capabilities enable the company to gain a long-lasting competitive advantage, even in a fast-changing market situation.

However, whether knowledge can be easily disseminated within an organisation has been debated. According to situated learning theory, sharing tacit knowing may only be possible through social practice by solving tasks and therefore staying within the practice (Wenger 1998). For organisations to develop new knowledge or novel ways of knowing, social interaction and interplay between reflection, thematisation and experience may be required. Thus, building on the premise that knowledge is inherently personal and will largely remain tacit, MNCs' management may try to move employees between their different business units in order to transfer their local embedded tacit knowing. This view builds on the assumption that learning and knowledge development is more likely to take place between individuals when they are located at the same place and under circumstances that will encourage them to share their ideas. Even though this approach is considered an easy way to manage their tacit knowing, this approach is also associated with risk, since the company may lose their knowledge if employees decide to leave the organisation.

These capabilities are distinct to each subsidiary and have often emerged over time in a certain geographical setting, influenced by MNC units' corporate environment and accumulated and stored in organisations' routines (Nelson & Winter 1982). In addition to subsidiaries' own unique capabilities, MNCs' units may also share some of their capabilities between units (routines and manuals). Since capabilities are path dependent and developed over time, the transfer of capability depends on the codifiability of the capability and is therefore not easy to transfer between MNC units. The company's ability to learn may be related to the way it is organised. Thus, it has been argued that the movement away from the hierarchical structure towards a flat structure with a horizontal flow of information enhances organisational learning.

Knowledge sharing

Transferability is related to how much the knowledge is reliant on the present context and a consideration of how much meaning may vanish in a case if parts or the whole context is removed. Explicit knowledge or codified knowledge refers to knowledge that is transferrable in formal language and can be easy formulated by means of symbols and by digital tools. This kind of knowledge can thus, with relative ease, be transferred to others by the use of information technology across organisational and national boundaries. Tacit knowing includes cognitive and technical elements. The cognitive elements centre on mental models such as beliefs and viewpoints and may help individuals define their world. The technical element of tacit knowing induces know-how, craft and skills. Thus, tacit knowing is personal, context specific and therefore hard to formalise and communicate, and it is not easy to transmit within a firm, let alone across national boundaries within an MNC.

The role of communities of practice (CoP) in the process of learning and knowledge generation has received increased attention related to intra- and inter-organisational knowledge transfer (Amin & Roberts 2008). Social contextual learning approach, also understood as CoP, highlights learning constituted by actors who take part and interact in a social context (Lave & Wenger 1991). Accordingly, CoP may be an important place for learning, negotiation and identity developed over time in relation to another CoP. Three dimensions of relations may contribute to coherence of a community. First, through mutual engagement, members may develop norms and relationships. Second, they are bound together through an understanding of joint enterprise; and third, through a shared repertoire by developing routines and artefacts.

Explicit and tacit knowing can, under certain conditions, be converted to each other. Accordingly, tacit knowing may be converted to explicit knowledge through an externalisation, and may be transferred and learned within MNCs' units by the same means as explicit knowledge. In order to enhance learning, it may be necessary to dis-embed, translate, interpret and incorporate the tacit knowing. Hence, social learning theory considers knowledge to be socially constructed, strongly tied to practice, and not an object that can easily be passed physically between people. Learning is likely to take place when individuals engage in a shared activity, have a common interest in a subject or area and collaborate over an extended period of time. This implies that knowledge sharing within an MNC's different units is more likely to take place when employees in different units working together engage in social interaction in close co-operation.

When learning is arranged in programmes or reports, it can be effectively exchanged or passed on to new representatives. Therefore, institutionalisation and documentation of exercises are an important mean of exchanging information, as they let the information stream more easily in all parts of the firm. Inferred information is harder to exchange than unequivocal information. The above discussion is intended to illustrate the fact that the MNC has available strategies to overcome the divide between generalised knowledge and locally embedded knowledge. It is argued that tacit knowing may flow across regional and national boundaries, as illustrated by the two cases. If organisational or virtual community proximity is strong enough, it may be considered as an effective strategy for overcoming geographical separation among MNC units.

The two cases

To illustrate the argument, we have presented two different MNCs. Both multinational companies share some of the same strategy by developing new technologies and adapting complex systems to different local conditions worldwide, and innovation often has emerged in a practical situation as a solution to recognised problems among their customers. Case A is a leading global provider of drilling solutions and services, which runs company units in 20 different countries on five continents. Our study of the two cases looks at challenges they met while trying to transfer local and global knowledge to subsidiaries abroad. In Case A, the management decided to close down the R&D department in Kristiansand, Norway, which raises the question of the importance of local knowledge. Case B is a manufacturing company that produces aluminium wheel suspensions for the automobile industry. The case describes the strategic decision as to why the company internationalised and the knowledge challenges the company faced while building up a new assembly line in the Montreal area, Canada, in 2002.

In Case A, tacit knowing does not flow rapidly between the MNC's units. Part of this knowledge is developed from processes of interaction and dialogue and repeated trial-and-error games, which have formed a shared experience and understanding over time within these companies. However, it seems that moving employees may be an efficient way to transfer tacit knowing among subsidiaries by restructuring information and applying it to similar tasks in a different context. Thus, this study reveals the importance of relationships and the strengths of underlying similarities, rather than geographical proximity per se, in determining the effectiveness of knowledge sharing among MNC units. This case also confirms that knowledge transfer necessitates quite intensive (face-to-face) interaction and co-operation in order to succeed. It is a prerequisite that employees are motivated and willing to share their knowledge. Based on findings in this study, it does not seem that this has always been the case.

Case A has succeeded in building up a unique knowledge base in Kristiansand, Norway, around the control system, which is technology-specific, but the most important knowledge is the local knowing and experience acquired by delivering these packages. This knowledge involves know-how – how to use the machine over time and in operation. They argue that this type of knowledge may be very difficult to transfer between individuals. Most of the technological development is based on the modification or improvement of their products, and often happens in close co-operation with their customers, a process that has lately become even more important. These kinds of activities require some codified knowledge related to companies' technical solutions or engineering work, but the most important knowledge involves the experience gained by employees at the workplace.

Through historical processes of socialising and by cultural appropriation, the milieu in Kristiansand may seem to have developed a form of common understanding, also known as *encultured knowledge*, which may affect the way individuals behave and interact with others in groups in different situations. This type of knowledge involves the company's collective tacit knowing; it is thought of as "the way we do things round here" and may only be available to the members' part of the group. Based on their experience of moving knowledge abroad, related to their control systems, part of the problem seems to be related to their cultural differences. People involved from the department in Kristiansand and people from the department in Houston seem to have different cultures and have their own way of doing things. There may also exist a conflict of interest between the group and subsidiaries, creating a knowledge barrier, reducing knowledge sharing and knowledge creation. Knowledge exchange between subsidiaries cannot be easily forced or directed by headquarters but may depend on the employee's motivation to acquire knowledge and to share it. Except for long-lasting interaction with their customers and some suppliers, the company has not utilised network-based knowledge, such as knowledge from local research institutions or the local university, even if they have been important in providing a well-educated work force.

For the establishment of the Canadian factory, Case B received help from the Canadian government. It helped the company to better tap into Canadian society and culture. After some investigation, it became apparent that the new company needed a Canadian CEO. After interviewing several candidates, the case company found a candidate who understood organisation as a social partnership, a concept that is deeply rooted in the Nordic Model. After interviewing the former leaders that made this appointment, it became clear that they give the new CEO in Canada much credit for the Canadian project's success.

Many of the employees in Canada went to visit the Norwegian company to learn. This learning and teaching went on for months, laying the foundation for a

CoP between the two workforces. The Canadians improved what they had seen in Norway and developed their own routines and way of doing things. These smart solutions were picked up by the Norwegians when they revisited Canada or when they talked to their counterparts on the phone: Allowing such interaction to develop meant that both companies improved their efficiency and effectiveness. Some of the shared knowledge was indeed tacit, in the sense that it was not written, just orally shared. However, it seemed that the Canadians were better at formalising some of the shared knowledge, resulting in them taking the leading role in some areas of production. Tool changing was such an area. The Norwegian CEO called for a project for the Norwegian company to learn from their sister company; however, this was not straightforward. Some years had passed since the Canadian factory had been built as a copy of the Norwegian factory. This meant that the direct transfer of knowledge and procedures was complicated. In addition to this, the CEO pointed to the social phenomena that the teacher now should learn from their former apprentice. The project highlighted the challenges of CoP. Leading a company with a focus on knowledge exchange and continuous improvement is difficult in itself; combining these efforts across two different companies in two different countries is even more challenging. The social feeling of being reduced from master to apprentice was felt in the tool-change project. The explanations offered for this were the use of different machinery; the fact that the development department (located in Norway) liked to experiment with the Norwegian lines; and different measurement practices, which meant that the downtime variable could not be compared. Many of the arguments were valid, but at the same time the leadership strongly believed that some exchange of procedures and knowledge should be beneficial.

Despite managers seeming to be aware of the benefits of knowledge sharing, there seems to be a misunderstanding of tacit knowing and an underestimation of the time it takes to transfer this type of knowledge, as employees are not taking enough time to transfer the tacit knowing. Lack of time may prevent knowledge sharing. In addition to avoid time "constraint," for a closer coincidence between the local and global interest, it may be necessary with financial incentives. While the subsidiary managers are more concerned with optimising their local subsidiary performance, headquarters managers rather want to optimise the performance of the whole organisation, creating a principal–agent relationship. Thus, in order to encourage knowledge sharing inside MNCs, it may be necessary for subsidiaries to manage compensation to be more tied to the overall MNC performance goals.

Prior to the establishment of the Canadian factory, governmental interest and support was essential for placing the factory in Canada. Mexico was an alternative location that was considered. Besides governmental interest and support, the overall industrial competence of the population was another important decision point. Interestingly, closeness to the customer seemed not to be a strong argument even when the decision went in favour of Canada, closer to the GM factories. At the time of establishing the Canadian factory, the Norwegian mother company experienced major financial difficulties. They used the Canadian factory as a hostage in order to get some financial aid from GM. According to the case company CEO at that time, GM did not issue any orders on the location decision. They came with advice and help in order to build a successful establishment. They helped with contacting government contact points in the United States, Canada and Mexico.

MNCs and local economies

Multinational corporations may be considered as unique global distributed knowledge systems, building up their competitive advantage through external knowledge tapping in different business contexts by taking advantage of the particular capabilities of local personnel and the other local institutions with which the subsidiary is embedded, as well as their internal knowledge distribution (vertical and horizontal). MNCs will therefore play an important role in the future in both supporting local economies and in exchanging knowledge across local economies. MNCs are confronted with critical strategic decisions as they must decide a point of convergence towards one of two essential strategies, multi-local or global. However, gaining access to knowledge in these various locations often requires a physical nearness, since tacit local knowing is embedded in the context (Polanyi 2009), in contrast to scientific knowledge, which can more easily be decontextualised. Thus, strong local embeddedness with various local institutions such as suppliers, customers and research institutions may more easily provide access to important knowledge and thus allow the exploitation of market differences both in terms of available resources and customers' preferences. In comparison with the multi-local strategy, a global integration strategy will emphasise competitive advantages through scale economies by increasing production volume and scope economies from sharing resources and costs over products, market and their business.

Box 3.5 The Kodak moment of globalisation

The disruptiveness of change:

Globalisation can imply sudden, disruptive consequences for local economies.

The knowledge one failed to use:

Politics for local economies need to have deeper understanding of the logic of MNCs in order to see how they can be more resilient to change. This implies a criticism of the assumptions that globalisation as a threat can be countered by its unique competencies.

Ability to adjust to future changes:

Local economies have to develop strategies ahead of disruptive changes. A resilient institutional structure has to be considered. The competencies that the MNC represents can be utilised before crises occur.

The opportunity in the changes:

The local strategies need to acknowledge global forces and develop more comprehensive responses to global challenges. From a strategy or policy perspective, both MNCs and local economies need to develop comprehensive strategies that develop resilient institutions and balance social, technological and economic factors.

MNCs may often try to gain the benefits from both strategies by emphasising global integration while at the same time being responsive to the various local needs. However, implementing such a system may be difficult, since some of these challenges are related to their different knowledge regimes and rationalities. For the local economy, the challenge is different; one would need to embed competencies in structures that are firmly located in the region but are also dependent on the dynamics of developing competencies that MNCs provide. Table 3.1 offers a way to perceive the relation between the local economy and MNCs. It defines three levels of organisation: the region or local economy, the industrial environment or cluster in the region and the MNC that attends the cluster. On the horizontal axis are shown three different perspectives of the key factors that determine the exchange of knowledge: CoPs, which can be understood as a social mechanism; dynamic

TABLE 3.1 Local economy response to globalisation

Ways of thinking organisations/ Levels of social structure	SOCIAL Community of practice	TECHNOLOGICAL Dynamic capability	ECONOMIC Transaction cost economy
Region	Core competence in local environment that can enhance firms' competitive advantage	The region's ability to be a dynamic place for creative thinking and social renewal	The region's ability to provide economically competitive solutions
Cluster	Groups within clusters that have a common interest in sharing and developing knowledge relevant to their own work and business	The cluster's ability to provide learning and sharing of knowledge	The cluster's ability to develop an economically competitive environment
MNC	Groups inside the subsidiaries or even within the organisation, but across borders	Ability to see opportunities at home and globally and to mobilise resources for value creation and innovation	Resources and activities inside the firm are transformed to transactions measured at a certain cost

capabilities, which that can be understood as a technological mechanism; and transaction cost economics, which can be understood as an economic mechanism.

We contend that the presence of various knowledge sources can never completely clarify the information exchange. As opposed to transferring information, learning is developed through community efforts. With respect to intra-MNC knowledge streams, this implies, in the perspective of the social learning hypothesis, that such "streams" will be conceivable just where people working in various units of the MNC are socially connected. Information is unequivocally fitting exercises or practices outside which it has little importance. Learning happens where people work together on common tasks. This is the quintessence of communities of practice, which develop by people working firmly together to solve common tasks. The argument that can be read from Table 3.1 is that both for local economies and for MNCs, there is an integration of factors – social, institutional, technological and economic – that defines the total utility of local competencies and knowledge. For the future, the local economy and its ability to withstand the pressure from globalisation will be dependent on its ability to host clusters that provide both social resources, learning capability and economic advantages that are competitive. It is not one of these factors alone but the combination of factors that is essential. This implies, seen from a strategy or policy perspective (which we discuss in more detail in Chapter 4), that both MNCs and local economies need to develop comprehensive strategies that balance these factors.

4

COPING WITH ECONOMIC POLICY

Innovation policy in times of disruption

Hans Christian Garmann Johnsen, Jan Ole Rypestøl and Ann Camilla Schulze-Krogh

Coping with the market

In an increasingly competitive world, innovation policy instruments play an important role in initiating and supporting innovation activities within and amongst firms and industries, and in aligning national and regional competencies with business opportunity. As instruments, these policies supporting initiatives could influence future industrial development in three main ways. First, they could aim to correct system failures; second, they could aim to form, cultivate and renew the present industry portfolio; and third, they could aim to influence future industrial development by identifying and promoting new and promising industries. Thus, policy instruments relate to the market in three different ways: correcting it, chasing it or paving the way for it.

Today's society experiences times of rapid disruptive market-driven changes within most areas of everyday life. Some of these changes are relatively easy to adopt, like changes in user technology or communication, while others are more complex and have a more path-breaking potential, like digitalisation, robotisation and artificial intelligence. Furthermore, we experience some challenges related to climate and sustainable distribution, which are so wide ranging that they could potentially threaten our future as humans. Our take on innovation policy in this chapter builds on the approach presented by Edler and Fagerberg, 2017, as we define them as policies intended to support economic growth and development, targeting both the system and the actors within it. As the intention of innovation policy is to interfere with the market-driven distribution of innovation, two important questions arise:

a. Are the policy instruments used in the past also suitable to the future knowledge economy?
b. If not, how should we design, implement and govern innovation policy instruments in order to support innovation activities that will benefit a sustainable, desired future?

In this chapter we focus on how innovation policy has coped with the market over history. Using Norway as representative of small European economies, we examine how national innovation policy has changed from 1900 until today. The picture drawn is a non-linear development, moving from an overall modernisation project (1900s) via a strong planning economic structure (1950s) followed by an era of opening up and moving into a more co-ordinated market economy (1970s), before ending up with an era of smart specialisation strategy (2010s). Furthermore, we discuss whether concurrent innovation policies will help us cope with the future. Finally, we reflect on the challenges of defining economic policy in a disruptive knowledge economy. Our main purpose is to initiate a discussion related to the advantages and disadvantages of such policies in times of rapid change and disruptiveness. We argue that current innovation policies have some challenging preconditions, which have to be modified in the future.

> **Box 4.1 Silicon Valley**
>
> Silicon Valley in California, primed by defence funding, has developed by recruiting migrant workers from around the world and by working with university research institutes. This has resulted in an unrivalled critical mass of companies at the forefront of technology development. Many nations have tried to copy Silicon Valley, but without success. The reasons why copying the Silicon Valley story will potentially never succeed is related to its uniqueness: the cultural, historical and economic conditions that made Silicon Valley develop into a technological driving force. As such, the question is not how to copy the success story, but how to relate to it as US technological dominance will influence the world economy. A way forward will be for other regions to diversify in relation to their own unique knowledge and regional conditions.

As there seems to be an overall agreement that leaving economic development strictly to the market is the wrong answer, coping with the market is high on the agenda in all economies all over the world. Even if we have this overall agreement, the rational, the preferred form of, and the extent of market interference differs between nations, as well as between regions within national boundaries, because they have different institutional setup, as discussed in Chapters 2 and 3. These variations occur because nations and regions provide different answers to questions like how to stimulate employment and economic growth and how to deal with economic crisis. Issues like these have been on the political economy agenda for centuries.

Innovation policy

So, why is it that nations and regions have different answers to the same questions? Why do some nations argue in favour of a strong state intervention, while others are more restricted in their interference in market mechanisms? The answers provided by economists could be roughly divided in two groups. The economists in the first group argue that the differences are strictly a result of deviation from best practice, while those in the second group argue that the differences can be explained by variation in the institutional framework of nations and regions. The second group argues that these institutions are differently formed through history and that these institutional differences are manifest in all layers of the organisation, as we discussed in Chapters 1 and 2.

This chapter is not about the variety of capitalism and political economy. However, policy is a kind of phenomenon that links some overall perspectives and conditions and some institutional arrangements, as well as common resources with specific activities aiming to stimulate social and economic progress. Policies are a sort of reading of a situation, linking conviction with practice, and they have the ability to align both institutional arrangement and resources. The downside of policy is, however, that if it fails, it can mean a tremendous loss of resources.

Innovation, in the narrow sense of the term, could be defined as "the implementation of a new or significantly improved product (good or service), or process, a new marketing method, or a new organisational method in business practices, workplace organisation or external relations" (OECD 2005, p. 46). It is commonly accepted that innovation is crucial to secure jobs, economic growth and prosperity, and so innovation policy becomes an important tool in governing the allocation of resources needed to stimulate such processes. As a government has a slot of resources, policies can contribute to shaping the future by stimulating and allocating such resources amongst actors. In a globalised world, this ability, if you are a small state, is limited, but in a more naturalised world, that ability increases.

Even if innovation is as old as mankind itself (Edler & Fagerberg 2017, p.3), the term *innovation policy* was not commonly used until the turn of the millennium. Prior to innovation policy, we therefore had separate policies aiming to stimulate technology research, science and industrial development – while from the millennium onwards, innovation policy fused these policy areas into one. The nation state economics appeared and was strengthened by the strengthening of the nation state after World War I and again after World War II (WWII). Keynesianism and national economic planning led, in western Europe, to national industrial policy, public ownership of capital, control of investments and exploitation of natural resources.

In Norway, fiscal policy and state control of the economy through industrial investments was a main policy area after WWII. However, it was a policy that collapsed at the beginning of the 1970s. Still, *The Economist* (2010) argued that state industrial policy has returned after the financial crisis. Today, knowledge about the importance of innovation, how firms innovate and how systems of innovation work has contributed to putting innovation policy high up on the political agenda.

To address the advent of policy development, we start by tapping into some political economic shifts in Norwegian history. The shifts are illustrated by brief descriptions of their political and economic "projects." Our starting point is the early twentieth century, when Norway separated from Sweden and became an independent nation. As a new nation, Norway focused its political attention on the construction of a solid organisational and institutional framework. This framework of formal and informal organisations, rules and regulations was highly relevant for the process of generating economic growth, as economic actors aligned with the national and regional system of institutions. The second shift in history is found in the post-WWII period, characterised by a renewal of the nation-building project, resulting in a top–down planning economy approach. In the third period, the decade between 1970 and 1980, economic politics took a more liberal market approach. In the period from 2000 onwards, there has been an ongoing transformation from a resource-based to a more knowledge-based economy, most recently materialised as policies with a smart specialisation core.

The period around 1900 was marked by a great modernisation and nation-building project. Norway is one of the smaller countries in Europe. Nation building and industrial development have been two parallel processes. Prior to Norway's dissolution of its union with Sweden in 1905, Norway was more modernised than Sweden. In 1875, 40% of its economic activity was related to non-primary industry, compared to about 30% in Sweden. Closing in on 1900, Norway was still in the lead with 53% compared to Sweden's 30% of economic activity outside primary industry (Berg 2008, p. 109). However, the Norwegian modernisation project was small-scale, with the Norwegian state as a huge contributor. The state was not really properly rigged for industrial development or operation. Based on its bank structure, company laws (set out in 1848) and technical universities, Sweden was much better positioned to set forth its modernisation project in the early 1900s. Thus, from 1870 to 1910, income per person grew by 131% in Sweden, compared to a 61% growth in Norway (Sejerstedt 2005).

In 1950s, in the post-WWII area, planning economy was a prioritised area in political circles. Norway, like most European countries, was economically exhausted after WWII. From being focused on how to regain its sovereignty, the country needed to unite on how to rebuild the nation. The modernisation project was high on the political agenda, and the Labour party's strong position in the post-war period preached for top-down steering, arguing against the development of a capitalist elite. To succeed, the economy needed planning.

A central theme in the first period of reconstruction was which economic model would be most suitable to create jobs, income and economic growth. In the inter-war period, a school of economists had emerged in Norway, led by Professor Ragnar Frisch (1895–1973) and later Professor Trygve Haavelmo (1911–1999) and Professor Leif Johansen (1930–1982). This milieu, labelled as "the Oslo school," strongly disagreed with leading economists at that time like William Beveridge and John Maynard Keynes, who argued that full employment could be achieved by the use of an active state in a market economic system. According to Frisch and his companions, even a strongly managed market economy would be ineffective to create jobs and future economic growth. The best way to optimise such processes would be to bridle the whole national economy. Thus, the Oslo School economists argued that a controlled and tailored national economic development could be secured through a set of economic regulations, and that these regulations could be managed by economic modelling. Economics, they argued, is like engineering. A country possesses a tool box containing economic instruments that can be used to create any desired outcome (Johnsen 2014).

The unique model of a planned economy was gradually implemented during the 1950s and 1960s. The main idea of the system was to engineer national economic growth through a scientifically based tailored system of investment regulations and, at the same time, to gain macro-economic balance between finance credit and income. The foundation of the system was a regulated, low interest rate that should secure a high rate of return from fixed capital investments in prioritised sectors of production.

The focus of the post-war industrial policy strategy in Norway was to support the transformation of small and medium-sized enterprises (SMEs) to more large-scale capital-intensive corporations (Fagerberg, Mowery & Verspagen 2009).

In short, this should be done in mainly two ways. First, the nation should finance and own its own large factories. Second, it should attract international investments (FDI). The rational for this strategy of large-scale corporations was to better exploit the cheap electricity and other resources provided by nature. This industry-building policy strategy resulted in massive investments in (amongst others) aluminium, steel, electricity, coal, mining and fishing. Due to major investments in factories and power plants, Norway developed as a nation of some industrial strength, even if the strength was less than what could be expected from its level of investments. Compared to Sweden who allocated (the private) capital to cities, Norway allocated (the public) capital to the workforce in rural areas. The political reasoning behind this was to populate rural areas by locating national funded factories in these areas. During the 1950s and 1960s, the national economy of Norway was under considerable pressure from international firms and industries, and the economic system came close to breakdown several times. To maintain national industrial competitiveness, the government had to use strong means to control the economy, like substantial subsidies, subsequent freezing of prices and wages and even devaluation.

In the period 1970–1980, we see a shift from plan to co-ordination. On Christmas Eve 1969, Philips Petroleum reported the discovery of the *Ekofisk* oil field in the North Sea. This discovery changed the national economic development significantly. From that day on, Norway gradually transformed into an oil-producing nation. During the 1970s, significant investment was made in order to build the new industry, and in this period of industrial growth, the historical legacy and culture had major impact. Norway had no former experience as producers of oil and gas, but it did have a history of strong public intervention, public ownership and an institutionalised acceptance of governmental decisions and regulations. Furthermore, Norway had a long and successful history of exploiting natural resources, starting with the licensing legislation of hydropower in the 1900s. This heritage was important in the first years of oil-industry building, especially when it came to claiming public ownership of the natural resources and to building a publicly owned firm that ensured Norwegian interests in a rough international market.

During the 1970s, it became clear that the results of the detailed state planned economy were rather poor and, together with most counter-cyclical policies, the strongly regulated Norwegian economy broke down during the late 1970s. In 1977, a government-appointed committee concluded that a shift to a decentralised market economic system would serve the national economy better, and during the early 1980s, Norway gradually moved away from its direct state intervention politics and became more liberal to market economic principles. This change of economic system, and the rise of a totally new oil and gas industry, soon created an urgent need for new knowledge creation. Building the new industry raised challenges not previously experienced in history, and therefore it soon became evident that innovation was needed in order to succeed in a highly competitive global market. A doubling of the technical research and development (R&D) efforts in addition to a significant increase in education were needed in order to increase the chances of success in a rapidly changing world market of oil and gas. Investment in education was particularly important within the area of analytical disciplines. The committee further argued that private firms should be rewarded and stimulated to increase their own R&D budgets.

This *first generation* technology-push innovation strategy strongly emphasised that future industrial growth had to be created from new products or completely new industries more than from incremental changes in existing products and industries. Identifying these winning industries became important. The Norwegian government identified information technology (IT) oil and gas, biotechnology and fish farming as future winning industries, and policy instruments were targeted to support R&D within these industries. In an effort to bridge the gap between private and public-sector innovation, a New Public Management (NPM) wave arrived in the 1980s. NPM was based on private sector management methods and innovation processes and was introduced to improve and make public administrations more efficient (Hood 1995; Christensen & Laegreid 2001).

In the 1990s, this "picking the winner" strategy of industrial policy support was replaced by a broader perspective on innovation policy support. Due to a series of industrial crises in strategic industries, and fuelled by new research on the field of innovation, a *second-generation innovation policy* aimed to *make* winners more than to *identify* them. From being mainly focused on supporting possible industrial path creating innovations, the policy support system changed in favour of supporting more incremental changes and the diffusion of new technologies on a broader basis. As part of this process, the Lean method of innovation was introduced as important for maintaining competitiveness within firms and industries. Another difference from the first to the second generation of innovation policy was the move away from a regional distribution policy towards a regional innovation policy. Regions became more involved in the decision making as to who should be granted policy support within their region. This systemic approach to innovation argued that innovation is a place-specific phenomenon of interactive learning, and that a "one size fits all" (Tödtling & Trippl 2005) approach to innovation policy is not sufficient. Thus, regions focused on building sustainable regional innovation systems to support regional cluster initiatives and to make winners out of regionally existing advantages.

From 2000 onwards, Norway acknowledged the need to shift from a resource-based to a knowledge-based economy. In 2015, an officially appointed commission argued that the experiences of high economic growth in the previous decades are not likely to continue in the years to come. There are several challenges ahead for Norway. The overall challenge is related to the transformation from a resource-based economy to a more knowledge-based economy. The wealth of resources is a scourge for innovation and entrepreneurship. A comprehensive crisis in the oil and gas sector (c. 2015) was an urgent reminder of the need of restructuring industries and work force. Another challenge is related to knowledge development and research. Already in 2008, an OECD report reviewing innovation policy in Norway rated the country's performance of R&D activity to be low in an international perspective. Despite its economic performance and high GDP per capita, Norway lagged behind other comparable countries (OECD 2008). Six years later, a Productivity Commission pointed to some of the same tendencies: a relatively low percentage of the population with higher education, few universities at international excellence level and relatively weak scientific communities. Norway is far behind Eastern European countries such as Poland and Estonia when it comes to educational level among the population. Moreover, the report identifies the challenge faced by business communities to keep up with the rapid changes in technology. Innovation in the public sector is needed, as fewer resources and higher efficiency demands will require a restructuring of public administrations. The OECD report initiated policy efforts that still persist, designing various instruments to foster R&D activities in industries as well as tighter interplay between R&D communities and firms. The Productivity Commission's report is high up on the policy agenda, leaving little doubt about the effort being made to include the report results in new policy approaches.

Today, the regional system approach to innovation is more evident than ever. Policy instruments are regionally tailored, and their main focus is to support regional knowledge sourcing and co-creation amongst sub-system actors represented by R&D organisations, firms and support organisations. Even though policy instruments are more regionally focused than ever, and innovation is no longer seen as a result of a linear process fuelled mainly by R&D, some of today's priorities share a resemblance with earlier initiatives. Influenced by the European Union's (EU) Smart specialisation approaches (RIS3), regions all over Europe are encouraged to diversify in accordance to their core competences. The core idea in this approach is that regions need to diversify in order to be competitive in the long run, as no region can be competitive in all industries, but most regions can compete in one or in a restricted set of industries.

The shifts in economic policy in Norway may be illustrated by Figure 4.1, with two different dimensions illustrating the relationships between the economic policy and market adoptions. The nation-building process that started around 1900 was

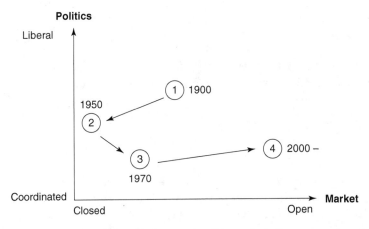

FIGURE 4.1 The relationship between politics and market.
Source: Authors' own.

a point of departure for economic and political decision-making continuing up till today. The political economic history shows a non-linear development moving from the overall modernisation project (1) via a strong planning economy structure (2) to an era of opening up and moving into a more coordinated market economy (3) characterised by a corporate governance structure. Finally illustrated by the ongoing transformation from a resource-based economy into a knowledge based economy (4), recently influenced by the RIS3 approach which is more in depth discussed in the next section.

Specialisation and diversification

Research and Innovation Strategies for Smart Specialisation (RIS3) is a policy concept founded in the European Structural and Investment Fund interventions for research and innovation. In order to receive funding from the European Regional Development Fund, all member state regions are required to have a RIS3. The rationale behind this requirement is an overall need to co-ordinate both funding and innovation initiatives in Europe, to make the EU more competitive and to avoid similar and duplicate specialisations and innovation attempts throughout EU regions. This policy approach concentrates its effort on the development of certain and particular areas, firms or industrial fields believed to be important enough to ensure regional economic development. The methodology that also comes in the RIS3 "tool box" is based on bottom-up processes of entrepreneurial discovery processes, including a broad range of actors (including knowledge of market potential) (Foray 2015). However, the policy concept has not until recently had a theoretical framework or theoretical rationale.

To start with, RIS3 is not about specialisation but about diversification. Through regional branching, regions should diversify their existing strengths and move into related areas. Regional branching is understood as the development of new industries based on knowledge of existing and related industries in the region. Regions need to identify areas of potential and existing competitive advantage through "entrepreneurial discovery," which is what the term "smart" refers to. Entrepreneurial discovery processes should be interpreted in a broad way, including all actors that may potentially discover domains of existing or future competitiveness. These actors can be entrepreneurs, organisations, firms, universities and regional development agencies. As of today, most European regions have developed, or are in the process of developing, such strategies. These include some Norwegian regions, even though Norwegian regions are not at all required to do so, since Norway is not a member of EU. As pointed out by advocates of RIS3, including scholars whose theories rationalise the approach, concentrating efforts and resources into specific fields, technologies and industries may have many potential advantages. These advantages may include expanding knowledge towards new domains of R&D and innovation, building capacities for diffusing knowledge and competence and improving the performance of selected industries or sectors.

However, as a tool for prioritising certain industrial paths according to some – and in theory broadly and well-founded – preferred fields, it may also pose some disadvantages. The collective experiment (entrepreneurial discovery) process, which has been laid as a basis for a successful smart specialisation strategy, is among other things conditioned by tighter collaboration between the private and public sectors. Arguably, there are some challenges ahead in this collaborative sphere.

The smart specialisation strategy is not an easy and straightforward strategy to adapt and implement. In order for nations and regions to qualify, they need to fulfil a wide set of regulations, follow strict procedures and handle a wide set of concepts and processes. As such, they need to qualify at a relatively high level of abstraction in order to prevail in such a system, and this qualification process causes a divide between those who manage this system and those who do not. The smart specialisation strategy is different from previous innovation strategies in one important respect. The decisions made on the basis of the policy also include the political system itself. In previous times, innovation policy was hammered out by the political system to influence the market. Today, innovation policy also includes the political system itself. Innovation in the public sector constitutes an increasing domain.

The rationale behind RIS3 is an overall need for co-ordination. As a whole, the EU needs to be more competitive, and the strategy for reaching a higher level of competitiveness is to force regions to diversify. The process of diversification should be broadly based and from a bottom-up initiative, but still, regions have to convert their competences and knowledge into certain prioritised areas. In this way, the EU will have less internal competition and will increase the overall level of expertise. This strategy might be potentially dangerous to regions within the union, as highly specialised regions face the risk of being locked in. From the literature on old industrial districts and specialised RISs, we know that prioritising will narrow the knowledge flow and gradually institutionalise in a manner that will promote extension over renewal and creation.

Prioritising as suggested by RIS3 could confirm and enhance existing trajectories. This could lead to path exhaustion, which is a confirmation and enhancement of existing trajectories, potentially leading to a reduction of growth. This goes for both industrial development and development within the policy domain. Sustainable innovation policies can thus be interpreted as policies that fulfil the objectives of contributing to economic and social growth for societies.

The regions in Norway have responded quite differently to the advent of smart specialisation. There are differences in to what extent they use it as an active instrument for developing new policies through engaging actors and stakeholders in the region. Despite this variable take on RIS3 in Norway, as well as a national reluctance to embrace the methodology and proposed "novelty" of RIS3, Norway has identified industrial areas of possible success, which are gaining special attention from the policy support system (see Box 4.2). The government has developed national strategies to support several industries like marine, maritime, travel, environmental technology and energy and generic technologies like nano- and biotechnology. By identifying its competitive advantages, the level of ambition has once again been raised to identify winners. However, the risk of making the wrong choice means the stakes are higher than ever because the evolution of knowledge and technology is changing even more rapidly.

How can we cope with the market in times of disruption?

There are several challenges ahead in relation to concurrent innovation policies and new policy approaches aiming to stimulate innovation and economic growth. First, as illustrated by the historical development of innovation policies in Norway, nation-states are extremely path dependent. This means that breaking out of old trajectories, even when required in times of economic decay, is an extremely strenuous affair. The success of smart specialisation strategies throughout Europe is conditioned by industrial and historical configurations already present and institutionalised in a specific region or a specific nation. Second, the entrepreneurial discovery process of RIS3 proposes to diminish the border between markets and politics as a methodological approach. What about democratic institutions? Are they disconnected as a result of this? Third, how can we be sure that these collaborative efforts choose the best areas, field and industries for the future (non-neutral manner principle)? Fourth, what are the consequences of such strategies in the long term for regional industrial development and, finally, what are the organisational and governmental capacities needed to address these complexities and uncertainties in the suggested challenges?

RIS3 is more about methodology (how to model/frame the strategy) and less about values and institutional configurations. It could be argued that the smart specialisation strategy is a quasi-solution between market and politics. To rephrase the smart specialisation strategy is neither market nor politics. It is at the borderline of both, as the policy approach is undemocratic but anchored in democratic processes, and it is not market-driven but aims to predict the outcome of market mechanisms. We will therefore point at some areas of conflicts resulting from a smart specialisation innovation strategy approach and initiate a discussion related to the advantages and disadvantages of such a strategy in times of rapid change and disruption.

As with Norway, more and more countries are increasingly reliant on knowledge as their main driver of productivity and economic growth. The learning economy is characterised by, among other things, a need for workers to acquire a range of skills and to continuously adapt these skills (OECD 1996). This has implications for governments and new policy approaches in terms of developing this important asset of "knowledge." Knowledge, and how we define what knowledge is, has become something that is held by the whole population and not only by a smaller scientific or political elite (as in the example of planning economic systems). However, it seems that the inherent regime-changing implications of talking about a knowledge economy have not yet really been acknowledged. Knowledge is often defined and used as if it is a resource of the same kind as natural resources. Thus, the complexity of a knowledge economy is seen as knowledge being both specific and dispersed. The second part of this book puts the focus on this issue. Knowledge is defined by some as a stock that can be purchased, earned and produced in the equation of "knowledge economies." Knowledge is a key input to innovation, and innovation is key to economic growth and development. Thus, governments are highly concerned with how to increase their knowledge assets, which is often materialised through different innovation policy efforts.

Box 4.2 The Digital Norway initiative

The initiative Digital Norway (Toppindustrisenteret) may be used to shed light on the difficulties to address the complexity of new knowledge development in order to realise policy objectives.

The Digital Norway initiative has recently gained great political backing and financing. Norway has several high-tech industrial environments, for instance, in Agder, in Raufoss and in Kongsberg, whereas the latter community and industrial elite within the maritime and defence sector came up with the idea of a cross-industry national centre. The idea is based on "Toppidrettssenteret," where sport talents are fostered in an overall organisation for sports from all areas. In their formal statement announcing the launch of Digital Norway in spring 2017, the organisers said that "Norwegian business needs guidance, arenas for co-operation and facilities to create new business models, methods of production, customer interface and services" (retrieved from www.digital-norway.com/). Besides backing from the Norwegian government, twelve of Norway's larger firms are currently behind the centre. Together with industrial, public and research partners, they will create three platforms for knowledge development and exchange: First, a network of talents within areas of digital technology, business models and leaderships; second, a digital platform for sharing competences and resources; and third, a test lab. The lab will be instrumental in testing disruptive services and business models across sectors and value chains.

Digital Norway is aligned with recommendations in terms of an overall goal of creating tighter relations between R&D and industry and fostering excellence and innovation in industries, as well as finding measures to meet the challenges of rapid technological change. There are reasons to question whether such large national initiatives also may be a fallacy in relation to vested versus non-vested interests, succeeding at the expense of other potential initiatives and contributing to impoverishing other parts of Norway. With the national government's blessing, the initiative is currently driven by relatively large and well-established firms, connected to different nodes of clusters located in larger cities in Norway. Larger firms and clusters as important driving forces may prove successful, but they may also be a barrier preventing smaller and less established environments from gaining the same support. Allocating support and resources to an initiative with already "handpicked winners" (in, e.g., clusters), may prove a situation of comfortable numbness and risk aversion. A central question is who are best positioned to predict which

> environment or clusters of firms will succeed to overcome the challenges and contribute to ease the process of moving from a resource-based economy to a knowledge-based economy. Who shall decide which environment can grow, while another cannot? What are the criteria for national public support? OECD has called the Norwegian dilemma a challenge of a triple transition imperative (OECD 2017). This means, to start with, that Norway needs to transform the economy into one that is more diversified. Second, in order to do this, the innovation system needs be strengthened. And finally, Norway needs to build research and education capacity that can cope with the larger societal challenges of aging, health and safety and climate (OECD 2017). The success of Digital Norway will thus depend upon how resources and knowledge are leveraged, managed and diffused.

Following this way of thinking on the knowledge economy, knowledge is just a new resource according to the same basic way of thinking that has governed economic policy for the last century. Knowledge has always been important to economic and social development, but the very essence of knowledge, and how we capitalise on it, is new compared to the very beginning of the nation-building era. Still, the transformation from resource-based economies to more knowledge-based economies has merely changed the discussion to talking about available resources for innovation. There are two ways to challenge this. One way is to argue that the current times of digitalisation and technological revolution may alter our previous knowledge of economic growth and welfare. These changes are, as we mentioned earlier, described as the fourth industrial revolution and are termed *industry 4.0*. According to analyses that are discussed in the media, 50% of existing jobs will disappear and 1/3 of existing revenue will be gone in the coming years. The third part of this book focuses on this. Such changes are disruptive by themselves. However, we argue that disruption with a more fundamental meaning will become visible by looking deeper into the concept of the knowledge economy.

In Figure 4.2, we have tried to show the gaps between different innovation policy strategies and times of change. In times of a stable economy, picking the winners may be a good strategy, which can be exemplified. There was no big risk involved for Norwegian society to invest in oil drilling and exploitation as long as carbon fuel was the main source of energy. Thus, in a resource economy, it is easy to pick the winners. True, it might be riskier today as we may be entering a post-carbon-fuel area. Still, this risk can be calculated. In a knowledge economy, picking the winners is more complex. The knowledge economy is more fluid, unclear and complex in terms of available knowledge forms. Applying a concept of knowledge that reveals its inherent social nature will make this argument more visible. The next part of the book goes deeper into this discussion of what knowledge is. For our discussion, we would like to suggest that the move to a knowledge economy might represent a systemic shift.

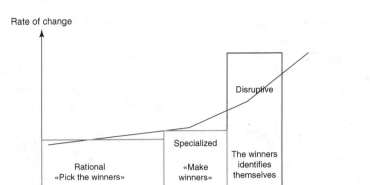

FIGURE 4.2 Innovation policies and change.
Source: Authors' own.

Box 4.3 The Kodak moment of economic policy

The disruptiveness of change:

Economic policy has tried to be ahead of the market or has at least supplemented or moderated market changes. The ambition in terms of national economic policy has been to position the nation in the international competition. With the increased disruptiveness of change, this policy will meet some serious challenges.

The knowledge one failed to use:

There has been criticism of assumptions that economic policy is something one can just decide and implement and thereby modify and be ahead of the market. Overambitious policy thinking will often exaggerate the possibility of predicting the market. Alternative ways of thinking might imply the development of general competencies that are flexible towards change.

Ability to adjust to future changes:

The possibility of developing flexible and more generic competencies implies that one does not respond to immediate market changes but rather builds an institutional capacity over a wide range of topics and skills.

The opportunity in the changes:

It should be acknowledged that economic policy historically has had an ideological basis and, in more disruptive markets, it cannot pretend to be ahead of disruption.

We have tried to trace economic policy thorough the recourse phase period, using Norway as a case study. This case has demonstrated that economic policy is defined by normative and ideological convictions. We have in addition looked at one of today's main economic policy instruments, RIS3 or smart specialisation. We have argued that smart specialisation strategies throughout Europe are conditioned by cultural, industrial and historical configurations already present and institutionalised in a specific region, or a specific nation. The entrepreneurial discovery process of RIS3 proposes to diminish the border between markets and politics as a methodological approach. However, RIS3 does not address institutional innovations. Rather, its thinking presupposes a collaboration within a rather traditional institutional landscape. This raises important questions like

- What about democratic institutions? Are they disconnected as a result of this?
- How can we be sure that these collaborative efforts choose the best areas, fields and industries for the future (non-neutral manner principle)?
- What are the consequences of such strategies in the long term for regional industrial development?
- What are the organisational and governmental capacities needed to address these complexities and uncertainties in the suggested challenges?

Answers to all these questions are related to the fact that knowledge is a social phenomenon, moulded by social institutions and context. It is this inherent constrictive and deliberative aspect of knowledge that has to be acknowledged in order to see how economic policy can lead to a larger change to a knowledge economy and knowledge society. Our argument is a critique of a policy that tries to run after, and even ahead of, the market. This is an idea from the natural resource area. In a knowledge area, economic policy will have to contribute to a discourse about the comprehensive challenges facing society, including how to preserve its basic values and ideals.

The core of this first part of the book has been to argue that there is an interestedness of politics, policy, institutions and local practices that defines the specific response to future challenges. A common challenge facing society is that of knowledge development. As we will argue in the next part, this development is strongly embedded in the institutional landscape. Subsequently, in the next part of the book, we turn to the questions of what knowledge is, how it is developed and what we can know about the future. Addressing this, we argue, will give input to understanding the institutional innovations needed in order to cope with the future.

PART II
Knowing the future

5
COPING WITH WAYS OF KNOWING
A pluralist perspective on knowledge

Hans Christian Garmann Johnsen and Olav Eikeland

We live in a time when Western societies are often called *knowledge societies*. Knowledge is a key resource that defines how we utilise other resources and how we organise our social activity. It defines the values we prioritise and the judgements we apply. What is knowledge, and what is it to know something?

Compared to an arguably monolithic understanding and monopolised production of knowledge typical of the period of modernity in the West, roughly from 1650 to the end of the twentieth century, the perspective we present here is a pluralist perspective on knowledge. Still, our perspective is hardly "post-modern" or relativistic and reducible to current or dominant social, cultural, psychological or economic forms. Pluralism does not mean that "anything goes," associated with P. Feyerabend's (1975) arguments "against method." Questions concerning the validity of knowledge: reason and method, are just as important, but definitely differently conceived, within a pluralistic perspective like the one presented here.

Philosophical discussions about the true nature of knowledge have followed science since its beginning. A. N. Whitehead (2010) even claimed that the European philosophical tradition amounted to no more than footnotes to Plato. Whitehead's claim may not be entirely true for Plato alone, but if we add Aristotle and even Stoics and other ancient philosophers, it comes close to truth. Historians of science and philosophy have often used Plato and Aristotle to identify two main positions through the European tradition, idealism (or rationalism) and empiricism. In a way, both are united in modern science through mathematics and empirical research joining hands. This "unified science" model, originating from the seventeenth-century revolution in natural science, has in turn been problematised continuously through the twentieth century, especially concerning the social sciences, changing the mainstream view and "standard of measurement" from a form of cross-disciplinary monolithic "positivism" to a form of "post-modern" relativism. As indicated, we problematise this change.

In referring to the ancient Greek discussion, two main positions have often been identified and personalised in Plato and Aristotle respectively. Instead of identifying Plato with idealism and mathematical modelling, and Aristotle with modern empirical research and deductivism, we propose to emphasise other aspects of the two. Although both in fact have a share in either side, focusing on Plato as a dialogical philosopher and Aristotle as a philosopher emphasising and articulating different ways of knowing (tacit, relational, skills-based, etc.), a different but still unified image emerges; not an indeterminate pluralism tending towards "anything goes," but a determinate and distinct pluralism to be explored here. These aspects of Plato and Aristotle are not only more relevant and accurate today, they also represent important contributions, at least for discussing the social sciences, the humanities and professional competence in our current situation.

In this book, we present several perspectives on knowledge. First, we argue that there is an asymmetry between the knowledge of the past, present and future, as indicated by Table 5.1. Second, we introduce the full spectrum of ways of knowing, elicited from the works of Aristotle (Eikeland 2007, 2008).

This implies that we have knowledge about different things in different ways and, therefore, different kinds of knowledge. Although we see knowledge as a social

TABLE 5.1 Knowledge and time

Past	Present	Future
Experience	Judgement	Vision
Things you know and can analyse the effects thereof, but cannot change	Things you can do, and thereby make a change, but do not overview all consequences	Things you hope to do and with affects you hope will materialise

phenomenon, this does not necessarily imply relativism or a reduction of knowledge to something merely socially determined.

We are interested in how society forms knowledge, since, necessarily, all growth and development of knowledge starts with individuals situated somewhere, sometime; historically, socially, culturally, and in other ways. Knowledge is anchored in the individual, and it is the individual mind that knows something. This individual mind builds on things that exist in society: language, history and concepts. What, then, is the relation between individual knowledge and social knowledge? If there is a convergence from different starting points, where, how and when does this happen? Are there emergent "universals" submerged in the different cultural, historical and various other starting points?

Many typical validity challenges in modern research methodology and philosophy of science are connected to specifically modern concepts of theory, methods and experience (or "data") and their institutional embeddedness. In order to solve or to dissolve the challenges, these modernist concepts must be transcended and transformed. In order to break the one-dimensionality of modernism, different ways of knowing need to be mustered and examined within a broader perspective on knowledge. In the following, we suggest how this can be achieved through demonstrating an alternative unity of Plato and Aristotle. Plato's belief in and defence of separate ideas is not at all clear in his dialogues. Also, although no doubt in favour of mathematics, there is hardly any maths – at least not in mathematical form – in Plato's dialogues. Plato cannot be identified merely with idealism and mathematical modelling. On the other hand, although Aristotle wrote the First and Second Analytics describing formal and deductive reasoning in detail, there is hardly any formal and deductive reasoning in the surviving *Corpus Aristotelicum*. Although Aristotle undoubtedly did empirical research, his concept of experience was quite different from the "dataism" of modern empirical science. He cannot be identified with modern empirical research and deductivism. Instead, we focus on Plato as a dialogical philosopher and Aristotle as a philosopher emphasising and articulating different ways of knowing (tacit, relational, skills-based, etc.). The practical approach of both was more inductive and dialogical than traditionally seen. For both, moving "up" or "in" to an articulated insight in basic principles (common patterns, forms) in any fields of activity, starting as novices and/or from how things appear to us phenomenologically here-and-now, goes through practice-based critical dialogue or dialectics, sifting and sorting, gathering and separating (Eikeland 2008).

Ways of knowing: Knowledge forms

Table 5.2 presents ways of knowing extracted from the traditional Corpus Aristotelicum (cf. Eikeland 2006, 2008). Differently from modern epistemology, Aristotle's theory of knowledge is a gnoseology, explicitly multidimensional, non-reductionist and relational, where episteme is split and takes a position among several other forms of knowledge. There is always a knower and something known involved, related to each other in specific and different ways that define ways of knowing; these relationships are also specifically required to acquire certain kinds of knowledge or competence. Certain relationships between means and ends, specific to the different ways of knowing, are also implied. As explicitly relational, the ethico-political implications of different ways of knowing are immediately brought to light as well, complicating considerably the modern ambition of keeping research "value neutral." Ethics deals with relations between people, and the ethical aspects of the

TABLE 5.2 Ways of knowing

Basis	Way of knowing – gnôsis form	Associated rationality	English equivalent
Aísthêsis (perception)	1. Theôrêsis = epistêmê$_2$	Deduction, demonstration, didactics	Spectator speculation (*observation*), dispassionate explanatory, predictive modelling
	2. Páthos	??	*Suffering*; being affected/influenced passively/"passionately" from the outside
Empeiría (practically acquired and accumulated *experience*) and *enérgeia* (activity/ actuality)	3. Khrêsis	*Tékhnê* (calculation)	*Using* external objects as instruments without changing them
	4. Poíêsis		*Making/creating*; manipulating external objects as materials, forming materials according to our preconceived plan
	5. Praxis$_2$	*Phrónêsis* (special form of deliberation)	*Doing*; virtuous *performance*, practical reasoning, ethical deliberation
	6. Praxis$_1$	Critical dialectics/ dialogue as reflection. The way from *novice to expert*, from *tacit to articulate* knowing	Practice, rehearsing, training for competence development, mastery, and insight (*theôría*)
	7. Theôría = epistêmê$_1$	Dialogue, deduction, deliberation	Insight, understanding forms/patterns

different relational knowledge forms, normally kept in the dark by modern ways of thinking, emerge when they are implanted among people – when some people know (about) others in the different ways presented below. The relational starting point also shows how the different ways of knowing are impossible to reduce to one basic form, differing merely in precision along one dimension. Although ultimately, praxis permeates the other forms, as will become clear as we proceed, the different ways of knowing are mostly independent from each other, with their own ways of acquisition and with their own validity criteria. Hence, both the modernist unity of science dream of transforming and reducing all kinds of knowledge to one basic form and level, and the "post-modernist" tendency to make all kinds of knowing indifferently valid or equivalent, were alien to Aristotle. However, his gnoseology allows for reconsidering and reintegrating ways of knowing: traditional, practical, tacit, emotional, experiential, intuitive and so on.

An Aristotelian theoretical attitude is to respect the nature of what is studied. An Aristotelian theorist is interested in knowing and understanding things "in nature" and "according to their nature" without artificially altering them. It's a non-interventionist knowledge form. This unites both forms of theory and separates them from the table's intermediary non-theoretical knowledge forms. Still, the two forms of theory should be kept apart.

The first form, called *theôrêsis* or *epistêmê²*, is based on non-intervening observation at a distance. Theôrêsis relates to external objects separate from the knower. It is based on *aisthêsis* or sense perception, or, rather, on a combination of knowledge from different sources, that is, perceptual knowledge input ("data") and knowledge from other (interpretive) sources producing educated conjectures ("theory"). The knower projects pre-conceived concepts and theory on to externalised observations, to predict or interpret movement, change or behaviour in the objects observed. The relation implied between knower and known is one of difference, distance, non-interaction and non-interference; this is sometimes because interference or intervention is impossible (as with remote stars) but equally often justified by the intent of studying things as they are naturally, in themselves, on their own.

The intellectual movement or thinking "down" in the theôrêsis model, from theory to "data," experience or practice, is primarily formal and deductive. In its deductive form, mathematised astronomy and physics have served as paradigms, as discussed here. For social and historical reasons (i.e. the rising success and social prestige of natural science), this paradigm gradually conquered the whole field of epistemology, science and research from the seventeenth century on. Attempts at modelling knowledge generation in most fields, based on this example, have formed the institutions of modern science and research in fundamental ways. Because of its status as a basic scientific paradigm in the modern period, almost all philosophy of science and research methodology has made theôrêsis under different designations (like "covering law," "hypotheticodeductive" method/HDM) its starting point and framework. For Aristotle, however, it was a model for the application of knowledge, not for developing basic insight and understanding.

By means of the distinctions in the table, it becomes possible to remain critical of this theôrêsis kind of theorising, while retaining the second form below (*theôría*). Mainstream social research, however, in mostly abandoning experimentalism and action research, and basing itself merely on reading, observing and questioning, has remained within this broad ideal of uninvolved and intentionally uninfluential theory and science. The experiential base for theôrêsis is registered collections of "data" as bits of information or observations taken at face value. Its relationship to "data": collecting them without influencing them, is non-critical and noninterventionist.

Generating theoretical explanations – moving "up" from "data" to theory – within theôrêsis is somewhat mystical and creative. Strictly inductive approaches (enumerative) have been abandoned logically since David Hume, and the abductive strategies (suggested by Ch. S. Peirce) attempting to make "inferences to the best explanation" have hardly advanced beyond educated guessing (conjectures). But according to Popper (1979), it does not matter from where and how you get your explanatory theoretical ideas. Theories are always hypothetical and merely required to provide falsifiable models (mathematical, graphical, physical or linguistic) that may explain the data, that is, predict the behaviour of the observed phenomena or events by deriving them logically from a theoretical scheme. The explanatory principle really consists in "saving the phenomena" instrumentally by reducing or assimilating the data or explananda to an explanans or interpretans as something already and better understood, subsuming the data under theory as singular instances of something more general. However, the real challenge of "theory pluralism," indicating how an endless number of hypothetical theories (true and false) might validly produce (i.e. "explain") a specific set of data as results, is not solved in this model.

However, with Aristotle, theôrêsis was not the only model for episteme – that is, for knowledge that was stabilised and pretty secure – about subjects that were for the most part or always stable and regular themselves. At the lower extreme of the table, we find the other epistêmê form, which in certain ways represents the extreme, opposite knowledge form to the first. With Aristotle, not only what we normally consider sciences were forms of epistêmê. Boxing, music, grammar, orthography, medicine and other skills and disciplines were also called epistêmê, because there was a certain patterned stability and regularity, a certain discipline, in what they represented. This patterned regularity is different from modern "laws of nature" and their derivatives.

In line with both Aristotle and Wittgenstein (1953), we may use grammar as the paradigm example for this other kind of epistêmê or theôría. *Theôría* translates as "insight." In grammar, the relation between the knower and the known is quite different from the corresponding relation in astronomy. Grammar is basically about ourselves as native speakers, proficient practitioners, of a language. It expresses and organises certain aspects of our linguistic practice: the more or less stable forms and patterns that repeat themselves in certain ways in our performance. Grammar is descriptive and analytical, but it is also normative, since it sets standards for correct speech and writing, describing topographies of language use. The basis for grammatical knowledge is not primarily hypothetical conjectures about artificially collected singular "data" of sense perception observed from the outside and at a distance, but the practical competence, or patterns and structures (forms) in the acquired practical experience of the knower herself. Grammar primarily describes and analyses the linguistic practice of the knower, not that of strangers as "the others," known only or primarily observationally (like the stars) through collections of singular "data." It is based on practically acquired *empeiría* (= Erfahrung) as accumulated practical experience exercised.

The table's in-between forms of *khrêsis* (using) and *poíêsis* (making) relate to external or externalised objects, as does theôrêsis, but not merely at a distance from a non-intervening spectator position. Khrêsis and poíêsis intervene actively in external objects as instruments used or as material formed respectively, making tools and materials move, change or behave artificially. Hence, their "artificial" principles of movement, change and development are in the knower (as user or manipulator), but outside the known.

Grammar also exemplifies what in the table is called praxis knowledge, where the relationship between the starting point, the means, and the end or objective of our actions is one of formal equality. As in playing an instrument or in dancing, what we do as novices; what we do on our way to perfection, as means; and what we do as perfected virtuosos are all formally the same. The end or objective is entailed in the activity itself as its own perfection, making it autotelic (meaning: carrying its end or *télos* within itself). Hence, praxis forms as activities are, in a sense, endless. *Ars longa, vita brevis*! As activities, they are not merely formally different and limited technical means for external and separate ends, inserted between a starting point and an end point, and stopped or put aside when the formally different aim is achieved. In praxis, there are no technical or instrumental "methods" or "tools" formally different, delimited in-between and separate from the starting point and the end. In perfecting a practice, or in attempting to perform virtuously (as in acting courageously, fairly or honestly), the aim and end is carried with and inside the activity.

This, then, represents genuine development as unfolding implicit (potential), emergent forms and tendencies, different from instrumental and technical modern "practice" causing artificial changes in external(ised) objects as khrêsis and poíêsis. Praxis knowledge is the primary base for theôría. In contrast to theôrêsis (and to both khrêsis and poíêsis as well), praxis-based theôría is knowledge shared, in common between thinking individuals through language. Praxis is shared or shareable as theôría.

As indicated above, quite different things may all "work." For example, human beings, or parts of totalities more generally, may be co-ordinated in quite different ways. The Aristotelian praxis-based concord or *homónoia* as being "practically of similar minds" – sharing common understandings, consisting in and created through lógos or reasoned speech, not only in face-to-face relations, but within large linguistic and conceptual communities – seems to be ignored when social co-ordination is attempted, reduced to secondary "mechanisms" like markets (trading and bartering), hierarchies (power) or networks (loyalty alliances). Praxis knowledge regulates, or organises, the relationships between equals. It constitutes and requires a "we" of peers, literally as a community with common standards of conduct and excellence, and a common practical mastery and understanding (as in grammar), and it regulates relations among "us."

In theôría, the thinking way down and out from "theory" to "practice" is also different. With grammar, the practical enactment is often spontaneous in fluent and proficient speakers. We usually do not think twice before speaking, and we sometimes act as if we were merely acting according to given rules, recipes, precepts and prescriptions. However, mechanical, machine-like and inconsiderate rule-following is not proper praxis. Praxis is defined in relation to its own internal standard of perfection (as skill and performance), maybe never or only momentarily fully attained in concrete action. In other more complex fields where the practice is not equally standardised and "automated," for example in ethics, the "application" of general competence or knowledge of principles provided by virtues like justice, courage, friendliness and honesty needs discretion and deliberation, that is, practical reasoning or *phrónêsis*, trying to find out how to act in the most just, fair or reasonable way towards someone here and now. There are no fixed rules or precepts for knowing when the *kairos* or right moment arrives, and for exploiting it in hitting the target in action, acting for the right reasons, at the right time, towards the right people, in the right way, taking all things relevant into consideration.

In poíêsis, movements and changes in the external object depend on us as knowers-manipulators. The change is not natural. The knower makes the changes according to preconceived plans in the knower's mind. Hence, poíêsis clearly intervenes artificially in its material, "going between" what would otherwise and "naturally" have happened to it. It creates or produces something from a material that depends on external intervention. The product or result would not otherwise come to be. Trees do not become chairs, paper or books naturally. A chair is made when a carpenter intervenes in the wood, making changes according to his concepts and plans. *Qua* carpenter, he is only interested in those aspects of wood relevant for making houses, tables, chairs and other artefacts from it. His interest is not theoretical, and he needs very little botanical theory in order to become a good carpenter.

When such poíêsis relationships are transferred and inserted into human relations, they do not always look as attractive. As with khrêsis, the art of changing and manipulating others is hard to defend ethically on a general basis, although some people are good at it. The art of medicine is clearly an ethically justifiable case of poíêsis or intervention, in relation to the human body aiming at correcting nature gone astray; restoring health.

Both khrêsis and poíêsis are based on technical calculation of effects in instruments and materials for reaching the aims of the actors. Their articulation is *tékhnê* or "technique." It works independently of any understanding by the ones subjected to treatment. When a specific cause is applied, certain effects can be calculated to follow. Technical relations can be mechanised through technology. Both khrêsis and poíêsis relate to external things, even to human beings in organisations, communities, and families and as individuals as external objects, as tools or instruments for use or as material for manipulative "making" or "conditioning." Both khrêsis and poíêsis employ means (instruments, tools) that are different formally and in kind, both from the starting point and from the end or objective of the act. Both have their aims in a product outside the technical activities in themselves. Unlike praxis, they are both heterotelic, meaning that their end is a separate object, state or objective presumably achieved when using (formally different external instruments) and making (from external material) have stopped.

From individual knowledge to social knowledge

We can argue that there are different ways of knowing, but that knowing becomes knowledge in the process of being validated. At a social level, what we in society regard as knowledge is defined by what is accepted as valid in the social process. The methodological argument related to this will be elaborated in chapter eight. So, how does society form knowledge? Social epistemology is about the general, prevailing understandings that exist in society. In the introduction, we presented the idea of society as a knowledge system. The argument is that knowledge becomes institutionalised and is related both to culture and social structure. There are power and interests related to knowledge. However, the point we make here is not about the sociology of knowledge development but the epistemological role that social knowledge plays in the process of forming knowledge.

As an illustration of the relation between individual knowledge and social knowledge, we use the argument made by F. A. Hayek in his famous article *Economics and Knowledge* from 1937. Here, Hayek argues that the knowledge that the individual needs in order to make rational decisions and contribute to market order involves insight into other people's plans. A simple example might illustrate the point. Say you plan to buy a car. For planning, you need to know something about the price of the car. This price is defined by what cars, and how many cars, other people buy. So, to be able to do rational planning, you would need to know what other people plan to do. At the moment you buy the car, these expectations have been revealed. The price of the car is now a fact. But before you closed the deal, the uncertainty was there. If you see the story from the point of view of the car producer, the challenge of making rational decisions is even more apparent. If you need some time to plan for buying the car, the car producer needs even more time and investments in order to be able to produce and deliver it. For the car producer to be rational, he or she should be even more dependent on knowing the knowledge of others. If we skip individual rationality, what is the alternative?

> Since our whole life consists in facing ever new and unforeseeable circumstances, we cannot make it orderly by deciding in advance all the particular actions we shall take. The only manner in which we can in fact give our lives some order is to adopt certain abstract rules or principles for guidance, and then strictly adhere to the rules we have adopted in our dealing with the new

situations as they arise. Our actions form a coherent and rational pattern, not because they have been decided upon as part of a single plan thought-out beforehand, but because in each successive decision we limit our range of choice by the same abstract rules.

(Hayek 1967, p. 90)

This argument, we argue, can be extended and used as claiming that individual knowledge is dependent on social knowledge. According to Hayek, this relation goes through what he calls "abstract rules," that is, ways of organising our thinking in a structural way. These abstract rules, Hayek argues, are not necessarily deliberately designed, but have evolved and seems, from an experience perspective, to be rational. They are inherent in our practices. Rationality, therefore, does not imply stability or that the future is like the present.

> There seems to me to exist a sort of rationalism which, by not recognising these limits to the powers of individual reason, in fact tends to make human reason a less effective instrument than it could be. This sort of rationalism is a comparatively new phenomenon, though its roots go back to ancient Greek philosophy. Its modern influence however begins only in the 16th and 17th century and particularly with the formulation of its main tenets by the French philosopher Rene Descartes. It was mainly through him that the very term "reason" changed its meaning. To the medieval thinkers' reason had meant mainly a capacity to recognise truth, especially moral truth, when they met it, rather than a capacity of deductive reasoning from explicit premises. And they were very much aware that many of the institutions of civilization were not the inventions of reason but what, in explicit contrast to all that was invented, they called "natural," i.e. spontaneously grown.

(Hayek 1967, p. 84)

Hayek thereby agrees with the critique of making formal, deductive logic the basis for knowledge. At the same time, Hayek links the knowledge of the past to the knowledge of the present, through institutions. A similar way of thinking can be found in Habermas' philosophy. For Habermas, the relation between individual knowledge and social knowledge goes through what he calls *communicative rationality*. This communicative rationality is deliberative, and comes as a result of dialogue. Habermas writes:

> There is a systematic relationship between the logical structure of science and the pragmatic structure of the possible applications of the information generated within its framework [...] Therefore, the technical and practical interests of knowledge are not regulators of cognition which have to be eliminated for the sake of the objectivity of knowledge; instead they themselves determine the aspects under which reality is objectified, and can thus be made accessible to the experience to begin with. They are the conditions

which are necessary in order that subjects capable of speech and action may have experience which may lay a claim of objectivity. [...] The underlying "interests" establishes the unity between this constitutive context in which knowledge is rooted and the structure of the possible application which this knowledge can have.

(Habermas 1964, pp. 8–9)

Individual knowledge, based on these reflections, is embedded in a social reality. It is from this reality that we form knowledge, and the instruments we use in forming knowledge are themselves embedded in this reality. Therefore, individual rationality and objectivity have to be acknowledged within the realm of the social reality that we live in. This does not make Plato and Aristotle irrelevant. Rather, what they teach us is the basic nature of knowledge. As indicated, one can reconcile the two, in the sense of seeing them as addressing different aspects of knowledge and knowing. Knowledge can strive for truth, but the truthfulness of different kinds of knowledge and knowing might come from different sources: The truth about the universe is different from the truth about my personal experiences. What this implies is a society that allows for both the subjective knowledge formation and truth seeking, and at the same time to have institutions that allow for sane and valid collective discourses. The first require reflecting individuals that critically relate to the world around them; the last requires institutions and structures that bring reason and rationality to the forefront of the public understanding.

How can we, based on these reflections and references, know something about the future? Our knowledge is based on what we know from what we have experienced and learned. However, we argue that even though the philosophical debate about knowledge and epistemology is ongoing and divided, and even though we acknowledge the social embeddedness of our deliberations, we maintain that human beings have a capacity to know both what is concrete and abstract, what is present and what is durable. The fact that we have a conception of time and space, as Kant noted, implies a capacity to see beyond the current, as we discuss further in Chapter 8.

Therefore, in the same sense that the capacity of individuals to develop reasonable knowledge about what they experience is based on both insight into matters and the ability to recognise the different nature of things as well as being able to have a critical reflection, social deliberation and institutional building need to do much of the same at a collective level. At a collective level, institutions will have the role of transferring knowledge from the past to the present, and our current knowledge is part of forming institutions that will have an impact on the future.

As knowledge is basically a social product, based on deliberation and conceptualisations that happens in the public domain, the main challenge becomes one of utilising the rationality and insight of all individuals in the social deliberation. This requires mechanisms and structures for securing the exchange of knowledge among citizens. The way to sort out what belongs to dispassionate explanations and predictive modelling versus what belongs to being affected or influenced passively, or using external objects as instruments without changing them versus making/creating – manipulating external objects as materials – can only be sorted out in a rational discourse that allows for critical discussion and dialogue. Taking part in such a dialogue is a form of virtuous performance, including practical reasoning and ethical deliberation, which is not in conflict with developing competence and insight in the form of theôría, meaning understanding forms and patterns. Handling these different knowledge forms, or ways of knowing, is the challenge of a knowledge society.

Box 5.1 The Kodak moment of knowing

The disruptiveness of change:

A knowledge society is a society that is critically dependent on utilising knowledge. Knowledge is embedded in individual minds and exposed in social processes. As knowledge is manifold and can be manipulated, a democratic society can easily end up making terrible decisions.

The knowledge one failed to use:

It is important to acknowledge the plurality of knowledges and forms of knowing and to apply them in the right manner. Not all phenomena can be understood in the same way or reduced to one kind of exposing knowledge.

Ability to adjust to future changes:

A society has to give attention to its knowledge developing processes. This implies a criticism of assumptions that knowledge is one thing, and that ideas like fact based policy, or evidence based decisions as a remedy against manipulation of knowledge, build on a narrow and wrong understanding of knowledge

The opportunity in the changes:

Acknowledge that knowledge is a plural phenomenon that gives meaning in a social context, and thereby is dependent on democratic dialogue.

Therefore, knowledge development has to be seen in a pluralistic perspective, where individual knowledge is embedded in a social context and where knowledge has many and different forms. This does not imply that knowledge cannot be objective, abstract or general. On the contrary, a pluralistic perspective on knowledge allows us to discuss the validity and relevance of knowledge.

6

COPING WITH DECISIONS

First I imagine, then I know

Carla Susana A. Assuad and Hans Grelland

The art of imagining

Jules Verne, in *Twenty Thousand Leagues Under the Sea*, imagines a machine that travels under the water for years, completely and sufficiently, without the need to replenish food or energy to keep alive the humans that travel in it. Verne was probably aware of the development of that kind of technology when he wrote the book in 1870. The first experimental submarines had already been built, and the idea of machines that could travel under the water had existed for two centuries. This had, however, not yet led to any technological development of the kind Verne had in mind. It had become possible to submerge a device, but not anywhere close to the advanced level that is described in Verne's book. Today, almost 150 years after the publication of the book, submarines with features like the one described by Verne are a reality. The case of the submarine is not unique; science fiction and storytelling have inspired many technological developments, and will continue to do so.

> **Box 6.1 Electric cars**
>
> Countries are setting target dates for switching to electric cars. The UK government has announced that it plans to ban all sales of new petrol and diesel cars from 2040. People woke up to the news. How will they cope? How can they charge electric cars? What will happen to the value of houses where cars cannot park outside to be charged? Has the government considered the implications of the policy? The French and other governments are making similar announcements. Norway has set a date of 2025. As electric cars achieve greater range and reliability and lower price, there will be challenges to the internal combustion engine. Solar panels and new generation storage batteries can power electric cars.
>
> - Automobile manufacturers revise strategies.
> - Countries fund research and conversion strategies.
> - Policies are needed on existing vehicles and pollution.
> - Infrastructure issues, such as charging, must be addressed.
> - The value of Tesla overtakes Ford and General Motors.
> - Companies decide where to locate construction plants.
> - Problems arise for companies making conventional vehicles.
>
> Driverless cars: A new generation of driverless cars are reaching public roads, raising issues of safety, responsibility, transport policy, employment, town planning and so on. Significant pilot projects will be unveiled, with many implications.
>
> - Accidents will provoke debate.
> - There will be a high-profile accident, causing deaths.
> - Pilot redesigns of urban areas will be rolled out.

In this chapter, we use this and other literary cases to discuss how we can have imaginative, and yet rational, thoughts about the future, and we consider the relevance of this question related to how organisations and managers make decisions today that have implications for the future. We do not know the future, but to cope with it, we have to make rational, and at the same time creative, decisions concerning this unknown.

The relation between knowledge and rational thinking

As we have seen, imagination is necessary for making decisions, but maximum use of the knowledge available is of course a condition for the decisions to be sensible and appropriate. One should use knowledge to choose between given alternatives or to look for alternatives when they are not given. The way a decision is taken is what we call its *rationality*. Knowledge and the rationality of decision are both crucial factors, since the same knowledge can produce very different outcomes, depending on the type of rationality that is used to make the decision. The type of rationality that is used depends, among other variables, on the time horizon to the expected outcome. The longer the time horizon, the less we know, and the more we need to imagine the unknown. Thus, our imagination shapes our rationality about today's decisions that have long-term effects. In this chapter, we will explore the knowledge and rationality that is used when making decisions in the long term, and how imagination interacts with knowledge and rationality in our attempts at coping with the future. We aim to shape reality to match our imagination.

Rationality has been mainly studied in philosophy, economy, psychology and sociology, and it has a specialised definition in each field. In general, one can define rationality as *the behaviour an individual has towards achieving a goal or solving a problem based on beliefs and reasons* (Foley 1987). It is the way in which an individual reasons when making a decision. The main point of division among the different interpretations is the frame of reference in which one defines when an action is rational or irrational. For instance, in classical economics, the *outcome* of the decision-making is the frame of reference, whereas in psychology it is the *process* (Simon 1980). Rationality can be related to decision-making when it refers to choosing from a pool of alternatives to a course of action in order to achieve a goal. It can also be related to the process of searching for information to find alternatives or new ways of doing things to solve a problem. Economics and psychology normally refer to decision-making when referring to rationality.

From ancient Greece to the Enlightenment, rationality was primarily a subject for philosophers, and it was mainly related to the creation of knowledge. Rationality was mentioned in the works of ancient Greek philosophers like Aristotle, Pythagoras and Plato. However, it was René Descartes in the seventeenth century who laid the foundations of what has become known as the classical understanding of rationality. For Descartes, all real knowledge is the result of reason only, without the need for any sensory experiences. Only the truth that can be accepted by reason or intellect alone can be catalogued as *knowledge*. Thus, Descartes created the school of thought known as *rationalism*, in contrast to *empiricism*, which defended the view that all real knowledge was based on sense experience. Other philosophers contemporaneous to Descartes, like Baruch Spinoza and Gottfried Leibniz, developed further the understanding of knowledge creation by the use of reason. During the Age of Enlightenment (the eighteenth century), the use of reason became the norm as the primary source of knowledge and authority. Immanuel Kant, who tried to formulate a synthesis of rationalism and empiricism, found a middle way between reason and practice in the process of knowledge acquisition. Kant introduced rationality into the concept of morality, claiming that moral principles are only determinable by use of reason, and that such principles are needed in order to make the right choice (Cummins 2012). Later on, in the twentieth century, sociologists like Weber and Habermas developed alternative understandings of rationality immersed in a theory of society. Herbert Simon introduced the concept of bounded rationality, and it is critical for the classical understanding of rationality; it assumes a human brain with unlimited capacities to find the optimal choice. This limited brain capacity has been further explored by psychologists like Kahneman and Tversky (1974), showing how humans do not behave according to the expected logic theory. Jon Elster (2009) has developed a rational choice theory.

There is thus a close relation between rational choice and knowledge. Habermas points out that two subjects can use the same type of knowledge in different ways, producing distinctive outcomes. The subject's belief in the reliability of such knowledge is one factor that contributes to the determination of the outcome (Habermas 1984). Human knowledge about the future is limited, its reliability is always open to question and it becomes more uncertain the longer the time horizon. The position a subject or an institution takes regarding the reliability of knowledge about the future will influence the outcomes from rational thinking.

Making a rational choice means making the right decision at a given situation, based on the available knowledge. However, the same available knowledge can obviously lead to different outcomes. In the same way, different outcomes can lead to different evaluations of the rationality of the decision maker. It is not unambiguous how the person making the decision evaluates if he or she has made the right decision, or whether the evaluation is guided by an external preconceived definition of the right decision. It could be a very subjective evaluation if the perception of the decision maker is the only variable in consideration when performing the evaluation. On the contrary, if the top–down understanding of logic, profit maximisation and statistical probabilities is used, then the evaluation will seem very external and does not consider the individual subjective preferences. This demonstrates the importance of defining the frame of reference when evaluating rational thinking. Such reference is not static or linear. It changes according to the situation, the time horizon for the outcome of the decision and the level of knowledge at the moment of the decision. This suggests that there are different types of thinking rationally, depending on the frame of reference.

Max Weber mentions the multiplicity of rationalisation processes that co-exist in specific situations. In his extensive analysis of rationality, Weber suggests that there is more than one way to be rational (Kalberg 1980). For the purpose of analysing the relation between knowledge and rationality, we will consider two types of rationality: constructive and ecological rationality. The first one assumes that humans or institutions follow the rules of logic, have unlimited calculation capacity and have complete knowledge about outcomes and optimal designs (Smith 2003). The frame of reference for constructive rationality is external optimal designs and the rules of logic and statistics. When a decision maker chooses wrongly (in relation to the rules), it is because he lacks the knowledge and therefore is acting irrationally (March & Simon 1993). The second one, ecological rationality, assumes that behaviour emerges from cultural and biological evolution, there is a limited capacity of knowledge and there is no conscious human design but human interactions (Smith 2003). The frame of reference for ecological rationality is the mental process and the environment. It does not consider the term irrational but the utilisation of the wrong heuristics in a certain environment (Gigerenzer 2010). Both rationalities can co-exist. However, when considering long time horizons for the outcome of the action, one could presume that ecological rationality is naturally used because it does not assume complete knowledge.

This chapter acknowledges the existence of multiple types of rationality and uses the concepts of constructive and ecological rationality for the analysis of the cases. It also assumes that for coping with the future both rationalities co-exist, but ecological rationality is the prevalent type when considering long-term effects of today's actions.

Knowledge about the future is to an extent unreliable and limited. We try to predict the future, but we do not know with certainty what will happen. Predictions get weaker the longer the time frame that is considered. Near-future predictions are based on information about present and past events and current trends. The near future is somehow foreseeable. Long-term predictions, on the contrary, are of lesser use due to the lack of assurance about repeating trends and the existence of unexpected events. However, it is unavoidable to use certain types of knowledge when making decisions, or to have an idea about how the future will look like a consequence of current actions. We argue that imagination is used in order to be rational today about long-term outcomes.

Looking forward: Short and long-term perspective

Looking forward, there is a difference between a short-term and a long-term perspective. In the short term, the future is somehow foreseeable, and current knowledge is useful for understanding the consequences of today's decisions. The challenge arises when making decisions with long-term outcomes. There is less knowledge available about that distant future, because it is further removed from the conditions we live in today. Between the present and the distant future, there are developments and changes that we cannot know with any certainty. There is an intrinsic relationship between knowledge and rationality: Knowledge is used to make rational decisions. Now, at this given point in time, there is knowledge available in the form of accumulated facts and scientific developments representing what humanity knows today. Then one can wonder what can replace accumulated knowledge in the process of making rational decisions with long-term effects. Our answer is that imagination, which of course has a role to play in any form of decision, even in the short term, becomes much more crucially important in dealing with the long-term future. Therefore, we will consider how imagination, as a representation of what the long term looks like, is used in decision-making faced with the lack of knowledge about the future. Imagination in this chapter is interpreted through science fiction (sci-fi) literature.

How can imagining the future help us to cope with it? We ask how literature (and other kinds of art) can stimulate creativity and inspire new solutions and new ways of thinking, and how the interaction between knowledge and imagination can be rational in today's actions concerning the distant future and in the effect of today's actions on the future.

So, what is imagination? We can say that imagination is the mode by which the human mind can relate to something non-existing or incompletely known. This obviously applies to the future; without imagination, we would not be able to have a relation to the future at all. We can also say that imagination is the source of creativity, of doing things in new ways. However, it is not such that imagination is independent of knowledge. We could rather say that every image of future situations always has a built-in structure or skeleton of knowledge (what we know today about the kind of situations we try to imagine). We can add to this structure of knowledge the creative dimension of imagination. Although it may make use of the knowledge available, an image will always be a product of free creation.

There is thus something non-robotic about human imagination, where knowledge about the circumstances or facts of today is transformed, through creative imagination, into a window of how reality could look like in the future. Somehow, that window of the future colours the decisions we make today, which will eventually create in the present that we call future now. This balance between knowledge and creativity will, as has already been pointed out, obviously be different when dealing with the short-term, the medium-term and the long-term future.

In this context, it is useful to remind ourselves of what Jean-Paul Sartre writes in his classic *The Imaginary* (Sartre 2004), where he points out that imagining some object is originally a relation to that object, not a relation to the image created of it. The image is just a means for relating to the object itself. Thus, imagining the future is a way of relating to the future, not to our own fantasies. Moreover, relating to the future is possible *only* through imagination, and this imagination *always* has a creative component.

We reflect on this by considering cases analogous to Jules Verne's submarines, cases where imagination became the starting point for developing new technologies and social systems, and how images affected the decisions that were made. We also look at the current narratives about imagining our future, and how that could affect the rational decisions made today. We discuss the role of knowledge and rationality when we imaginatively make decisions for the future. Hopefully, with a better understanding of the relationship between knowledge, imagination and rationality, we will be better equipped for coping with the future. First, we consider the imagination as such.

Imagination: A source of knowledge

The uncertainty of predicting the future is rooted in the undisputable fact that the future does not (yet) exist. So, the main problem is: How can we relate to the non-existent future?

A major question considered by Sartre (1969, 2004) is the general question of non-existence, the absence, or what he calls the nothingness (*le néant*), in human life. He points out that what makes it possible for us to relate to something non-existent is precisely the faculty of imagination. While our senses, our perception, connects us to the existing now, and memory connects us to the given (and, in this sense, existing) past, imagination is a form of consciousness by which we can relate to what does not exist, including the future. In the following, we build on Sartre's phenomenological study of the imagination in *The Imaginary*, which is still one of the best studies of the subject.

Even when we imagine something that exists, like the Eiffel Tower, we relate to it in its *absence*. The absence of the object is essential to the act of imagination, and this has the implication that imagination is independent of the object's existence. To imagine the Eiffel Tower implies the production of an image of it. This act of producing images is interesting, for it demonstrates a mental power of making something absent present in our minds. Even if I have never seen the Eiffel Tower and have only heard it very sketchily described, I am still able to produce a mental picture of it for myself. This mental picture is a result of applying both knowledge and creativity. Somebody has described the tower to me; thus I have some knowledge of it, and my image is partly shaped by this knowledge. However, the description is incomplete for the mental image, and I have to invent the rest in an act of free creativity. This duality is typical of imagination.

All conscious acts, including imagination, are directed towards some object, which we are conscious of. Sartre points out that imagining an object, like the Eiffel Tower, is a way of relating to the object itself, in this case the Eiffel Tower, not to its image. The image is just a *means* to relate to the existing or non-existing object. Sartre calls the image an *analogon* of the object. An analogon does not have to be purely mental; we can also produce physical analogons, like a drawing or a steel wire model. But Sartre points out that pictures and models become pictures and models of the object only through being "animated" by our imagination. A steel wire model of the Eiffel Tower is not in itself a model of something. In itself, it is only a steel wire structure, a physical object, but my imagination turns it into a model of the Eiffel Tower, and thus an *analogon*. When we read a novel, the reading depends on our imagination, and we can say that the text itself is an *analogon*, in the same way as the wire model of the Eiffel Tower. However, the medium of the text extends much wider than wire models and similar constructions. Texts make us imagine not only physical things, but also abstract, emotional and in other ways psychological phenomena. This is important in relation to literature.

A single physical object, like the Eiffel Tower, has a physical appearance that can be pictured both mentally and physically – physically by drawing or painting it or making models. We are also able to imagine more complex or abstract objects, like global climate change. Even if we consider climate change up to now, which is an existing physical phenomenon (including past facts as in some sense existing), it is something we cannot look at with our eyes like a single physical object, and thus it is not something we can make a simple image of. Nevertheless, the fact that the climate change cannot be simply seen makes it all the more necessary for us to use our imagination to relate to it. We somehow have to put together facts associated with climate change into what we can call a *conceptual image*. Again, this conceptual image is a means of relating to the real phenomenon out there in the world. In this way, we can imagine situations, trends and other abstract and complex phenomena.

So, imagining an object is primarily a relation to that object. It is not a relation to the image we create of it. The image is a *means* for relating to the object. This may sound like a simple and reasonable fact for an existing object, like the Eiffel Tower or the climate change. What about non-existing objects, like Captain Nemo in Verne's novel, or a future situation? As we have pointed out, the faculty of imagination works equally well for such cases, because it always relates to its object in its absence, and hence existence is not a condition for imagining something. We can assume that the engineer Alexandre Gustave Eiffel imagined the Eiffel Tower before it was built, and our image of it will still be able to be activated after it is destroyed. Thus, imagination can be a relation to purely imaginary objects, which got their names from this fact. Imaginary objects cannot be seen, heard, documented or remembered; they are only present to us through our imagination. For this to be possible, we must create the analogon, a visual or conceptual mental picture, of that object. The mental picture, the image, is our means for relating to the non-existing object.

This implies that, since the future does not exist, our imagination is basically the only way of relating to it. Since the images we create in our minds are the means by which we relate to the future, they are also the means by which we can cope with it through making decisions. Our decisions are based on our knowledge, and, in the case of the long term, that knowledge is to a greater extent replaced by images.

As in the simple case of the Eiffel Tower, of which we may only have sketchy knowledge, our images are combinations of knowledge and free creativity. The creativity component also represents a freedom to vary the mental image to explore different possibility. Knowledge of the future is about assumed regularities and laws, which make the future partly predictable. Examples are the computer models for climate change or the construction drawing of a house to be built, which is based on the architect's knowledge of the properties of materials and of the mechanics of construction.

While in the conscious act of imagination we relate to the object we imagine, we can also, in a *different* conscious act, make the mental image itself the object of awareness. This act is called *reflective* consciousness. In the reflective mode, we can consider what image lies behind our rational reasoning in making a decision, and make plans for the future.

In the case of the steel wire model of the Eiffel tower, the construction is obviously both an *analogon*, analogous to the mental image in other imaginations, and a *model* of the Eiffel Tower. We can always look upon our mental images, including the conceptual images, as well as other forms of analogons, as models of the object imagined. One of the functions of the reflective act is to consider this model and to ask, for example, if it is adequate for our needs.

However, the creativity in planning the future is based on the creative part of the images we produce of it. This is where we think that art, for example, literature, is a help to work on and develop the creative part of our imagination. We will present some cases of how reading novels can help us relate to the future in new ways by developing our ability to create our means to relate to the future: the mental images. One example of this is the novel by Jules Verne. This and further examples will be considered in what follows.

Science fiction that shapes the future

Jules Verne is known as the father of science fiction, even though the term itself was only coined in the 1930s (Smyth 2000). A special characteristic of Verne´s writing is the frequency with which the scientific knowledge of the day was referenced (Unwin 2000). When writing *Twenty Thousand Leagues Under the Sea*, Verne must have had access to technological advances in underwater machines. In 1800, the French Army tested the first functional submarine, named *Nautilus* (Burgess 1975), which also was chosen as the name of Captain Nemo's ship in *Twenty Thousand Leagues*. The French Army continued with the development of underwater ships, and in 1863, seven years before the publication of Verne's book, the *Plongeur* was the first submarine to be mobilised with mechanical rather than human power.

However, Captain Nemo's *Nautilus* is far beyond the limitations of the technology in Verne's days. Verne imagines a much more advanced machine that is able to go for months under the water without coming to the surface, and it is self-sufficient. Modern submarines reflect that vision, using nuclear power and being completely independent of air, which allows them to stay submerged for long periods of time and to travel at high speed.

Verne's imagination is not unique in terms of advancing knowledge and science. Many are the examples where the creativity of science fiction writers serves as an inspiration for scientific advance. For example, Peter Hamilton in his 2004 book *Pandora's Star* imagines traveling in space through tubes or wormholes. Modern physics has discovered that a network of tubes in fact connects planets (Stewart & Davey 2012). The knowledge was first imagined and then realised.

All decisions that were involved in all those years developing the submarine were certainly not only driven by Verne's book. However, the visualisation of what a future submarine could look like was available, presented in a way that was designed to stimulate the imagination, and thus motivate and inspire new designs and new technological solutions (Unwin 2000). If the kind of rationality used through all those years of development had only been based on the current state of knowledge regarding the future of the ship, the decisions made might have led to a different outcome. Some would try to maximise their profits and design a master plan to develop a machine that was optimal for their needs, but not necessarily the needs of society in 200 years. Others would use their heuristics learned from previous experiences or inherited in order to adapt to current changes in the environment, but not naturally towards a desired environment. The process of making decisions involves an imaginary vision of the outcomes, no matter what type of decision-making rules are used, and such a vision needs to be based on something that is known. In the short term, such knowledge is foreseeable. In 1870, a submarine propelled by mechanical power was already possible, so it could be conceived that in 1878 the size of the ships and the length of the trips would have increased. However, it was impossible to know that in 2016 there would be nuclear power submarines that do not need to be refuelled during their 25-year lifetime. In retrospect, one could say that Verne's imagination was the knowledge of the future.

Selective rationality: Predictions that never happened

There are also several imaginations about the future from science fiction that never happened, for example, the possibility of getting the equivalent calorie intake for a day's worth of food in one pill. The first person to be recorded imagining this was the suffragette Mary Elizabeth Lease, who wrote an essay commissioned by the American Press Association for the upcoming World's Fair in Chicago to imagine the world in 1893. Lease thought about a world where people would eat food in small condensed pills, liberating women from the task of the kitchen (Faulk 2015). Since then, the idea of food pills has been part of science fiction literature. It can be found in the works of Isaac Asimov, Ray Bradbury and J. R. R. Tolkien, among others (Faulk 2015). This also captured scientific thinking in order to solve the problem of overpopulation and agricultural production (Belasco 2000).

Some techniques for concentrated food were already known in 1856. Gail Borden, for example, developed condensed milk and concentrated meat biscuits (Belasco 2000). Chemists like Justus von Liebig and Ralph Waldo Emerson had the idea that anything could be synthesised from basic chemical elements; they later worked on synthetic substitutes for breast milk. In 1894, Marceline Berthelot, also a chemist, based on the fact that synthetic forms of some foods were already available, like butter (margarine), sugar (saccharin) and vanilla (vanillin), affirmed that a "beefsteak in table form" was going to be realised very soon, and that it would be safer and would taste better.

However, Lease's imaginative thinking about feeding with a pill has not yet happened. Faulk, in his book *The Next Big Thing*, attributes this failure to the physical limitations of condensing high number of calories and fibre in such a reduced size. Besides that, he argues that the cultural barriers towards synthetic food have been an even stronger reason that this idea has failed (Faulk 2015). Belasco also reflects on the latter factor, adding that eating is a social behaviour and that innovations should be adaptable to the existing social structures. Besides, the act of eating has some psychological components regarding the texture, colour and form of what is being ingested, the most important being that it looks natural (Belasco 2000). Another factor also highlighted by Belasco is the political influence that the food industry has; with the existence of a pill, lots of jobs will be lost, and capital will be obsolete. They argued against the meal in a pill, pointing out that is impractical and unhealthy. This sentiment was reinforced in the 1970s with the food movement; synthetic products were seen as part of the pollution and ugliness of the industrial revolution. In 1973, the science fiction movie *Soylent Green* showed a dystopian future with global warming and overpopulation where humans have to eat synthetic food made of human corpses (Faulk 2015).

The fact that a meal in a pill still is not a product that is out in the market suggests that somehow society in the long run has a filter, or it is selective as to what it is willing to know. The cultural and possibly even biological evolution of rationality has organically removed the imagined concept of feeding humans with pills, despite the attempts to design a solution for achieving feminist equality, feeding an overpopulated planet and conserving nature by reducing agriculture areas.

On the other hand, liquid meal replacements are emerging as an alternative to the meal in a pill. There are no limitations to our imagination, but is there a limitation to what we can know? Or is it just a matter of time before knowledge catches up with our imagination? The answer to that question is challenging to answer with certainty. Take the example of the flying car, another vision that until some years ago was tagged as another failure of science fiction (Barr 2003). In 2017, Chinese and German start-ups are developing prototypes that are getting closer and closer to a commercial aircraft that resembles the sci-fi vision of a flying car (Hawkins 2017) the technology is almost available, but the regulation and cultural adaptation of the product are still to be determined.

What do we imagine about artificial intelligence and genetic engineering?

In 1950, Isaac Asimov published a collection of nine books portraying the relationship between humans and robots, titled *I, Robot* (Asimov 1950). Science fiction has produced many stories where robots develop to be stronger and smarter than humans, taking over many humans-only tasks. Most of the time those stories end up in dystopian futures where robots take over and undermine human superiority, while in more recent ones, the robots help humans to achieve a prosperous future, taking care of elders and physical heavy jobs.

Robots that move and solve cognitive problems are a reality now, as discussed in Chapters 9 and 10. Intelligence and robotics have developed enormously in the last 20 years. Manufacturing in developed countries is financially viable, thanks to the use of highly efficient, low-maintenance robots. Boston Dynamics, an engineering and robotic company that works extensively with the US military, has developed so-called humanoids (human-like robots) that are able to perform advanced physical feats like walking on uneven terrain, jumping and grabbing heavy boxes (Patel 2015). Machine learning techniques equip computers with the skills that allow them to write reporting news to online newspapers (Jenkin 2016), or autonomous cars that do not need a driver (Pesce 2017).

Another future imagined by science fiction is the one where humans use genetic engineering to create super humans. In 1931, Aldous Huxley in his novel *Brave New World* developed a plot wherein reproductive technology is at the centre of the storyline. The technology known as *crispr* today offers the possibility of changing the DNA of a living being in order to correct genetic mutations or unwanted characteristics (Ledford 2016; Specter 2017). Engineering life is becoming a reality. The argument in Chapter 10 is that the science fiction literature can make us aware of what is at stake in the future and thereby help us sort out the best values to live by.

Still, we are not yet where Isaac Asimov or Aldous Huxley imagined we would be. We are still in the process of converting imagination into knowledge. Most of the imagined robotics or genetically modified futures in science fiction involve tragic endings, with the human race suffering under the superior forces of our own invention. In 2014, Stephen Hawking, one of the most brilliant scientists of our time, warned against artificial intelligence, saying that it could be the end of human kind (Cellan-Jones 2014).

On the other hand, there are many supporters of the development of this technology, arguing that it will make life easier for humans. If we shape reality to our imagination, then we should be able to imagine a future where robots and humans work together, instead of destroying each other. Current science fiction is quite diverse in this aspect; the trend of imagining apocalyptic endings is still ongoing. There are also works that show human relations between genetically modified organisms and artificial intelligent humanoids, like *A Closed and Common Orbit* by Becky Chambers.

Regarding artificial intelligence and gene modification, we are at the stage where we make decisions based on what we know, and what, we imagine. Those decisions can either be a result of a centralised design that believes it has full information about the outcomes of its actions, in order to shape the future it wants; or the product of an organic process, where there is not one single choice that shapes the future, but a combination of small emergent choices that are made in ignorance of the future they are going to cope with.

The role of imagination

How can we have rational thoughts about the future (which is unknown), and what is the relevance of this question related to how organisations and managers make decisions today that have implications for the future? We do not know the future, but to cope with it, we have to make rational decisions concerning this unknown.

We have pointed out that imagination is the mode humans are in when relating to the future, and that such imagination has a component of knowledge (what we know today about the situation we are imagining) and a creative component. We have also suggested that we have different modes of thinking/imagination when dealing with the short-term, medium-term and long-term future.

How is the interaction between knowledge and imagination of the unknown to be rational today, concerning the future and the effect of today's actions in the future? Knowledge and imagination merge in the minds of the decision makers, perhaps unaware that their rationality is built upon that hybrid knowledge. Decisions that have long-term effects are made in an iterative process, where the future is built while adapting to changes in knowledge and imagination, as described by Piaget, assimilating and accommodating them (Chelini & Riva 2013). This iteration process is what creates the possibility of both shaping and coping with the future, where humans imagine and re-imagine situations and technologies according to the knowledge they get and the place where they want to be.

In the book *The World in the Model*, Mary S. Morgan (Morgan 2012), explains in a very elaborated way the interconnection between conceptual and visual images, which she calls *cognition* and *visualisation*. She argues that in economics, researchers imagine the economic world and make an image of it in a model. Then the model is used to understand both the model itself and the real world. Economists use their imagination to create a model version of the world, as a way to explore their ideas about how such a world works. In the context of understanding the effect of our decisions in the long term, imaginary worlds like the ones provided by sci-fi can be the model for testing today's decisions or within the imagined world and into reality. They can be interpreted as a tool for reasoning today about the consequences of the long term. One of the interesting characteristics of this tool is its flexibility, because, as explained here, the rationality to make decisions in the long term is iterative and changes according to the environment.

Imaginary models are used to replace the lack of knowledge about the future and simulate alternative worlds; to help us understand better, in a collective way, the structure and behaviour created by today's decisions. Since it is a collective action, there is a big chance that is an unaware process, and that is a complex matter to precisely define how it works. Kim Stanley Robinson, the author of *New York 2140* (Robinson 2017), a sci-fi novel that portrays a New York in the mid twenty-second century that is trying to cope with the rising sea levels produced by climate change, which makes it the Venice of the future, reflects about this in a podcast (Molinsky 2017). Stanley discusses the double effect that a dystopian science fiction novel can have on people. According to him, showing only the wrong side as a warning induces complacency and the feeling that "this will happen to others, not to me; things will never be that bad." On the other hand, he tries to show the positive side, in order to induce people to go for that future where we adapt and cope with the changes. He is aware of the power of creating a model of the future and the effect it has on the readers. This is especially relevant in the case of creating knowledge in social science (see Chapter 4); the social simulations possible with imaginary worlds somehow become benchmarks or anchors to compare to or create hypotheses. One could also say that science fiction literature could have some influence on the creation of or demand for economic and public policies that we discussed in Chapters 1 and 4. For example, with the election of Donald J. Trump as president of the United States in November 2017, sales of dystopian books like *The Handmaid's Tale* by Margaret Atwood and George Orwell's *1984* exploded. This could be interpreted as a sign of a need to visualise how the world could look like with a government that has a leader with attributes that this president demonstrated in the election campaign.

In the context of organisations, leaders could be more aware of the role imagination has on their decision-making process. This will make the process stronger and will open discussion about where they want to go, confronted with what they are leading. Organisations set goals and visions in order to have a sense of or visualise where they want to go. In the process of planning, more credit should be given to imagination, because in order to have visions and goals, organisations need to create a picture of a future that is unknown, but that they want to somehow achieve. Being more playful with imagination, and understanding it as an input for a rational process of decision making, could allow the simulation of alternative futures and create different models of development, idealisations of what they would like to see with reality checks of the model itself. Companies like Tesla and Uber are good examples of the role of imagination in developing new products. Tesla has created an electric car and batteries for solar energy with increased storage capacity; Uber has changed the concept of how transportation works in cities by shifting the mental model of owning a car to sharing a car.

Box 6.2 The Kodak moment of rationality

The disruptiveness of change:

We need to understand that rationality is different from just looking backwards or only considering what we know as facts. However, rationality in decisions change character as we set the target forward in time.

The knowledge one failed to use:

If we have a too narrow perspective on rationality, we will fail to perceive the long-term effect of what we are doing. However, this also implies a criticism of assumptions that we can form rational knowledge about the future.

Ability to adjust to future changes:

We need to acknowledge that the future is dependent on our ability to anticipate and imagine and thereby see different realities and their consequences.

The opportunity in the changes:

Imagining a more sustainable future can be an inspiration for innovations today that help in developing a better life for all.

Imagination is also useful for becoming able to cope with *black swan* events, events that are rare, that have extreme impact and are usually retrospectively predictable or explainable. Imagination is a tool for being prepared, less vulnerable and aware of the fragility of organisations in the face of extreme situations. There is a need to be creative and imaginative to contemplate alternative futures and reason backwards, in order to understand the dynamics that arise today. It does not mean that uncertainty about the long term will be reduced, but that we use imagination more explicitly to cope with the lack of knowledge about the future. Since we do not have any knowledge of the future, we propose to find a substitute that is created by imagination, because it is flexible and permits iterations, characteristics that allow for adaptation and learning to a changing environment. However, that absence of knowledge is normally replaced by risk analysis and predictions using constructive rationality. That gives a fake sense of security about the future; then, when a black swan happens, we seem to be surprised and wonder why all our calculations did not see that coming, since they looked so precise and rational at the moment. That is what Nasim Taleb has called the *ludic fallacy* (Taleb 2009).

The main thesis of this chapter is that fictional literature is useful for developing and reflecting on our images of the future. Since, as we point out, imagination is a necessary part of relating to the future to cope with it, it is both fruitful and important to work on our imagery of the future. Literature develops our imagination, and it also functions as a field of experimentation. From literary experiments, we can reflect on how we develop our images, what kind of knowledge we include in our images and what kind of knowledge we leave out, our own emotional reactions to the different possibilities imagined and so on. Thus, we can develop better abilities to deal with the future in a creative and responsible way. In other words, we can develop our rationality to make better choices and contribute to a better future. Instead of pretending to predict the future, we suggest developing strategies and methodologies to cope with it in its unpredictability.

7

COPING WITH SUSTAINABILITY

The need for non-instrumental thinking

Karen Landmark, Hans Grelland and Christian Johnsen

> *We cannot solve problems with the same thinking that we used when we created them.*
> Albert Einstein

The sustainability challenge

Against the backdrop of a planet in peril, this chapter presents a critique of the instrumental thinking that dominates the world of business today and looks to philosophy in the effort to develop an alternative mode of thinking about sustainability. We argue that instrumental thinking is insufficient for dealing with the seriousness of the environmental challenges we are currently facing. The complex nature of the grand societal challenges we confront necessitates a critical view of all aspects of our human existence and its consequences for our planet. More specifically, this chapter borrows insights from Martin Heidegger and Arne Naess in order to outline suggestions for how to deal with sustainability within a corporate setting. To do so, we ask: how can Heidegger's concept of care be related to Naess's philosophy of deep ecology? Is there room or a need for philosophy in business today? How can philosophy enable us to think differently about sustainability within a corporate setting?

Underneath these questions lies a deep concern for the contemporary condition of our planet. Taking into consideration the severe effects of climate change, ecological degradation, failing eco-systems, increased migration and conflicts linked to scarcity of natural resources, it seems unavoidable that we must alter the course of our global society. Most global economic, social and environmental indicators show a troubling negative trend, one that will surely be exacerbated by a rising world population.[1] Change is needed on an individual, organisational and societal level. We will argue that the necessary change is deeply linked to how we perceive ourselves in the world, or as part of the world.

Sustainability in this context is based on the principle that everything we need for our survival and well-being depends, directly or indirectly, on the natural environment. Hence, sustainability creates and maintains the conditions under which humans and nature can co-exist in productive harmony. Ideally, this harmony should allow for the satisfaction of social, economic and other needs, both for the present as well as future generations. Sustainability is concerned with making sure that we have, and will continue to have, water, materials and other basic resources that are paramount for protecting both human existence and the natural environment. In other words, sustainability is a precondition for human survival on planet earth. To do so, it is necessary to make sure that we organise society in a more sustainable way.

The way we perceive and relate to the world influences how we relate to sustainability on an individual, organisational and societal level. We worry about a marginalisation of the challenges relating to sustainability facing humanity today. Put differently, we are concerned that the speed and pace of our sustainability efforts do not match the seriousness of climate change and environmental degradation. We believe that this is connected and interlinked with human's relationship to nature and the way we perceive ourselves as part of nature – or not. In dealing with sustainability issues, our mode of thinking makes a difference. As Albert Einstein once said, we cannot solve problems with the same thinking that we used when we created them. This is a relevant starting point for discussing the potential consequences instrumental thinking may have on corporate sustainability efforts.

Corporate sustainability efforts today

The global context is rapidly changing. Climate change, loss of biodiversity, environmental degradation, the redistribution of life on earth, pollution of the natural resources and the atmosphere and increased migration due to conflicts and resource scarcity are all interlinked, and they represent systemic challenges that affect all parts of society, including how we trade and conduct business.[2] The role of business in this context is complex, but as institutions playing a crucial part of the global society, there is an obvious role for business to contribute to sustainable solutions and the sustainable development of our commons. Today, most organisations and leaders know that flexibility and willingness to change is crucial for securing economic growth and competitiveness on the market, and hence corporate sustainability ranks high on the corporate agenda (Laasch & Conaway 2014). This can lead us to think and believe that corporate interest in sustainability issues automatically leads to a change in corporate behaviour. However, it remains uncertain how "deep" this understanding really is and how and if it really affects corporate action, since corporate action still and undoubtedly rests on a growth paradigm, and this paradigm is in conflict with a planet of infinite resources.

Box 7.1 Climate change

Rising temperatures are linked to rising sea levels and new climate patterns around the world. Disasters can strike, with irreversible effects.

- major floods in low-lying coastal areas
- changes required in agriculture
- changes required in planning, for example, housing and flood plains
- debates on responsibility and international action
- major flood disaster in Bangladesh
- new opportunities for vineyards in Northern Europe
- Venice under water

Renewable energy: Economic viability of renewable power generation increases, that is, wind and wave power.

- threats to other energy sources
- cancellation of major building projects
- changes in economic power relations

- renewable energy becomes financially viable: business opportunity
- solar energy to power electric cars: business opportunity

Nuclear power: Costs of nuclear power are rising, while renewable energy prices are falling. There are links between civil and defence use of nuclear energy.

- controversy over an international plant: safety and cost
- cross-border implications discussed
- allegations of military links for civil nuclear power, requiring international response
- cost escalations for nuclear power generation; should projects be abandoned?

This dilemma of growth was first properly addressed in the famous report "The Limits to Growth" (Meadows, Meadows, Randers & Behrens III 1972). The report examined the five basic factors that determine and limit growth on planet earth: population increase, agriculture production, non-renewable resource depletion, industrial output and pollution generation. Sadly, the work still holds relevance today; the global system of nature on which we all depend probably cannot support present rates of economic and population growth much beyond the year 2100. Although it is criticised and challenged, the idea of infinite growth seems to rest solidly on an instrumental paradigm in a contemporary organisation of capitalist society and still dominates business efforts on sustainability.

Most of the literature on corporate social responsibility (CSR) and corporate sustainability looks at the role of business in society from the perspective of the firm, thereby reinforcing the instrumental orientation towards the world. At its core lies the question of what impacts companies may have on society, either positive or negative, and the extent to which, and how, companies need to address, or even utilise further, these impacts (Torjesen, Rodvelt & Landmark 2015). Still, there are several ways to think about the role of companies in relation to society that may expand our thinking on sustainability. Painter-Morland and Bos (2015) distinguish between discourses linked to instrumental attempts at providing assurances that environmentally friendly practices will eventually pay off in terms of financial gains our ultimate survival as a human species or the organisation's image as good citizen or political agent. Further, some have argued that corporations have certain social contract duties, while others have made appeals to deontological principles. According to Painter-Morland and Bos (2015), these normative arguments have limitations because they share epistemological assumptions with instrumentalist thinking.

Instrumental thinking in relation to sustainability is preoccupied with figuring out how companies can maintain their activities, while at the same time refrain from damaging the natural environment. To do so, focus is placed upon the efficient use of natural resources. However, in doing so, instrumental thinking fails to address the very idea of using nature for commercial purposes and avoids asking if businesses have a right to do so. As well, this approach proceeds on the basis of a fundamental distinction between the company and the world. Painter-Morland and Bos (2015) show that this way of viewing the world is built on a "means to an end" relationship to nature. Business leaders typically talk about their companies' sustainability efforts from a financial point of view: Producing environmentally friendly products will eventually pay off. Occasionally, they argue from a purely ethical point of view, stating that going green "is the right thing to do." Both views reflect an instrumental way of looking at the world and represent a kind of "sustainable development without tears" approach. We will care for the planet as long as it does not affect our bottom line in a negative way. From a Heideggerian perspective, both "world-views" distance us from the very world we are a part of and prevent us from experiencing ourselves as embedded in the world, and they subsequently limit the effect of the efforts made to enhance sustainability.

From nature to environment: The instrumentalisation of the world

Man's relationship to nature has changed over time, yet our dependency on our eco-systems for food, water and air remains crucial. In what follows, we present a critique of the instrumental thinking that seems to dominate the human–nature relationship, and subsequently and interlinked corporate sustainability efforts. We seek to explore how this way of thinking creates or underlines a dis-connectedness to nature and hence a distance from our own efforts in dealing with pressing environmental challenges.

The modern way of thinking can be characterised by the transformation of nature (depicted in European traditions as a "wild, untamed," often hostile force) into environment (more "manageable" and "goal directed"), as pointed out by Banerjee (2003). For Banerjee, this conversion of nature into environment implies that the variety of meanings that the former concept bears gets lost in the latter. Hence, while nature contains a myriad of different connotations, the concept of the environment represents a system of resources that can be managed by humans. In other words, the environment is something "out there," the natural world an object that remains external to human affairs. Yet, it is a system that can be controlled, monitored, exploited and governed by us.

Heidegger was already aware of this tendency towards externalising the world within modernity. For Heidegger, what characterises modernity is the emergence of what he calls a *world picture*. However, Heidegger acutely notes that "world picture does not mean 'picture of the world' but, rather, the world grasped as picture" (2002, p. 67). What is unique about modernity is the conception of the world as a picture. Another way to express this idea is to say that modernity is permeated by the logic of representation. The world is something that is represented, thereby making the world an object that is viewed from a distance. We might ask: Who views the world? The answer is the Cartesian subject who always looks at external objects from a distance. Following this account, we are not part of the world, but rather observers of the world. Hence, Heidegger elaborates: "The world picture does not change from an earlier medieval to a modern one; rather, that the world becomes picture at all is what distinguishes the essence of modernity" (2002, p. 68). The importance of this remark consists of revealing the distinctness of the modern way of relating to the world. In the Middle Ages, according to Heidegger, the world was not grasped as an object perceived by a subject. On the contrary, the world was created by God, and within this created world, man occupies a specific rank. In modernity, man is no longer situated in a created world. Instead, man observes the world from a distance. Man is a spectator.

What this shows is that the current way of addressing environmental issues operates within instrumental thinking. As Painter-Morland and Bos (2016) note, instrumental thinking represents the world by making use of a set of distinctions, such as fact/value, means/ends and subject/object. Following instrumental thinking, the environment is an object out there, one that human subjects can use as a mean to achieve certain ends that are dictated by our sets of values. This is what connects instrumental thinking with the world picture. For Heidegger, "the essence of technology is by no means anything technological" (1977, p. 4). What Heidegger alludes to here is that we cannot understand the significance of technology by considering it solely from a technological point of view. Instead, we must grasp how the essence of technology lies in its manner of framing the world in a particular way. For Heidegger, this signals an important transformation in the way of thinking that characterises our time. If everything is framed within a means/end relationship, then it follows, Heidegger acutely notes, that agriculture becomes nothing but "the mechanised food industry" (1977, p. 15) and the river nothing but a "water power supplier" (1977, p. 16).

We can see here that the concept of the environment belongs to the age of the world picture. The natural environment is frequently conceptualised as something external to the internal operations of the organisation. As such, we find here a distinction between the organisation and its environment, a distinction that is premised on the assumption that those who populate the organisation stand at a distance and observe their surroundings. For this reason, the environment is always portrayed as an "object" (Painter-Morland & Bos 2016, p. 551) that remains external to the organisations and society. This object, however, can be managed through human interference. This reduction of nature to the environment therefore has a two-fold consequence. On one level, the environment, or what is often called the "natural world," becomes a specific system that operates within what Rockström and his colleagues call "planetary boundaries" (Rockström, Steffen & Noone. 2009). These planetary boundaries can be transgressed, resulting in climate change, loss of biodiversity and other forms of ecological degradation. Hence, the environment is a system that should remain within a balance that is defined by certain parameters for how much CO_2 that can be emitted, water consumed and resources extracted from the world's ecosystem. Beyond this, the reduction of nature to the environment frames the horizon in which we can perceive possible solutions to ecological degradation. If the ecological degradation is caused by the transgression of certain planetary boundaries, then the solution consists of restoring balance in the environment. Such refurbishment can typically be achieved by introducing eco-technologies, such as renewable energy sources, that can help to restore the balance of the ecosystem.

Predominantly, we see that the manner in which the current ecological crisis that we are witnessing is being addressed is through the paradigm of technological optimism (Böhm, Bharucha & Pretty 2015). The basic idea here is that environmental problems, including climate change, loss of biodiversity, depletion of natural resources and pollution of the ecosystem, can be solved by inventing new technologies that allow us to maintain our current way of living while simultaneously protecting the natural environment. In other words, technological advancements will allow us to disconnect economic growth from environmental degradation (Jackson 2016). Consider, for example, Tesla's new Solar Shingles. Tesla has recently produced a new tile that, according to CEO Elon Musk, offers several advantages, including the ability to generate electricity through being a solar cell, longer durability due to its quality fabrication, cheaper price and superior aesthetic design. In the words of Elon Musk: "So the basic proposition will be: Would you like a roof that looks better than a normal roof, lasts twice as long, costs less and, by the way, generates electricity? Why would you get anything else?" What we see here is a typical example of how technological advancements are supposed to offer "win-win solutions" (Cohen & Winn 2007). Both better environmental performance by creating renewable energy and economic profits by being cheaper. Consequently, we are led into the idea that it "pays to be green" (Orsato 2006). In a recent case described from the point of view of the Norwegian business cluster, it seems obvious that the dominating instrumental thinking is present at the CEO level. In this case, the CEOs in the cluster were asked to specify their motivation for working with sustainability and elaborate how they perceived the world from the perspective of sustainability. Thus, they were asked questions such as 'Do you trust science?' 'Do you endorse global agreements?' 'Do you have positive or negative future outlooks?' and so forth. This study reveals that the majority of the CEOs acted according to the mantra that "it pays to be green." They reinforce technological optimism by placing faith in their companies' ability to create innovative solutions that can reverse ecological degradation. To do so, they work towards placing their company in a competitive position for further financial growth in a zero-emission society and in a circular economy. Viewed from this perspective, environmental degradation therefore signals a business opportunity for creating new technological solutions that can boost the economy, make companies thrive and save the environment.

This is what Jackson (2016) calls "the myth of decoupling": Economic growth is supposed to miraculously be disconnected from environmental degradation. Undoubtedly, such a solution to the problem of ecological degradation is attractive, because it basically requires us to make no major shifts in the way we conduct business. Or, as we call it, it is sustainability without tears. To be more precise, this solution requires us to simply wait until a technological breakthrough occurs that will save us from climate change, restore biodiversity and allow us to maintain our current lifestyle without making radical changes. In the meantime, while we wait for such revolutionary technologies to emerge, we do not have to do much besides maintain business as usual. For this reason, Jackson (2016) laments this belief in the "decoupling" of economic growth and environmental degradation as a "myth," claiming that such a solution fails to address problems that we are currently facing. For Jackson, technological optimism fails to address the crux of the matter, namely the fundamental organisation of our current way of living. What we need, according to Jackson, is not to retain belief in technological optimism, but rather to address the way we currently live, the organisation of our society, including the way we trade and do business.

What can we learn from philosophy?

Can philosophy offer an alternative to instrumental thinking? Is there a way for humans to connect more deeply with the world, and can this connection lead the way towards a more holistic approach to sustainability? In other words, is it possible to develop a non-instrumental way of interacting with the world? What would non-instrumental thinking look like?

In Heidegger's (1962) thinking, we can find basic insights that are helpful for the purpose of going beyond the purely instrumental way of approaching environmental problems. Heidegger develops a precise language for describing the kind of being that humans are. He points out that we are "thrown" into this world, not just as observers at a distance from our surroundings, but to cope with the world, which, in an existential sense, we are not only surrounded by, but to which we belong. In other words, we are interwoven with the world to such an extent that Heidegger calls the human being simply a "being-in-the-world." Moreover, we are in-the-world in a certain way, and he identifies this way as care (German: Sorge). We are basically a kind of being that cares; it cares for itself, and also, it cares for others and for the world that it experiences as its world. For Heidegger, it is not the case that there is a distinction between, on the one hand, isolated human beings and, on the other hand, the world which we inhabit. Thus, care is not a relation between two autonomous spheres: us and the world. Instead, we always already take part in the world or dwell in the world, and care is basically our way of existing in the world.

According to Heidegger, our existence is always directed towards the future. A human being is not something substantially fixed, not even something substantial that may change in time. Instead, we exist as a possibility that is realised by our motion into the future, but we never stop being a possibility. We are, in other words, something that comes into being, but which never settles in a certain fixed form. Coping with the world is all about coping with the future. Care, which is something directed towards oneself, others and the world, is also directed towards the future; it is about carefully coping with what is going to happen. Here, instrumentality also has its role to play in this, as a means to attain selected goals, but this is what we could call an instrumentality that is driven and sustained by care. It is when instrumentality is in the lead that things go wrong.

The relation between the existential level, considered by Heidegger, and the normative level, dealing with what we should do, or how we should live, can be illustrated by an example. We sometimes explain the traits of being a loving or a hateful person by childhood experiences; whether the person has been raised in a family that is loving and caring, or the opposite. This does not mean that, in the first case, the child loves because it learns from the environment what love is and what is loving behaviour. It is rather that love is a natural ability of the child, so it understands intuitively what love is and recognises it when it experiences it. The loving family creates an environment where love, which is natural to the child, is allowed and expressed, and the child learns how love is practiced. In the second case, it is not such that the child is does not understand what love is or is unable to love, but its inborn ability and tendency to love is suppressed, leading to a state of mind with an unfulfilled desire for loving and being loved. The love suppressed is replaced by hate, which we consider as a learned faculty. In a similar way, while the attitude of care is basic in the human being and shows itself wherever a person cares for something and someone, care is also suppressed or un-learned by attitudes acquired from the culture and, among other things, by misplaced instrumental thinking. If care were not pre-given as the basic way of being-in-the-world for humans, it could not be learned, because care, like love, is beyond definition or rational explanation. So how do we deal with suppressed care or love? This is where normativity enters. In normative philosophy, we develop the theory of how we should behave, given our crippled state of mind. Normativity fills in what instrumentality lacks: values. Nevertheless, the existential analysis is still important, because care is still the motivating factor in the normativity necessary for overcoming our lack of care. We need to go from how we basically are, to how we should live.

We find this kind of normativity in Arne Naess's (1989) *ecosophy*, which deals with human beings' relationship to the whole, to nature. This philosophy aims at revitalising our natural concern for life – human life as well as other forms of life – by bringing in a non-instrumental way of thinking of our interaction with the world.

The starting point is that care in the subject corresponds to value in the object to which the subject relates. When I care for X, then X appears to me as valuable. Here language itself is misleading, so we must treat the sentences we use with caution. At first sight, our statement above may mean two different things. One is that X has value because I care for it. This would mean that X does not have a value in itself but only a value given to it by me, who could detract the value from the thing by not caring any longer. Thus, I would be the master, deciding what has value, and thus what is right or wrong regarding this matter. This has also been the traditional attitude since the Renaissance: Man is nature's master. Or, it could be that X has a value in itself, and by this given value it brings me to care about it. Then my care would be something induced from the outside, not from myself. This is certainly a normative position, leaving only the question of where this externally given value came from. What ecosophy is all about is, however, a third alternative, a holistic one, which cannot be expressed by any of these sentences. Thus, we are at the limit of what we can say, at least in a conventional language. The only linguistic way of handling it is to say that both alternatives are true at the same time, and because they both are true, each of them are also untrue, because each sentence represents a fragmentation of a whole, which is the truth. There is a correspondence between my care, which is part of my free relation to the world, and the value of X, being an aspect of X itself as it appears in the world, which is both subjective and objective. In this way, when we say that life has value in itself, it does not mean that value is something that can exist without appearing to a caring subjectivity, but it means that the value is not created or destroyed by the individual subject by a free choice. The value of life is discovered, not constructed, but it is still an aspect of life's appearance to a caring subjectivity that relates to it.

This is a philosophical consequence of the view that we, ourselves, are a part of the whole, call it Nature or the Universe, and at the same time we are able to relate to this whole of which we are a part, passing judgements, discovering values and, most importantly, acting in a conscious and intentional way.

In our opinion, ecosophy is the most consistent philosophy of life as having value in itself, combined with awareness of reasonable practice, thus avoiding the dangers of fanaticism or excessive rigour. Contrary to the science of ecology or the philosophy of ecological thinking, which are both purely descriptive, ecosophy is a normative philosophy based on the connection between and the inherent value of all life. Since values cannot be derived from factual descriptions, ecosophy cannot be derived from the science of ecology alone, but needs another foundation, which Naess calls *mythical*. We find this way of dealing with the question of foundation too vague and unspecific and suggest instead that we found our normative thinking on Heidegger's concept of care. Care leads to normativity, and the normativity of ecosophy is an expression of care for all life.

Since the beginning of the industrial age, human activity has steadily destroyed animal species, in addition to the costs to human health and life caused by industrial pollution. According to Naess, this makes it a reasonable assumption that at the beginning of industrialism the ecology of the earth was at an optimal state, from which human activity has cased steady decay. The optimal state means a state in which a maximum of species is supported by the ecological system. In recent years, we have become aware of the kind of pollution that only causes damage indirectly through climate change. We can see this as a continuation of the negative influence caused by industrialism in general.

This does not mean that we suggest a dramatic reduction of all industrial activity as a solution to the problem. Rather, we see the only realistic solution to be to change industry into an activity that causes less damage, and which is sustainable in the long run. Furthermore, when we stress the number of species existing on the earth as a focal point, it is mainly as an indicator of the state of the life system in general. To care for ecological variation and the manifold of species is not necessarily always instrumental for human needs or aims, but it expresses our respect and concern for the whole of which we are a part. Of course, the human suffering and politico-economic problems caused by industrial pollution and climate change are also a concern in ecosophy. The interesting approach is to see these problems together, based on a concern both for human life and for all life. Naess (1999) sums up his ecosophy in a few principles that can be seen as useful ethical guidelines that include embracing life itself, that manifold of life forms, as well as arguing for quality rather that quantity in life, which, he argues, goes hand in hand with the transformation into a greener economy. We find that Heidegger's philosophy of care – focusing on the individual acting subject – and the principles of ecosophy – focusing on the relation between the responsible individual and the whole of which we humans are a part – are complementary, and the synthesis of the two gives a reasonable alternative to instrumental thinking.

Back to Nature or Sustainability with some Tears

In the beginning of this chapter, we asked whether business is receptive to philosophy. We further asked if our thinking of ourselves in the world, and as part of the world, matters in handling sustainability issues from a business point of view. The reasons for asking these questions were to build an argument for a new basis for ecological thinking, a thinking that to a larger degree allows a deep human–nature relationship and that goes beyond the dominating instrumental thinking in business today. We have tried to show that the human world is "richer" than instrumental thinking reflects, and that subsequently that the corporate language or corporate sustainability efforts are "poorer" than they need to be and, in consequence, too weak to deal with the seriousness of today's complex societal challenges. Moreover, we have argued that philosophy may offer a way of thinking that can redefine the relationship between humans and nature, and hence affect business sustainability efforts.

Box 7.2 The Kodak moment of sustainability

The disruptiveness of change:

The world might experience a sudden and threatening shortage of resources or a threat to existence from pollution, beyond what can be managed.

The knowledge one failed to use:

There has been criticism of assumptions of instrumental thinking and a need to acknowledge the imaginary aspect of preparing for a future.

Ability to adjust to future changes:

The picture or images of the future threats and possibilities has to be shared in order to provoke action.

The opportunity in the changes:

We should rethink the basis of our thinking, acknowledge how it is embedded in our social context and thereby consider reality beyond this context.

The combination of Heidegger's concept of care and Naess's ecosophy offers new reflections on the relationship between humans and nature and hence also potentially a new way of approaching sustainability. The contribution to the sustainability discourse is linked to the development from a purely instrumental way of dealing with the world towards a more human–nature approach, where the starting point is an acknowledgement of our systemic interdependency. We also argue for a normative approach: allowing values to guide our actions. This very mode of thinking can potentially be nurtured in an organisational setting, allowing leaders to approach sustainability in a more human-centred way. Coping with the world is all about coping with the future. Care is not only about being concerned about the present state but also about being directed towards the future and being concerned about what will happen. Here, instrumentality also has its role to play as a means to attain selected goals, but this is what we could call an instrumentality that is driven and sustained by care. It is when instrumentality is in the lead that things go wrong.

In an uncertain and rapidly changing world, organisations should strive to be "the loving family" that allows us to care, in a Heideggerian sense, about nature in a deep sense. Organisations should be a place and a setting that allow us to feel that our inter-dependency with nature is our natural state and one from which we should let our decision be guided.

We have seen that the concept of the environment belongs to the age of the world picture. Looking into the future, we are challenged again to look for a deeper connection with nature, a connection that allows us to acknowledge our interdependency with all ecosystems. It is time to move from the environment and back to nature, to avoid the pitfalls of technological optimism and to challenge the very idea of infinite growth.

Notes

1 www.nature.com/nature/journal/v461/n7263/full/461472a.html?foxtrotcallback=true
2 http://courseresources.mit.usf.edu/sgs/geb6930/module_3/read/competative_advantage.pdf

8
COPING WITH METHODOLOGY

Validity and knowledge about the future

Hans Christian Garmann Johnsen, Jan Ole Rypestøl and Mariann Berge

Rethinking methodology

This book presents a critical perspective on the tendencies and forces that are shaping contemporary reality for society, business and work. We are looking at real time issues, but with a forward-looking perspective: What can we do today that will be rational from the perspective of tomorrow? The methodological aspect concerns how we get knowledge about the future. We address three aspects of how social science contributes to knowledge development.

First, social science is, to a large extent, focused on real-time issues. However, understanding the future is more complex than understanding the present, even though that is complex. Focusing on the future, and the expectation that social science can help us cope with the future, raises complex methodological challenges and questions about knowledge development. The philosophical issues discussed in Chapter 7 are related to fundamental questions about how we conceptualise things, our world picture, what values and assumptions we hold and how these values and assumptions guide our future actions. Fundamentally, this is also about knowledge. Subsequently, the question of coping with the future challenges knowledge at a practical, methodological and philosophical level. Second, social science is fragmented. How can we overcome this fragmentation and the fact that social scientists often are locked into paradigms? Third, how is it that social science knowledge integrates with, influences and contributes to the development of knowledge in society?

In short: What is the methodology of coping with the future, and why does social science have so little to say about the future? Solid scientific knowledge is supposed to require documentation, to be built on facts. What is valid knowledge in social science? The answer is related to the philosophical discussion of what knowledge is, what true knowledge is and what science is, as we addressed in Chapter 5. These are some of the oldest and unresolved questions in both philosophy and science: How do we know that something is true? Despite the fact that methodologies refer to the instruments and techniques we choose to acquire knowledge and are independent of the ontological and epistemological questions, they still tend to be linked in practice. Thus, while the positivistic approach in social science often seeks unambiguous data, concrete evidence and rules ("hard methods"), the more interpretive approaches open up ambiguity and contingency, and recognise the interplay between the researcher and the object of research, requiring "softer" methods.

The traditional approach in positivism presumes that explanations in social science should be similar to those in natural science and may therefore use the same methods. Positivists also argue that metaphysics does not belong to science, and that the world exists as an objective entity, outside the mind of the observer. Researchers within this approach are separated from the objects of their research, and may therefore be able to describe and analyse this reality in a natural way without affecting the observed object. Thus, while some of these assumptions are less strict within the neo-positivism/post-positivism approach, the reality is still considered to be objective (external to human minds), even if some phenomena are not governed by causal laws but by probabilistic ones. The validity of what has happened is sometimes hard to establish. What about the validity of what will happen?

This chapter builds on the three former chapters in this part of the book. Going back to Greek philosophy, we look at the epistemological foundation of social science. Epistemology is about our perceptual and cognitive capacity. It is a capacity that is related to individual thinking and reflection. It is also a capacity that can be built into organisations and society. There is a collective dimension to epistemology. What role can social science play, given that it is embedded in a social reality, and how can it contribute to valid and relevant knowledge about a sustainable future?

Social science in the post-positivist age

In 1962, two important but completely independent books were published that had tremendous impacts on thinking about science, written by Thomas Kuhn and Jürgen Habermas. They had a parallel in addressing the role of science in the post-war period. They also had a parallel in promoting the approach to science that we can call *sociology of knowledge*. Science and society are integrated realms, and a discussion about science may take its social realty as a point of departure. Thomas Kuhn (1962/1970/2000) makes this argument. In defence of the argument that sciences develop through paradigms, he argues that this historically is the case both for natural sciences and social science. However, he also argues that there is a difference between the two, as the constant development of new paradigms is more apparent in social science than in natural science.

A paradigm can be defined as a research tradition with consensus on method, empiricism, epistemology or theory. Paradigms, or research traditions, limit the methodological, thematic and/or epistemological perspectives. Within paradigms, there is a normal scientific discourse. Thomas Kuhn talked about scientific revolutions, when there is a shift in a paradigm. Discourses can be seen as different language games, that is, linguistic practices within a set of rules, norms, customs and traditions. A discourse is a constitution of legitimacy of an intersubjective practice. In the preface to *The Structure of Scientific Revolutions*, Thomas Kuhn wrote:

> Particularly, I was stuck by the number and extent of the overt disagreements between social scientists about the nature of legitimate scientific problems and methods. Both history and acquaintance made me doubt that practitioners of the natural sciences possess firmer or more permanent answers to such questions than their colleagues in social science. Yet, somehow the practices of astronomy, physics, chemistry, or biology naturally fail to evoke controversies over fundamentals that today often seem endemic among us, say, psychologists or sociologists. Attempting to discover the source of that difference led me to recognise the role in scientific research of what I have since called 'paradigms'. These I take to be universally recognised scientific achievements that for a time provide model problems and solutions to a community of practitioners.
>
> *(Kuhn 1962/1970/2000, p. viii)*

This position can be called *anti-positivist*, in the sense that it questions the idea both of the unity of science and of the progress of science. One of the problems approached by anti-positivists is related to using natural science as a role model for social science. Anti-positivism has taken many and different forms. Some anti-positivists have been antagonists to conventional, positive science, and we should not hide the fact that these debates have been highly conflict ridden. A general position in anti-positivist controversy is that over time, grand ideas and systems have developed into discourses. Science as a discursive process could be used as a general description of the theory of science debates that occurred after World War II, and not least the debate that followed Thomas Kuhn's concept of *scientific paradigm* (Kuhn 1970). What Kuhn showed, by making some historical analysis of science, was that what at one time was regarded as truth was at other times overthrown. Normal science was the type of scientific activity that happened within a framework of accepted truths; however, scientific revolutions might overthrow these truths. Put differently, any normal scientific activity happens within a paradigm, and as there are paradigms, there are also competing paradigms. Even Karl Popper observed that:

> 'Normal' science exists. It is the activity of the non-revolutionary, or more precisely, the not-too-critical professional: of the science student who accepts the ruling dogma of the day.
>
> *(Popper 1979)*

Lakatos and Musgrave (1970) used the term *research programme* to describe how scientific activity happened within frameworks, and Feyerabend (1975) coined the term *anarchy* to describe how different positions within science compete on truth claims. The position that science basically is a discursive process includes Peter Winch's work on science (Winch 1958/1985) and similar arguments posed by Stephen Toulmin (2001). Social science is a discourse among other discourses, and a discourse in society. It is an argument for democratising science and research (Bourdieu 1977; Habermas 1964). Science has been atomised into disciplines and research programmes. Research programmes imply that science is moving between observation and reflection within frameworks. These frameworks are not necessarily correct; rather, they reflect the particular choices of that scientific group.

Habermas takes as a starting point a sociological perspective on science; that is, he regards science as a social practice in its own right. The value of freedom or objectivity of science is defined by the institutional and social process within science. It is a negotiated truth. The value question, Habermas argues, can be termed as the relation between facts and decision, or the dualism of *is* and *ought*. He writes:

> The dualism of facts and decisions corresponds, in the logic of science, to the separation of cognition and evaluation and, in methodology, to the demand for a restriction of the realm of empirical-scientific analysis to the empirical uniformity of natural and social processes.
>
> *(Habermas 1971, p. 145)*

The question, then, is whether we can separate knowledge (facts) from evaluations (decisions). This question highlights a problem or question: Is there a continuum between theoretical (scientific) knowledge on the one hand and practical processes on the other? Popper's answer is that scientific knowledge is distinct, because it must have the property of being falsifiable. Habermas disagrees that this is a universal criterion, because he regards this criterion as in itself a (social) norm. This leads us to Habermas's main point that even (social) science is a social activity and is performed within the framework of institutions, norms and pre-understandings. There is no such thing as pure theory. The circle of arguments that this leads to is that even criteria of value freedom are socially constructed (a product of social processes). He argues:

> Within a life-reference fixed by everyday language and stamped out in social norms, we experience and judge things as human beings with regard to specific meaning, in which the un-separated, descriptive and normative content states just as much about the human subjects who live in it as it does about the objects experienced themselves.
>
> *(Habermas 1971, p. 166)*

This perspective corresponds with, and supports, the general argument that science is a social practice and has to comply with the same control, critique and social questioning that holds for society as a whole. Habermas does not take an extreme anti-positivist standpoint. He recognises different ways of studying society and different ways of theorising. He discusses and compares two approaches to society as a system, that is, system as understood by Hegel, implying that individuals are part of a comprehensive whole (society), so-called dialectical theory; and system as understood more technically, as a deterministic, functionalistic process. He discusses this relation along four themes: The meta position is that no system can study itself, so all system approaches have to be regarded as some sort of social sense-making, or what he calls an *ordering schema*. On the other hand, he holds that any such general perspective that the scientist has will influence the research that he or she does; it has an indirect impact on our perspectives. And he proclaims:

> For we know hardly anything about an ontological correspondence between scientific categories and the structure of reality.
>
> *(Habermas 1971, p. 133)*

Furthermore, in comparing the functionalist systems theory with a dialectical systems theory, he argues that functionalist systems theory is analytical-empirical based (ref. empirical sociology), while dialectical system theory is experience based. Habermas explains the difference between the two systems approaches as follows: The functionalist system presupposes society as if it was a natural phenomenon that we can observe, where one element is a functional part of the whole, and where we get the same result independent of how we research it. This implies a direct relation between science and practice. The dialectical approach acknowledges the dependence of individual phenomenon upon the totality but rejects that this can be perceived in law-like terms. From this perspective, social phenomena are not constants but particular concrete events that must be understood in their application (practice). Social laws become a reality in this practice, that is, as a result of individuals' interpretation of the concrete situation. In this sense, social structures and laws are objective, in the sense that they are perceived as real by individuals in a particular situation. This points in the direction of sociology as interpretation (*verstehen*). Following this, the dialectical approach implies that we must distinguish between theory (science) and practice and, not least, meaning and interpretation. Given the above points, analytical social theory can only be regarded as partial in the sense that it is restricted to some interpretations. Furthermore, the dialectical approach implies that science must explain (and legitimise) itself and reflect on its own practice. How can we theorise on social phenomena, how can we get knowledge and what are the constraints of this knowledge?

Historical traits

Some historical traits can help us understand the current discourse within science. René Descartes (1596–1650), to whom we referred in Chapter 6, was seeking secure foundation (axioms) from which other truths could rise. According to Descartes, we are capable of knowing when things are evidently true; thus he acknowledges both that reality exists and that it is accessible to us. Therefore, phenomena have their own existence, independently of how and when we view them, and they remain as such long enough to be measured. David Hume (1711–1776), for example, was a strong critic of rationalists like Descartes (and therefore of deduction). He thought that moral science could develop methods (induction) that were different from, but still similar to, natural sciences, thereby developing true understanding of human and society (Levison 1974). He accepted the split between moral science and natural science but also believed that one can systematically understand human beings. At the same time, Hume destroyed some of the optimism created by the inductive approach. He was a *scepticist*, and took some of the principles laid down by the empiricists very seriously. He argued that the only things we can know for sure are the things where we have an immediate sensing. When I sense something and start putting it into a category, I make a deduction or assumption. Let us say, I know my desktop. So, I know for sure that there is some hard material there. When I classify that as a desk, I do so because I have learned that things that more or less look like the thing my computer is placed on are desks. This is practical knowledge I have; it is not a truth in itself.

> Hume is not concerned with any recognisable utility of the particular action, but only with the utility a universal application of certain abstract rules including those particular instances in which the immediate known results of obeying the rules are not desirable. His reason for this is that human

intelligence is quite insufficient to comprehend all the details of the complex human society, and that it is this inadequacy of our reason to arrange such an order in detail which forces us to be content with abstract rules; and further, that no single human intelligence is capable of inventing the most appropriate abstract rules because those which have evolved in the process of growth of society embody the experience of many more trials and errors than any individual mind could acquire.

(Hayek 1967, p. 88)

So, Hume argues that most of the ideas we have about things come from social learning, norms and habits. We should therefore not exaggerate our perception of knowledge, and we should distinguish between hard facts and socially accepted knowledge. This implies that the battle over the right way to do science was not over. Empiricists' rejection of *deduction* and embrace of *induction* had not settled the debate. The man that would try to put the whole picture back in place was the German (Prussian) philosopher Immanuel Kant (1724–1804). Kant took Descartes' divide and dialectics as a starting point. He also acknowledged David Hume's critique of induction. And he agreed with all those who argued that science should not be based on metaphysics. So Kant, roughly speaking, divided our thinking into *pure reason* and *practical reason*, and he wrote two of his most important works as a critique (discussion) of the two: *Kritik der reinen Vernunft* (Critique of Pure Reason) from 1781, and *Kritik der praktischen Vernunft* (Critique of Practical Reason) from 1788.

Kant responded to Descartes' question: Where does thinking come from? But he denounced Descartes' metaphysics. However, he agreed with Descartes that our knowledge is not about solving the ontological question: What are things? But also the epistemological question: How do we get knowledge about things? Kant thereby developed what we today will call the *epistemological position*; our study of the sources of our knowledge.

> Kant was the first modern philosopher to recognise that Newton's monumental achievement in physics specifically his formulation of the law of universal gravitation – required the recasting of philosophical inquiry about knowledge. As geometry was Plato's paradigm through which he explored the nature of knowledge, Newtonian physics was Kant's. He regarded aspects of Newtonian theory as necessarily true – specifically the assumption of universal causation, and the reality of space and time. But he also agreed with David Hume that such necessity was not given, or seen, in experience. Thus Newton's truths: Kant's paradigm of a knowledge claim, could not be accounted for by saying that the mind conformed to reality, rather the mind had to provide these necessities. This is the beginning of Kant's famous, or for some infamous, intrusion of the knowing subject into the object of knowledge.
>
> *(Southerland, Sinatra & Matthews 2001, p. 329)*

Kant started out by arguing that *space* and *time* have to be categories that are already installed in our mind, in order that we can perceive things. Perception requires some structure, and this structure cannot be part of perception. Kant calls this *pure reason*, and argues that since the things that are pure reason cannot come from sense impressions or experience, they have to be of a very abstract and general kind. This is why we can know things in abstract form: It does not come from experience but existed as categories that are fundamental to our thinking. Kant's concept of pure reason, metaphysics and Descartes' "the first philosophy" are basically the same concept. They all refer to knowledge that cannot be proven by observation. Kant formulated it this way:

> That all our knowledge begins with experience there is no doubt. [...] But although all our knowledge begins with experience, it does not follow that it arises from experience.
>
> *(Kant 2001, p. 24)*

The ambition of the rationalist tradition is that our thinking has some sort of superiority. Thinking is separated from experience so that we can think about experience and hold it against more abstract ideas we have on what is right and wrong or meaningful or meaningless. In fact, the Kantian position implied that we have many different categories of knowledge. Table 8.1 illustrates this point.

We can know something *a priori* (before it is experienced) but also *a posteriori* (based on experience). The idea that a priori knowledge is analytic, that is, purely abstract, is not very controversial. That a posteriori knowledge is synthetic is not controversial. The controversial part is the synthetic/a priori and the analytical/a posteriori knowledge. How can something that is thought and reasoned without any empirical foundation say something about the practical world? How can we claim abstract, true knowledge that is based on contextual experience? The first of these was the main focus of Kant; he believed that there are universal truths, like human rights, that can be proven right from purely abstract thinking. The second part was to some extent the preoccupation of phenomenology and its social science version, hermeneutics. It is about coming to a deeper understanding of things starting form observation.

So, how do we understand things? Hermeneutics is in general a method providing meaningful understanding and interpretation by considering the whole

TABLE 8.1 Knowledge and mind

	A priori	*A posteriori*
Analytic	Tautology: True by pure logic but empty of empirical content	Rationalism: Logical inference or deduction (Descartes)
Synthetic	Epistemology: Universal, transcendental reason (Kant)	Ontology: True by empirical evidence: simple observation (Hume) or induction (Bacon)

or context of a human life, with the aim of arriving through language at a common understanding or shared vision. However, central in hermeneutics are the terms *pre-understanding* and *prejudice*. Pre-understanding is composed in tacit knowing as well as articulated elements, and involves personal experience, concepts and so on. It is important that researchers who interpret and understand the meaning of phenomena have a reflective attitude to their own pre-understanding, and be aware of the elements of the understanding toward which they do not have a conscious and reflective attitude. However, our horizon of understanding is constantly changing. Gadamer (1975/2010) supposes that history, tradition and culture are all crucial, and that our values, assumptions and beliefs help us to colour any new understanding. Through the hermeneutic circle, we may constantly assess whether prejudices and prior understanding are part of the hermeneutic circle. Prejudices are integrated, and one can constantly have elements of these up for revision and change.

Conversation and dialogue is intersubjective, and a function of the interactions that generate new knowledge and understanding. According to Gadamer, a successful understanding is an amalgamation of the various horizons. "To decide a question is the road to knowledge" (Gadamer 2010, p. 328). It is through dialogue with questions and arguments that we articulate tacit knowing and prejudices, which in turn should lead to a revision of our understanding horizon. Having these epistemological positions as a background, and building on the discussion of knowledge in Chapter 5, it can be asked: How can social science approach social reality? In order to approach this question, we present two perspectives on the concept of knowledge. The first perspective we find presented in the book *The New Natural Resource* (Johnsen 2014), and the second concept of knowledge we find in the book *Territorial Development and Action Research – Innovation Through Dialogue* (Larrea & Karlsen 2015). These two perspectives on knowledge are partly contradictory ways of understanding knowledge, as knowledge in the first case is understood as a *one-dimensional concept*, while in the other case knowledge is a *two-dimensional concept*. To highlight and discuss these differences is important, because how we understand the concept of knowledge will influence how we deal with knowledge creation, knowledge diffusion and knowledge sourcing processes. We can observe these two positions in the former table. The one-dimensional position can be regarded as what we have called spectator/observer, abstract knowledge. The two-dimensional can be seen as participant/concrete, practical knowledge in Table 8.2.

TABLE 8.2 Knowledge and levels of analysis

	One-dimensional concept of knowledge	*Multi-dimensional concept of knowledge*
Actor level	Analytical: Seeking true knowledge	Synthetic: Seeking useful knowledge
System level	Analytical: Seeking general, abstract knowledge or institutional conditions for truth	Synthetic Identifying conditions for learning and knowledge development

The one-dimensional concept of knowledge

The line of argument for the one-dimensional conception of knowledge starts by stating that knowledge has to be different from "not knowledge". If it was not so, the concept of knowledge would be worthless. Without being able to separate A from B, there would simply not be something called A or B, but only the mix of A and B. If we agree that knowledge is something different from not-knowledge, we should also agree that we need some mechanisms to sort out knowledge from not-knowledge. If knowledge actually is different from not-knowledge, these differences have to be stable despite contextual preferences. If A is different from B, the two variables have to be different, no matter where in time and space we are located (Table 8.3).

Knowledge is a neutral concept. In order for knowledge to be different from not knowledge, regardless of context, knowledge has to be a neutral concept. This implies that the differences between knowledge and not knowledge have to be possible to detect regardless of cultural factors, institutions and subjective interpretations. The knowledge-sorting mechanisms are constituted of open discussions in society. Even though knowledge is a neutral concept, we do not live in a divine system. We (as humans) are not socially deterministic but social beings rooted in various contexts, in various times of existence, and therefore differently rooted and differently shaped. Even though we are different, humans are born with the ability to reflect. This ability to reflect includes reflections as outsiders, not only as insiders. The reflection as outsiders includes the ability to emphasise and to view an argument from several angles, and it includes the ability also to reflect on the system itself.

As knowledge is a phenomenon fundamental to humans, humans need to be involved in this selection process of knowledge separation. The way we are involved is that we communicate and discuss. In open and free societies, knowledge is the result of knowledge-sorting procedures, consisting of free and open discussions in society. In such societies, there is a complex relationship between individuals and society, where both spheres influence each other. These procedures, sorting out fantasies from knowledge, can be understood as communicative rationality. Claims of truth have to be made explicit. Knowledge is not the same as truth, and neither is it just facts. Knowledge and truth are connected in that way that knowledge is what is considered to be the right understanding of things. This "right understanding of things" is compared to what is considered to be "the false understanding" of things; or, in other words, knowledge is separated from not knowledge. In order for people to be involved in open discussions on what should be determined as the right understanding of things, there has to be something to discuss. Some claims to knowledge have to be raised, and these claims have to be open to contradiction. If not, there is nothing to discuss. However, in order for claims to be put forward, and in order for claims to be part of the discussion, the claim has to be made explicit. The claim of knowledge, or the claims of truth, needs to be translated from our minds and made explicit, into something that can be understood and argued. It has to be "de-personalised".

TABLE 8.3 How social science can influence society as a knowledge system

	Power: The social position or role dimension	Beliefs: The dispositional dimension	Position: The interactive-situational dimension	Institutions: The knowledge-institutionalisation dimension
Conscious (explicit knowledge held by the individual)	What are the dominant strategies	What values and assumptions are underlying dominant strategies	Who are gatekeepers for dominant strategies	What institutions exist
Objectified (explicit knowledge held by society or an organisation)	What is the social position of the organisations – their ability to influence	What is considered relevant	Who are the influencing institutions	What is the strategy of the institution
Automatic *preconscious* individual knowing)	Who has the knowledge	How do people interpret	What is people's position and personal networks	How do institutions preserve knowledge forms
Collective (highly context-dependent knowing that is manifested in the practice of society, institutions or organisations)	Who are in power to decide over knowledge	What is the nature of social deliberation	What is the network structure	How inflexible are the institutions

Source: Based on Johnsen, Hauge, Magnussen and Ennals, 2017.

Knowledge is a social process. Even though we have a de-personalised process of claiming knowledge, our existing language restrains our ability to argue our claims of truth. In this process, we use words that already exist, and which contain a specific meaning that is individual. Thereby, the discussion of what is knowledge and what is not knowledge becomes a result of dialectics between individuals and society. The world consists of several sub-groups, and these sub-groups have their own discussions of what is knowledge and what is not knowledge. Because these dialectics will be different, the final decision as to what is regarded as knowledge (most certainly) will vary. One group in society could agree that a certain statement is true, while another declares that it is false. The conclusion from this is that knowledge is a social process and that what is regarded as true will differ among social groups. As such, a one-dimensional concept of knowledge defines knowledge as what is (socially) regarded as a right understanding of things.

Based on this definition, and in other words, knowledge is a phenomenon that is recognised on the basis of what society at a certain point in time regards as true. This definition of knowledge as a socially explicit phenomenon frames the concept in a way that makes it possible to elaborate on certain distinctions of the knowledge concept. First, from the definition, we can argue that knowledge is distinctly different from truth. There is a link between knowledge and truth, but knowledge becomes what is regarded as true and not what is objectively truth in itself. From this, we can have a situation where knowledge is completely false.

Second, knowledge is not an objective truth; it is not fixed. Knowledge is still what is considered true by society at a certain point in time, and as new claims of truth are constantly entering the social dialogue, what is considered true today can (easily) be declared false tomorrow. New arguments or new proofs are constantly launched, and the constant dialogue in society makes knowledge development an eternally ongoing dynamic process. When new claims of truth prove existing knowledge wrong, this particular claim of truth shifts status as it goes from knowledge to not-knowledge.

Third, there is a qualitative dimension to knowledge. This qualitative dimension results from the fact that society is a rather blurred framework. It does not mean that everybody in society has to agree that something is knowledge, and it does not even mean that society has to agree as a whole. There is no democratic process, in the sense that what is considered true by most people is the defined truth. The consequence is thereby that the same claim can have status as both knowledge and not knowledge within different sub-groups of society. This is, however, not a problem for the definition of knowledge. The qualitative dimension grades the degree of knowledge, even if it does not influence the definition of knowledge itself. Knowledge is still what society regards as truth at a certain point of time, but in this way, a claim to truth could be held by both a minority and a major part of society.

This way of defining knowledge also has certain implications. As knowledge is a result of an ongoing evaluation by society, knowledge creation is the result of a dynamic, non-totalitarian process. Yes, knowledge can result from claims of truth being forced to society by totalitarian regimes, but the process of knowledge development leans heavily on individuals. As such, totalitarian regimes might press claims to be regarded as true by society, but they can never eliminate individual thinking. As times shift, new arguments are again put forward, and what was regarded true under one regime now becomes false.

This definition of knowledge also gives arguments for social change through the accumulation and creation of new knowledge. Because knowledge is separated from truth, and as knowledge has a qualitative aspect, society can support processes of change by investing in certain types of knowledge. We, as a society, can decide to increase our knowledge within certain fields by investing in knowledge development in these areas, and as we become more knowledgeable, we will change. As we can invest in knowledge, we will also be able to identify what gain from trade we can harvest from this investment. The result will be visible in our competition with others, and as such, geographical limitable areas will increase or decrease their competitive advantage through knowledge generation exploited in incremental and more radical innovations.

The two-dimensional concept of knowledge

In territorial development, the creation of new knowledge is crucial, and knowledge-creation processes are often analysed and reflected upon from an inside–out perspective. From this perspective, researchers may play an important role as participants in action. This constructivist approach introduces a term that represents a different aspect of knowledge, namely *knowing*. Knowledge and knowing cannot be separated from one another as they represent double meanings that interact and are rivals in the process of knowledge generation and knowledge diffusion:

> There is a difference between knowledge and knowing. In English, the word "knowledge" is a noun, while "knowing" is a form of the verb "to know". As a noun, "knowledge" can be interpreted as a stock. As a verb, "knowing" can be interpreted as an action or a process. Knowledge presupposes a fixed point in time when some insight or belief qualifies as knowledge, while knowing is what continuously unfolds as we make use of knowledge in action.
>
> *(Larrea & Karlsen 2016, p. 64)*

From the above quotation, we observe that action is presented as the process needed in order to transform knowledge to knowing. The relationship between knowledge and knowing is that "knowing is what continuously unfolds as we make use of knowledge in action" (see citation above). So, "A" (knowing) is what you get when we use "B" (knowledge) in action. That means that knowing is different from knowledge.

It can be argued that the concepts of knowing and knowledge in fact are various facets of the same phenomenon. We discussed this in Chapter 5. The Aristotelian concept of different kinds of knowing, as presented in Chapter 5, is also represented in Ryle (2009) and his distinction between "know-that" and "knowing how", and also in Polanyi's dichotomy of tacit and explicit knowledge (Polanyi 2009). It supports the argument that both these concepts are presented as inter-dependent dimensions of knowledge. Ryle (2009) argues that "know what" and "know how" are two dimensions of knowledge, and that these two dimensions are inter-dependent. This inter-dependency is also highlighted by Polanyi when he introduces the tacit and explicit dimension of knowledge. This inter-dependency between the tacit and explicit dimension of knowledge is made explicit in his most famous quotation, "we know more than we can tell" (Polanyi 2009, p. 4). What we know (knowledge) thereby consists of two dimensions that are inseparable, namely, the one part of knowledge that we can articulate (explicit dimension of knowledge) and the one part we cannot articulate (tacit dimension of knowledge). Polanyi himself highlights the importance of both facets of knowledge in knowledge creation processes when saying:

> The declared aim of modern science is to establish a strictly detached, objective knowledge … [but if] tacit thought forms an indispensable part of all that knowledge, then the ideal of eliminating all personal elements of knowledge would, in effect, aim at the destruction of knowledge.
>
> *(Polanyi 2009, p. 20)*

Knowledge and knowing are deeply interwoven and also impossible to disconnect. This is where it gets complicated: Knowledge and knowing are separate elements, but they are both manifest in action. So, being in the action is crucial, if you have the ambition to understand change and development processes. Knowledge-creation processes often involve several partners, and learning takes place at several organisational levels. One of these levels is the region, and at a regional level, various development processes are launched in order to try to increase the competitive advantage of that particular region. Such processes normally involve actors representing various parts of the regional innovation system, and the intended outcome of such interactive learning processes is to generate mutual understanding and collective knowledge as foundations for action that will increase future growth and development. "Knowing" at an aggregated level then becomes important, called *collective knowing*, and defined as follows:

> Collective knowing is the *social process of creating common ground for action and for acting in alignment with others.*
>
> *(Larrea & Karlsen 2016, p. 22)*

According to this definition, collective knowing is a social process that involves generating "common ground" within a group of people. One can explain this term with reference to the concept of social capital in general, and the concept of cognitive social capital in particular. Social capital is highlighted as important by several fields of research dealing with interaction at both a micro and a macro level, according to Putnam (2000), when he argued for the importance of public governance in the education sector. From here, the concept of social capital has developed through the thoughts and ideas of several authors. Among these authors, Bourdieu (2011), Coleman (1988) and Putnam (2000) stand out as some of the most important contributors. In recent years, two other authors have made their mark within this line of research. Nahapiet and Ghoshal define social capital as:

> the sum of actual or potential resources embedded within, available through, and derived from the network of relationships possessed by an individual or social unit.
> *(Nahapiet & Ghoshal 1998, p. 243)*

Nahapiet and Ghoshal distinguish social capital as having three different dimensions, namely a structural, a relational and a cognitive side. The cognitive dimension of social capital is referred to as:

> those resources providing shared representations, interpretations, and systems of meaning among parties.
> *(Nahapiet & Ghoshal 1998, p. 244)*

Building on this definition of cognitive social capital, it could be argued that building collective knowing involves the same elements needed in order to increase cognitive social capital.

If one understands knowledge as a two-dimensional concept, action research is a particularly suitable and important research method in territorial development processes. This point is further elaborated in chapter eleven on social learning. The knowledge concept includes both an implicit and explicit dimension, and collective knowing is built gradually from the process of interaction between the two dimensions. Territorial development is about creating collective knowing, and in order to do that, new knowledge has to be extracted and refilled into the process. If researchers intend to understand the knowing part of these processes, they have to get involved in action. They simply have to be part of the process; otherwise they will not possess knowing. However, researchers involved in action have a particular responsibility as they possess both knowledge and knowing and as, at the same time, they also hold the competence, knowledge and networks needed in order to reflect, discuss and create new input. As so, researchers involved in action are those most suitable to refill and restart the process with new elements.

Comparison of the two concepts

Knowledge as socially explicit means arguing that knowledge is to be understood as an either/or phenomenon. Either the claim to knowledge should be accepted as knowledge, or it should be accepted as "not knowledge". There are no such things as facets of knowledge or "partly knowledge". From this argument, we can conclude that knowledge is a one-dimensional phenomenon. However, the one-dimensional approach to knowledge does not support the argument that there is one objective truth. There could be various conflicting claims of truth that all are accepted as truth by various groups of people. The important issue is that society can easily identify the claim of truth as it is made explicit, and from there make the claim a part of a social process, where discussion acts as the sorting mechanism that separates knowledge from not-knowledge. In this line of argument, knowledge is neither facts nor skills. Knowledge is simply claims of truth accepted as true by society. Arguing that knowledge is a two-dimensional phenomenon, however, means arguing differently, as this concept argues that a dualism exists within the concept of knowledge. Knowledge is two dimensional as it consists of one implicit type of knowledge and one explicit type of knowledge labelled "knowing". These two dimensions of knowledge are inter-related and cannot be separated. In a process of knowledge generation, the inter-relatedness between knowing and knowledge is crucial in order to generate collective knowing. Collective knowing is the knowledge accepted as true amongst the group of actors involved in the knowledge generation process, and this type of collective knowing is the result of a time-consuming process involving a high level of trust, commitment, regularity and frequency among the actors involved. Theoretical knowledge and practical knowing are both facets of knowledge, and as such, both facts and skills can be included in this knowledge concept. Action is of particular importance as it presupposes collective knowing. Collective knowing is a capability that develops over time, from dialogue between different actors.

Knowledge as socially explicit separates knowledge from truth. Knowledge is what is considered to be true, but it does not have to be true for eternity. What is considered to be true is then socially determined. Therefore, what is considered to be true at one period of time could easily well be regarded as false in another period of time. As times passes, what is regarded to be true is challenged by somebody who claims they have some more true knowledge. Over time, society has some sort of rationality in order to sort out the better from the false. According to this definition, no one can claim absolute knowledge, and so, knowledge is a result of a non-totalitarian process of sorting out truth from not-truth. Knowledge as two-dimensional, on the other side, highlights the process of generating collective knowing as a process of constant change. The changes are a result of knowledge put into action, and the result of this process is the way regions could build cognitive social capital. What is regarded as collective knowing can change. Through reflection and discussion with the outside world (through academic papers, etc.), collective knowing is challenged. New information, new facts and new experiences are developed, and the refill of such new knowledge challenges the collective knowing and pushes it forward as a dynamic process. In this process, consensus is not needed. However, a significant number of participants have to agree. If not, the existing collective knowing will remain in play. Based on these arguments, truth is decoupled from knowledge in both concepts of knowledge.

Within the concept of knowledge as a two-dimensional phenomenon, collective knowing is a result of a dialectic process between the explicit and the implicit type of knowledge. In order to create common ground for mutual understanding, trust is crucial. Trust between actors makes agora a more "safe" place, and as such, trust is important in order for actors to reveal their "true" selves and in order to speak the truth instead of the things "itching the ears of others". Openness, trust and confidence are factors that will make the process of generating collective knowing go more smoothly, even though it is not enough in itself. Collective knowing is generated from dialogue, and trust will make this dialogue less turbulent. Trust is, however, not an important element in the conception of knowledge as socially explicit. Here knowledge is what is regarded as the truth by society, regardless of whether the society has a high level of trust or not. Dictatorships have knowledge in the same way as democracies have knowledge. Knowledge could differ between the two societies, but nevertheless knowledge is what is considered as true in a society at a certain time. That means that groups can have their own truth and groups can disagree on their belief of what is true. Truth can be measured at various levels, and at the chosen level, the majority of actors define what knowledge is.

In order to foster smooth processes to generate collective knowing, a high level of commitment from the actors is vital. Creating collective knowing is a result of a dialectic process wherein the explicit and the implicit types of knowledge are combined in action, and as such, having loyal and dedicated actors will help make the process smoother. A high level of commitment tends to increase the effort put into the process, and as such, a high level of commitment will increase the chances of creating collective knowing. Commitment is not very important in the concept of knowledge as socially explicit. The dialogue in society goes on regardless of who participates, and it is not necessarily positive that actors have a high degree of commitment. Less commitment opens the dialogue for more voices and thereby also more claims of truth. Society thereby has more variety, and more arguments to consider in their democratic dialogue, when sorting out knowledge from not-knowledge.

Regularity is important in the processes of generating collective knowing. Regularity between actors in the agora makes the dialogue less fragmented and disjointed, and as such, dialogue between partners meeting regularly makes the dialogue proceed more smoothly than dialogues with less regularity. Regularity helps make the process predictable, and as such has a positive impact on the process of generating knowledge. Regularity amongst the actors is not important to the concept of knowledge when knowledge is conceptualised as socially explicit. Society consists of whoever society consists of, and the regularity of actors involving in the debate of sorting out what is true from what is not true is not important. What is knowledge is determined by society from the information spread and accepted.

Collective learning is a capability defined as "a learned pattern of collective action where the actors in the agora systematically modify their actions over time, through the learning process in the agora" (Larrea & Karlsen 2016, p. 68). To create mutual identification and norms is not easily done, and such processes normally require a long timeframe filled with discussions and reflection. To rush the learning process will most certainly lower the probability of exchanging and combining knowledge, and thereby will also lower the expectation and motivation of the participants. When knowledge is conceptualised as socially explicit, time is not an important factor when it comes to generating knowledge. What is defined as knowledge today is what the majority of society agrees is truth, regardless of what might actually be the pure truth. So, knowledge is in most cases a constantly evolving phenomenon, and as such, whether the actors involved in the knowledge creation process have a short or a long timeframe is of little importance. What is important is what the majority of society argues to be true at a certain point in time. How to make the process of knowledge generation better, in order to make more valid knowledge, is another question, and when it comes to the validity question of knowledge, the timeframe becomes more important.

Actor and system

The point about the one and the two-dimensional concepts of knowledge is that they not only represent a divide between definitions of knowledge but also have an implication for methodology. You go about it in different ways if you are applying the one versus the other concept of knowledge/knowing. Before we draw further conclusions from this dichotomy, we will introduce a second major divide in social science, that between actor and system. Knowledge from the perspective of the actor is often oriented towards understanding and interpretation, giving meaning for the subjects. The actor's view implies that the socially constructed reality consists of different levels of meaning structure, and that language is given different meanings in relation to these levels. Knowledge is dependent on the individual, but also on the observer, by trying to understand relations among (constitutive) interpretations made by various actors in relation to different level of meaning structures in a dialectic relation to each other. To be precise, this involves interpretations, and factors are mutually and in constant transformation, mutually influencing each other in a continuous developmental process in which reality is socially constructed. Thus, as a result, the reality exists only as a social construction and is not dependent on its observers; the social world is made by the actors in interactions. Since the reality is socially constructed, a central assumption within the actor approach is that the world is subjective. Thus, reality is not considered as independent of us, but consists of an interaction between our own experience and the collected structure of experiences, which we have created over time together with others.

As a researcher, the knowledge ambition of the actor view is to provide knowledge that extends the understanding of the complexity of the human society by denoting meaning and the idea of how social reality is constructed. However, these complexities cannot be divided into simply relations (determinism), since we will then erase human complexity, which we instead intend to understand. This means that social science, in comparison to natural science, studies phenomena that consist of concepts, involving the actors' conceptions of their experience. The main instrument of creators of knowledge within the actor's view is dialogue. Dialogue as a method is based on nearness, authenticity and willingness to emancipate, and as a central part of the creator of knowledge, it requires humility and attention as well as a genuine curiosity. The methodological purpose with dialogue may be either be to clarify differences (thesis/antithesis), in which the participants can reflect their original opinions, or it may be used to go beyond the original options (synthesis) by entering the dialogue as a participant.

The systems approach is a holistic approach. A system implies that the components of the system have an impact on the performance of the whole. However, the whole is something different from its parts. The performance of each component in the system depends on the performance of at least of one other component part of the system; therefore a component can only be analysed within the context of the whole. The links between the elements consist therefore of different relationships between the elements that can contribute to synergy that exists between system components, and this is considered as one of the key elements of the systems approach. The way the parts are put together may therefore provide important information, as the interaction between each component may cause a synergy effect. As a result, the parts may create more or less than the sum of the individual components, depending on whether the synergy effect is positive or negative. Since the term *system* relies on many interactions, parts and feedback loops, systems may be considered abstract and also difficult to observe in practice.

Emile Durkheim is considered as a central thinker related to the development of a systemic, structural analysis of society (Durkheim [1893] 2014). His analysis attempted to create a functionality between structures in society, and between these structures and the individual action. Thus, despite the fact that system thinking is still heavily disputed, most of the critique has been directed towards the older system theory. The younger system thinking that emerged in later years considers systems to be non-linear and complex. An analysis of the systems approach is looking at forces that may have an impact on a particular system as a whole, by providing a better understanding of the particular whole is created. From a methodology point of view, the systems view therefore seeks system-dependent knowledge and is not reductionist but holistic, as opposed to individualistic. It means that all the properties of a given system cannot be determined, explained or understood by the sum of its component parts alone, but the system as a whole determines in an important way how the parts behave.

It can be claimed that systems thinking and the actor perspective may be considered as two aspects of the same subject, complementing each other rather than being two incompatible opposites. However, as this theoretical discussion has highlighted, it is not straightforward to combine insight from those two different perspectives (actor and systems), since they are built on different assumptions. However, different strategies have been suggested in order to overcome these difficulties. Some of the strategies that have been highlighted have been promoted to use different methods to complement each other, also known as *triangulation*, or merging elements from different approaches into a single approach, also known as *synthesis*. However, even though it may be possible to synthesise different methods and techniques, these strategies are less relevant when it comes to synthesising different epistemologies based on different assumptions about social reality and knowledge. Another strategy may be to consider the two perspectives as dualism and thus to discuss a dialectic between them. In practice, this involves a movement where one viewpoint is contradicted by another, contributing to develop a third view. The recognition that there exist different understandings, different knowledge and different perceptions of reality may contribute to establishing a superior officer joint perspective. Thus, looking at the differences as dynamic and the various positions as a criticism may result in better understanding.

Thus, based on this discussion, we have seen that knowledge developed within the system approach depends on systems, and that the whole does not equal its parts because of synergies and where parts may only be explained (understood) by the characteristics of the whole. This is opposite to the actor approach, where knowledge depends on individuals, and where the whole only exists as a meaning structure, which is socially constructed.

Methodology for coping with the future

We discuss in this book what the future of society, organisations, networks and leadership might look like. From a systemic change perspective, we see today's structure as a result of historical conditions. We argue that a discussion of a sustainable future has to learn from history and the processes that brought about the structure we see today. In a change perspective, we can identify the individual actor, but also systems, and we can take a long-term as well as a short-term perspective. This implies that we can talk about change considered at many different levels and time scales. There are several strategies available, but it seems difficult to combine these different methodologies. However, since there may be several interpretations of a situation, dialogue may offer one possible solution by representing multiple perspectives, where a situation may have more than one interpretation according to how we view it. This solution is quite common in social science, by going back and forth between different theories and cases. By sharing each other's knowledge and points of view, this strategy could provide a better understanding, and that reality consists of more than individual elements, but also relationships between the elements that are important for the results.

Our main argument is to bring together the two dimensions that have been discussed: the concept of knowledge and the level of analysis. Methodologies build on assumptions about knowledge. The two dimensions of knowledge/knowing and actor/system give us, in combination, some ideal types of methodological approaches.

The different chapters in this book position themselves within this set of typologies. The discussion on sustainability and rationality exemplifies the actor/one-dimensional position: What is the true nature of knowledge in an analytical sense, one that can cope with the future? Our discussion about systems and structure is also to a large degree analytical in terms of knowledge. The chapter on learning is multi-dimensional at an actor level, as is the chapter on leadership. However, the chapter on work can be seen as multi-dimensional at a system level. As these are typologies, they cannot easily be combined. As methodologies, they are based on different assumptions. This is the case with most social science; it is pluralistic in its approaches. What implication does our discussion have for the challenge of doing research that is relevant for the future?

Box 8.1 The Kodak moment of methodology

***The disruptiveness of change*:**

Social science constructs knowledge based on assumptions. These assumptions have to be acknowledged. If the output of social science is taken for objective facts that can be implemented by politics, one might end up making terrible mistakes.

***The knowledge one failed to use*:**

The hypothetical nature of scientific knowledge has to be acknowledged, and subsequently the science/society dialogue has to be improved by accepting the need for a broad dialogue including different scientific positions.

***Ability to adjust to future changes*:**

There should be criticism of the assumption that social science can provide facts and true knowledge for making decisions that can guide us into the future.

***The opportunity in the changes*:**

It should be acknowledged that social science is a way of producing knowledge, and that it is socially embedded, thereby acknowledging the limits to social science knowledge development.

Social science, in this way, produces knowledge within a social context that can be described as a *knowledge system*. The impact of social science is not only the scientific discovery itself, but also how it is perceived and interpreted in the social process. The question is how can social science contribute to increased rationality and reason on issues related to economic and social development, business and work. As methodologies, these different positions produce insight and results that cannot be compared directly. However, at a societal level, we argue, these findings contribute to a social discourse. They are arguments in an ongoing discussion, where validity and relevance are mediated. How this process of receiving and relation to social science, seen from society, can be perceived was discussed in our book *Applied Social Science in a Regional Knowledge System*. We would like to refer to this book, as the argument therein corresponds to what we argue here. Table 8.3 is developed in that book, where we identified some main dimensions in the social knowledge system and how social science influenced it.

The table tries to describe, in a simple way, the many forms in which knowledge and knowing are institutionalised and socialised. It can be used to understand how knowledge at an individual level (up to the left in the table) contributes to the social and institutionalised field of explicit knowledge and tacit knowing. One way of reading the table is to argue that the most robust kind of knowing is when something is collectively taken for granted and institutionalised (down to the right in the table). The point with the model is to illustrate that if society is to change knowledge, it can do so in different ways, but that structures, opinions, power relations and positions can counter knowledge development in each other's domains, and each of these domains can have reason to reject new knowledge if it threatens them. This means that knowledge development is only likely to have a real impact to the extent that knowledge changes in all domains.

Social science produces knowledge about the past, present and future, based on different assumptions and approaches. It provides a repertoire of insights and ideas that play into the social domain as part of the discussion about social and economic development. Methodology in an extended understanding includes how this knowledge is perceived and used in the social and public domain.

PART III
Future technology, organisation and work

9
COPING WITH TECHNOLOGY

A future of robots?

Halvor Holtskog, Lars Harald Lied and Geir Ringen

What is technology?

People use technology every day, and almost every minute of their daily activities, without thinking about it. A presenter at a conference illustrated this with two pictures. The first one showed the crowd waiting for the 2005 papal election. People were standing and just waiting. The same picture taken at the 2013 papal election was quite different. Everybody had a phone or iPad in their hands, taking pictures or filming this historical event. Technology changed how people experienced the same event just a few years apart. Taking pictures or filming have changed dramatically over a short period. Often the opportunities and usage of a new tool or technology are natural to people. They do not even reflect much upon it. However, when technology is changed, people notice and sometimes get scared. A common frightening thought, shown in many movies, is when robots are no longer servants but are in charge of society. Movies like *Robocop*, *Terminator*, *I Robot* play with fear of technology taking over our lives and make decisions on behalf of humans. Science fiction movies illustrate one extreme view of the future. This discourse in the technological discussion is addressed in the next chapter on humanity. Here, we look into the relation between technology and industry, and discuss technology as something social with requirements in markets, business development, public support and social adaption.

The history of technology runs in parallel to the history of humanity; humans since the Stone Age have invented tools and techniques to make life easier or even possible. One can see technology as an enlargement of human senses and organs. We see more through a microscope or through a telescope; we move faster in a car; we even fly in a plane; we hear more with loudspeakers than we could without the technology. So, technology can be seen as the ambition of human beings to reach further than nature had made possible. Beyond this, technology has become a denominator in human existence, and sometimes has even been able to define that existence: Technology in medicine can keep a person alive. Technology has also had a sociological impact. The machine in the industrial area has defined work and the organisation of labour. Our ability to live and work in different places has changed with technologies that have made commotion possible. Large metropolitan areas would hardly have existed without technology; neither would skyscrapers, if there were no lifts or electricity or equipment able to build them.

The current debate about technology is highly influenced by the *digital revolution*. Beyond expectations, even those of experts, only some decades ago, digitisation and information and communication technology has had tremendous impacts on the lives of people in most of the world. It has enabled information transmission to a degree that few foresaw only a short time ago. The special thing about digital code is that it allows information to be stored, used and transmitted at a speed and at a distance previously unknown. In the 2011 book *Race Against the Machine* by Erik Brynjolfsson and Andrew McAfee, it is argued that this will have tremendous impact beyond what we have seen this far. What we already see is that this new technology creates platforms that make new network patterns possible. It opens new ways of doing business. There is a high-tech avenue where new advanced systems can replace conventional technologies, but there is also a low-tech dimension in this, where anyone with a computer and internet connection can mike their own business, publish or engage in networks on the new platforms.

The digital revolution is to some extent exceptional. Most technologies have emerged gradually. In complex society, technology is difficult to sort into groups, but recombinant innovation is thought to play a significant role (Wilson & Kirman 2016). Innovation theory divides innovation in technology into at least three different groups. The first is continuous improvement, whereby small steps in improving existing technology are the main point. The second, and at the other end of the scale, is breakthrough technology, where developments totally new to humanity are in focus. When penicillin was introduced to medicine, it was a breakthrough. In the middle of the dichotomy is recombinant technology, where known technologies are recombined in new ways. Toyota's innovations in hybrid car technology are one example (May 2007), where they combined existing technologies, like existing combustion engine with existing electric motor and batteries. Combining technologies points not only towards complexity but also diversity (van den Bergh 2008). The iPhone is an example. Smartphones with internet connectivity and the ability to run applications had been on the market for years, but with no success. The introduction of the iPhone changed this. Apple combined existing technologies, like small touch screens, running application ability and the existing iTunes store (to mention some examples) into one easy to use mobile phone. Additionally, Apple made it possible to code small programs and to market or sell them efficiently to users. These combinations resulted in what the market thought of as a breakthrough product and a game changer. However, each technology was already known and developed. Most of the products that are regarded as game changers are the result of recombinant innovation. The same phenomenon is observed in the car manufacturing industry. "When new technology is core to a vehicle, Toyota distinguishes itself from the rest of the pack by diligently working to master the technology and becoming the best in the world at using it" (Morgan & Liker 2006, p. 195). In this case, it is the usage and how to combine it with what already exists that are in focus. What are the underlying mechanisms that determine how we use technology? We address three aspects of how technology is adapted:

- Business strategies: new technological solutions enable new ways of making business;
- Governmental incentives: saying that governmental intervention can play a significant role;
- Social organisation: social patterns as a response to technological change.

Absorption models of technology change

Acceptance and usage of new technologies have been in focus for the science community, especially information technology (IT). The result has been many different models for transforming and using new technology. In 2000, at the height of the e-commerce bubble, Earl provided a roadmap for businesses to become E-enterprises (Earl 2000). The roadmap argued for six stages that a company needs to go through in order to transform its operations for doing business electronically, starting with a simple homepage and then developing internal communications, setting up e-commerce solution for customers, adding key capabilities, providing decision-making information and transforming the business model. This model, and many similar models, follows a Guttmann scale (Guttmann 1950), wherein the response patterns of a survey are put into an ordered scale. If you agree with a higher item in the scale, it implies that you agree on the lower items. According to Earl's model, if you agree a phase in transforming e-business is decision-making information, then you also agree with the six stages. These Guttmann scale models are discussed and debated, but they illustrate an evolutionary view of implementing, accepting and using new technology.

The re-industrialisation of Europe, often framed as Industry 4.0, has drawn much recent attention. It is the fourth industrial revolution. The first industrial revolution is defined to have started around 1750 through the introduction of mechanical production facilities with the help of water and steam power; for instance, the machine invention "spinning Jenny" by James Hargreaves was introduced to the cotton industry in 1764, the power loom by Edmund Cartwright in 1787 and the steam engine by James Watt in the 1760s. Moreover, new processes for heating iron more quickly accelerated the building of machines and railroads. All these efforts greatly improved productivity and changed the way people lived and worked.

The second industrial revolution was another great leap forward in technology and society, during which innovations in steel production, petroleum and electricity made mass production of complex products available to the public as well as development of cost-effective infrastructure. Historians define the years of the second industrial revolution from 1870 to 1914, and its inventions include the light bulb, the telephone and the internal combustion engine. The first two industrial revolutions brought increased welfare and urbanisation among people. From the late 1960s, the third industrial revolution kicked off with the introduction of the first programmable logistic controller (PLC), which enabled automated production through the use of electronic and IT systems. This era is identified by the shift from mechanical and analogue electronic technology to digital electronics and computers, and their connections through the internet and to people as we see today.

Now, we are said to be at the dawn of the fourth industrial revolution. The term *Industry 4.0* encompasses a promise of a new industrial revolution, the fourth such transformation in the history of manufacturing. The term was first coined in 2011 at the Hanover Messe trade fair, which was the subject of a presentation by an Industry 4.0 working group established by the German federal government. The Germany Trade and Invest (GTAI) defines Industry 4.0 as:

> A paradigm shift … made possible by technological advances which constitute a reversal of conventional production process logic. Simply put, this means that industrial production machinery no longer simply "processes" the

product, but that the product communicates with the machinery to tell it exactly what to do.[1]

(GTAI 2016)

These revolutionary phases show similar thought of evolutionary acceptance and usage of new technologies as the Guttmann scale models, with Earl's model being an example. As we go through these so-called revolutions, it is interesting to note that they all have time spans of decades, indicating that there is a sum of innovations over time that we, in retrospect, like to refer to as distinct breakthroughs. The revolutions are phases in the evolution. It can be seen as a counter to disruptive technology (DT). This view is too simple. The disruptiveness has three different aspects: learning/knowledge, timing and choosing. The latter deals with choosing the correct technology when there are several to choose from. Back in the early days of video cassettes, there were several different systems or technologies to choose from. Many regarded Sony's Beta system as the best technology; however, it lost to the dominant VHS. Timing is about when to choose. First-mover advantage got much attention in the early 1980s. Nobel recipient Michael Spence (Spence 1981) built his argument on the learning curve and competition. Early movers would have learned to use new technology and gained an advantage. This argument was supported and further elaborated on in the works of Gilbert and Newbery (Gilbert & Newbery 1982) and Reinganum (Reinganum 1983). The disadvantages of first-mover strategy were described as free-rider effects (late movers can drop research and development [R&D] expenses or other learning costs), resolution of technology uncertainty (the market is created for late movers), shifts in needs or technologies (create a better product, better satisfy the market needs) or incumbent inertia. The latter is caused by a company being locked in to specific fixed assets, not cannibalising existing products or being organisationally inflexible (Lieberman & Montgomery 1988). The e-bubble exploded in the early 2000s, but with the smartphone and the introduction of Apps or Widgets, it seems that e-commerce has made a comeback. The first bubble lacked an important piece of technology: the smartphone.

A driver for the use of new technology is a company's effort to gain competitive advantage. Technology is an important factor in the race for market share or success. The usage of technology and type of technology are often at the core of the company strategy or business model. From a manufacturing point of view, Freyssenet, Mair, Shimizu, & Volpato (1998) defined six profit strategies or business models found to be operative in the automotive industry. These models were used to describe the social and institutional characters of productivity, and we use these as a framework for further discussion of the implications of Industry 4.0. The following list presents the basics behind productive models:

- Quality strategy: This involves focusing on quality in all steps of the value chain and maintaining a skilled work force that identify themselves with the product/service. Profit margins are based on the product's reputation of being top of the range.

- Diversity and flexibility: This is a model where profit margins are based on rapid adjustment of costs to demand fluctuations, which in turn requires a work force that is autonomous, flexible, mobile and willing to accept intensive systems.
- Volume: This is a model that benefits from producing increasing quantities of relatively standard products/services. Work processes and operations are divided into pieces requiring undifferentiated and repetitive work by a not-so-skilled work force. It is defined as a top-down management approach, relaying on economics of scale.
- Volume and diversity: This represents a combination of economics of scale and economics of scope, where products are differentiated by what is visible, favouring a manufacturing strategy of modularisation and platforming. The work force tends to be polyvalent and with opportunities to develop their skills.
- Permanent cost reduction: This is a risk reduction model where continuous improvement and fact-based decisions, are inherent throughout the organisation. The work force is defined as semi-skilled and used to be benchmarked according to global production networks; this is an accepted model so long as employees feel involved in processes and improvement programmes.
- Innovation and flexibility: The work force is seen as entrepreneurial and opportunistic with an emphasis on expertise and responsiveness. Profit margins are based on delivering a continuous stream of new and innovative products as a response to perceived new expectations.

These business models within the automotive industry are not an exhaustive or static classification but a framework wherein many manufacturing companies can acknowledge and possible identify their strategy. It is also a framework where strategy is aligned to choices of product and process technology, as well as how the different models transform context and work life in organisations. The framework also indicates how the business model is linked to the scale representing the distinctions between regulation and radical change. In the "innovation and flexibility" business model, organisations focus on rapidly developing and producing new products that are commercially relevant and not immediately subject to being copied. Boyer and Freyssenet claim that such a strategy needs to be supported by developing employees who are curious, take initiatives, develop expertise, imagine future opportunities and so on, who, in return, enjoy a more reflexive type of work, good working conditions and career promotions. On the other hand, the "Volume" perspective tends towards regulation thinking, providing less job content and possibilities for the development of new skills and expertise, resulting in low-motivated jobs and high rates of personnel turnover.

Box 9.1 The car industry

During the 2008 financial crisis, the automotive and automobile industries were hit hard, creating a new awareness among managers dealing with radical changes. Prior to the financial crisis, there was concern about overproduction, escalating costs, the huge selection of different car models and stiff price competition. When the crisis hit the industry, the "Big Three" (General Motors, Chrysler and Ford) soon faced serious difficulties, resulting in bankruptcy for two of them, with a governmental bailout. It had a tsunami effect on the rest of the industry. Suppliers laid off highly educated people, there was a greater concentration of ownership, efficiency expectations increased dramatically and there were tough price negotiations.

Following this, we have seen the emergence of electric cars on the global market. The el-car has been on offer for a long time. Until 2008, the el-car had very limited range, poor safety and handling. It was a vehicle for enthusiasts. Tesla introduced its Roadster in 2008, offering good range, better safety features and sports-car handling, with limited success. However, it illustrated for the market that el-cars could be interesting and an actual alternative to combustion engine cars. 2012 saw the introduction of the S model, which became an instant success; this was a family car with great handling and range, good safety and sports-car power.

As a newcomer in the automobile industry, Tesla had its focus more on the market than on the actual production. They bought the old NUMMI factory from Toyota, and some equipment cheaply at auction (Ricketts 2010; Wire 2011). Their car model was in 2012 the most innovative el-car, with long range, new dashboard solution and other innovative design features. Tesla won several awards for their model S. They had managed to make a new, innovative car with old equipment. New production technology did not play a central role in making this ground-breaking car. The disruptiveness was in the long range, battery pack and design features. These made the car stand out from the crowd. It served as an example of market orientation in the "Innovation and Flexibility" strategy category.

Since then, other car manufacturers have introduced models with alternative powertrains. However, the market share for el-cars is not very impressive, globally standing at 0.9%. The el-car has a market share in the US of 0.7% and in the UK of 1.0% in 2015 (EIA 2017). These countries have few governmental incentives for el-car buyers. In the Netherlands and in Norway, the picture is different, with 9.3% and 23.3% (Ibid.). Exception of registration fees, road taxes and purchase tax (only in Norway – 25%) are incentives that motivate people to consider an el-car. The International Energy Agency predicts that the market share of el-cars will rise to 5.1% in 2020 (Ibid.). This and other estimates have car manufacturers focusing on the development of new technologies. During the summer of 2017, Mercedes and Porsche announced their entry into Formula E in motorsport, which is the test bed for electric technology. In addition, many countries are notifying a planned ban on fossil fuel–driven combustion cars. The UK and EU talk about doing this in 2040 and Norway in 2025.

This has resulted in a new landscape, where old truths like the benefits of higher education, providing job security and the benefit of local ownership, have suddenly vanished. Still, little or no research has considered what this all means for different regions and countries. Understanding of managerial decision-making in times of high uncertainty is underdeveloped.

As we write this book, legislators in California are about to allow self-driving cars on public roads. New cars might not only have no driver behind the wheel, they might not even have a steering wheel. California alone has 27 companies testing self-driving cars, not because it is the hub of the automobile industry, but because it is the hub of the information and communication technology (ICT) and electronic industry; cars have become ICT (SFC, March 12, 2017). For car-producing countries, the transfer to electric cars, accelerated by a ban on combustion engines, will have dramatic implications for trade balance and employment.

Mass production, commonly exemplified by Ford's assembly lines, aims to achieve economies of scale by offering large quantities of standardised products made by dedicated machines and strict work routines. Hence, this is an attractive model, as long as customers adapt to the product and not vice versa. Today, a customer in Germany can have a new Ford Fiesta configured in a trillion ways (Schaffer, Schleich, Reis & Fernandes 2008), where numerous choices related to the exterior, interior, driveline and trimming add to the number of variants and the total complexity of manufacturing a modern car. Individualised products and consumer perception of tailor-made configurations have been a trend for decades. From the manufacturing standpoint, these trends have been responded to by launching new products more frequently and by building flexibility, re-configurability and transparency into production lines and distribution throughout the value chain. The most advanced manufacturing industry has responded by utilising electronics and IT to automate production, both of which are core elements of the third industrial revolution. Boyer finds responses to increased demand for variation in two out of six productive models; "Volume and Diversity" and "Innovation and Flexibility".

The first model refers to Sloan's market strategy, where General Motors developed the product platform philosophy, making interchangeable parts, invisible to the consumer, between car platforms. Thus, differentiation and product segmentation could be carried out by visible exterior based features. This strategy is still viable and is to be found in the approach of many manufacturers globally. The way this strategy impacts conditions of relevance for labour, and how employment relations to management, strategy and manufacturing system, has minor differences from the pure volume strategy.

The second model tries to combine the mitigation of risk in developing new and innovative products with the ability to adjust volume and variation quickly. Such a strategy has typically been adopted by newcomers to an existing market, but in the context of today's turbulent market conditions and the need for individualisation, it may work as well as a long-term strategy and productive model. It may also serve as a basis for taking the next step towards implementing Industry 4.0, adding a new dimension to the term *flexibility*. Innovations are risky by nature, and the risks can be related to time, cost, resources, technology and the market. How can Industry 4.0 contribute to risk reduction?

Time to market is continuously under pressure for most firms, where R&D efficiency becomes the next focal area. The time where a factory lost sight of the product at the gate is over. Product developers will in the future have access to enormous amounts of data from the product life cycle, and they will be able to analyse component behaviour and make better decisions about next-generation products. Gains will likely emerge from extensive simulation, data integration, big-data pattern recognition and real-time feedback loops, not only for product developers but also at process and operating level. Digital innovations will make product and process development more efficient, flexible and cost effective. For instance, costly and labour-intensive physical prototypes can be reduced by improved simulation tools and data integrity. Connecting the product to all machines and devices along its way, as well as interconnectivity between machines and devices, brings new opportunities. Exploring these opportunities requires new ideas about how we organise the factories of the future. Skills concerning digitalisation, communication and decision-making across professionals, business units and the entire value chain will play an essential role in how the degree of innovation and flexibility develops further.

Most of what is written about Industry 4.0 focuses on the impact expected on the factory floor. While plant operations and workers will experience disruptions due to digitalisation, this industrial revolution may have its most profound effects on the support functions: white-collar staff. Recall the regulations versus radical discussion above, where intentions for change can be questioned. This discussion can be related to the concept of Industry 4.0: is this concept driven by technology, or is it based on the demand for building products faster, better and cheaper? Assuming the latter is true, and the concept is dependent upon technological progress and our abilities to utilise the technology, real-time information about customer demand, production capacity, operational performance and product quality will enable decision-making that dramatically improves process efficiency and reduces human support functions. Algorithm-based decision-making will probably emerge into a new level within functions such as R&D, product launches, pricing, planning, despatching and purchasing.

Industry 4.0 at its most mature level seems disruptive in nature for many companies, but changes can also create opportunities. Utilising these opportunities will require flexibility, willingness to acquire digital knowledge, training and experience, so people begin the transition to roles that rely on human problem-solving capabilities and creativity. Such new capabilities can be addressed to support core business, but they can also represent a platform for evolving digital capabilities to create new business models and revenue streams for the company. It is all about how workers, white or blue collar, can adapt to a new and connected environment.

Box 9.2 Different pathways required by a transition to a state of Industry 4.0

Example number one concerns a company founded on an idea of producing complex lightweight parts by an innovative additive manufacturing process. Considerable R&D has been directed towards generating new knowledge about the specific and patented manufacturing process the last five years in order to scale up production to reach customer tact time. The new process aims to save time, cost and material usage throughout the extended value chain, which can rapidly and seamlessly be configured to a broad portfolio of new products for different market applications. The transport sector especially, and particularly the aerospace industry, will benefit from successfully bringing this technology to an accepted readiness level. Much effort is devoted to industrialising the processes into a stable and repetitive production system. There is no or little room for launching product errors as a newcomer to a relatively conservative market for critical and structural components for use in, for instance, the aerospace industry. Thus, developing, utilising and combining enabling technologies to create a zero-defect manufacturing system is of crucial importance for a manufacturer of high-value, high-performance and custom-designed parts. The case company has now qualified, by a top-tier original equipment manufacturer (OEM), as a first-tier supplier for level 8 on a Technology Readiness Level scale from 1 to 9. The final step is assumed to be achieved in short term, and after this it will be qualified to start part qualification and serial production of actual components. The market outlook views opportunities for a growing number of component variants, which need to be met by flexibility in manufacturing and a set-up for frequent product introductions. The market demand for products from this process is expected to grow by 6% per year in the years to come, especially due to the high strength/weight ratio of the material, in combination with increased demand for lower weight and less pollution from the transportation sector. The knowledge base of the company is strong in terms of formal education and experience, with many of the employees having a PhD and master degrees. Extensive front-loading is to be found in the company, where nearly 60 employees are in place before any products are sold. These people are organised into functional departments, not in a more expected entrepreneurial way, responsible for different parts of the value chain, where they have outlined a strategy for building an integrated value chain from raw material to finished products. Thus, developing a strong supplier base is not high on the agenda. The existing network is the extended R&D efforts into improving material properties, critical processes, and manufacturing efficiency.

Example number two is about a company that develops and manufactures air brake fittings and couplings primarily for the commercial vehicle market globally. The production volume can be categorised as mass production, but the number of variants are increasing, so the production system is challenged

> by the flexibility criteria. Production is fully automated, and the factory is designed to run unmanned for periods of time. Further ambitions are to reduce cycle times and to produce according to zero-defect manufacturing principles, where quality to an even larger extent has to be built into the product and the process to achieve in-line and real-time quality control. These processes need to be interlinked through an automated component handling system, and each separate process needs to be reconfigurable to a new product variant within the timeframe of one cycle due to required flexibility and volume. An interesting feature is that the company, in order to be an attractive and challenging workplace, has kicked off a programme aiming at enabling operators, maintenance personnel and technicians to design and build next-generation machines and equipment. The reasoning behind such a programme is that these human resources have the best knowledge about existing capabilities and requirements, and are hence able to convert these experiences to build robust machines producing zero defects. This new and integrative way of working aims to combine both technology utilisation and attractive work content, in line with the Industry 4.0 concept. The company is organised as a relatively integrated product, process and production unit, but one where support functions such as product development, quality and performance are reporting into a global matrix structure. The main strategy for the subsidiary, among many others in the company, is to produce as cost effectively as possible, and with outstanding quality, to attract new and existing customers, as well as to give internal positive attention towards getting new investments and products to produce. The market is stable in the Western world and growing in Asia, but the case company aims to take a greater share of the existing market as their products support light-weight criteria in global environmental regulations. Networking is important to the company, especially related to extending R&D efforts. Numerous R&D projects with external research institutes and universities have been conducted in recent years to improve products and processes combined. Collaboration with suppliers also takes place, especially for developing critical tooling parts.

There will be different trajectories towards approaching Industry 4.0, especially given the maturity of the firm, its place in the value chain, the type of industry and the level of absorptive capacity to identify, extract, translate and exploit new knowledge towards creating value. The two examples discussed here illustrate that leveraging to an Industry 4.0 level is about determination and about taking the necessary technological steps, whether the example is about penetrating an existing market with a breakthrough new manufacturing technology or about conducting innovation by summing up a number of continuous improvements by structural combining product and process development. The latter is an example of a mature industry with well-established value chains, where the company structure, core competence focus, performance and incentive systems underpin an incremental path for major innovations. This is in line with the claim that the focus on variation reduction and search for incremental improvements in routine will lead to increased incremental innovation, exploiting existing capabilities. The first example demonstrates that bringing a technology from a low to acceptable technology readiness level, at the same time as it intends substituting for a functioning and well-proven technology, is time and resource consuming. The capital needed is considerable, and the number of risk factors brings about an organisation that focuses strongly on R&D. Despite the search for a breakthrough innovation, the mature market they operate within forces them to follow a very structured innovation and product development process; contrasting theories say that such innovation journeys should take on a more explorative approach.

An example of this strategy category comes from an Austrian-owned company in the automotive industry. They decided to move their factory from China back to Europe. The reason was a lower total cost of production. In total, they estimated that a quarter of the cost in terms of people, investment and time is needed in production in Europe versa China due to newer production technology, higher educated workers and closeness to the actual market. Their estimate turned out to be right.

New business models in the service sector have their basis in employment/use of artificial intelligence or robots. The initial contact with the customer can be handled by a robot. It guides the customer to the right product after asking specific questions. Customised product configuration can be done online with artificial intelligence. Search engines can be taught to find the lowest price for a product. These are just examples that already exist.

The banking sector in Norway is an example of a more sophisticated solution. It started as a collaboration in the bank sector to develop a common transaction system. This system has steadily been developed over the years. The largest bank looked at the biggest Danish bank establishing itself in Norway. They had a developed an app as a payment solution for ordinary users. It inspired the Norwegian bank to develop their own app for their customers. This app made it possible to pay a friend only by knowing his/her phone number. Small businesses and ideal organisations could also use it to sell goods or tickets. Little or no pre-installation is needed. The market responded very positively to this. After just two years, this easy-to-use solution has over two million users. It has changed how consumers pay, and the need for cash has dramatically dropped. The local bank, with people giving advice and handling accounts, is under threat. Many of the local offices are closing and the people working there must find other jobs. The whole idea of banking has now changed, with internet sites and mobile apps.

Implications for policy and social organisation

A story from the third industrial revolution sheds light on how the introduction of robots in production lines was influenced by governmental incentives. The big feat was that robots would take over jobs. In Norway, the government supported joint efforts between the union and the Confederation of Norwegian Enterprise (being the employer side). In every major factory, a rationalisation representative was elected. Her work was to make the transition to the new industrial revolution (the third) as painless as possible. The main argument was that there would not be jobs for everybody, and all the unemployed could not sit in an office. In the aftermath, jobs were changed and different tasks occurred. The employment rate went down in traditional industry, but new jobs were created. Small and medium-sized production companies were formed and provided service to the big companies. These new companies could handle prototypes, small series, special series and so on, which the big companies could not handle due to the switching cost in automated lines.

Now the fourth industrial revolution is underway, and the same argument is resurfacing. Loss of jobs is a major concern. However, there are signs that do not paint a dark picture. A company in the automotive industry, making brake couplings, is insourcing the design and building of their new machines. They can do this with some support from different governmental programmes for re-educating the workforce. The UK idea of catapult centres is discussed in many other countries. A catapult centre is a network and physical testing place for innovations and new technologies. Such centres represent a collaboration between government, research and education and businesses. The goal is to put the UK in the lead in development in specific areas. In Germany, learning factories have been a way of connecting education and manufacturing. There are many ways of setting up a learning factory (Mavrikios, Papakostas, Mourtzis & Chryssolouris 2011). One way is to create a copy of an actual production line at the university and use it for education. Students learn how to produce actual products and serve the company. In these ways, the disruptiveness of the technological change is eased. At the same time, governments try to influence the direction of change and provide the capability to gain the desired knowledge to make the change.

Research funding repeats the governmental effort to guide research in a direction where they think it is most needed in order to achieve more breakthroughs, discoveries and world-firsts – by taking great ideas from the lab to the market. Priorities for building the EU's future forms the backbone of the EU's research program, Horizon 2020. It finances projects from 22 themes or areas, ranging from agriculture and forestry to space. These areas are then linked up to sections, which cover more than one area. Adding to this, there are different financial tools for supporting research and innovation in different sizes of companies. The idea is to help companies in their competitive struggle in the marketplace with research-driven results. In addition to the huge program, Horizon 2020, the EU has established EUROSTAR, specially tailored to small and medium-sized companies with great ideas close to being introduced to the market.

The EU's example is repeated in many countries with programmes tailored to address specific issues for the country in question. For instance, Norway has established the User-driven Research based Innovation programme, helping Norwegian companies with their industry-oriented research. All of these programmes and initiatives are based on the idea that research should help the country's interests and support its companies. From the innovation theory, it is known as Mode 2 (Nowotny, Scott & Gibbons 2001; Nowotny, Scott & Gibbons 2003). Later innovation research has tried to link system theory with clusters and networks, calling it Mode 3 (Carayannis, Campbell & Rehman 2016). These argue for holistic thinking when it comes to research, helping the companies first. Closeness to market and faster implementation of technology are two central points. Basically, it is believed that fast technology implementation helps companies' competitiveness. The funding helps companies to tap into the knowledge generated in research laboratories and universities, and in this way to be competitive.

Governmental initiatives or incentives play an important role in technological development and in directing research efforts. This argument supports the policy perspective we discussed in Chapter 4. However, technology development also has a social side, and one should not overlook the effect of the digital technology on social organisation. What we have seen so far is at least two different streams: the one is high tech, and the other low tech. The organisational and social efferent of the two are partly contradictory. The high-tech stream is related to new applications and is a main driver in the creative economy. It requires highly skilled people and insight to develop, and it attracts young, talented people as we see in Silicon Valley. The high-tech stream can produce solutions that could seriously change the workplace and remove a lot of existing jobs. It seems to flourish in urban, metropolitan areas with specialised skills that can pool together to develop breakthrough solutions.

The low-skilled track is of a different kind. Here you have platforms that everybody can join if they have access to internet. You can start your own publishing activity, you can join discourses across distances, you can engage in the sharing economy; in short, it is a platform for new forms of occupation. It is likely that the speed with which the new digital economy has expanded is partly due to the adaptation in terms of new social forms of interaction and communication. The longer perspective on the implications of these new social forms is more difficult to foresee.

Box 9.3 The Kodak moment of technology

The disruptiveness of change:

New technology can have disruptive effects on societies and markets.

The knowledge one failed to use:

Criticism of the assumption that technology is something independent of social reality that social reality has to comply with.

Ability to adjust to future changes:

Have a more detailed insight into the value chains and structures that new technology presupposes and effect. Have a broad debate on the future of technology, and how to adjust the social system without compromising basic values.

The opportunity in the changes:

Take a more interactive approach to technology, acknowledging that it is a social product and should be the issue for a broad social dialogue.

Technological development happens over time. Sometimes it goes very fast; at other times, expectations are not met and development pauses. How we use technology and see the benefits of using it is key. The service sector has started on what seems to be a radical change with the new technology usage ahead of development. New services will be introduced to the market fuelled by new technological possibilities. Even traditional industry is going through dramatic changes. The old race for cheap labour is being questioned. Radical changes to business models will come. Even if you talk about radical change, it need not happen as A revolution. The best way to cope with change is to understand and engage with new technologies. New opportunities are created through these technologies and will provide new jobs that we do not see today. This theme is further developed in Chapter 14.

The main argument of our chapter is still that technology is mainly a social phenomenon. It is in the adaption of technology that its effect becomes reality. Its adoption is a deliberate process, even though the individual can experience being forced into a new trajectory. Thus, coping with technology is about having a social dialogue on how we relate to technology, how we adapt it and use it and what it means for us as human beings.

Note

1 Germany Trade & Invest, "Smart manufacturing for the future"; National Academy of Science and Engineering, "Securing the future of German manufacturing industry."

10

COPING WITH HUMANISM

A Posthuman future?

Evi D. Sampanikou and Hans Christian Garmann Johnsen

What does it mean to be human?

What does it mean to be human? The question has concerned philosophers and others for as long as we know. A strong modern reference is seventeenth-century French philosopher René Descartes. Descartes is famous for his statement "Cogito ergo sum" (I think, therefore I am), a conclusion of his scepticism by which he questioned what he could know also about his own existence (Descartes 1996). Descartes ended up making the great divide or dualism between the mental world and the physical (the soul and the body). In today's terms, we would say that he placed humanness in the soul and the body as part of nature. Being human was therefore something beyond nature. Descartes' dualism has been debated, and few find it easy to understand how the soul can be separated from the body. Still, few are able to locate humanness as something strictly material. Current discussions neurology about what is conciseness, what is mind, struggle with these issues.[1] The theme has become more relevant as technology moves into the body and replaces human parts, thus creating Transhumanism: Where does the human part stop and the machine/technology take over? This chapter deals with the Posthumanist/Transhumanist discussion: Is the borderline between humans and non-humans (technology) becoming blurred? If so, what does that imply for future humanist thinking?

Posthumanism and *Transhumanism* are terms recently in official use, explained through an amazing variety of meanings (See Sampanikou 2017; Tuncel 2017) and at present mistrusted by the mainstream academy as the "wrong" successors of Darwin, Nietzsche and Postmodernism. To be more specific, Posthumanism is now conceived as the main successor of Postmodernism, taking different directions from Transhumanism, which is mainly engaged with human "enhancement" via biotechnology with no special moral dilemmas about creating new forms of beings. We must always bear in mind that Posthumanism and Transhumanism are not identical.

The best way to deal with Posthumanism is to analyse it, in *cultural* terms, as a philosophical trend that opens the frames of exclusively anthropocentric Humanism to embrace all forms of natural existence (e.g. the animals, the environment), but also to approach, critically but open-mindedly, other forms of existence (e.g. artificial intelligence) and to defend the rights of all. We can thus accept that Posthumanism is the ideological expression of *a contemporary cultural and political theory* born immediately *after* Postmodernism (Sampanikou 2014, pp. 241–242). Taking into consideration its openness, to accept another dimension of Posthumanism: sustainability, as a logical balance between humanity's existence and technology, with distance from both Eurocentrism and colonial imperialism.

Posthumanism and Transhumanism are thus, as new philosophical and interdisciplinary terms, an integral part of contemporary audio-visual culture. Are they really new? Scholars are very much engaged with recognising and attributing Posthumanist ideology and ethics as a big part of the cultural production of the past, arguing, for example, on the relations between Nietzsche, Darwin and even Heidegger or Habermas and Post- and Transhumanist thought (Sorgner 2011, online). Our text focuses on the example of the science fiction (SF) genre, with main references to comics and graphic novels either inspired by SF literature or not. The same stream of thought is however not fully absent from other, more "realistic" works, socio-political or autobiographical comics and graphic novels, for example. As a rule, and as we can see in other fields of contemporary culture, Posthumanist topics and character models are built on the denial of dualisms, on taking the interaction between human beings and technologies for granted and on analysing this interaction from a more sociological or anthropological point of view. On the other hand, Transhumanist topics and character models criticise the meaning of being "human" in environments ruled by technology, and societies organised by enhanced or totally mechanical ex-human beings who sometimes preserve or acquire the qualities and ethics that humanity has lost.

We are searching for how Post- and Transhumanist ethics affect one of the most expressive contemporary arts (born however in the nineteenth century) – comics and graphic novels – and how they include broader, not exclusively anthropocentric, values, that tend, however, to be humanist but not in the Enlightenment sense. During recent decades, since the 1980s, comic-book stories tend to follow different directions according to the decade, analysing things in specific ways influenced by the ideology of the times. Usually, in stories written during the 1980s, a Transhuman hero who also interacts with a Transhuman setting proves to be keeping or have kept human values and ethics at the same time that the behaviour of real humans tends to become more machine-like or animal-like. Expressions of this attitude are also met in cinema production: Ridley Scott's *Blade Runner* (1982), for example, inspired by, but so different from, Philip K. Dick's *Do Androids Dream of Electric Sheep* (1968), no matter if the central hero is the same in both, bearing the symbolic name Descartes.

Similarly, in stories written during the 1990s, the Transhumanist environment is the background setting, but the message is more Posthuman; we usually meet human heroes who revolt against the anarchy and chaos that technology has brought and seek ways to re-invent humanity, human values and nature on a new basis and new terms. As comics perfectly interact with cinema, an example from cinema for this period could be movies by Terry Gilliam, the early *Brazil* (1985) or *12 Monkeys* (1995).

Subsequently, in stories written during the 2000s, including Euromanga productions, Posthumanism seems to characterise most of the (European at least) production: Transformed or recreated heroes, most of them human – though their origin does not really matter – act in a Messianic way to lead the human race back to Posthuman values and awaken them from being ruled by machines or Transhumans. The *Matrix* trilogy (though the first movie came out in 1999, the second and third came out in 2003) could be the best example from cinema from this decade.

Our methodological approach

In order to approach the term *Humanism* in today's society and in the future, we are looking for the political vision of the being called the *Posthuman*. Politics is a crucial point of contemporary graphic novels and includes serious moral concerns about the social landscape, the natural environment, sustainability and the essence of being human at a time when the term has to be re-defined. The dignity, freedom and free will of the individual, contrasted with traditional or "mutated" forms of power that are common science-fiction philosophical concerns, are also at the centre of this discussion.

Since *Humanism* is a sort of ambiguous term, provoking endless philosophical discussion, we have chosen two methodological approaches. First, we analyse cartoons that portray a Transhuman world. The idea here is that we get an understanding of Humanisms by describing its opposite (inhuman) behaviour. By looking at what androids or Transhuman or half human creatures might do, as portrayed in cartoons, we might get a clearer idea of humanness. It might also help us understand the challenges we could meet in a Transhuman future.

Second, by using cartoons, we are into the fields of fables and myths. There is a long history of using myths or fables in social science. One of the classical examples is Plato and his use of the myth of the cave in his book *The Republic*. Here, Plato portrays life as living in a cave, where we get light from the outside but cannot access that light because it is dangerous to leave the cave. The light outside is the truth, and the absolute truth is something we cannot access. However, based on the light we have in the cave, and the shadows it creates on the walls, we can know a lot and we can speculate, based on that, about the truth. There are many aspects of this myth that Plato plays with through his political thesis. One of them is that the light is reduced the further into the cave one goes. Put differently, some people are close to the entrance and, subsequently, they are more enlightened than those deeper into the cave. Being deeper into the cave is more secure than being at the entrance. Enlightenment is risky, so only the brave ones will dare to be at the entrance. Through this, Plato also argued that political leaders should be those who were brave and therefore also enlightened.

Another good example is Bernard Mandeville's *The Fable of The Bees: or, Private Vices, Public Benefits*, which includes the poem *The Grumbling Hive: or, Knaves turn'd Honest* published in 1705. Here, Mandeville tried to show how bees are able to create structure and order in spite of the fact that an individual bee does not oversee this order: Each individual does his or her part, and the overall order (the beehive) is not something that anybody designed but still is the result of everybody's action. Thus, order in society can come from natural instinctive action and is not dependent on somebody's design. In addition, he argued that even bad behaviour could have good consequences, which is implied in the phrase "private vices, public benefits". This myth had a tremendous impact on the thinking of David Hume and Adam Smith. It made us aware that what we see in a social order or social structure is not necessarily the same as the intention of each individual within that order.

Also, Nietzsche's *The Birth of Tragedy from the Spirit of Music* from 1872 is an interesting discussion on the role of myths (Nietzsche 2000). Nietzsche's project was a critique of rationalism in the Enlightenment movement. He wanted to show how human existence goes beyond the rationalistic project started by Plato. He finds this in the pre-Plato tragedy, where human destiny and sentiments, as well as emotions and primitive instinct, are expressed. Nietzsche's thinking inspired modernist art as well as existentialism,

Similarly, Max Horkheimer and Theodor W. Adorno's *Dialectic of Enlightenment* (2002) uses myths as a key to discuss the nature of enlightenment. They discuss Odysseus, who they see as an archetype of the modern man; a man on a journey, seeking meaning, as part of a very egocentric project. They see him as the modern individualist and use him to discuss the dialectics of the modern project or modern society; how it has the potential to be both emancipatory and destructive.

These examples are meant to illustrate how myths and fables can be regarded as *ways of theorising*. They are illustrative and add some dimensions to normal theory building: They can take in a larger number of elements, they can put these into a social situation or context and they can exemplify some hypothetical ways in which a very complex play may turn out, so they might illustrate the long-term consequences of certain actions or choices by individuals. It is from this perspective that we refer to some of the stories below and how they might illustrate Humanism in a Transhuman world.

Coping with Humanism or Humanism re-invented

A good way to start discussing Posthumanism and Transhumanism in comics could be to consider Alan Moore's (script) and Dave Gibbons's (design) famous graphic novel *The Watchmen* (1986–1987),[2] which, since its first publication, has been recognised as one of the first "mature" comics[3] bearing elements that can be interpreted as a transition from Postmodern to Posthuman thought. There is a famous frame in *Watchmen* where Ozymandias is sitting in front of hundreds of screens in a room[4] where he enjoys glory and the reality he and other ex-heroes have literally constructed. He is a monster, a tycoon adored by the media, who advertises himself as the incarnation of Nietzsche's Übermensch and leads the life of a multi-millionaire and feels he is an Olympian God; he even dresses like one. Ozymandias is the most successful of a team of seven ex-superheroes, six (actually seven) men and one woman (actually two women), with no real superpowers, the six now being old and rather marginalised by a law forbidding superheroic actions in Margaret Thatcher's world, a world that does not seem to need them anymore. Ozymandias will be largely responsible for the mass destruction that has been approaching since the beginning of the novel and makes the atmosphere, page by page, more and more menacing. To underline this menacing atmosphere, Moore has written a parallel story into the book, a dark pirate story read in chapters (in similar sequence to the chapters of this graphic novel) by a little boy who just happens to be in the setting as a neutral person, reading it.

Alan Moore has posed several ethical and political problems in *Watchmen* that make this graphic novel a perfect model of Posthuman thought. Pelliterri thinks that Moore wonders what happens if, in a real or at least "realistically designed" world, a number of individuals decided to become costumed vigilantes and act outside the law. It would certainly create a world "strongly oriented towards right-wing political ideologies". This world would be ruled by right-wing politics, because the United States and Great Britain are right wing, and superheroes are an Anglo-Saxon cultural product bearing the same dominant ideology.[5]

> **Box 10.1** *Watchmen*
>
> In *Watchmen*, the story follows the Postmodern trend of superheroes who do not really have superhuman powers, unless they are mutant superheroes like *X-Men*. While *X-Men* stories should mainly be perceived as examples of Transhumanist thought, the *Watchmen* could really be their Posthumanist opposite, as, no matter how tragically wrongly these "superheroes" lead their lives to a dead end, their initial purpose has been to defend humanity and traditional human values. Even the two far right-wing members of the team, Rorsach and The Comedian, bear elements of humanity deep inside, while the only mutated hero among them, Dr Manhattan – the ex-human scientist Jon Osterman, who had a nuclear accident – is a new atomic creature carrying all Osterman's memories and personality. Dr Manhattan has been transformed into a god, surpassing all the limits of space, time and human nature. He is a creature of Transhumanised form and at the same time the main evidence of the eternity of human spirit and soul, as he chooses to rebuild his ex-body and receive a human aura, among millions of other possibilities he now has.[6]

Another great example from the late 1980s could be a Batman story, *The Killing Joke* (1988), written by Allan Moore and designed by Brian Bolland (art-cover) and John Higgins (colour). This is a story about madness and the limits of human reason, owing so much to Foucault's *Madness and Civilisation* (1965), more than one could originally tell. Valereto[7] attempts an interesting reading of the story as the evolution of the Joker's madness and its analysis through not only Foucault's, but also Derrida's and Deleuze's, thought.

> **Box 10.2** *The Killing Joke*
>
> One of the most interesting points in the story is how a sane and moral human being like Jim (Commissioner Gordon), a crime prosecutor and Batman's close friend, can momentarily turn to madness when his dignity and personality are violently attacked by the Joker, who kidnaps and imprisons him among circus monsters (mutated beings?) after shooting his daughter Barbara, trying to lead him to madness: "Memories can be vile, repulsive, little Brutes ... Memories are what our reason is based upon. If we can't face them, we deny reason itself! Although why not? We aren't contractually tied down to rationality!

There's no sanity clause! ... Madness is the emergency exit".[8] Moore puts these words into the Joker's mouth when he leads Jim naked to the cage, with the intention of keeping him there forever and driving him mad. Memory is, however, the Joker's own concern in the story, a memory of him being a family man[9] before turning into this hideous "mask". Moore underlines here the strong connection between memory, reason and the human condition, difficult to deny even by a monster like the Joker or even by Batman himself, who does everything to keep human feelings at a distance by wearing the Bat costume but who however turns to be rather "addicted" to human values. Batman is thus the main bearer of posthuman ethics in the story.

The Killing Joke's designer, Brian Bolland, living and working in Britain, is also one of the main designers for *2000AD* comics' *Judge Dredd*, created in the mind of John Wagner (Dredd's original writer, who also wrote under the pseudonym T. B. Grover) and Carlos Ezquerra (design);[10] it was first published in 1977 (year 2099 for Dredd's world) and has run through all the following decades.[11] Dredd is a merciless cop and judge in a future society called Mega-City (there are numbered Mega-Cities, 1, 2, etc.). The Judges are an order that rules this world; they have the right to arrest, judge and kill all the trespassers and outlaws, and you can become an outlaw for no reason in this society. Dredd has no mother and father; he is a clone produced in a lab (this is the state politics for the production of judges) and is trained not to have any feelings but a perfect sense of justice and a Protestant notion of punishment that has to be imposed on anyone that does not follow the rules.

Box 10.3 *Judge Dredd*

According to his designer, Brian Bolland,[12] Dredd is a fascist and also a parody of fascism. He's also an allegory for Margaret Thatcher's politics[13] as well as a perfect example of how a Transhuman creature would really look. Brian Bolland's team of writers and designers have, however, managed to make Dredd a more complex character,[14] turning him into a rather likable hero, hiding a human soul under his very official judge uniform. They have also made him completely human in terms of aging; in 1977 (2099 for the comic), he was over thirty, and nowadays (2134 for the comic) he is more than seventy years old. Strangely, he has not had any genetic improvements so far. In a short story, "Vienna", first published in *2000AD* # 116 (1300), the readers learn that Dredd has a niece, a daughter of his ex-judge cloned brother Rico, who had become an outlaw and was killed by Dredd. Dredd cares for and visits his niece; he even plays with her and he also rescues her when she is kidnapped by one of his enemies. In a more complicated and rather long story, first published in a series of *2000AD* issues in 1980 (March 15, 1980), "The

Judge Child" (progs. 156–181; epilogue in 182),[15] Dredd wanders in several enemy lands, wild societies where the law is unknown, putting his life in risk countless times, to find an adolescent that oracles say is destined to be the greatest judge of all. He finally finds the child, but when he is about to take him to Mega-City, he decides to leave him behind. This decision is an outcome of Dredd's own free will. After so many years as a judge, Dredd starts to discover human values; he violates his orders, because he sees so much hate and cruelty in this child's eyes that he is actually afraid of making him a judge. Step by step, Dredd increasingly recognises the importance of being as a prior necessity to being a judge. Dredd is a hero of a Transhuman origin that has gradually been transformed into a Posthumanist.

Moving a little further south from the Anglo-Saxon world, in Italy in 1985, Paolo Eleuteri Serpieri created the character of Druuna in a series of albums under the titles *Morbus Gravis* (=Serious Disease) and *Druuna* (or: *Morbus Gravis I* and *II* according to some editions), followed by five "sequels".[16] Druuna is an exceptionally attractive Posthuman being, bearing not only the qualities of a dynamic survivor, but also an expressive Mediterranean femininity. The posthuman atmosphere of the story is supported by the excellent artwork, placing the action in a diachronical post-industrial architectural setting. This setting of place and time in the story is related to a spaceship named "The City", existing at an unspecified time in the future, a long time after the final destruction of Earth that has brought civilisation to an end. Most of the inhabitants do not know what the city is and what lies beyond. The human species faces extinction. Religious fundamentalism, based on a dark order of robot priests and an uncountable number of ex-human mutants, having been transformed into carnivorous octopus-like monsters expanding the so-called "disease", are the main elements of this world.[17]

Box 10.4 Druuna

Druuna's desperate search for the serum, the medicine, under horrible circumstances of disorder, criminality and sexual violence sets the directions of the main plot. The mysteriously healthy Druuna, who was born after Earth's destruction and has never been part of any organised human society, living exclusively between robots and mutants, is revealed to the reader as the Posthuman counterpart of a post-Transhuman environment created by scientific advance, with no moral limits. She thus becomes the heiress of the notion of humanity, preserving all the humanistic behavioural attributes, even the loss of morality under certain circumstances, but never the loss of reason, compassion and solidarity. For example, she does not hesitate to provide sexual services to buy the serum, but at the same time she helps others whenever she can and she does not leave Shastar, her lover and companion, when he is seriously attacked by the disease and becomes one of the countless mutants gradually turning to an octopus-like creature. Shastar leads her to the upper city before his final mutation and asks Druuna to kill him. It is then that she meets Lewis, led by a voice in her head. Lewis, the last wise human being on the ship, an ancestor who was born long before the destruction of Earth – or rather his preserved brain in his "talking head", fed by the bodies of the "lucky few" who had won a pass to the upper city – reveals to her the truth: The ship city is ruled by a computer program that has gone mad, gradually preparing, through the disease, its own destruction. He assigns Druuna the mission to stop the computer; she is the only one that can give madness an end. Druuna turns thus into a Posthuman defender of humanity.

The 1990s are perfectly represented in Posthuman thought by the French-speaking works related to the famous writer Alexandro Jodorowsky,[18] especially in his extraordinary collaboration with the designer Juan Gimenez, which resulted in *The [Saga of] Metabarons*, inspired by science fiction literature; and epics like Frank Herbert's *Dune* (1965). *The Saga of Metabarons* is a graphic novel series published from 1991 to 2003.[19] Jodorowsky has also co-operated in the past with one of the most famous designers, Moebius (Jean Giraud, b. 1938)[20] on *The Black Incal [L'Incal Noire]* series, from 1981 to 1988. The futuristic atmosphere of the design in both series of stories intensifies Jodorowsky's Posthuman irony in many aspects. For example, the psychedelic atmosphere inspiring both the designs of the *Metabarons* and *The Black Incal* clearly criticises the Transhumanist approach to the future. The stories co-operate. The main character in the *Metabarons* series, Otto, was first born in The *Black Incal*.[21] The semi-heroic atmosphere of the *Metabarons* dynasty comes into strong contrast with the anti-heroic humorous tone of The *Black Incal*.[22]

Box 10.5 *The Black Incal*

In the *Incal* stories, *Moebius* follows the 1980s attitude and style. The notion of a big subterranean metropolis with an upper and lower world, a motif we meet in a number of science fiction stories of the times, a city guarded by robot-cops, is once more present in the story. There is even a "suicide square", a place where anyone can jump into the void, be shot by others while falling and finally melt into acid. Mutations are humorously criticised in the story. A good example is the case of the extraordinary beautiful aristocrat lady (aristocrats have the privilege of bearing a technical nimbus around their heads, the same nimbus we see in holy icons) who visits the lower city, under the protection of the rather idiot protagonist of the series, the detective John Difool (a parody of Harrison Ford) and has sex with the Wolf, a huge mutant with the body of a supernatural human male being, with a huge penis and the head of a wolf. At midnight, the beautiful lady turns out to be the product of a strange drug-based mutation as she turns into a horrible aged woman, frustrating the Wolf, who chases John Diffol into the lower city's labyrinth channels, areas belonging to crime syndicates and staffed with mutants, monsters and replicas.[23]

In the *Metabarons* series, which reflects ideas on Metahuman existence, a combination of Ancient Greek tragedy, classical science fiction and old tribal myths, the main themes are artificial intelligence (the story is told by two robots, the dominant species at the time the story unfolds, who are telling stories to each other);[24] the isolated racism of a safe fortress meta-city (the *Metabunker*) supported by all kinds of technology; and, finally, the issue of biotechnology and prosthetics, which has created improved human body parts that comprise a tradition for the *Metabarons* sequential generations.

Box 10.6 *Metabarons*

The heroes belong to a special aristocratic cast of the future destined to be leaders of planets and galaxies. They are supernatural but human, and their actions are recorded for posterity on an epic scale. To become a real man, each male member of this cast has to suffer a specific rite of passage when he comes of age: He must accept mutilation by his own father and then immediately replace the missing member with a technical member that will stand powerfully in the position of the former. Otto, the first hero of this saga, has his ear and inner lobe and part of his brain violently extracted by the hand of his father, accepting this suffering without even changing his facial expression or shedding a tear. His father is proud, because he himself could not avoid leaving a tear drop when he underwent his own mutilation. Arms, legs, even penises are thus sacrificed to make the perfect aristocrat warriors, who, gradually, generation after generation, tend to become less human and more and more biotechnological beings. They even replace their sex or turn into both sexes to rule; Aghora the Father-Mother is an example of this (Book 7, 2002). They go even further; Steelhead, one of the last Metabarons (Book 5, 1998), has become almost entirely mechanical, as he was decapitated and has an iron head and brain. The ironic element in the story is that Steelhead tends to be a Humanist! He will defend the human race as none of his predecessors has ever done. It has already been stated that the script is clearly influenced by *Dune*, while the expressionist industrial colours underline the Transhuman atmosphere of the plot.[25] Even the work process of the designer, who works directly on the computer, as only few designers of his status do, seems to bear Posthuman qualities.

The 2000s were the Euromanga decade, and Franco-Belgian productions were the first to welcome the Japanese influence. Needless to say, Japanese tradition and production was actually the first to turn to a discussion on technology and the future of the human race, long before Europe and the United States become engaged with Posthumanism and Transhumanism. Katsuhiro Ottomo's *Akira* (1982–1993), for example, could in fact have been recorded as the first manga and anime engaged with Posthumanist issues.[26] As far as it concerns Europe, a wonderful and relatively recent story and a perfect example of how European Posthumanist thought was translated into comics scripts and images is the French Euromanga *Wake* (*Sillage*) by Philippe Buchet (designs) and Jean-Pierre Morvan (script), first published in 1998.

> **Box 10.7 Euromanga**
>
> The protagonist of the whole series is a girl named Navis, the only descendant of the human race, a child discovered by the Alien Forces Fleet [Wake or Sillage] on the surface of an evacuated planet. They rescue her as a protected species, the only rescued representative of the human race, having inherited all the biological characteristics of her ancestors. As a creature of "unusually special intelligence" for the aliens, she grows up enjoying a high reputation in the Wake, undertaking, during her teenage years, several missions on planets. In one of her missions, in a story officially recognised as *steam-punk* and published in album 3/part 3 under the title *Engrenages [Unexpected Events]*, Navis visits a planet of human-like creatures in a setting similar to the cities of Earth during the early industrial era. For a while, she hopes she will satisfy her deepest strong desire, which is to meet creatures of her own species. However, the human-like citizens turn out to be Puntas, a goat-like but intelligent species that have been transformed into human beings by a scientist from Earth who has actually "produced" them in the lab, fertilising with his own semen one of the Queens, female creatures that are fertilised like bee queens and are the mothers of all the Puntas. The original Puntas are now living out of the human cities, keeping a peaceful reconciliation with nature and actually continuing an ecological behaviour that bears Posthumanist qualities in many aspects, respect for the lives of animals, for example. They never kill for food, and they do not have any sense of pleasure in killing. They do not go hunting, but they accept buffaloes that are about to die, who become their food immediately after.

What makes the human-like race human is a serum the Puntas' species need to keep human characteristics. The serum is produced by scientists who work in a secret laboratory, where the man from Earth, the father/ancestor, has also lain for hundreds of years, preserved with the help of cryonics. He regains consciousness, "waking up" whenever it is required to take serious decisions on the evolution of the human-like race, who ignore everything about him and the importance of the serum. Navis arrives on the planet in an era when the human-like politicians, initially under the scientist's influence, have become too oppressive, and a revolution starts against them and against the obligatory receiving of the serum. The rebels believe the serum is a drug that makes them submissive. Navis will help rebels go to the serum factory and reveal the secret and she will, for the first time, meet another human being, the awakened scientist, under conditions of tragic irony, as he is immediately killed by the leader of the rebels.

In one of the early graphic novels by the famous Enki Bilal (b. 1951 in Belgrade, living and creating in France),[27] based on Pierre Christin's script, *La Ville qui n'existait pas [The City that Never Existed]* (1977), the motif of the happy isolated world, created as an experiment on a dream of political utopianism, can nowadays be read as a Posthumanist text. Melancholy is the dominant characteristic in both the story and Bilal's design. The story is also a critique of Marxism and, mainly, of the Communist regimes of the Eastern Bloc, which still existed at the time.

Box 10.8 *The City that Never Existed*

The plot takes place in an industrial town, mainly inhabited by workers at the local factory, which turns into an experimental working class "Paradise" watched over by the crippled granddaughter of the founder of the industry, who believes she is creating an ideal world. The futuristic and colourful town, protected by a huge dome from the external world, a dome no one can thread without a pass, offers every possible facility for its inhabitants and their children and a modernised working environment. It becomes a "golden cage", however, and workers start leaving the city, thus making it something that "never existed". A main topic in the story is human revolt against the authorities' madness and the revenge of perfection acting as a boomerang to its creators; therefore it can also function as an additional contemporary criticism of Transhumanist thought and the contemporary notion of mechanised perfection.

However, it is *Le sarcophage [The Sarcophagus]*, for which Bilal created the artwork as an experiment based on Pierre Christin's script in 2000 in the form of an illustrated exhibition catalogue rather than a comic book, that actually reflects Posthuman ethics. The story is about a museum of the future built in the heart of a nuclear power station, Pylon 4 in Chernobyl, the exact site of the 1986 nuclear accident. It is interesting here that Bilal questions and criticises the role of the museum in the twenty-first century: It must be "a museum about life and death".[28] The details are more emblematic.

Box 10.9 *The Sarcophagus*

The museum is composed of four building sections: The first is the "Relics of Memory", containing the rooms "Glasnost", "Taliban",[29] "The Great Suk" (The Great Market), "Zoo", "Monuments" and "Last Congregation". The second section of the museum is "The Modernist Industry", a critique of the notions of both Modernity and Postmodernity, containing "Cosmetics", "Drugs", "Sports", "Rich People" and "Poor People". The third section is "The Future", containing "Chemical and Nuclear Weapons", "Videogames" and a room named "Immortality", dedicated to "Cloning, Biotechnology and Human Will for Immortality".[30] The fourth section is in the heart of the Chernobyl atomic pile, covered by cement since 1986, in the shape of an ancient sarcophagus. It is the place of Life and Death, a Sarcophagus, a vessel containing everything. It is, at the same time, a graveyard, a place of entertainment and a lab. Christin and Bilal make a clear statement by signing this work: the end of Postmodernism calls for a re-invention of Humanism, transformed into Posthumanist thought.

Another case of Posthumanist production originated in Greece in the 2000s and, similarly to the bulk of comics and graphic novels production from the year 2000 and after, derives from manga archetypes. Constantinos Papamichalopoulos (b. 1975) is a typical representative of the Greek generation of the 1990s, and his North American and manga influences become more than clear in both his script and his design. Papamichalopoulos interprets the contemporary world through violent, suffocating black-and-white images. He draws them as monumental size figures in big blocks of black ink, projected on huge all-white backgrounds. He owes the noir atmosphere of his stories and the monumental size of the figures to his favourite United States designers Jack Kirby and Frank Miller. On the other hand, he owes the facial characteristics of his protagonist and the name of his work, *The Japanese*, to his manga influences.[31]

Box 10.10 *The Japanese*

The Japanese (2000–2008) is a two-volume adventure about a Metahuman being in Athens somewhere in a distant future, in a society that is at the same time familiarly Greek and also reflects parallel contemporary political realities. Both albums function in three ways at the same time: (a) as expressions of Posthumanist ideas, (b) as political criticism and (c) as a tribute to manga. The Japanese is at the same time human and cyborg. In his era, man and machine have been so assimilated that they have become a new hybrid human breed

> in a machine-ruled world. The Japanese is a stranger in a strange land, the land of Greek decadence and pessimism, where he has to fight in order to survive. The plot is difficult to follow as it is based on poetry. In the first album, the Japanese enters the Athenian underground, where entrance is prohibited, after fighting a huge machine cop, whose size is duplicated every time he shows off his authority. This notion of the police as servants and keepers of a corrupt system that denies entrance to anyone who is not a part of it, apart from bearing Posthuman elements, is common to both anarchist and left ideologies in Greece. In the first pages of the second album, the Japanese escapes being killed by an armed and swearing Orthodox priest, while later he returns armed with a hyper-weapon to kill the priest. The whole story evolves like a videogame, with cops and priests setting ambushes around the Japanese and swearing at even God himself, while the Japanese challenges them and answers their swearing with poetry verses.[32] The Japanese battles their "monstrous" face and their hypocrisy.

Apart from being Japanese,[33] the hero also bears the facial characteristics and style (e.g. shaved head) of the designer himself, thus denoting the issue of artistic isolation and the search for identity. This is also a way for the artist to express his commitment to manga as an *otaku* ("devoted follower paying respect" in Japanese) and his respect for the Japanese culture, the first that can really be recorded as Posthuman. In the first album, the human Japanese is transformed into a human–machine cyborg because he "is bored of this miserable life in an unpleasant city surrounded by unpleasant people". To escape this, he becomes a cyborg and heads to Eleusis[34] to find the truth. Cops transformed into cyborg creatures will try to stop him countless times, and he will even fly, acquiring machine wings to fulfil this escape.

Moreover, the Japanese has to implant a chip into the back of his head in order to understand Balkan languages and gain introduction to "the System of Athens". To get in, he has to meet an "identity donor", a guy who commits suicide to offer the Japanese his place in the system, because "for every tourist that arrives, one of us has to die to create a place in the system". "I don't mind" he says. "After all, *everybody* is now a tourist here".[35] Before leaving Athens, the Japanese will also destroy all the "violent, idiot and audacious micro-investors".[36] The Japanese will fulfil the crossing by the end of this volume that will come with the Japanese saying, "Despite all this, Athens is a beautiful city with visible and touchable enemies. Life gets a meaning when you have enemies".

The most Posthumanist and interesting part of *The Japanese* is the second album, *The Japanese. Deuteronomion* (Deuteronomy – The Biblical Book), published eight years after the first (2008). This is the story of a return or a passage ritual from *myesis* (rite of passage) to fight against all aspects of New Hellenic reality. The enemies here are not only the cops and the priests, but all "Neohellenes". From this generalised aspect, Papamichalopoulos gets deep into both Nietzsche and Transhumanist thought, viewing the intellectual artist as Übermensch. Therefore, a series of sequential battles in the album comprise a necessary and "holy" war: the private (?) war of the Japanese that is seeking the Greek origins of ancient cults, against the enemies of the strange country. Posthumanism turns here into a Greek issue, related to the preservation and prevalence of ancient values.

In *Deuteronomion*, the Japanese is older and different. He has organised into his inner self the holy war he has started in the first album, following the method and ritual of a Samurai warrior or a Japanese monk: building his serenity and silence with wisdom, floating into knowledge and poetry, safely controlling his titanic explosions of anger. The Japanese is now acting as an avenger on behalf of a parallel reality: the reality that returns to Humanism and is entrenched into intellectuality against the intolerance, prejudice, ignorance, fanaticism, villainy, savageness and violence of everyday reality. *Papades* (the priests), borrowed from another comic series by Papamichalopoulos,[37] are symbolically used in this album as the official representatives of all these vices. They become the official enemy accompanied by smaller enemy groups: those who lost their money in the stock market, the "unlucky Barbies" or the pathetic TV watchers – in other words, all those that a Posthumanist intellectual would really hate.

Box 10.11 *Deuteronomion*

Deuteronomion is a series of stories that could be understood either as the sequential chapters of an action story or as independent stories, despite the fact that they are actually designed as *chapters*. The album is comprised of two preludes and eleven chapters. Prelude I introduces the reader to the poetry of Yannis Ritsos (1909–1990),[38] which is read loudly (as the really big letters imply) by the Japanese, contradicting the wisdom of the poem with contemporary ignorance and violence. In Prelude II, Ritsos's poetry leads to the magnification of one verb, EIMAI ("I AM"), through visual means, and the layout of the pages is indeed masterly here. Chapters I, II and III represent, in equally dramatised visual ways, the phases of the Japanese's counterattack against the strengthened populism of *Papades*, comparing the wisdom of a Samurai to the aggressiveness of the priest, to the sound of the poetry of Miltos Sachtouris (1919–2005).[39] These chapters reveal, in my opinion, the overall narrative, visual and cultural influences of the artist: from Jack Kirby's drawings to the epic dimension of the manga creation that includes the comprehension of theoretical key points of Japanese culture, from classic Samurai stories in the Japanese cinema to even Tarantino's stylish interpretations in all of the *Kill Bill* movies, all of which could also be viewed as alternative Posthumanist stories.

> In Chapter IV, the Japanese is declared, by a TV priest, the enemy of the State and the Order, while in Chapter V, the reading of the nineteenth-century poetry of Dionysios Solomos[40] (who is Greece's national poet, as some verses of his epic *Hymn to Liberty* are used as lyrics for the national anthem) literally transforms the Japanese into an organic hyper-weapon. In Chapter IX, the angry Japanese, to the sound of Sachtouris's poetry, again will accept the ultimate attack from the System that, in Chapter X, will lead to the extinction (?) of the Japanese. After this attack, his fortress, The Library, is flattened to ground zero, a great metaphor for all the attacks against all forms of "the civilised world", from the burning of the ancient Alexandria Library in Egypt to 9/11. It also functions as a metaphor for the attacks of ignorance against intellectuality.
>
> By the last pages, the reader is not sure whether the Japanese is dead or not. Into an atmosphere of open hypotheses (is the hero cloned? Is he merely reborn? Is he metaphorically present as a force and an idea? Is he a ghost?), the Japanese returns into a Messianic shuffle that gets superficial dimensions by reading the verses of *The Mad Rabbit* by the Greek poet Miltos Sachtouris: "Wings sprang out of my shed blood: all the awesome birds, into the sea". Balance has, for the moment, returned. The narrative is empowered by the idiosyncratic visual *maniera* of Papamichalopoulos, which establishes the black-and-white reality of *The Japanese* to an absolute One, with the literal visualisation of the poetic discourse in an attempt to illustrate esoteric qualities. This is one of the few occasions on which we could literally speak of the "power of the image": coarse in terms of design, but so tender in its isolated elements.

The Japanese's suffocating world also bears elements of Phillipe Druillet's influence. Tribute to the famous French designer has been paid by several Greek designers so far. Known for his adaptation of Gustave Flaubert's *Salambo* (1862) in a series of graphic novels, Druillet has created the perfect Posthuman protagonist, Matho or Matosh (according to Flaubert) and his alter ego Lone Sloane (according to the designer), a space traveller and warrior. Druillet published his first Sloan stories in 1966 (first album in 1972)[41] and later moved into the graphic novels *Salambo* (1980), *Salambo 2 – Carthage* (1982–1984) and *Salambo 3 – Matho* (1986). *Chaos* comes many years later, as an independent continuity. In the story *Chaos*, published in 2000, Druillet introduces us to a Meta-human world: "Fascinating monsters, idle intellectuals, beauty lovers satiated by ancient treasures; their palaces, like ancient caravans, are flooded by Cashhan treasures. Their museums are temples. Their gardens are the planet. Their oracles are memory collectors. Their religion is the ultimate art. Madness, for once more! They seek immortality before death. In vain, however. Time is against them. For ever".[42]

> **Box 10.12 Cashhan**
>
> Cashhan is the eighth planet of the Shaan system. Shaan, who is the prevailing evil force and this world's ruler, is the eternal enemy of the just warrior Sloan, who disappeared ten years previously and is now considered dead. The cast of Azure Barons called "the holy collectors" are now Shaan's deputies. They actually rule a waste land, addicted to drugs and collecting ancient treasures on the surface of their planets, leaving them rot away under acid rain.
>
> However, Sloan, who is partly "dead", rises again. Still under Shaan's witchcraft, he has to destroy Shaan's ring and let virtue occupy his own soul. Loved by a noble higher priestess, Thryli or Thouli, Sloan gradually becomes less violent but more powerful, his thoughts ingrained with philosophy and poetry: "Is there a dinosaur playing music? A lizard thinking like Kant? A spider dreaming of Mozart? A wise man who thinks he's a butterfly? Life is a music symphony of the world, and we all are its heart and soul".
>
> Sloan will finally win, and virtue will prevail. The religious and philosophical syncretism running through the whole story is more than evident. Apart from the easy recognisable (for the Western reader) Christian references, there are also strong connections with Buddhism, a religion also bearing Messianic content; and Shamanism, a cult incorporating the Messianic element into the highest powers of Nature. From this perspective, *Chaos* can be read as a Posthumanist graphic novel.
>
> Moreover, Sloan does not return unharmed. His face bears the scars of the universal conflagration he has taken part in. Sloan becomes thus an angel of the post-technological era. Chaos is the ultimate mutation, and the warriors engaged in it cannot have purely human physiognomy and nature. Sloan's risen body has been reconstructed. He is a compilation of prosthetic surgeries; therefore, his body is technically "improved" but physically disfigured. As with the aforementioned Metabarons, he faces the tragic irony of getting distance from human nature in order to comprehend and conquer it.

Posthumanism in times of Transhumanism

To create a better understanding of ideas and values reflected in the stories bearing Post- and Transhumanist qualities, please see Table 10.1 wherein we can trace a consistency between morality, sustainability and culture and Humanism, while technology, violence, power and religion stand on the other side as the Transhumanist Other.

The stories presented above summarise the centrality of the notion of producing a *new meaning* in contemporary comics and graphic novels in Posthumanist terms, and they underline (a) the need for an ultimate "beginning" for all through a return to the roots of philosophical thought and creative imagination that comprise the core meaning of being "human" in a meta-technological era; (b) the need for art

TABLE 10.1 Transhumanism and Posthumanism in cartoons

	Watchmen	The Killing Joke	Judge Dredd	Jodorowsky and Moebius	Euromanga	Enki Bilal	The Japanese	Philippe Druillet
Transhumanism	Social environment	Super-evils, (i.e. The Joker)	Social environment and beings produced in labs or mutated, (i.e. Dredd himself)	Social environment	Cyberpunk social Environment	Social environment, mutated evil characters	Physical beings	Environment and beings
Posthumanism	Posthuman beings	Batman	Dredd's mind and critical ability	The Metabarons and John Difool	Steampunk social environment	Genetically transformed humans and their memories	Social environment, technological beings, (i.e. the Japanese)	Memory, ideas, culture
Process	Freedom	Sanity versus insanity	Power, technology, fascist regimes	Fascist regimes, class struggle	Technology, ecology and the future of human beings	Memory as revolt against Transhumanism	Culture, natural and urban environment versus violence and religion	Eternal battle between good (represented by intellectual beings) and evil (represented by technology)
Humanism	Free choice, social activism, morality, sustainability	Morality, sustainability	Humour, family bonds, morality, sustainability	Humour, decisions, sustainability	Technology and sustainability	Memory's preservation of the historical process of human beings, sustainability	Power of words, poetry, individual revolutions, sustainability	Eternal reoccurrence, memory, sustainability

to become "dangerous" once more and spread philosophical ideas – Posthumanist ideas on this occasion; and (c) the need for a new Humanism, in Greco-Roman and Renaissance terms. According to Edgar Wind,[43] Plato would be jealous of the condition art has fallen into nowadays, as the terrible demon of imagination he so hard tried to exorcise, had lost its disastrous powers, and art is becoming harmless. Hegel has on the other hand explained that, when art moves into a safety zone, it can be very popular, but its influence on our lives will disappear.[44] This is not the case with comics and graphic novels nowadays, which represent a "dangerous" art filled with Posthuman thought.

Box 10.13 The Kodak moment of Posthumanism

The disruptiveness of change:

In the interface between technology and the human body, we can see some new threats to Humanism.

The knowledge one failed to use:

Still, we present a criticism of the assumption that Transhumanism and Posthumanism are only a threat to human existence. However, it provokes us to rethink some human ideals and values.

Ability to adjust to future changes:

It is important to engage in the debate on Transhumanism and Posthumanism and the conditions for Humanism under new technological regimes.

The opportunity in the changes:

Science fiction literature can help us become aware of the need to re-define and re-state human values and Humanism under new technological conditions. The interconnectedness of social structures, political regimes and technology, and the fact that they can reinforce each other in ways that are difficult to identify, makes it important to have deep debates about this issue.

What fiction can tell us about is the potential interconnectedness of different factors that are difficult to identify in real-world stations. They can help us see, in a caricatured way, the mutually reinforcing effects of political, social and technological changes that might influence how we evaluate things, and what values and opinions are exposed. They expose the potential dilemmas of the ethical and pragmatic kind that these changes might force. They can also make us aware of how humanness might be threatened in sophisticated ways by these complex interactions.

Notes

1. See: Nigel Warburton: "The portrait of Erica, the Japanese android, raises the question of what it means to be human. In today's secular age, how can we find an answer?" *The Observer*, September 10, 2017.
2. Moore & Gibbons 1987.
3. Kawa (2000), pp. 211–213.
4. #XI, 2.
5. 2011, p. 86. Also, Robichaud 2009, pp. 5–17.
6. DiGiovanna 2009, pp. 109–111.
7. 2011, pp. 69–80.
8. Moore, Bolland & Higgins 1988, p. 21.
9. Robichaud 2008, p. 79. Also, Valereto 2011, pp. 75–76.
10. And also Pat Mills, the editor who developed *2000AD* in 1976.
11. In 2008, prog [story] 1595, Dredd is diagnosed with benign cancer.
12. Bolland 2010, p. 18–20.
13. How 2000, pp. 226–230.
14. "The Day the Law Died", *2000AD* # 108.
15. For a list of all Dredd stories: http://upload.wikimedia.org/wikipedia/en/6/6c/Dredd2AD.pdf.
16. *Creatura* (1990), *Carnivora* (1992), *Mandragora* (1995), *Aphrodisia* (1997), *La Planète oubliée* (2000). All seven albums were republished in 1999. A first appearance of a woman Druuna-like character and octopus-like monsters took place in 1981, in a short (16 page) comic story by Serpieri, "In His Likeness"; see the site www.druna.net.
17. The same elements are usually met in SF/horror films. See: Creed 1995, pp. 127–159.
18. The Russian–Chilean script-writer is actually also a designer, a director, a writer and a mysticist. The best guide to Jodorowsky's work, containing the complete series of *Incal* and *Metabarons* albums, is the official *Les Humanoïdes Associées* site. Jodorowsky is one of the founding members. See: www.humano.com.
19. The stories published by *Les Humanoïdes Associées* in France are: (1) "Otto the Great-Great-Grandfather" (1992), (2) "Honorata, the Foremother" (1993), (3) "Agnar, the Great-Grandfather" (1995), (4) "Odda, the Great-Grandmother" (1997), (5) "Steelhead, the Grandfather" (1998), (6) "DonnaVicenta, the Grandmother" (1999), (7) "Aghora, the Father-Mother" (2002), and (8) "Nameless, the Last of the Metabarons" (2003).
20. Jean Giraud created the character of *Blueberry* in 1963, in *Pilote* (script: Jean-Michel Charlie). Giraud is rather "classicist" in design. On the other hand, Moebius, his alter ego, is a modernist SF creator.
21. Jodorowsky comes back to develop this character ten (!) years later. It must have been an obsession to him.
22. There are eighteen albums so far in total; thirteen of them are already out, comprising a series of *Before Incal, Incal* and *After Incal* thematics.
23. There is also a series by Jodorowsky &Janjetov under the title *The Early Years of John Difool*, published from 1984 to 1994.
24. Robots continue to play a secondary role in SF comic book stories.
25. The Argentinian designer's former studies in industrial design are evident.
26. *Akira* takes place in New Tokyo in 2030. A Third World War has devastated society and the world; violence and disorder are the rule. Some teenage bikers accidentally discover an important secret military project, the consequences of which are inconceivable.
27. There are hundreds of international newspaper and magazine articles on *Enki Bilal*. Most of them are now concentrated on internet sites. Some of them are on the designer's official site: www.bilal.com; www.humano.com, the official site of *Les Humanoïdes Associées*; www.scifi.com; and www.desbois.com. Also see Bilal's full bibliography and work in: www3.sympatico.ca/ans.beaulieu/Bilal/Bilal.htm. For exhibitions and interviews see: www.enkibilalandeuxmilleun.be and www.lesinsomniaques.com/bilal/bilal.htm, with three video-clip interviews.

28 Sampanikou 2001 and 2004.
29 An ironic (and prophetic) reference to the 21st century, months before September 11, 2001.
30 Christin & Bilal 2000.
31 Papamichalopoulos, a talented Fine Arts graduate, is also a visual artist. His artistic work is highly influenced by black and white photography, a tribute to the era when art became the product of mechanical reproduction through photography, sharing Walter Benjamin's ideas as indicated in his classic famous essay written in 1936 (see Benjamin 2008).
32 These battles against the priests reflect strong disapproval of the Greek Church's involvement in political and social life, as some of the major political and economic scandals in Greece that have come to light involve Church people and politicians.
33 According to everyday speech in Greece, a "Japanese" is a person that keeps a stranger's attitude in any situation, e.g. 'Stop playing the Japanese to me!' (in an angry voice).
34 The ancient Greek city, a religious centre in antiquity and the place of a famous sanctuary, now an industrial suburb of Athens.
35 This metaphor works like a strong pessimistic and ironic reflection of a feeling, among young people especially, of living in a country that has more facilities for tourists than for local people.
36 This image reflects political criticism and a rather pejorative idea of politicians and their followers. There are also memories from the days of one major economical scandal known as the "stock-market" scandal (in the late 1990s), in which thousands of micro-investors lost their money in favour of big-money investors with political connections.
37 The 9 Magazine was published from 2000 to 2010 as a weekly comic magazine by the newspaper *Eleftherotypia*. The "Papades" series by Papamichalopoulos appeared in the magazine from May 9 to October 15, 2001.
38 The well-known Greek poet was a candidate for a Nobel Prize in 1968 and received a Lenin Prize in 1977. See Ritsos & Yannis (1982). Ritsos has been translated into English and other languages.
39 Sachtouris, Miltos (2000).
40 On this occasion, the Japanese is reading verses from *Eleutheroi Poliorkimenoi* [Free Besieged], another major poem by Solomos. His poetry is concentrated on the philosophical question of what liberty is and how human beings perceive or use it.
41 For Druillet visit: http://www.chez.com/druillet/bd.htm.
42 Druillet, p. 2.
43 Wind (1986), p. 22.
44 Hegel, *Forlesungen über die Aesthetic* I, εκδ. H. J. Hotho, 1835, 134 κ.ε.

11

COPING WITH SOCIAL LEARNING

Social and economic change through engagement

Richard Ennals, Björn Nelson, Anders Ingwald, Viktoria Johansson and Victor Lagercrantz

Learning and innovation through dialogue

There is much that we do not know about the future. We can agree that people will continue to have a central role; it will not be enough to depend on technology. In short, our students and children will just have to cope with the future. We cannot offer them certainties, but we can provide environments and experiences today that can empower them to rise to new challenges (Wolsk 1975). This applies both within and outside formal education, affecting the future of work and society. Learners need to be equipped to cope with unpredictability. This requires a transformation of the learning process.

This argument links to the discussion in Chapter 5 on knowledge. It also links to the discussion in Chapter 8 on the two-dimensional concept of knowledge. Common to these discussions is that knowledge is seen as embedded in practice and thereby is activated in social processes. The argument in this chapter relates to how one can organise learning processes that manage to activate this embedded knowledge and develop it further by exposing it in social deliberations. Thereby, this chapter deals with the question of how dialogue and learning can build a capacity to cope with the future, with learning including reflection on action. This question is now being asked around the world (Gustavsen et al. 2007; Johnsen et al. 2015). Here we try to learn from a particular case, described in a way that enables readers to reflect on their own situations.

Our case is based at Linnaeus University (Sweden). How can tacit knowing, learning from practice and dialogue form the basis for coping with the future? We know that the future is uncertain. How then can we prepare through conventional teaching, as has been done in the past? Can we remodel relationships and processes concerned with teaching and learning, with an emphasis on empowering learners? We need to put alternatives to the test of practice. Rather than just addressing global changes, which are effectively beyond our control, we also focus on the local level (Gustavsen et al. 2007). We explore learning through engagement in social action, which we can call *social learning*.

The Linnaeus case represents a bottom-up approach to innovation. Learning comes from experience of active engagement and dialogue, combined with reflection. Based on work in the Department of Skill and Technology, in the Faculty of Technology (Ennals et al. 2016), we offer new cross-disciplinary perspectives. The university has encountered enthusiasm from external partners at the levels of municipalities, regions and companies, which can be enabled to join a growing movement. There is innovative work on Vocational Teacher Education and Sustainable Regional Development at Linnaeus, as well as a Master's programme in Skill and Technology, which is adapting to embrace the expanding scale of practical applications. Here we explore some radical features.

The focus on collective and social learning can be contrasted with more individualised conventional approaches to education, where the emphasis has often been on formal academic inputs. Here we recognise the importance of the local community and distinctive cultures of dialogue and development (Gustavsen 1992).

Recent developments in pedagogy and distance learning enable universities to address and engage in such cultures. We recognise the contribution of learning to processes of regional development. Perhaps most importantly, collective learning can help people to cope with the future.

The Småland region has traditionally had a low level of participation in higher education and an economy that has been dominated by the local forest environment. There is strong regional feeling, and a distinctive tradition of efforts in regional development and innovation. There have been concerns about people leaving the region to move to big cities, and a corresponding need to attract, welcome and integrate newcomers, including refugees. There have been previous regional development projects in Småland, linked to international partners (Brulin 2012).

Box 11.1 Sustainable Regional Development

At Linnaeus University, "Sustainable Regional Development" (as a course, a project and a movement led by the Department of Skill and Technology) is working in a region that is increasingly aware of the need for development in the context of rural depopulation. Students work in Circles in association with local villages, building on their experience of Study Circles in Swedish schools. There is a central role for Dialogue Seminars, and there has been an accumulation of experience and expertise. Dialogue Seminars have changed in focus, from philosophical rationale to practical implementation, giving fresh reality to concerns for practical knowledge. Having written for and spoken in seminars, students tend to be more prepared to act.

In the counties where Linnaeus University has campuses (Kalmar and Kronoberg), there were more than 25,000 companies in 2012, the majority being small and medium-sized enterprises (SMEs). In some sectors and areas, the percentages of employees with academic qualifications are very low. OECD reports on this part of Sweden say that in theory, many companies should not be able to survive. This has raised the question whether there are other factors, apart from formal knowledge, that make enterprises in the region competitive.

"Please do not bring professors out into the region telling the enterprises who they are." This view from a regional entrepreneur leads us to John Shotter (2006) and the importance of talking from "Within" rather than talking "About". Perspectives from "Within" have led development at Linnaeus and are used in many courses and programmes at the university. Later in the chapter, it will be seen how this has been used in education, where forest enterprises, vocational teachers, SME companies in different branches, teachers and regional developers have attended.

During the period from 1998 to 2008, there was very positive evaluation of our courses from both companies and students. Our problem was that we did not have tools to articulate why this was. This threatened the hidden tacit part, which is both worth keeping and changing. There was an obvious need for a new research paradigm that could deal with explicit and tacit knowing, linked to experience based knowledge and complex thematic challenges (Göranzon et al. 2006).

The subject Skill and Technology was built up at the Faculty of Technology at Linnaeus from 2008. Originally this research paradigm was created at the Royal Institute of Technology (KTH) in Stockholm. The conventional philosophy of knowledge, emphasising the limits of explicit knowledge in propositional form, which could be handled by computers, was challenged. There was a focus on what could not be captured through explicit knowledge and computers. A central tool in the subject is the case study, where personal tacit knowing and collective tacit knowing are studied. Typically, these are taken from working life.

The main method in Skill and Technology is based on "Dialogue Seminars" wherein inter-subjective meetings between students convert experience to practical knowledge by reflecting. The "Dialogue Seminar Method" (Göranzon et al. 2006) means in short that students present their experiences by writing a short reflective text and reading it to others. The text is inspired by a collective reading of classic literature, language philosophy, experiencing works of art and so on. The Dialogue Seminar follows the distinctive method where students read and reflect, by having a dialogue about their own and others' experiences. The objective is communication rather than agreement.

From a focus on research at KTH, the challenge for us at Linnaeus University was to incorporate Skill and Technology into courses at a practical level. Over the years, this has led to the insight that we could develop different meanings, using the Dialogue Seminar Method to create a supportive environment and learning opportunities (Alvunger et al. 2014; Ennals et al. 2016).

Following the remark from the entrepreneur quoted above, the question arises: What did the attenders react to when they were told who the visitors were? Many of our students are middle-aged and highly skilled and have not been in education for a long time; perhaps meeting us was the first time. They now meet us as partners. Academics should not adopt a superior attitude.

The importance of dialogue

We stress the importance of dialogue in our courses. A challenge when meeting the students was facing their picture of what knowledge and academic work could mean. Their picture is often traditional, where theoretical knowledge counts as "the truth". Our belief is that the deepest form of knowledge in working life is tacit, personal and collective and cannot fully be formalised. The importance and balance between explicit and tacit knowing is therefore a challenge in our courses and programmes. "My experience from my work counts at the university" has been said in different ways in evaluations over the years. Of course, this picture could be put forward from our lectures in theoretical terms, but soon we found out that the way students and lectures met at Dialogue Seminars meant that different definitions of knowledge could be shared. Working life provides a common reference point.

We offer distance courses, where we meet the students three to four times each semester, one or two days each meeting. The first time we meet the students physically, they are prepared for a Dialogue Seminar. The aim is to create the environment for dialogue, where mutual respect for different kinds of knowledge can emerge. A key factor for successful education at this stage is that the students dare to rely on their own experience as one crucial basis for their further development of skill. Regional development is not merely a matter of economics and innovation policies. Crucially, we see students as the "human face" of regional development, as they go on to seek employment after graduation. They are in considerable demand from employers, who would like them to remain in the region. Kalmar region has recognised this, with a new project to support the regional role of the Student Union.

Students can be used in many ways in regional development: They can be used as the link between the academy and the local region, where they help new knowledge spread into the local economy. This will benefit regional development, as well as the students who are working in co-operation with local industry. This co-operation between the local region and the students can take many forms; the student can work directly with a local partner and produce an academic paper, or a group of students can work with a case from a local village. The Student Union are organising new meeting places between the students and the region of Kalmar (Persson et al. 2016) and are trying to find working procedures for collaboration between the groups. This will include field trips out in the region, where students can meet local business and other actors.

At Linnaeus University, 70% of the students come from outside the region. The university is one of the biggest reasons why young people move to the region. The problem is that most of these young people leave the region after finishing their higher education, and they have never been outside Kalmar or Växjö. The students do not know if they are needed by the region, and the region does not know how to use the students. According to the OECD report, the region has a problem: Young people with higher education tend to leave the region for the conurbations; meanwhile, the young people who stay in the region are not interested in higher education. This will have a big impact on the local economy and on industry in the region. This means that one of the key factors for regional development is discovering how to get the students to stay.

The Student Union are working together with the local municipalities and their role in regional development. In the region, the municipalities have different needs, and therefore the work with students must be adapted to them. The working procedures can shift from working with local policies, and how the policies can be implemented, to how we can keep young people interested in higher education. The project also has the intention of showing the region to the students, to show them that you can live a good life in the region, and that they can have an interesting working life. There are many implications for courses and support activities.

The project started in the spring of 2017, and it is in the process of finding partners outside the university and how they can work with students. During this process, and in the dialogue between the Student Union and its partners, the idea of how local business can work with students has changed. Before, the local business were looking for students who could help them develop their specialty or something similar. In many cases, these students do not exist, or do not know they exist, because the logic is different between university education and working life. The dialogue between the Student Union and the local partners has given a new perspective on how they can work with students. Instead of trying to find students who can develop their strong sides, the idea is that students can help local business to develop their weak sides. This can help the local businesses to develop, and the students will form a closer connection to their future working life. This will give the region a push in regional development and give the students a better memory of the region for the future.

There are new projects led by the Student Union, with partners in the counties. We can also discuss current and potential collaboration with other partners such as the Linnaeus Foundation and the Kamprad Foundation. Engagement with and through the Student Union can be presented as making a vital contribution to the development of individuals, the university and the region. Over time, this should change patterns of decision making in business in the region.

We can take Victor, Student Union president from 2016 to 2017, as an example. He comes from the region and has international experience of both working life, as a chef, and monastic life, returning to the region to study, lead the Student Union and develop initiatives in regional development. He has helped to secure external funding, and he has found a way to continue to contribute to the development work while undertaking Master-level studies. Helen is another example, playing a leading role in the Student Union and working with a Circle of students in Sustainable Regional Development, addressing the needs of a local village. Her competence and confidence have increased greatly through engagement. The Student Union elects a new board each year. Careful succession planning is required if there is to be continuity in the conduct of a growing set of projects and activities. Learning by the Student Union requires more than simply a few active individuals. A culture shift is needed.

Collaborative advantage and development

It is significant that a large proportion of Linnaeus University academics, at all levels, are themselves from the region. In common with local company managers, many of them are also forest owners and are personally engaged with the culture of forest and wood. They play an active part in a "region of meaning", rather than pretending academic detachment. The link has been strengthened through many years of courses on Forest and Wood and Sustainable Enterprise. It is now a great potential source of collaborative advantage. Småland has had distinctive approaches to development (Ekman et al. 2011).

In the Linnaeus region, most SME companies are forest owners; most owners do not live on their farms, and many have other occupations. The forest industry is the leading sector in Sweden in terms of net exports. The approach of linking sustainable regional challenges and needs has a history at Linnaeus University in the development of academic courses named "Sustainable Forestry". Four different faculties worked together with forest owners and their organisations from 1996 to 2001. In a normal academic approach, courses are built up from traditional academic subjects. Now a new approach has meant that researchers and lecturers have learned and internalised the needs of the enterprise as a starting point for new courses. This was made possible due to the fact that some lecturers were forest owners, and by a group of forest owners. The aim was to discover how theory and training could be linked to one case: the forest owner's own enterprise. The result became a 30-ECT course that took students through ten linked challenges, handled by developing sustainable forestry. Over the years from 2001 to 2017, approximately 20,000 students attended different courses, giving them 7.5 to 30 ECTs. (In terms of individual students, we are talking about 5000–6000 students).

Linking dialogue and learning are new development processes in the university and the region, with important potential. One interesting outcome has been "the weaving of a regional web" through work with four case-study villages on the Sustainable Regional Development course, and the dialogical process that made that possible. Student Circles researched the past, present and future of the four villages, aided by local residents as Circle members. They submitted reports from the Circles, and each individual wrote and presented a reflection paper on the work of a different Circle, leading to a dialogue involving all participants. The discourse was multidisciplinary, and dialogue was taken forward by the enthusiasm of the participants.

The outcome of the course showed common understandings across the region, with a common vocabulary and set of attitudes. In terms of social science, this is an extremely important outcome, providing evidence of social capital formation, linking to research in regional development (Gustavsen 1992; Putnam 1993; Scase 1977). In the literature, this has usually been suggested as an outcome of academic analysis; we have been able to demonstrate it operating in practice. We facilitated the creation of the regional dialogue. All of the students on the initial course want to continue the work and may join the Master's course in Skill and Technology. Potentially, we are building a new movement. This offers a fresh interpretation of Development Coalitions, which bring people and organisations together in order to pursue common objectives (Ennals 2014; Ennals &Gustavsen 1999;). There has been marked instability and unpredictability in the region. Småland has had experience of poverty and large-scale emigration in the past, typically to the USA, as well as the international success of IKEA, which was founded and based locally. IKEA is a major company in an area dominated by SMEs.

Recently, many of the local villages in the Linnaeus region have been experiencing "Kodak moments", with sudden closures of long-established industries.

In Lidhult, a long-established truck factory closed. In Boda, the traditional glass industry closed, to be replaced by the Glass Museum. Student Circles have explored possibilities for positive initiatives, for example, finding new uses for old buildings. They encounter great interest among local residents, who would like to find ways of continuing traditional industries. The way forward is rarely as straightforward as they would hope. Problems of employment, education and housing are linked; fresh thinking is needed, developing initiatives that may have radical implications.

Development of isolated enterprises is often also linked to regional and global conditions. To ensure development, there has been support nationally and from the European Union (EU), which has resulted in different projects. Looking at related projects, a fragmented picture often emerges regarding how those projects interact with the aim of causing long-term effects. Results from small projects are often not taken up. We need to build sustainable alliances with such projects.

One problem that has been noticed in different local meetings is that there is a lack of plans for places outside the main city, in each of several different municipalities. This means that there are problems in terms of suggesting directions for new development efforts in local villages, as well as taking care of existing results. Skill and Technology works thematically, and one aim is to deal with complexities, taking perspectives from "Within". After discussions with different partners such as companies, boards of municipalities and individuals from villages, the new course was developed, Sustainable Regional Development, 7.5 ECTs. The course took perspectives from the Linnaeus University Students Union and from the agendas of local residents.

Taking forward sustainable regional development

The partnership with the Linnaeus University Student Union, which is one of the largest in Sweden, has considerable potential. The students are voluntary members and expect various services to be provided. The Student Union is part of the design and delivery of the Sustainable Regional Development course, and its members are now co-designing a follow-on course, to be co-led by experienced students, and they are pressing for the development of a new Master's course in Sustainable Regional Development (SRD). This could be a pathway within the Master's in Skill and Technology. Active interest from the students is changing the rules of the game. They do not just rely on the official catalogue of courses.

Linnaeus University has good basic conditions for a Master's in Regional Development. This is because they already have subjects that have developed into regional courses, for example marine biology and ecology. The work done in Skill and Technology is interesting and could be used as the basis for a new Master's programme. Regional development is interesting for many academic subjects and has many aspects. Therefore, the students think that a Master's programme in SRD should be open to all types of students with a bachelor degree; this provides a basis for cross-faculty working. All students could have courses in theory and method in regional development and how it can be interpreted. The students also think that the students should work on some type of case study. The cases do not come from industry but instead from local villages or similar actors in the region. These cases should provide the theme for the programme and should be the foundation for the students' Master's thesis in their own subject. Courses during the programme could be up to the student to choose, as long as they are associated with regional development or the student's subject; or the student can have an internship. In principle, it would probably be best if the Master's was offered in both full-speed and half-time modes, so it can attract both students in employment as well as regular students. Some courses can use both student groups in seminars and dialogues.

We learned a great deal from the first four village Circles from the SRD course. Earlier we outlined the stages of the work of the Circles, with reports on the past, present and future of the chosen villages. They provide rich material. They have linked with the national programme "All Sweden shall live". They discussed fresh uses for rural buildings for community use. In Oland, they considered the importance of restaurants.

Skill and Technology, which could have a home in any academic faculty in the university, has enabled us to develop insights that cross disciplinary borders. The common starting point is a reflection on human skill, highlighting the importance of experience and tacit knowing. We need to go beyond explicit knowledge and deal with tacit knowing. We can gain access to some of that tacit knowing through dialogue, for example through the "Dialogue Seminar Method", developed by Göranzon et al. (2006). Göranzon's focus, in a series of six volumes on Skill and Technology published by Springer in 1988–1995 and now available electronically, was mainly on individuals reflecting on their own skill. His work with the companies Combitech and Vattenfall showed how Skill and Technology can impact on company culture. Dialogue was a means of creating a shared understanding and competitive advantage. This has been developed further with the Master's in Skill and Technology. Building on foundations established at the Royal Institute of Technology in Stockholm, the Master's in Skill and Technology was developed at Linnaeus University. Strong philosophical principles are complemented by practical experience from working life. The scope of the Master's programme is now to be broadened to take account of work at Linnaeus on SRD and Vocational Teacher Education. This reflects the increasing range of practical applications of Skill and Technology.

At Linnaeus University, great progress has been made in Vocational Teacher Education (VTE), where individual teachers develop economically important skills, both in working life and in educational communication. The programme has a national reputation and a large active network of teachers. This is extraordinarily important if a culture of skill is to be developed and maintained in the region and in Sweden, with teachers recognised as essential. In a changing and uncertain world, young people need to be able to think, act and reflect. The use of Dialogue Seminars in VTE provides a link with the work of the Master's in Skill and Technology and in SRD There is a core of common approaches and methods. A majority of the students of VTE are practicing teachers, and those who are not already teachers often find work as teachers during the course.

The VTE is a part of the Teacher Education programmes at Linnaeus University, and it includes a total of 20 weeks of teaching practice placement spread over four courses (periods) of 2–6 weeks. By addressing each of the teacher practice placement periods, this allows the student to formulate a target for teacher practice placement, based on the goals and the experiences of the student. To be able to formulate their goals, students must take an active part in the syllabus and study guide. Efforts targeting formulation acts as an *invärdering* (framework) before the teacher practice placement, and it is a way for a supervisor and mentor to determine where the student is in his or her development. The corresponding documentation takes place at the end of the period, when an assessment is made on the basis of the student's own goals. There is a case for applying this approach in SDR and the Master's programme. Invärdering is a concept that has been introduced at Linnaeus University in Växjö in connection with a project on teacher practice placement in distance learning.

The individual targets may be rooted in a development that has already been initiated at the school where the student teachers are based for their daily work. Sometimes the student's individual goals and the exercises in the VTE make the schools aware of an area that needs to be developed. An important aspect of planning is that the student and the supervisors together make a time plan for the teaching practice placement period, which is then reconciled with the mentor at the university. The time planning should indicate details of the teaching practice placement, when the guide talks will take place and what activities the student will participate in/carry out in order to achieve the objectives of the teacher practice placement period. In this work, the supervisor has an important role.

The evaluation of the student's goals and the time planning at the end of the teacher practice placement period provides the supervisor, the mentor and the student with recommendations for the next teacher practice placement period. A supervisor is a teacher who is working at a school and has a competence in supervising trainee teachers. A mentor is a teacher at the university who supervises a group of fifteen to twenty students during the VTE. This recommendation is then used along with the goals of the curriculum when the student formulates his/her goal in the upcoming teaching practice placement period. This creates continuity and progression between the teacher practice placement periods. Vocational teaching and regional development have converged. This experience from VTE provided many key elements of the SRD course. There will be a vital role for regional development through bottom-up initiatives, together with coalitions of partners. We can then learn from that experience.

At Linnaeus University, the way forward could involve increased collaboration with the Linnaeus Technical Centre, which works with companies across the region through a network of sub-regional nodes and links to university faculties. European funding supports the development of company networks, which take on functions such as research and technology transfer, previously undertaken by the university. This involves major changes in working relationships in the region. Companies and communities learn new ways of working. In Skill and Technology, we have opened up new possibilities for regional collaboration, including with the Student Union and the community.

Learning to cope with local challenges

In our work with the Student Union, we respect the experience, skill and tacit knowing of the students, which has been demonstrated in practice. Many students have experience of working life. We recognise that the Student Union can present an important human face for regional development, as our students seek employment in the region after graduation. This enables us to add value to regional development programmes. In terms of Regional Innovation Policies, we can move from the "Triple Helix" (government, universities and industry) to the "Quadruple Helix", adding the voice of the community and civil society. This development is of interest to international researchers and to those who are interested in democracy in practice.

The Student Union has taken a lead, establishing the new Linnaeus Students for Regional Development. This joins the VTE network and networks arising from courses in Forest and Wood, Sustainable Enterprise and SRD. We can link these cases as part of a common approach based on partnership and dialogue with the students. As we try to cope with an unpredictable future, it becomes apparent that we should not place complete reliance on technologies that are based on only partial understanding of complex areas of knowledge. Explicit knowledge can only ever be partial. We need to empower individuals to draw on their own individual and collective experience, skill and tacit knowing. We need to develop suitable structures. Actors in society need to be able to learn from active engagement and to develop the capacity for collaborative working. This should be a central theme for new programmes in Civil Engineering, now under development.

We can offer a fresh and unifying account of learning and development. Dialogue must be more than skin deep. We argue for active engagement rather than academic detachment. Regional partners co-develop the new courses and projects and participate in the dialogues that are at the centre of the courses. In the Department of Skill and Technology, we are bringing together academic theory with practical engagement in education and regional development. We recognise that tacit knowing is a major issue in social and collective learning. This contrasts with a traditional and more instrumental approach, which has often been concerned with competence (observed performance) rather than skill. Our students, of all ages and backgrounds, are empowered to cope with the future. In Skill and Technology, learning means empowerment, with a central place for reflection on skill as a vital resource.

How can practical experience form the basis for sustainable strategies for the future? This represents a departure from conventional approaches to teaching and learning. It requires a culture change and a recognition of the limitations of our knowledge of the future. This implies possible changes in career paths for teachers, with increased recognition of the importance of working life. Mobilising local engagement and learning is an alternative to imposing predefined top-down models for change. It means taking risks and building relationships of trust with partners outside the university. The boundaries of the university have changed. It also requires a strong and consistent support culture, both inside and outside.

The argument is that individual knowledge and experience, mediated in local learning processes, with an in depth understanding of the contextual conditions and with experience of collaborative working, is increasingly well fitted to coping with the future. There has been a change in the balance of power between academics and students. We are partners, with much to learn from each other. There are potentially radical implications for the working of the university. The challenge is to organise the processes in a constructive way. This includes working with new external partners. This gives new reality to the Quadruple Helix engaged in development: universities, government, industry and civil society. For universities, it is not just a matter of interpreting the world from a safe distance. We need to be prepared to engage with, and change, the world. Here, we have learned that we must work as partners with the Student Union, who represent students as stakeholders. We do not know what the future will bring. The students will have to cope. We hope that they will support us in our old age!

We offer a fresh vision of the university as an actor in the process of coping with the future. The approach is bottom up rather than top down, and it has a potentially significant role for the Student Union. It does not present explicit knowledge as holding all the answers; this means that access to tacit knowing is vital. At grassroots level, people work together in Circles, tackling problems identified by Circle members. The attitude is that problems can be addressed. In some cases, they can be solved in technical terms. In other cases, we can learn to live with the problems. The university with this vision can be a powerful catalyst for development in the region: intellectual, social and economic. In order to solve problems, it needs to engage the right people – with their experience, skill and tacit knowing. They need to be empowered to develop and implement policies in an environment of democratic dialogue.

We might regard this as a key element of democracy in the knowledge society. It helps to redefine the set of processes that are required. It also highlights the importance of Development Coalitions, as organisations and their members decide to work together to pursue common objectives. In this way, the university can be a leading force for development in the region. We can give fresh clarity to the arguments of "Higher Education in a Sustainable Society" (Johnsen et al. 2015). We point to the role of underpinning dialogue in enabling the development of mutual competence, often bridging academic disciplines and linking theory and practice. In addition to changing work and thinking inside academic disciplines, we are reminded of the traditional concept of the university as an academic community, with parity of esteem. Of course, details of the process will be affected by the participants, their power relations and their objectives. Principles of democratic dialogue apply, ensuring the right of all participants to contribute their ideas and to be accorded respect. The sustainability of the process will not be achieved overnight; trust must be built up incrementally, and conclusions must be open to challenge.

> **Box 11.2 The Kodak moment of social learning**
>
> ***a) The disruptiveness of change:***
>
> Enterprises can collapse and close, with drastic consequences for communities.
>
> ***b) The knowledge one failed to use:***
>
> Experience, skill and tacit knowing developed through work can be lost at the time of change.
>
> ***c) Ability to adjust to future changes:***
>
> Individuals and communities need to be able to make sense of new situations, coming together to collaborate and form development coalitions and engaging in dialogue.
>
> ***d) The opportunity in the changes:***
>
> Social dialogues and organised, open learning processes can mobilise embedded knowing. Social deliberation can create a space for common reflections as a basis for common action in a community. Individuals and communities need to be empowered to take new initiatives, reflecting on and sharing experience.

Dialogue processes should lead to some collective conclusions, but with ongoing scope for disagreement and dissent. The process may highlight the case for separate institutional structures where there is no natural agreement. Institutions have diverse histories and objectives. Discussion of social and collective learning may help to focus the debate. This vision can be contrasted with the orthodox approach to Quality as Compliance, where universities are seen as corporate organisations, managed top down, within a culture of New Public Management. Those driving New Public Management claim to know what the future will bring, and they require compliance with their standards and indicators today.

Social and collective learning, associated with a university, could be seen as a hybrid of individual and organisational learning. It need not involve following a conventional curriculum. It need not be constrained by the requirements of a particular organisation. It has much to do with people working together, pursuing common objectives and engaging in dialogue. It can cover people from different organisations working together. The organisations provide backdrops, making context specific. When we talk of organisations "learning", we use the analogy with human learning. How human learning works continues to be controversial. We imagine that we understand human learning when we use the analogy. In fact, there are many approaches, but often they use the same words. We cannot expect precision. Ambiguity will continue; it is an important resource.

Within Skill and Technology, the first case studies concerned individual learning and skill. We then considered various collective contexts where there are shared ways of thinking. We might refer to "language games" played by people in particular "forms of life". As people continue to interact, they can share vocabulary, then engage in joint activities, then share meanings. This has been the experience of VTE and of SRD. This hybrid approach to learning may provide an excellent preparation for coping with the future. Changes can take shape gradually, emerging from the mist, so we need the experience of feeling lost and then finding our way. On occasion, changes will be radical and fast. Our experience, skill and tacit knowing are vital resources. That has been our experience at Linnaeus University as we have combined courses and projects, resulting in building a new movement in which dialogue is a way of life.

12

COPING WITH ORGANISATIONS

Socio-technical, dialogical and beyond

*Hans Christian Garmann Johnsen,
Ida Lervik Midtbø and Richard Ennals*

The role of organisations

Organisations play an important role in modern society. Their role is probably underrated, because we often talk about markets or social processes as if the actor is an individual. However, the acting object is often an organisation or an individual acting from within an organisation. Perhaps one of the great inventions of modern society is the formal organisation. Prior to the modern area, there were structures of power related to family, tribe, religion or feudal power. The modern company is none of these. The British *Joint Stock Companies Act 1844* is often regarded as the first modern company law, followed by the *Limited Liability Act 1855* and the *Companies Act 1862*. By this type of legislation, a company became a person in legal sense. It could act, take responsibility, hire people and own things, but it was not a person. It came to change the structure of society.

Marx and Engels write in the Communist Manifesto:

> The manufacturing system took its place. The guild-masters were pushed on one side by the manufacturing middle class; division of labour between the different corporate guilds vanished in the face of division of labour in each single workshop. Meantime the markets kept ever growing, the demand ever rising. Even manufacturers no longer sufficed. Thereupon, steam and machinery revolutionised industrial production. The place of manufacture was taken by the giant, Modern Industry; the place of the industrial middle class by industrial millionaires, the leaders of the whole industrial armies, the modern bourgeois.
>
> *(Marx & Engels 1848/2002)*

The description by Marx and Engels of how modern industry created a divide between workers and owners, and how this divide also became a source of alienation, contributed to forming the modern conception of the role of organisations. Part of the picture is that present-day organisations have a much more integrated role in the modern society than they had earlier. In modern welfare states, your welfare and pensions are defined by your affiliation and work. Organisations are tax collectors on behalf of society, and social work and social networking happens within organisations. Organised work is so central to the modern state that people outside organised working life are seen as a "problem". At the same time, people are concerned about what organisations might do. We argue here that there is a potential in reconsidering the organisation. This potential can be seen as an innovation opportunity. It can create a space for entrepreneurial engagement. Here, we argue why we think this is an opportunity.

Our main argument is that current organisational thinking is a response to the social and economic environment in which it was developed. Therefore, much organisational thinking originates from the second stage of industrial development, the mass production stage, while the criticism and moderation of classical organisational thinking has been developed within the third stage of industrial development, in the post-capitalist or knowledge society.

A considerable part of the organisation theory that developed after World War II had the classical divide between labour and capital (owners, managers) as its background, and at the same time, it tried to show how to overcome the divide. The remedy, to large extent, was to make work more meaningful and to utilise human resources within the organisation. McGregor's 1960 book the *Human Side of Enterprise* can be taken as an example. He talks about theory X and Y, where X is the thinking about people based on the ideas that organisations are technical systems, and people are part of it as part of a machine. Theory Y is the modification of X where more attention is given to human needs. As we argue here, organisational thinking is still influenced by this divide and takes that as background for the conceptualisation and discussion; organisations are both formal and dialogical.

Why should we rethink the way we conceptualise corporation? One argument is that it can make organisations more innovative. For example, the re-industrialisation of Europe is due to companies integrating in value chains and helping develop value throughout the chain. This requires competences of communication, dialogue and innovation. Companies in high cost countries, in order to meet global competition, combine management concepts and methods with specific contextual, historical and cultural patterns. In the Norwegian case, this means combining insights from both dialogical and structuring organisational processes, and the dialogue extends beyond a narrow definition of the value chain. Companies are increasingly focusing on continuous improvement and are involving employees. Many have adopted business development ideas, like business systems, but often in a pragmatic way. This continuous improvement activity has resulted in cleaner production processes, more sustainable work places, increased dialogue and compliance with local environmental needs. However, this way of approaching workplace innovation and development requires a balancing of business-design principles, where both formal structuring and dialogical participation play important roles, as we argue in Box 12.1.

How relevant is the divide from the earlier part of the industrial era when discussing contemporary and future challenge for organisations? Organisations are still about organising labour in a productive way, but can we think of more innovative ways of doing this. The question is not new. Already we see that the growth of more network forms or organisations and new internet platforms has created a new platform economy. However, our focus is the organisation, and even in network or platform economies, there are organisations. Neither are we proposing abandoning organisations; our focus is on how to renew them.

There is a divide between human interests and organisational interests. It is a good idea to align organisational structure to utilise competencies within the organisation. We are now experiencing a more network based society. Are people linked to organisations, and do they identify with the organisation as they used to? Are organisational boundaries as relevant as they were before? Will organisations play the dominant role, as they do today, in the future? These are pending questions that we will try to address in this chapter. How can we move beyond the divide in analysing organisations? Technocentric and managerialist accounts have been the norm in business. This runs counter to the views of Adam Smith in his *Theory of Moral Sentiment* (1759), as he recognised the human implications of technological change. Today's companies are thereby facing conflicting calls to respond to the challenges of innovation and workplace development. Some of the conflicting ideas have roots in different knowledge regimes and rationalities. They are partly embedded in structuring decisions in the company, like business models, and partly in the beliefs, opinions and decision-making. Seeing the relation between human development from the perspective of theological change requires a certain way of thinking where human learning and cognition as well as practice is seen to be interrelated with the physical reality (Dreyfus & Dreyfus 1986).

An earlier example of this is Burns and Stalker, who in their 1961 book *The Management of Innovation* made the distinction between *mechanistic* management and *organic* management. With mechanistic management, they implied that there are differentiations of functions according to tasks, defined as abstract categories, differentiations between hierarchies in the organisation, a precise definition of rights and obligations, and rights and obligations translated into methods and responsibilities in functional positions. This implies a hierarchical structure of control and the localisation of specific knowledge in the hierarchy, with interaction being mainly vertical. This resembles many aspects of Max Weber's ideal type of bureaucracy (Weber 1947). With organic management, Burns and Stalker (1961) challenged the ideas of Frederick Winslow Taylor and his *Principles of Scientific Management* (Taylor 1911). Taylor's book became a standard reference, partly because large organisations such as Ford used it as a reference for their mass production plants in the auto industry, utilising economics of scale. Taylor, an engineer, argued that one could, through scientific methods, identify the optimal and most resource-efficient work routines. His argument resembled that of Auguste Comte (1798–1857), two generations earlier, who had made similar arguments in favour of the philosophy of positivism (Comte 1988). In the modern discourse, we see this divide in the discussion between socio-technical and dialogical approaches to organisations. Behind this discussion, there are assumptions about the nature of organisations.

Box 12.1 The Norwegian workplace discourses

There is a particular workplace research tradition in Norway, based on democracy projects in the early 1960s. The democracy project came as a result of co-operation from the 1950s onwards between the social partners and government, establishing a research milieu for workplace development in Norway. There was co-operation with the Tavistock Institute in London, and both Fred Emery and Eric Trist, from Tavistock, favoured the socio-technical approach to workplace development and emphasised the importance of autonomous teams.

Autonomous teams are relevant organisation forms today. In matrix organisations, organisational roles are ambiguous. We find this in the sectors of maritime and oil and gas, where engineering is a crucial part of delivering the right product, at the right quality and on time. Projects are organised as autonomous work groups, given a mandate, a time horizon and a brief specification of the expected output. A person can be a leader and an employee in the same company; one can have many leaders related to the same task. The dichotomy of management versus employees now makes little sense. There can be flat and informal organisations, where employees significantly contribute to everyday and strategy decisions.

It was possible in Norway in the 1970s to develop workplace legislation that opened up participatory arrangements in companies without deep and dividing conflict, as seen in countries like Sweden and France. Participatory work systems and self-steering groups were seen as smart ways of organising businesses. The model was seen as the Norwegian or Nordic approach to democratic capitalism. In Norwegian work life in the beginning of the 1990s, most of the ideas of the democracy movement in the 1960s had been integrated into managerial practice. Decentralised solutions and participatory processes were absorbed into managerial recipes like Total Quality Management (TQM), Management by Objectives or Quality Circles.

Modern manufacturing companies combine expert knowledge and knowledge derived from praxis. Awareness of responsibility and sustainability issues has to be comprehensive. Future co-workers, given the further degree of automation and knowledge-intensive processes and systems, require the role of the expert and the "blue-collar worker" to merge. The learning perspective, with knowledge transferred from the expert to the others, becomes increasingly important. Dialogue is pivotal, linking bottom-up improvement processes and top-down strategy.

Many manufacturing companies adopt business systems based on Lean thinking. Business systems relate to daily routines and are task oriented at a level that the employee can influence. They integrate action and thinking, with an emphasis on action that can be measured, controlled and supervised, and so it resonates with more economically oriented management thinking. On the other hand, it is transparent and impersonal and creates a common commitment from top to bottom. It has the effect of redefining roles and power relations in the company. Everybody becomes subordinate to the "system". The introduction of business systems like Lean has happened without large conflict; management has acted as support, but the process is often driven at operator level, going from tacit knowing and production procedures to a formalised explicit system. Workers have seen the benefit of making the workplace safer for everyone.

We have observed that business systems have been adopted in a pragmatic way and are balanced with other features of the Norwegian work-life tradition, such as participation and union involvement. There is a value chain, not only in time but also across time. Unions and local community are culture carriers. Learning is central to organisations in the Knowledge Society and Knowledge Economy. Workers need to be empowered to use their own experience, skill and tacit knowing as engaged actors. Thus, Norwegian practice has balanced organisational design principles, bottom up and top down, with a focus on efficiency and innovation. These approaches to continuous improvement imply engagement and involvement, presupposing dialogue with employees and communities.

We have observed that although companies have adopted the new business system, they still retain strong elements of the dialogue tradition. In fact, we observe that companies balance different organisational design principles. The contrasts between the different approaches involved in this balancing act are based on different ways of thinking. For example, the business system seems to emphasise a form of operative and self-binding rationality, while dialogue is based on a reflective and sometimes self-expressive rationality (subjectivity, authenticity, etc.). This book discusses and explores these and similar rationality forms and how they compete or might be combined in organisations.

There may be problems ahead in Norwegian and European industry. Many companies are now foreign owned, reducing strategic co-ordination potential at local and regional level. Norway is a high wage, high cost economy, and production can be relocated. Norwegian industries, facing the challenge of global competition, need to emphasise the experience, skill and tacit knowing of their workers. If their focus is on ever-increasing automation, jobs may not stay in Norway. There are also challenges to Scandinavian and Norwegian models, such as that innovation should be socially responsible (Ekman et al. 2011). The model can promote stability. Tripartite co-operation in Norway exemplifies this, as does close collaboration between political authorities and companies (Johnsen & Ennals 2012). New technology, new information areas, and man/mashing relation, sustainable work places (Docherty et al. 2008), are some of the issues ahead for companies. The values and social foundations of Nordic societies are the basis of the discussion. Social values have equivalents in organisations through broad participation and democratic election of worker representation for the board of directors. These values meet the competitive demands of a globalised world, where innovation is central.

In line with the argumentation above, we argue that there is a series of divides in the discussion of organisations: organisations as self-centred versus social systems; as technologically driven versus human-driven systems; as irresponsible versus responsible systems; as background for social structuration and differentiation, creating social divides; as drivers for change versus obstacles for change. We also argue that the way we perceive the organisation has implications for how we perceive that organisation's ability to handle future tasks. We argue that this fundamental perception of the nature of organisations can be grouped into two main ideas: organisations as technical systems and organisations as human systems.

Organisations as technical systems

Modern companies grew out of industrialisation and modernisation in the early 1800s. The big leap in this development came when organisations were given the properties of a subject. Before that, organisations in the formal sense were firms, meaning the enlargement of a person. It was the signature of a person. The modern joint stock company is a limited liability company or a public limited company, meaning that the owner or the persons behind the company are only in a limited sense responsible for what the company does. At the same time, the company is given juridical rights. It can own things, make contracts, hire people, have opinions in the public debate and influence politics, to mention a few. In short, the co-operation, specifically when it is a certain size, becomes an actor in society. We talk about company interests, for instance.

Henry Mintzberg, in his 1979 book *The Structuring of Organizations*, captured this development well when he called one of the five organisational types he identified *machine bureaucracy*. One can emphasise *bureaucracy*, but one should also emphasise *machine*. Max Weber had around 1900 described modern bureaucracy as an impersonal social structure; however, the concept of a machine brings us closer to the core of the modern corporation (Weber 1947). Similarly, Chris Argyris in his 1957 book *Personality and Organization: The Conflict between System and the Individual* described the individual as a subject and argued that self comes into conflict with the non-human properties of the organisation.

A machine is a technical system that, when started, moves on its own. Humans construct it, but the machine often has power beyond human beings. Humans may try to steer the machine. If it is a car, a human can force it in different directions, but that machine also has power of its own and can turn out to be hard to manoeuvre. We argue that the machine is a good metaphor for more substantial aspects of the modern corporation. There seems to have developed a meaning of corporations and organisations as something that have an *essence of their own*. By this, we mean, that organisations in the form of corporations of different kinds have a place in society as something non-human we have to comply with, take into account and refer to. It represents a non-human voice in society. This perspective on organisations goes beyond the argument by Taylor about scientific management. Taylor described a sort of organisational determinism, wherein individuals had to comply with the requirement of the corporation's needs. The type of essence of organisations is related to how the whole concept of cooperation is constituted in our perception of reality.

It is partly as a result of this that organisational theory started, after WWII, to give organisations social and human properties like learning, memory, culture, knowledge, identity and resources (Argyris & Schön 1978; ; Brooking 1999; Fuller 2002; Hatch & Schultz 1997; March 1991; Penrose 1959; Schein 1985). We do not argue that these theories explicitly refer to organisations as technical systems; however, they have in common that they argue that the properties of organisations are not a result of a particular human being; they are not something that necessarily change when human beings leave or enter an organisation. They are properties of the organisation per se.

This thinking is consistent with the idea that organisations are something autonomous and non-human, which is what we refer to when we describe the organisation as *a technical system*. Understanding organisations in this way is to see them as a reality, as something we have to comply with, as something exogenous. It is to argue that organisations have some sort of *nature*. The classical work by Ranald Coase (1937), *The Nature of the Firm*, exemplifies this, as does the later work of Oliver Williamson (1981) on *Transaction Cost Economics*. Both try to identify the core of organisations, their necessary elements, things we have to comply with. One can see it as a form or realism or *naturalism*: Organisations have a core nature that define what they are, what they can do and what they are likely to do.

It is in line with this naturalism that organisational theory has tried to humanise organisations. *Corporate Social Responsibility*, *Creating Shared Value* and *Triple Button Line* (Elkington 1997; Porter & Kramer 2011) are concepts that in different ways address this issue, trying to make the corporation "beast" more civilised, or, as in the case of Porter and Kramer (2011), to argue that this civilisation is actually inherent in the corporation's nature. It is the same way of thinking that we find in *Human Relations* (McGregor 1960). As the core nature of organisations is inhuman, it has to be modified with a deliberate attention to human needs. This is also the background for socio-technical thinking in organisational theory (Trist & Bamforth 1951). Here, the idea is that the technical system has requirements that can be mended and adjusted or designed to meet human needs. This thinking is not completely technologically deterministic, but it is assumed that technology is a denominator for the possibilities in organisations, and thereby the challenge is to adjust it according to human needs as well as possible.

This implies that seeing organisations as technical systems is a way of thinking of organisations as reality and nature that we somehow need to understand and adjust. A large part of the debate about organisations based on this thinking is how this modifying can happen, how organisations can be civilised and if it is meaningful to do so. Some would argue that modifying the nature of the firm is only doing harm. Milton Friedman (1970) is often referred to as an exponent of this view. It is an argument with a certain logic; if you believe that there is a true nature of the firm, logically, firms should be true to their nature. Based on the same way of thinking, attempts to modify the working of corporations can be seen as simply a form for normative and ideological bias for which it is difficult to give an argumentative foundation. Those who believe in the nature of the firm would naturally question the modification of organisations in the same way as one can ethically question the right to manipulate or modify any other part of nature or humans.

Organisations as human systems

This is why an alternative to looking at organisations as technical systems is a necessary precondition for taking a completely different approach to what they are and how they work. Such an alternative is to see organisations as *human systems*. The emphasis here is not on systems but humans; that is, organisations and corporations are merely seen as frameworks that individuals make in order to work together. In this thinking, corporations start with people and end with people. People choose technology, people make decisions and people divide labour between them. There is no core of, or nature of, the firm or corporation beyond human decision. Organisations are human constructions.

A particular discourse within this framework is the "Human-Centred" discourse. The "Human-Centred" discourse was based on dialogue and initiated by manufacturing engineers. The "Skill and Technology" discourse had inputs from philosophers and diverse professionals, including engineers. It was acknowledged that "there is no one best way". Kuhn (1962/1970/2000) noted that those who challenge conventional paradigms are normally evaluated against those same paradigms. Human-Centred Systems approaches are not always successful in business terms (Ainger et al. 1995). They start with people, in contrast to major national programmes like the UK Alvey Programme in Advanced IT, which were technology driven. Another strand in Human-Centred discourse was the conversion from defence to civil production, which had implications for people and organisations and a political flavour (Ennals 1986).

A link can be made with work on language and discourse by Toulmin and others after World War II, with an impact across the disciplines. With a technical background in physics, Toulmin worked on wartime radar before returning to philosophy (Toulmin 1958). He was early to move on from positivism to an approach based on language. His work with his teacher Wittgenstein helped him to make the transition (Wittgenstein 1953). Austin (1962) and Searle (1979) took the debate on speech acts forward. Toulmin was concerned with argument and reason and their use. His focus became the history of ideas, in which he saw major thinkers in their human contexts, with human faces and frailties. He challenged the myth of an exact scientific language, and then worked on Action Research and Regional Development projects in Sweden. He was concerned with European Union (EU) policy development. In the focus on EU integration, the significance of globalisation had been understated.

The case for Human-Centred systems brings together theory and practice, with a strong base in manufacturing industry practice. Sections of industry are already precariously dependent upon machine-centred systems. Such systems are typically highly synchronised and co-ordinated but frequently lack robustness; they are inadequately equipped to deal with disturbances and uncertainties. Cooley (1987) has challenged conventional models of science. At Lucas Aerospace, he had urged a move from defence to civil production, with a focus on socially useful production, which required organisational culture change. Cooley challenged a characterisation of science in terms of repeatability and emphasised human insights and expertise, with cultural references back to the Italian Renaissance. He offered an agenda of socially useful production. Rosenbrock (1989), criticised the focus on explicit knowledge and highlighted the importance of the tacit knowing of expert engineers. Rosenbrock explained that he would not use computers and automation to reject human abilities and skill but would co-operate with them to make them more productive. He applied socio-technical design principles at a deep level in technology. Brödner (1990), based on his own extensive engineering experience, set out the model of Anthropocentric Systems. Cooley noted that the extraordinary success of German manufacturing industry and its export performance arises from the vast reservoir of skills and knowledge that employers are able to draw upon". For Brödner, the worker deals with qualitative subjective judgements, and the machine deals with quantitative elements. Corbett, Rasmussen and Rauner (1991) considered the social and engineering design of computer-integrated manufacturing (CIM) systems. The book discusses and develops concepts and methods of inter-disciplinary collaboration between engineers, social scientists and users in the process of developing "Human-Centred" production technology. Human-centredness was transformed into a more holistic, participatory and inter-disciplinary approach to Human-Centred CIM systems.

In the Human-Centred discourse, the focus is on individual professional skill and reflection along with tacit knowing, which is not captured by computer systems. It is a distinct epistemological focus and makes use of dialogue through Dialogue Seminars, which is discussed in Chapter 11. This pays less regard to formal academic disciplines and institutions as the basis of knowledge. The starting point is practical experience, skill and tacit knowing. Rather than precise explanations in terms of cause and effect, the intention is to find areas of mutual understanding, when we "know how to go on", with continuing dialogue. Among fellow residents in the same region, we may expect to find shared understandings and meanings. This is important for sustainable regional development. Thus, Human-Centred thinking focuses on dialogue as a source of knowledge. The relevance of the Human-Centred discourse relates to today's industry: The essential features of successful knowledge distribution derive from the participation and engagement of the workforce. Industry needs to maintain close awareness of the leading edge in science and technology but must recognise that management decisions result from interventions by managers who are engaged with the company and in dialogue with the workforce. This links to the discussion about responsibility.

A broader perspective on organisations as human systems, can be related to the thinking of Jürgen Habermas (1984). He sees the modern organisation as developed from pre-conventional via conventional unto post-conventional. The pre-conventional is related to an authoritarian system and interests activate co-operation. In conventional action, roles are more predominant and norms are guiding the activity. While in the post-conventional situation, action is related to discourse. It is supposed that these three levels of convention are related to an increasing level of rationality. The assumption is that critical discourse will remove irrationality since reality will dominate discourse, while authority tends to increase primitively: mysticism, and symbolism. Towards an authoritarian system, loyalty, relation to tribe, organisation of group, egocentrism and obedience of order are important moral elements, while in the discourse situation, voluntary interaction, respect for procedures and striving for truth are essential elements. In between these two extremes, there is conventionalism, wherein norms and the feeling of duty are essential. Thus, such a post-convectional organisation is a human system.

Habermas sees formal rules as stabilising the instability that might result from discussion where individual interests do not produce co-ordinated solutions and therefore threaten to ruin social stability and progress. As organisations are functional in a sense that creates an underlying tension in the employees' relation to them, contextual design has, in normative terms, to be made to make it meaningful for employees to be involved. This implies that an organisation can be a human system and still comply with formal rules.

The workplace is a functional context, a type of context that induces non-involved strategic action (alienation). In order to change this through communicative action, the context has to meet formal requirements. That is, formal structures (e.g. that secure participation), the use of power and the general culture of trust have to correspond with normative ideals of involvement. These are fair norms. Employees might be involved and still "live with pluralism" (Gustavsen 1992). The communicative dimension in Habermas's system is a direct contrast to the conventional idea of common culture and common values. For Habermas (1984), communication and dialogue do not require common norms in the sense of pre-defined and comprehensive values and goals. Rather, communication in the sense of an unconstrained dialogue requires some open-ended universal rules of just conduct. To the extent that common culture means more equality and less dissent, it will be contrary to communicative processes.

Still, somehow, the plurality of individual meanings and arguments has to be restricted by cultural values and norms in order for decisions and common actions to be made. Habermas's communicative theory is based on the fact that interests are not a pre-political phenomenon. Habermas sees democracy not primarily as a negotiation arena for pre-defined interests. Rather, interests are developed and formulated and reformulated in a discourse. With that, a division between two types of action emerges: communicative action and strategic action. Communicative action is aimed at one's own understanding and articulation of own interests in a critical discourse with others. There are also arenas for strategic action distinguished by interest articulation and interest negotiations, but these are distinctly different from communicative arenas. Subsequently, in a post-conventional way of thinking, corporations are human systems. It implies that concepts like CSR (Corporate Social Responsibility) or CSV (Creating Shared Value) have no meaning. and nor does socio-technical thinking. Organisations are by nature human discourses and decisions, therefore; any discussion about good and bad decisions is simply a matter of human discourse. This leads to a question of how these discourses are developed/evolving, how they are taken into consideration in managing the organisation and what implication this has for different organisations.

Beyond the divide

The two basic ideas about organisations and corporations underlie much of the discussion that we see today. There is considerable discussion within the two camps but very little discussion between them. The two ideologies or philosophies live side by side. The technical system ideas look at the human system ideas as a romantic idealisation of pre-modern society; the human system thinkers look at the technical system idea as a misconception of reality. However, the kind of mechanistic tasks described by Burns and Stalker (1961) are hardly seen as valid for employment in 2018. Especially in modern society, employees are required to not only undergo tasks but also to develop and improve these into more effective solutions. This calls both for changes in education, with more emphasis on creativity and critical thinking rather than reproducing the curriculum; and the argued autonomy of the employees. There are alternatives; post-structuralism offers an alternative way of thinking of organisation. Its proponents will see it as social constructions, as belief system and as artefacts. Also, Nicolas Luhmann (1981) has presented an alternative understanding of organisations as communicative systems that develop boundaries through meaning construction. Our argument is not that the two fundamental ideas of organisations – technical and human – are the only ones. Rather, the fundamental differences in understanding what an organisation and a co-operation are represent an obstacle for a constructive development of the discourse.

A further challenge we see in re-industrial era and modern (or postmodern) states is a workforce challenged by inter-disciplinarity. While at one time most colleagues had the same training and the leaders were the most skilled, we now face a situation of specialization where many workers have different competencies, skills and knowledge. The advanced technologies developed in the oil and gas industry would not be possible without different experts putting their heads together. It is not only industry that relies on workers skilful in cross-disciplinarity co-operation; as technology enters the sectors of health and care, inter-disciplinarity is called for. The notion of inter-disciplinarity changes the way many employees both execute their tasks and how the work should be organised. Tacit knowledge is a well-recognized phenomenon, but this is not sufficient to meet the challenges of tomorrow. In order to make use of tacit knowledge, organisations should make an effort to articulate these, not only to develop the organisation but also to empower each professional (alt. individual within the organisation.) This creates a space for autonomy, which can lead to a closer affiliation and more identity linked to the workplace. To articulate knowledge also opens the communication flow and expands both individuals' and organisations' knowledge base for further development.

An example of a description of a sustainable and responsible organisation can be found in Stilgoe, Owen and Macnaghten's (2013) framework for responsible innovation. This framework was originally designed for governing science and innovation projects for the UK Research Councils, but in several contexts it is applicable to other innovations as well, for example, organisational innovation. The framework claims four dimensions of responsible innovation, and for organizations' sake, this could be a way to undergo a process of responsibility: Anticipation, which demands a look into the crystal ball, imagining what the future might bring and the possible consequences of this; reflexivity, the willingness to take a critical stand on the organisations own practices and uncover the discourses in play; inclusion, not only amongst the members of the organisation but also of other actors and stakeholders connected to it, thereby creating a sense of ownership and involvement in order to develop the organisation further; and responsiveness, a crucial way of taking the above into consideration and actually changing in line with the content of the Norwegian model, described here.

Box 12.2 The Kodak moment of organisations

The disruptiveness of change:

In view of the knowledge society and technological change, one has to consider how one perceives the organisation.

The knowledge one failed to use:

Organisational thinking has emerged as a reflection of social and economic development and needs to adjust as these develop further.

Ability to adjust along with future changes:

In order to reconsider how we think about organisations, one has to be willing to set aside established assumptions. We have presented criticisms of the assumption that there is a divide between technologically driven and human-driven thinking in organisations and that human thinking should modify the technological and functional aspects of organisations.

The opportunity in the changes:

There is a need to close that divide and think of organisations as social phenomena with a role and responsibility in society, not as an add-on to their business but as their business.

Coping with conflicting perspectives on the organisation is a call for pluralism in organisational thinking, giving more room to individualisation and individuals. This should of course not be at the expense of having common goals. We have here described Norwegian workplace discourses. The argument we have developed from empirical observation is that in practice, there is a pragmatic adjustment of conflicting organisational principles. Practice, it seems, has moved farther than theory in coping with the requirements of the future. Our argument is that the future organisation and corporation cannot live in conflict with society and cannot be perceived as having a basic nature that is contrary to a sustainable society. The future needs an understanding of the organisation and the corporation that is consistent and in line with a sustainable society.

13

COPING WITH LEADERSHIP

The role of judgement

*Lars Harald Lied, Charles Barthold and
Hans Christian Garmann Johnsen*

Leadership in a disruptive world

We face a more complex and integrated world. The implication for organisations is that they should have a more comprehensive perspective on their activity than is often argued in management literature. What about the role of management or leadership? Is that part of the challenge? Is it causing problems or is it part of the solution? It has been argued that the financial crisis of 2007–2008 demonstrated the failure of many business leaders who were interested in immediate profit rather than thinking responsibly about the wider risks for society and their organisation (Stein 2013). In particular, Collateralised Debt Obligations (CDOs) demonstrated that leaders in the banking industry did not mind about destructive consequences brought about by the deregulation of financial markets. This led to a correlated "financialisation" of higher education and business schools, which led students and future leaders to think only about the best strategies to make money in the short term (Beverungen et al. 2013). This was connected to the fact that tuition fees increased considerably, forcing students to think as financial subjects in order to make a return on their investment in their studies. Studying would then be like managing a financial portfolio (Martin 2002).

Business schools are an important context in which to reflect on business and organisational leaders, because it is the higher education institution that trains them in many cases. Business schools give them the technical skills they need to perform leadership roles in organisations, such as accounting, human resources or management. Perhaps more profoundly, business schools shape their way of understanding society, politics and their role as leaders in order to contribute to an ethical and democratic society. The business school as structure was invented in the American context at the end of the nineteenth century to train future managers and leaders (Khurana 2007). The idea was to combine technical skills with a reflection on ethics and on what the role of the manager should be. In the same way that lawyers and doctors were trained in very specific ways that allowed them to constitute professions, with a degree of control from senior professionals on what should be taught and not taught or what represents a good practice or not, management was considered by many as a profession. However, after World War II and more rapidly from the 1970s onwards, business schools tended to sell products, in particular MBAs, to students who were treated as consumers as opposed to being future professionals. This led to an instrumental understanding of management knowledge that favoured the casting aside of the moral and ethical responsibility of managers as leaders. This was symbolised by the famous article by Milton Friedman in the *New York Times* (1970) which clearly mentioned that business ethics was not relevant, and that the only responsibility of business was to be efficient and make profits. This would contribute to the marginalisation of any thinking about the moral responsibility of leaders in business schools. Therefore, not surprisingly, business schools would train future business leaders to be efficient, irrespective of the ethical consequences for stakeholders. However, judgement is different from calculation, as had already been observed by Immanuel Kant (1788). It is the deeper quality of reflection, allying wisdom and making balanced decisions.

Thinking about changing business schools, and making them more able to train future responsible leaders, is relevant. From this perspective, the development of scholarship in sustainability and business ethics is positive. Another interesting line of experimentation could be to diversify the disciplines and the pedagogic approaches in business schools. For instance, Copenhagen Business School emphasises philosophy and humanities, so as to help business students develop their culture and their understanding of the social impact of business and management. This allows them, in particular, to understand ethical dilemmas or the challenges represented by economic and organisational problems. However, can we train judgement, even though the education of managers matters in shaping the psyche and the imagination of future leaders?

In this chapter, we try to argue and explain what this implies. Adam Smith, in his 1776 book *An Inquiry into the Nature and Causes of the Wealth of Nations*, argued that if everybody in the economy concentrated on doing their own, narrow piece of the activity as efficiently as possible, the *invisible hand* would see to it that the totality (economic order) would prosper. He had a good argument. As argued in the chapter on Humanism, even egoistic behaviour might have benign consequences. It was a theory that inspired Smith and also one that Friedman relies on. Many things in the economy are so complex that we cannot get the whole picture, even if we try to, so therefore it is a better strategy to concentrate on doing one's own job, rather than reflecting on consequences. Under certain systemic conditions, Smith's argument will work.

However, as has been pointed out by many commentators, Smith had some years earlier written a treatise, *The Theory of Moral Sentiments* (1759), wherein he challenges citizens to develop a decent, moral foundation for their actions. Much debate related to Smith is about the connection between these two sets of arguments: one calling for focus and optimising means against ends, the other urging people to see the wider context and principles they live within. One might argue for one over the other. Alternatively, one can see the two as two sides of a coin, an unsolved dilemma that we need to live with.

This dilemma becomes very visible in the discussion about *leadership*. Leadership is about getting things done, but it is also about making wise judgements. It is about pointing out direction and fulfilling a specific goal by utilising the resources available. The circumstances framing a situation will change in time and space, and bad leadership can create a Kodak moment with surprising and unwanted change. A contextual perspective on organisational leadership studies can help to ensure a direction and connectedness. A contextual approach frames the topic of leadership and gives it an understandable surrounding. Studies of leadership that do not address contextual impact may appear as the contrary (Zaccaro & Klimoski 2002). Leading a given situation calls for a combination of understanding the specific situation and the people involved in it, and the context in which it happens. It is about making things happen right here, right now, and creating organisational actions that promote defined goals, and at the same time knowing that these goals are sustainable. How should leaders think and behave in order to cope with the future? What traits will solve future leadership tasks, and what can be done to prepare for them?

Decomposing leadership

The scientific study of leadership study arose from the work of Max Weber, known as one of the founding fathers of sociology. He questioned status, legitimacy and authority and dedicated much attention to the tension between bureaucracies and leaders, arguing that the inevitable trend towards reasoning in every part of sociology made the leader's role not only increasingly important but also more problematic. Weber (1947) saw leaders in the role of a bureaucracy, where the main thing was to remove the randomness of individual judgement. Weber's idea of a modern organisation, part of what we earlier called the second stage in industrial development, had the mass production industry as an ideal; the reduction of waste, variation on the securing of equal quality throughout the production process. Routines, structure of command and predictability, were important preconditions for good leadership. Today, we might call this: management.

Compared with this classical idea of a leader, what is the contemporary discussion about leadership? One is critical approaches to leadership, which argues that leadership is a socially constructed phenomenon, which is always contested and actualised. Social interactions between individuals are the source of leadership as well as other organisational phenomena. Leadership, even if it is conceptualised as the ability of specific individuals to lead followers, is not something that can be understood outside specific cultures and social relations (Grint 2005). Individuals are recognised as leaders by followers because they correspond to a series of socially constructed values and norms. This aspect has been emphasised by many scholars whose work is described as Critical Leadership Studies (Collinson 2011; Gemmill & Oakley 1992). They have emphasised power and domination associated with leadership. Indeed, leadership legitimises and reinforces the power of specific individuals, as opposed to others (Calás 1993). This is associated with the fact that leaders are considered as heroes in a form of socialisation, which justifies their separation from the rest of the people or followers (Śliwa et al. 2013). In addition, leadership, especially in Western countries, tends to be articulated to a masculinist culture (Sinclair 1998). This implies that it is very challenging for women to become leaders because they do not fit the hegemonic norm of leadership. In the same way, it could be argued that leadership is racially constructed. In the Western context, individuals from ethnic minorities will find it more difficult to be recognised as leaders because they do not correspond to the mainstream norm. These potential problems associated with leadership entail a necessity to reflect about ways to democratise or distribute leadership (Gastil 1994).

The idea that leadership is judgement began to be discussed in Antiquity. The old Greek conceptions of *ethos*, *logos* and *pathos* might be a starting point. They were used by Aristotle in what is described as "ingredients of persuasion". They are known as "appeals" used in a rhetorical setting of persuading and influencing others to take a given point of view (Demirdöğen 2010, p. 191). Even though they have different meaning, all these old concepts can be embedded in the construction of the leader's role. They are modes of convincing the other part. Pathos (from the verb *pathein*) is about feelings. It indicates an emotion that arises in us independent of our own free will. It is "knowledge created from being passively affected by external sources" (Eikeland 2007, p. 352) and not something we do. Pathos is the emotional appeal to an audience where you try to create a response and a commitment based on emotions. By framing the message in a context that appeals to emotions of the recipient, the aim is to create support for an argument or point of view. This context can be transferred to the role of a leader when explaining common tasks and goals to achieve. Example: "This Company was built up over generations, and it is our common duty to develop it even further for our children."

Logos is a concept with different meanings. It would not be correct to reduce it to a modernistic, one dimensional, formal-rationalistic and non-lingual concept of reason (Papastephanou 2010). Without going into all facets of the logos concept, it would be natural to mention that the term "logic" is derived from it. The most common understanding of logos points to facts supporting a message. The receiver is convinced by reason and logical statements underpinning the point of view given. How can I persuade you to take my point of view by appealing to your sense of logic? Example: "She has won the six latest championships, and I find it likely that she will perform well in the next one too."

Ethos appeals to our ethical side. It is about the practical formation of a character (Papastephanou 2010). We all want to stand out as trustworthy individuals who conduct ourselves morally and ethically correctly, according to commonly accepted social guidelines. Ethic is derived from ethos, and it is about persuading someone through the credibility and the authority of the character giving the argument. If a person uses Ethos actively as a part of persuading, one can appeal to other values known as common in order to build support for another or new area of argument. Ethos is an important part of conducting leadership because it is an appeal based on credibility. This character appearance (Eikeland 2006) is important in creating loyalty to the leader as a person and to the decisions made. For example, when giving a speech, you choose the right vocabulary in order to underpin your line of argument in a way that is understandable to the audience. Pathos, logos and ethos constitute the characteristics that form the personality of a leader, and they belong to the generic part of being a leader. You as a co-worker evaluate your leader upon these concepts, and they influence factors like trust, dedication and motivation in a social interaction. These ancient descriptions of persuasion stand out as most contemporary, and we could argue "that most contemporary persuasion research is derived from the work of Aristotle in some way or another" (Demirdöğen 2010, p. 192).

Leadership seen from a work-life and socio-technical point of view is a matter of joining technological systems and social systems in a balanced way (Reason & Bradbury 2006, p. 80). There are both the personal and the contextual parts of leadership. The personal part is bound to the leader as a person, and it represents the characteristic of the leader that withstands the changes of time and space, the inner "core" of what we regard as leadership. Personal characteristics that form the foundation for trust and motivation are examples. These are core elements that we as humans appreciate regardless of the situation. They can be described as universal when it comes to validity, since they are commonly accepted and respected. The distribution between personal and contextual balance of leadership may vary due to the scenario and the people involved. There are many definitions of leadership, and to sharpen the focus of this chapter, two distinctive elements of leadership are included here. Zaccaro and Klimoski (2002, p. 6) argue that:

- Leaders' influence is grounded in cognitive, social and political processes.
- Organisational leadership is inherently bound by systems characteristics and dynamics, that is, leadership is contextually defined and caused.

Leadership, defined by traits and actions, should not be mixed up with administration or management, as pointed out by Philip Selznick in his 1957 book *Leadership in Administration: A Sociological Interpretation* (Selznick 2011). Kotter (1996) describes management as planning/budgeting, organising/staffing and controlling/problem solving. These administrative tasks form structures that create some predictability in a work-life situation. They help to guide us through the complexities of daily life. Leadership on the other hand is, according to Kotter (2008), establishing direction, aligning people and motivating/inspiring others. It is about the character arranging for change. It is about you and me influencing a process with our conduct (or lack of conduct) on the way to success or failure. Good overall results, in the long run, require a combination of both good management and leadership in order to gain sustainable solutions.

Taking an organisation into the future, identifying the opportunities that arise in the process and productively taking advantage of these opportunities are some of the things that are associated with leadership. Previously, leadership was linked to the steering and controlling of others within a hierarchy (top–down). Today, most organisations appear to be shifting towards a flatter structure emphasizing self-management, delegation and autonomy, with highly skilled workers and increasingly complicated products as well as services. The creation of opportunities by having less hierarchy with high levels of responsibility delegation has the potential to form new challenges with indistinct responsibilities in addition to power associations.

Leadership can be related to the virtue of governing within the framework of Plato's philosophy (Bloom 1991). Leadership in the context of management studies is related to the management of people and to the capacity to lead followers in an organisation. However, Plato usually does not mention leadership in the economic domain but rather in the military, as in *Laches*, or in the political domain, as in the *Statesman* (Cooper 1997). In Plato's *Republic*, philosophers govern the ideal city (Bloom 1991). Three types of citizens live in it: the artisans who produce it, the guardians who defend it and the philosophers who govern it. Therefore, the virtues of leadership would be those of the philosophers who govern the other classes of citizens. These virtues are connected to rationality and truth (Bloom 1991, Book VII). It is the love of wisdom, or philosophy, that provides the skills to lead. However, the skills of philosophy and rationality are learned through a careful training, starting with geometry and finishing with dialectic (the ability to reach truth through dialogue). Additionally, philosophers need to master discourse and rhetoric so as to persuade the other citizens of the city to perform specific types of activities. In particular, they can lie (Bloom 1991, p. 380b–c).

In other words, this is an idealist and elitist vision of leadership. Leaders need to master rationality and discourse; they need to know things and to persuade followers to act in specific ways. However, for Plato, the training to become a philosopher is the most appropriate route to a just leadership. In contrast, leadership, exercised by people mastering the art of discourse (rhetoric) but without the will to pursue truth, that is to say sophists or demagogues, would bring about negative consequences, and ultimately a republic without justice, for instance oligarchy or tyranny (Bloom 1991, Book VIII). This is related to Plato's critique of democracy (Bloom 1991, Book VIII), which, for him, would be a regime where demagogues through sophistry flatter the passions of the people instead of leading them towards a greater good, the Form of the Good.

Some insight into philosophy makes it easier to learn how to become a leader. In addition to wisdom, which is a specific virtue, philosophers need the virtues of courage, temperance and justice, which they share with the other members of the ideal city-state. This means that leadership, according to Plato, is not a natural gift like, for instance, charisma, as argued in social sciences (Weber 1947) and management studies (Bass et al. 1996). Plato argues that not everyone has the ability to successfully take the training to become a philosopher. In other words, leadership is a combination of nature and education. Finally, for Plato, there is a core of leadership, which is mainly wisdom (rationality) in addition to courage, temperance and justice. Unethical leadership would not be sustainable for Plato and might be equated to tyranny (Bloom 1991, Book VIII). The contextual part of leadership differs in time and space, and this is a major challenge. No single prototype of leadership applies to all situations (Lord, Brown, Harvey, & Hall 2001). These contextual elements tend to change more rapidly in a modern society as technology and information are taking their toll. These changes are inevitable, and they must be dealt with accordingly. Past, present and future leadership require different angles for approaching the task of leading.

Good leadership requires something from the person leading. One of the things is the ability to show empathy (old Greek – *empatheia*). When you show empathy, you put yourself into the emotional state of others. Seeing the world through the eyes of others "helps people to grow beyond egocentrism, so empathising with another is the antidote to human selfishness" (Reason & Bradbury 2006, p. 89). You use your own personal experiences together with the emotional expressions from the other person to understand their feelings. This is not based upon your own terms but on the other person's premises. Empathy creates social linkages and skills between humans (Day 2001). By listening to another person, you show dedication and genuine interest in that person's experiences (Reeve 2009, p. 436). The trait of empathy is an important part of social competence, and it is essential for our ability to socially interact. When you as a leader make decisions, you must take empathic evaluations into your considerations. How will this decision be understood and interpreted by my subordinates? Do they have previous experience that makes them vulnerable in this particular situation? Such reflections must be an embedded part of the leader role, and personal life experience is of great importance in this matter. Our emotional scale of feelings varies a lot between positive and negative emotions, and lived experience is most useful for a leader in this regard. A leader uses previous and personal experiences consciously and unconsciously in the daily practice of making decisions. You automatically compare a situation with your personal interpretation, and your reflections become part of the further handling. When a leader lacks the experience in question, s/he must make the decision without relevant references. Leadership is a craft with many dimensions, and missing personal experience may stand out as a missing dimension. A leader who experienced hardship and disappointments in life is better equipped, perhaps, to solve similar situations also in work life. The experience of coping with hardship is a dimension of leading that might be underestimated when it comes to learning potential. It is a kind of personal and tacit knowing, bringing more depth into the role of leading.

Leadership in a dialogical organisation

Dialogue as an instrument of improvement is well established in work life. Dialogical turns of development have shaped the work life we experience today (at least according to the Nordic Model), and democratic involvement and the need of autonomy have promoted this course. The involvement of all parties gives the opportunity to influence both processes and improvement work affecting your own work situation. Bjørn Gustavsen (1992) underlines that he derives theory from practice, and he "rejects a reliance on expert-led change" (top–down). This calls for the utilisation of knowledge from the shop floor or "bottom-up". The social interaction through dialogue facilitates better co-operation among the involved parties, and objectives appear more clearly. These are important issues to consider as a leader. The dialogue is also a medium for personal development, and a leader can openly invite personal feedback by the use of dialogue (authentic leadership). It is through others that you develop yourself. This active approach will help the leader to adjust the leadership conduct, and alignment to the expectations and the situation becomes easier. Practical examples showing dialogical impact will be commented on later.

The modern leader requires a good understanding of both the generic and the contextual part of leadership. Qualities that were previously considered to make a good leader may nowadays be considered less useful or outdated. It is about finding the right tool. Trying to provide a uniform definition of a good leader is unproductive. Modern leadership generally requires more adaptability to emerging changes. The generic part of leadership must be present. Coping with change is an element of modern leadership that is here to stay. Our ability and willingness to align to new and other challenges will determine whether we succeed in our future leadership.

The nature of work has gone through some drastic changes in the last century. Technical development has given us an increased access to goods and services. The ways we work, communicate and organise have been adapted along this journey. The rising need for knowledge and specialised jobs requires a different form of leadership compared to earlier days. Drücker (1994) refers to "The rise and fall of the blue collars" in his article "The Age of Social Transformation". Industrial blue collars' roles have been through an enormous transformation over the last 150 years. From being a peasant and then becoming an industrial operator, blue collars have become skilful and highly competent workers operating complex systems in an autonomous setting. This has resulted in the old-fashioned "top–down" leadership of controlling becoming outdated. Higher levels of competence and other organisational structures call for a facilitative approach when it comes to leadership. Employees are able to make good decisions by themselves, and future leadership will be based on sharing the responsibility. Co-workers trusted with responsibility usually step up and are eager to share leadership. This element of "sharing" does not apply only to the relation between the leader and the subordinate, but also to the relationship between the leader and the team (or other units). Shared leadership is a "dynamic interactive influence process in which team members lead one another to accomplish team goals successfully", and, according to Neck and Manz (2010, p. 96), "Shared leadership represents a next-generation model of leadership that holds promise for helping us as we work, play and live in teams." It is a precondition that the team members are able to lead themselves, lead others and be led in order to succeed in the practice of shared leadership. It must be managed correctly to avoid failures, but conducted properly: it has proven to be effective in terms of change management, research and development, military and top corporate executive teams. To develop the traits needed in future leadership, it takes personal maturation through social interaction over time.

Box 13.1 Diesel-gate

"Diesel-gate" in the VW industrial group may stand as an example. The Volkswagen (VW) Group was caught violating the US Clean Air Act. VW's Turbo-charged Direct Injection cars (TDI) produced between 2009 and 2015 were programmed intentionally to activate certain emissions during laboratory emission testing. This act was comprehended as a deceit by the market, and 11 million cars were called back for reprogramming. The economic consequences for VW were severe, and it need time to restore a trusted position in the market. VW stocks dropped by 25% as a result of the scandal (Cue 2015, p. 15). The VW Group hopes to overcome the problems by taking a new approach to sustainability. They plan to shift from diesel to electric and hybrid cars. Anyhow, the leader must stand out as a responsible representative on behalf of the company, and ethical issues will be important on the agenda of "tomorrow".

The four stages of industrial evolution referred to earlier have given us different changes in terms of social development. Social classes have arisen and then vanished. The industrial worker became a large group of the population as a result of industrial mass production. They organised themselves, and the unions became strong. New ways of producing emerged, and there was a need for higher and more specialized skills in production. The number of unskilled industrial workers has reduced considerably, and union power has been declining just as fast (Drücker 1994). In general, technological development has helped us to improve our standard of living considerably as compared to previous stages of development.

Leadership is directed towards humans. Humans have needs that must be satisfied in order to perform well. We are social beings that like to be a part of something bigger than ourselves. We enjoy being a part of a group along with others, and we are motivated by contributing to a common goal. The sensation of making a difference by utilising your own abilities is most important. To this could be added two factors that are an important part of good judgement: ethics and knowledge. Unethical decision-making behaviour in organisations has gained increased focus (McCabe, Ingram & Dato-On 2006). Customers want to act responsibly, and they will behave accordingly. According to Gini (1997, p. 34) ethics "is about the assessment and evaluation of values, because all of life is value-laden". The impact of ethics will increase also in work life, and leaders must meet these requirements by aligning (recall ethos). Taking responsibility as individuals and organisations is a part of the identity, and leadership by example is vital. In some examples, you will see the managing director playing an active part in the brand-building activities of a company. Your personal characteristics as a leader become a part of the company brand.

Practical knowledge is built on experience and can be harder to utilise since it holds characteristics that are often bound to a person. Practical knowledge can be developed through continuous evaluation in different stages of organisational development. A leader must make a balance between inputs from the past and the challenges of the future. One cannot enter future challenges back to front. Reflection as a tool of improvement can be used actively for both individual and team based units. A structural layout can be helpful in order to understand how to navigate between situations of reflection and levels. In Box 13.2, we give a practical example of how leadership is performed today: the Lean leader.

Box 13.2 The Lean leader

An example from Norwegian industry can be used to visualise the potential of reflection in leadership practice. It is a producer of high tech products for an international market, and the factory employs about 700 employees. As a part of the company's improvement work, the focus of Lean practice has been emphasised over a number of years. As a part of the improvement work, the company joined a national Lean Management programme in order to utilise leadership that supported Lean practice. "Leading improvements" was defined as the goal of the project, and the project started up in the autumn of 2016. One of the main goals was to produce improvements that have practical implications. Previously, Lean efforts were mainly targeted at process improvement within the production. This Lean Management project was about improving the leading skills needed to conduct and to facilitate good Lean performance within the production environment. Twenty-four leaders on every level were engaged, and the union was a natural co-partner as the project progressed. An action research based model of approach was selected. The principles of action research fitted the culture, history and identity of the company and therefore became an obvious choice. Involvement, practice and empowerment were defined as important criteria, and the participants' experience was given much attention (the average length of employment in the company was 21 years). During group sessions in the project, the leaders defined that visible and facilitative practices of leading within the frame of clear and visual goals were preferable. The company has a well-educated and skilled workforce on every level, and a major focus for these leaders was to utilise this potential in the production process. During the group sessions, the importance of the foreman role was highlighted. Their actions should underpin the good work already established in the teams. Facilitative skills stood out as an important skill a leader needs to master. A facilitative approach recognises the synergies and the potential of engaging the whole workforce. The capabilities of the employees are essential. The reflections on these matters also led to the confession that the leaders did not have the right skills needed to coach and facilitate for optimal (and defined) practice. Previous practice in leading was more focused on controlling (old-fashioned leadership), and it did not require such skills as coaching. It is not right to describe the leadership of the first-line leaders as old-fashioned or "Tayloristic", but the skills of coaching and facilitating were specifically defined as a "missing link" in the reflective process. The group sessions defined measures to fill in the gap, and the human resources (HR) department arranged a common leader training programme for both the leaders and the employee representatives. This training programme lasted seven days.

During group sessions in the Lean Management project, one of the first-line leaders came up with a good idea. He indicated that the company used appraisal interviews as a part of its improvement efforts. These dialogues take place annually, and they are organised as conversations between the leader and the employee (dialogue). Evaluation of practice and goalsetting are important subjects in these individual talks. The first line leader stated: "since we mainly organise our departments team wise, we should also organise these appraisals team wise. The object is to improve the team. This proposal indicates moving up from a "personal" to an "organisational" level in the "time and scope" table (Table 13.1). This issue was not followed up directly, but it is a good example of reflective awareness from a leader who has been in that position for 25 years! This leader also indicated that they lacked the right knowledge or experience to conduct a team-based appraisal. This statement also shows insight into one's own needs and limitations. Practical reflection can open vital doors if you organise for it. This goes for both the personal and the organisational level in the figure.

Experience from this Lean Management project (so far) shows that the leaders in the project were able to define the optimal knowledge base needed, reveal skills that were lacking and then come up with measures to fill in the gap. All those inputs to improve came as a result of the leaders reflecting on their own roles and conduct in retrospect. They were given time and space to reflect upon their own professional conduct, and the outcome showed a high degree of introspection. This insight turned out to be practically useful, and actions were defined in order to improve. The powerful tool of reflecting has diminished in a world marked by information and stress. Maybe we depend too blindly on technology and systems, and our self-reflective capacity has become less important. Donald Schön (1983) defined the expressions "reflecting in action" and "reflecting on action." He emphasised the practical learning potential in these settings for professionals, and these theories have been most influential ever since. Schön's theories have been interpreted differently depending on the position taken on them using his theories. This chapter uses his theories in the framework of improving the conduct of work-life leadership for the future. Since knowledge creation and experience are important inputs to the conduct of leading, it feels natural to link Schön's theories to practical leadership. These theories can be vital elements in succeeding with future leadership. They are most relevant today and in times to come.

Employees must be guided in a way that enables them to solve problems on their own. The reflective processes of the Lean Management project documented the same findings. Based upon the fact that our fellow co-workers are more skilful, the first-line manager should not solve every occurring problem. Co-workers are more than able to solve problems by themselves, and then the leader avoids involvement in this matter. "Monkey on your back" is a metaphor for a problem that besets you and will not go away. We are continuously in a process of change, and we must consequently align to it. The rising complexity of work life calls for a leader who is highly focused on a few goals, understands the influence of the surroundings and uses the principle of simplicity. They need to "go into themselves" and do some self-reflective inquiry. You are not supposed to solve all challenges yourself, but you need to engage your organisation in a way that accomplishes the goals set. Your handcraft as a leader should function as a catalyst to ensure that the right things happen.

The Lean Management project produced some practical and definite examples of what dialogue can produce. All departments use Lean Blackboards as a part of their Lean work. The production starts up with a co-ordinating meeting every morning. One of the first-line leaders experienced fewer requests for clarification after the introduction of these meetings. He stated

> that "suddenly my phone went silent". After a short discussion, the group concluded that the dialogue of clarification carried out in the Lean Blackboard meeting replaced what previously was looked at as stressful one-on-one clarification. The formal dialogue in the meeting produced practical results that made a positive impact on the situation of the leaders.
>
> Another summary from the experiences of the Lean Management project was the practice of visible leadership. The first-line leader realised through reflection that visibility is irreplaceable. You need to be physically present, and you must show your dedication by listening to your co-workers. Technological solutions or remote management does not fulfil the human needs of co-workers. "Go to GEMBA", and "Walk the talk" is crucial when it comes to first-line leadership in an industrial setting. Co-workers want close interaction with their leader, and that aspect is often shown in employee surveys as well. The issues of presence and visibility are important contributors in the socio-technical balance.

Flexibility and adaptiveness become more important due to circumstances that influence those situations we should lead. The changes that an organisation must deal with are increasing in pace and complexity (Yukl & Mahsud 2010). Technological complexity, new cultural values, a more diverse workforce and increased globalisation are mentioned as factors influencing our daily life. Schön argues that society overemphasises what he refers to as "technological rationality". Rationality based on technological advances and structures overshadows the ability to learn from practical surroundings. Technological rationality is, according to Schön, "the heritage of Positivism" and the "Positivist epistemology of practice" (Schön 1983, p. 40). From a technological rationality point of view, professional practice is a process of problem solving. The practitioner (or leader) must construct problem-solving solutions based upon situations that appear "puzzling, troubling and uncertain." Schön argues that we as practitioners must "convert" a problematic situation to a (specific) problem by making sense of an uncertain situation that initially made no sense. This theoretical description is to a great extent a definition of challenges we meet in our daily leadership.

Experiences from the Lean Management project showed that the leaders benefited from internal networking. Cross-divisional arenas boosting flow of best (and equal) practice. The establishment of such arenas was defined as one of several actions of improvement in the project. The reflections in the group sessions also indicated the importance of the leader taking an active part in facilitating flow of "best practice." Communication and leadership are strongly linked, and leadership communication is the "transfer of meaning by which individuals influence a single person, a group, an organisation or a community" (Barrett 2006, p. 21). Effective leadership is largely a matter of communication, and a leader must use understandable words together with actions that promote the right response among employees. Communication is often exposed to interference in an organisational setting.

Interference like poor formatting, unclear messages and cultural misunderstandings weakens the communication, and future leaders must counteract accordingly.

An important part of conducting leadership is setting direction (Kotter 2008, p. IX). The leader should visualise the targets for an organisation and draw up a clear picture of how they should be accomplished. The leaders participating in the Lean Management project clearly stated the importance of visual and attainable objectives. It is a part of telling everybody where we are going. We unite over a common objective. In society and work life, we are overloaded with information, both useful and useless. An important characteristic of the future is to separate out what you need and ignore everything else. Complexity is a challenge when it comes to leadership, and in his article "The coming of the new organisation", Drücker (1988, p. 7) underlines the importance of setting defined and few goals. Information-based organisations need simple and clear objectives that can be translated into particular actions. One or a few clear objectives help the organisation to navigate through the complexity that influences us as professionals. The leader of today and tomorrow guides educated and skilled employees who are highly capable of doing their specialised line of work. The leader must not interfere in professional details but rather focuses on motivating and creating a unity around a clear objective; compare it with a conductor interfering with a single musician in an orchestra. Even though Peter Drücker wrote his article in 1988, it is most relevant today and probably will also be so in the future. The utilisation of professional skills builds enthusiasm.

Experiences from the Lean Management project show clearly that the leaders feel short of time. There is always something happening, and strict priorities must be made. Statements like "I do not have time to lead" came up during the group sessions, and it describes a normal working day as stressful and full of administrative obligations. Filling in reports, statistics and other software-based activities have drawn our attention as leaders away from our employees and into the computer screen in our offices. We have become "screen leaders", with limited attention focused on the inter-human perspectives of doing business. Occurring problems are often solved by installing new software, and that is not a measure that solves the root problem. It is close to thinking about Donald Schön's technological rationality. Thus, judgement is something beyond this kind of rationality.

The leaders are responsible for establishing a vision, showing a few clear goals where knowledge stands out as important. The value and visibility of knowledge must be highly regarded at every level of the organisation. This overall directing of knowledge must hold an understanding for both technological and social knowledge that promotes both innovation and progress. The leader must actively organise for a company culture wherein knowledge is respected and acknowledged. The organisation of a workplace is important to how we succeed in creating and utilising knowledge in a professional setting. Without going into the details of how to organise for technological and social knowledge creation, it is essential that the leader brings this consciousness into every stage of doing business. Practical matters, of how you organise both the workplace and the social interaction in it, influence the creation and flow of knowledge. This goes for both explicit and tacit knowing.

Since knowledge has become so essential to us, it must be followed up by a leadership that empowers all employees. We have become highly skilled, and we want to use and develop our competence in a satisfying way. *Autonomy* is a key word when it comes to utilisation of empowerment among humans in a professional setting. Freire (2000, p. 101) says "Some work to keep the structures, and some work to change them". It is a responsibility of a leader to organise a structure that empowers the knowledge of the employees. Freire never uses the expression "empowerment" in his book "Pedagogy of the oppressed", but he strongly argues that people cannot be ruled by a "top–down" system that does not allow for learning and abilities to be used. Everybody must have the same opportunities. The dialogue is the medium for progress, and the people are challenged to bring their best argument to the table. This challenge makes people use their knowledge and experience in a stimulating way. They feel their contribution is important to the improvement process, and they sense that they are a part of something bigger. In many ways, psychological empowerment is built on inner motivation (Spreitzer 1995). Empowerment becomes even more important as the level of education and knowledge increases. A gap between yourself and the situation you are facing brings on frustration if you are not allowed to take part in closing the distance. Employees in a modern and professional setting want to feel free and to make use of their skills. A leadership that facilitates the use of knowledge is inspirational, managing to make knowledge productive and to make the organisation and its employees flourish.

The future leader must show good judgement

What will be the major changes in the future? What will be the leadership tasks solved by the leader of tomorrow? Kotter (1996) draws up a picture of the expected changes to come in his book *Leading Change.* Changes in organisational structures, systems and culture will impact our daily work life in a major way. The structures of organisations in the future will change from multileveled to fewer levels. Flatter and simpler organisational structures give less administration and other leader challenges. Together with this change, there will be less focus on bureaucracy and administration. The continuous change in environments calls for more adaptability in the organisation. Adaptability must be gained through flexible structures and supportive information, backing not only the top management but also the whole organisation. All organisational levels need equal access to relevant information due to specialisation. Decision-supporting systems will not be for leaders only; they will be a more common property. Human needs and technology must functionally be merged so the dialogical and socio-technological design balances out. As mentioned in Chapter 9, we see a dualism in today's work life separating technology and humans. Industry 4.0 and its human–machine interface characteristics will address this question in an even stronger way. The leadership of tomorrow has the opportunity to narrow this dialogical/socio-technological gap by putting us (the humans) in a strong and defined position. Our human needs must be aligned to the technology surrounding us in order to avoid alienation.

Companies and organisations often work within an international framework. Even local businesses, with local and domestic markets, often rely on international suppliers and connections. Specialisation impels networking and co-operation across borders. The "world is getting smaller" as technological development moves on. Global trends are not about producing the cheapest products any more. It is more a question of having employees capable of understanding what measures to use in order to succeed. How can we analyse available data in way that helps us to develop our organisations, activities and business conduct? How should we develop analytical business models that help us to succeed in global and domestic markets? One obvious way is to get access to the most gifted brains. Human capital is not expandable, and future fights over clever minds will increase. Attractiveness is and will be a key word, and organisations must offer a "whole package" in order to attract the best employees possible. Wages form only a fragment of this package, and issues like professional development, working environment and ethical profile will be essential when choosing your next employer. Building up an attractive profile of an organisation is a product of the leader making the right choices.

Globalisation of markets, labour and knowledge will continue to develop. Future leaders must accept and adapt to this contextual framework in the best way possible. This evolution creates new opportunities for those who understand and are able to utilise them. Mobility in the work force has become a common part of work life. Interaction between countries and companies creates together with social inequality a workforce in motion. Within this cross-cultural picture, a leader must deal with and take advantage of those occurring opportunities. Diversity is a capacity that a leader must understand, and some environments will experience a reduction in the homogeneity they have been used to.

All these contextual changes in the surroundings call for a continuous adaptation by the leader. Fixed leadership cannot solve complex and changing situations. "Authentic leaders foster the development of authenticity in the followers" (Avolio & Gardner 2005, p. 317), and authentic leadership calls for an open-minded attitude on the part of the leader. The leader demands feedback from the co-workers, and self-development is gained through interacting with others. This flow of feedback will support your development and the alignment needed to lead. Authentic leadership is based upon empirical knowledge, and it is only through practical experiences that you gain this type of insight. This practical experience will also be highly respected by your co-worker, since you know the problem through personal experience.

Leadership is workmanship, and it requires the use of the right tools. Due to complexity, the future calls for new tools, and you need to find them and use them in order to succeed. The creation of a good leader is supported by a person's ability to improve oneself through others. Social interaction helps such a development. Adult experiences influence our capacity to lead, and an active and self-critical approach will help us gain the inputs needed to solve future leadership challenges. This self-critical examination includes constructive and targeted use of reflection from action and the willingness to adjust your own behaviour. Time is a limited resource in today's work life, and difficult priorities must be made. These priorities do not necessarily mean that you reject your previously focused conduct, but you gradually adapt your actions as a leader to work differently and more "within" your professional setting.

Research indicates that we need to move beyond the traditional way of leadership practice. We organise our work life to be flatter and more team wise, and the average co-worker has become more educated and skilled. The role of leading has moved on from leading (and controlling) individuals to leading social processes, including groups and teams. The balance of power has changed along with this evolution, and modern leadership calls for more involvement and shared power. Impulses that bring us forward must pass both ways (top–down/bottom–up). The future leader must take these elements into consideration and try to involve the co-workers in a more shared leadership model. This calls for a stronger focus on the organisational level. It does not mean that a leader ignores the individual level, but it emphasises the importance of the teams as a common item in our organisational practice.

If you visualise leadership as a tree, the generic part would be represented by the roots. They grow slowly, appear strong and are less affected by external influence. Our personal traits form us as leaders and are represented by personality, knowledge and attitude. "This is who I am, and this is how I choose to do it based upon my experience." This generic part does also change, but not compared to the contextual part represented by the tree above the ground. Here you find all sorts of different influences. All those elements described previously will influence the contextual part of the leadership. The influence will change like the wind in terms of direction and strength. "Decisions under uncertainty has become a term of art" states Schön (1983, p. 239) in his book *The Reflective Practitioner*. In any case, we as leaders must meet any situation (the Kodak moment) with the right measures, and Schön's statement is and will be relevant in times to come.

We can summarise some of the dimensions and topics we have addressed in the chapter in Table 13.1. We have talked about leadership at a personal, organisational and contextual level. We have also addressed reflection, both personal reflection and reflection related to the situation and to the broader context of executing leadership. There is a scope and time dimension in leadership. When we talk about coping

TABLE 13.1 Leader strategies related to the time and scope dimensions

	Reflection in action	*Reflection on action*	*Retrospective reflection*
Person	Improve behaviour	Change leadership style	Critically consider what it is to be a leader
Organisation	The current organisation	Incremental organisational change	Radical organisational change
Context	The current business environment	Incremental changes in business profile	Rethinking business

with the future, we have a different time perspective than if we talk about leadership in a specific situation.

Judgement is based on reflection

We have so far indicated that the quality of a leader to a significant extent relies on his or her personal ability. Arguing that leadership is dependent on good judgement (Johnsen 2014) also implies the acknowledgement of the personal dimension in leadership and subsequently the fact that leaders make wrong judgements. We cannot guard ourselves against that, but we can perhaps increase the likelihood of good judgement. A key here is reflection. Practical experience and learning builds empirical knowledge, and the potential of reflection is often forgotten in a hectic work life. Reflection is a part of building empirical knowledge, and Swedberg (2014, p. 140) emphasises the importance of reflection. He says, "all theory worth reading arises from reflection about data". We underestimate its potential in the daily routine and may rely too heavily on systems, procedures and technologies. Those human sides of leading tend to drown in this jungle, and this chapter argues that we cannot forget the importance of satisfying human needs in this picture. Basic inter-human interaction based on trust and motivation between individuals must be fulfilled when you are leading. Leadership is a part of management, and management is a social function (Drücker 1994). Remote steering and technological solutions cannot replace the presence of and engagement from a leader.

Donald Schön (1983) used the concepts of reflection "in" and "on" action." These concepts are important in the understanding of practical knowledge creation. From a work-life perspective, they become fundamental because theories of actions are an important part of giving legitimacy to practical knowledge. Donald Schön engaged in the situation around the practitioner and established his theories on the uniqueness of every situation. A book cannot describe only the best practice. Respect and acknowledgement to the knowledge created "in and on action" must be bridged with theoretical knowledge. The leader must meet the expectations of the employees by being present.

"Reflection in action" is thinking about what you are doing while doing it. It is the use of cognitive qualities by observing in the moment. You consider different aspects of the situation taking place in order to learn from it. Something about the situation might surprise you, and you redesign your actions in the moment. "Action science" is a type of action research introduced by Kurt Lewin, and he highlighted the conduct of research usable in the world of practice. Schön describes "Reflection in action" as "Design as a Reflective Conversation with the Situation" (Schön 1983, p. 76). You evaluate in the moment of action. In order to solve a problem, you need to understand the nature of it. From a professional perspective, it is about capturing explicit forms of insight that can produce knowledge.

"Reflection on action" is thinking about the situation after it has taken place. You are no longer a part of the explicit situation but can think about what happened and try to learn from it. You bring experiences from the actual situation into this "Reflection on action", and they may appear more clearly in retrospective. Rethinking of input from "in action" is possible, and you may alter your initial impressions.

"Retrospective reflection" can be described by reflecting on situations further back in time (a week, a month, a year). This type of reflection gives you the opportunity to compare different situations with different experiences. This holistic perspective will add a deeper understanding to the issue, and conclusions may add value to the future conduct of and decisions made by a leader. A retrospective reflection contributes with an overall evaluation of more than one situation, and previous learning from reflection both "in" and "on" action are inputs to this reflection.

In Table 13.1, we have systematised these reflection forms in relation to different kinds of challenges facing the leader. These can be categorised at different levels, in the sense that some are directed towards individuals, some at organisational structure and some at the wider context of which the organisation is part.

Reflecting helps to adjust behaviour and decisions aligned with the situation you lead. Professional skills and insight into a situation gives a leader a foundation for trust. What Table 13.1 describes is that this judgement is conducted at different levels and is directed towards different aspects of the organisation. The main argument we try to develop here is that the future leader needs to be able to demonstrate good judgement at all these levels and areas.

Future leadership must counteract vulnerability and promote the utilisation of knowledge. Management education today pays little attention to the importance of practical knowledge. In order to succeed in practical work life, there must be a widespread combination of theoretical and practical knowledge; however, this combination has to be approached in the context of reflection. The education of tomorrow's leaders should focus strongly on solutions that merge these two worlds together in way that brings understanding to the individual leader candidate. Leadership is a practical function, and models of co-operation between academia and work life must be the focus for further development. The approach of combining theoretical and practical learning must be carried out through the educational system, and not only on the Master's or PhD levels; practice periods, Bachelor's/Master's thesis, lessons based on experience, industrial PhDs and other practical arrangements for co-operation between academia and work life should be highlighted. Education in combination with work is another important initiative. Such a combination can provide practical and experience-based knowledge to students together with theory. A stronger and more visible combination of theory and practice will bring a momentum to future leadership practice. Action-research-produced practical knowledge can be a strong contributor into this picture. One might obtain a better understanding of the working of a system when it is changing, compared to it being in some sort of stable situation. Action research therefore implies that one learns and adjusts actions, even as a researcher, as the process proceeds in time.

> **Box 13.3 The Kodak moment of leadership**
>
> ***The disruptiveness of change:***
>
> As employees become more autonomous and work is redefined, the role of leaders has to change.
>
> ***The knowledge one failed to use:***
>
> We can already see the direction of these changes and can start discussing the implications for leadership.
>
> ***Ability to adjust to future changes:***
>
> We present criticism of the assumption that leaders are commanders of some sort.
>
> ***The opportunity in the changes:***
>
> Leaders have to see themselves as part of a social dialogue. In doing so, a whole new way of interaction and knowledge development in organisations might be possible. The future leader must be able to reconsider the context of leading, reflecting on the complexity of the situation and assessing a comprehensive set of dimensions in order to make decisions based on good value judgement.

Many of the references used in this chapter are quite old, taking the pace of change into consideration. This has been an intentional choice, in order to emphasise that their original intentions are not outdated. They are of importance today, and they will probably stay relevant in terms of leadership in the future. We cannot shape our future leadership conduct on the basis of the past and present, but we need to learn from it. We must think proactively by tuning in our leadership based on experience and contextual impact. Leading is a social process, and a leader must manage to fulfil the requirements of both the generic and contextual sides of leadership. We cannot decide today what the future will bring, but we can make qualified assumptions based upon trends and so on. Under the premise that you as a leader understand the influence of your surroundings, a structural and targeted use of reflection (all stages) in combination with authentic, involving and focused leadership are the adaptations needed to solve future leadership challenges. As a leader, you have the knowledge and data needed to do a great job, but your greatest challenge is to realise it in practice by showing good judgement.

14

COPING WITH WORK

Redefining relations between work life and society

Thomas Owren and Migle Helmersen

The future of work

Work is changing. The tenuous balance between capital and labour seems to be swaying in favour of capital, creating a more precarious labour market. While globalisation processes provide new business opportunities and therefore also new opportunities for employment, they also contribute to destabilising traditional ways of organising labour, for example through:

- the shift and relocation of industrial workplaces between nations and continents;
- the changes to industry that have been termed the next industrial revolution, "Industry 4.0", marked by the introduction of robots and artificial intelligence technologies in production processes;
- the generation of new forms of work that transcend the boundaries of a traditional employer–employee relationship, such as the rise of the unpaid internship, the "zero-hour contract" and the independent contractor.

One effect is that while ideological trends, such as the UN Sustainability Goals and the Convention for the Rights of Persons with Disabilities, call for creating a more inclusive labour market and workplaces, the reality is that in many ways the labour market is becoming more exclusive, not less.

In this chapter, we start by tracing the history of the concept of work and the development of what we call the "normal model" of work: a model that specifies a certain relationship between work life and society, as well as standardising the parameters of what constitutes a "job". We proceed to examine some global challenges to this model, ranging from new modes of production, changes in the character of "manual work", and how the technological changes have cultural, geographical and racial dimensions to how they may undermine social protection and blur the boundaries between work and leisure.

The "normal model" of work also has educational dimensions. The knowledge society has increased the demand for formal skills. Parallel to the development of the knowledge society, there has been a sharp increase in higher education, accompanied by a pervasive belief in raising the level of professional skills in the population. While contributing to the development of the "normal model", it has also contributed to a divide between those who fit the "normal model" of work and those who do not. This divide is now widening further. We look in detail at some increasing imbalances within the "normal model" of work. For one, our societies and selection effects in the labour market seems to produce ever more "unhealthy workers" and "unhealthy youth", who are selected out and relegated to welfare systems (in some parts of the world) or poverty (in others). At the same time, other groups, for instance people with disorders such as an intellectual disability, may never gain entry to the labour market at all. In all three cases, one of the drivers is the development of the knowledge society and the resulting paucity of "low threshold, low skills" and "manual labour" jobs.

The new ideologies of social inclusion call for measures that counteract these exclusionary processes, not by reversing them, but rather by enhancing the "normal model" of work with options that promote accessibility. We look in some detail at what such inclusion may mean in practice: what challenges such enhancements may provide organisations, but also the potential benefits they can have for those who rise to the challenge. Making workplaces more inclusive and accessible may involve making changes to job content, to work processes or to the physical work environment. It may also involve adjusting social practices, a form of change that may depend on the organisation being willing and able to reconsider hitherto taken-for-granted routines, or the willingness of the members of the organisation to examine aspects of their social practices that ordinarily are just enacted. Thus, organisations wishing to become more inclusive organisations by not expelling "unhealthy workers" and becoming accessible to people presently excluded may need to develop internal arenas for discussion and negotiation, establish new collaborations with external actors and, to a larger extent, become knowledge producing, learning organisations.

We ask whether such processes of extending the "normal model" of work will suffice; whether such an enhanced "normal model" is sustainable and able to withstand the present challenges and potentially disruptive processes, or whether we are part of a larger upheaval, a systemic change that implies that we need to redefine work on a more fundamental level?

Development of the "normal model" of work

Industrial development in Europe and the US grew out of a society where production was mainly related to different crafts and farming. One of the primary work forms in this society was that of a master educating an apprentice in the process of production. Work and learning went hand in hand, and work happened mainly on site. Work had to comply with seasons, with the weather and with local conditions. This pre-industrial society was based on large families, farming and craft, and subsequently was integrated into the social structure. The Industrial Revolution started around 1790, and from then on there have been different stages in its development. Its consequences were beyond that of organising work. It had implications for social structure as well. The early industrialisation created industrial towns. Work had to move to the machine, and the machine was running according to the clock (not the season or weather), so it required a disciplined workforce that lived close to the machine. This new work situation created new issues in defining work. It implied, as the French sociologist Émile Durkheim observed in his 1893 doctoral dissertation *The Division of Labour in Society* (French: *De la division du travail social*), a new type of structuration: We got a new functional differentiation in society, and a new class divide with an increasing labour class. Production happened away from use, and work was only a small piece of the production process. Although one can discuss how to define these stages, roughly speaking, many commentators point at how industry developed into mass production from around 1870. This mass production made consumer society possible but also failed at a certain point, when the economy became more demand driven. In mass production, the divide between a middle class of engineers and a labour class doing unskilled work increased. Industrial towns became larger, more sectorised, and workloads could now be defined more actuarially. In this second stage of the Industrial Revolution, the social tensions increased, as did urbanisation and political radicalisation. Mass production had this double face; it created enormous output and made increased consumptions possible, but also increased tension in society. As pointed out earlier in this book, many commentators around World War II foresaw that this tension would destroy society. However, industrial development entered a new stage.

In this period, the "normal model" of work life was developed. It has some different national forms, to some extent defined by the level of political tension in the mid-war period, but gradually most European countries adopted this normal model. This "normal model" is a partnership between the state and the social partners. The idea is to build a social system related to work, wherein the state takes some responsibility for the young and the elderly and the sick, paid for by taxes on those who work. We can call it the *welfare model*, and it was partly inspired by the British 1942 report *The Beveridge Report: Social Insurance and Allied Services*. The logic of this model that we call the "normal model" is that there is full employment; that is, society is structured around work. The state provides support and education to fit work-life and production. After people finish their education, they work and pay taxes that are redistributed to the social services that make the population healthier and work more efficient, as well as education and pensions. The Scandinavian version of this model is perhaps more extensive than is found in other European countries, and there is national variation, but the principles of the "normal model" is the same in Western countries.

Some argue that from the period after World War II, between 1950 and the 1970s, we moved into a post-capitalist society, with increased production of services, more customised products, increased competition and internationalisation. In the Western world, industrial workplaces have been exported to Asia and other low-cost countries or have been replaced by technology. This third stage of industrial revolution is therefore also called the *computer age*: From the mid-1900s, computer technology started to have an impact. The city of Detroit, in the US, can serve as an illustration of the development from the second to the third industrial revolution. In 1950, it had 1.8 million inhabitants; today it has around 650,000 inhabitants. The mass production of cars, using a large number of unskilled workers, is now history. Today, production facilities are filled with robots, being served by a smaller and relatively skilled workforce. What is more, the new knowledge economy has also changed human geography. A new urbanisation has escalated. It is not the old industrial towns that expand, but more diverse, multicultural, tolerant and dynamic urban areas. This demographic change indicates new tensions between rural and urban areas (Florida 2002); the "Creative Class" has become dominant. At the same time, globalisation over the last 20 years has had an impact on wage distribution. The distribution between capital and labour has gone in favour of capital (Brynjolfsson & McAfee 2014).

The discussion is now whether we are about to enter the fourth phase of industrialisation, driven by new technology, robots and artificial intelligence. In a report on the impact of "Industry 4.0", the German Federal Ministry of Labour and Social Affairs (2015) launched the concept "Work 4.0". The report discusses how the "normal model" can be adjusted to the new work regime. The big question asked is whether the changes we are seeing are more than ordinary cyclical changes; is the "work" of work is changing for good? There are many challenges to the "normal model" as it has developed along with the industrialisation and bureaucratisation of society – with the idea that paid work with a fixed contract is the norm. As discussed in Chapter 2, the "normal model" has developed into a sophisticated set of laws and institutions that regulate much of individuals' relations to society and the state. However, it can be asked how resilient this model is.

Box 14.1 Global challenges to the "normal model" of work

The International Labour Conference (ILO) writes:

> New modes of production have facilitated the development of deeper and more widespread global supply chains, which are now a common means of organising investment and production in the global economy. This has generated opportunities for economic and social development and created employment, providing many workers with a toehold in the formal labour market and a pathway out of poverty in many countries. It has also increased productivity gains for the firms engaged in global supply chains. However, there is also evidence that global supply chains can affect different aspects of the quality of jobs, such as wages or the nature of work contracts.
>
> *(ILO 2016, p. 6)*

The *New York Times* (Tingley 2017a, February 23) writes that General Motors (GM) now operates 30,000 robots in their plants, 8000 of which are linked to the internet via cloud computing. And, further:

> The emerging face of the American working class is a Hispanic woman who has never set foot on a factory floor. That's not the kind of work much of the working class does anymore. Instead of making things, they are more often paid to serve people: to care for someone else's children or someone else's parents; to clean another family's home.
>
> *(Appelbaum 2017, February 23)*

The question is not only what technology does with work but also how the changes have cultural, geographical and racial dimensions to them. Manual work, in the age of computers and machines, seems to increasingly become service work. Furthermore, the education divide (Putnam 2016) may add to a new divide between low-paid, unskilled service workers and a higher skilled creative class. A German Ministry of Labour and Social Affairs report argues:

> While factory work usually has to take place at a certain time and place, many services and administrative activities can, using digital tools, potentially be performed from any location at any time. This opens up NEW SCOPE for a more self-directed way of working, and makes it easier to balance work, family and leisure more flexibly in line with individual needs. However, it is also leading to a breakdown in the boundaries on work, in terms of when and where it takes place. In a survey commissioned by the Federal Ministry of Labour and Social Affairs into quality of work and economic success, 30% of white-collar workers said that they work from home at least occasionally (manual workers: 2%). 12% of white-collar workers deal with work matters in their leisure time several times a week (manual workers: 4%).
>
> *(Federal Ministry of Labour and Social Affairs 2015, p. 64)*

Similarly, a federal report from the US argues:

> Engagement. Humans will likely be needed to actively engage with AI technologies throughout the process of completing a task. Many industry professionals refer to a large swath of AI technologies as "Augmented Intelligence," stressing the technology's role as assisting and expanding the productivity of individuals rather than replacing human work.
>
> *(US Government 2016)*

This picture might look different in different parts of the world. Globally, it adds to the issue of gender and of global economic growth and unemployment in general. The ILO writes:

> The world is faced with the formidable challenge of creating 600 million new jobs by 2030, the majority in developing countries, in order to return to pre-crisis employment levels, provide employment for the 40 million young women and men entering the labour market each year and increase the participation of women in line with internationally agreed targets.
>
> *(ILO 2016, p. 5)*

Furthermore, they write:

> As routine jobs disappear, new jobs are emerging in the knowledge economy, the green economy and the care economy, in both developing and

industrialised countries. ILO estimates show that the transformation to a greener economy could generate between 15 and 60 million additional jobs globally over the coming decades. While Internet enabled mobile and independent types of work facilitate the matching of workers and employers and offer flexibility, they also bring challenges in ensuring conditions of decent work. Without formal contracts, such arrangements can lead to excessive working hours and little social protection.

(ILO 2016, p. 5)

New forms of work relations seem to be emerging. One is "crowd work". The ILO maintains that

crowd work, which affords opportunities for Internet-based workers globally, raises challenges in relation to labour regulation and protection. New modes of production have facilitated the development of deeper and more widespread global supply chains, which are now a common means of organising investment and production in the global economy. This has generated opportunities for economic and social development and created employment, providing many workers with a toehold in the formal labour market and a pathway out of poverty in many countries.

(ILO 2016, p. 6)

In a report on crowd work, it is stated:

The proportion who had ever carried out paid work via online platforms work was 9% in the UK and the Netherlands, 10% in Sweden, 12% in Germany and 19% in Austria. However, for many of these respondents, crowd working seems to have been an occasional experiment. The proportion reporting doing such work at least once a week was between 5% and 9% of respondents, with 6%–13% doing so once a month. Crowd work is generally a small supplement to total income.

(Huws, Spencer & Joyce 2016 p. ii)

All these changes raise serious issues about how to cope with work life in the future. As the report to the German Ministry of Labour and Social Affairs asks:

How can the "humanisation of work" be achieved in the 21st century? What will the factory, the office, the production model of the future look like, and what are the implications for workers? How can socially responsible technology design ensure workers stay healthy, reduce mental stress and make work safe? How can the same level of occupational safety and health be guaranteed in the case of mobile working? Are the basic concepts of labour law (such as "employee" or "establishment") still applicable in the digital world of work?

(Federal Ministry of Labour and Social Affairs 2015, p. 67)

> Thus, the changes in work have social, organisational and legal and structural aspects. This is well illustrated by the Norwegian/Nordic case of development of work.

There are, in our opinion, two main challenges to the "normal model" of work: It is dependent on full employment and on the inclusion of the adult population in the workforce. However, increasingly, groups are excluded from employment, resulting in unemployment and a variety of health and social problems. At the same time the new, digital economy has created a new structure of work: more network driven, more dynamic and more based on temporary contracts or tenuous contracts. How can the model adjust to this challenge without compromising its basic values of organised work? We will first consider some increasing imbalances within the "normal model" before moving on to discuss how it may be adjusted to become more inclusive, and what this may mean in practice for businesses and organisations.

The new redundancies: The unhealthy worker and unhealthy youth effects

The *healthy* worker effect (HWE) seems first to have been described by Dr W. Ogle in an appendix to the Register General's report on mortality in England and Wales in 1885. He found that "the more vigorous occupations had relatively lower mortality rate compared with the death-rates in occupations of an easier character or the unemployed". Ogle identifies two kinds of selection bias: one present at the time of hire, the other present in the period of employment. The first selectively attracts or rejects new workers depending on the physical demands of the job and defined health criteria. The second forces people to leave their job if their health becomes too impaired to perform it. Ogle's description is more comprehensive than the commonly used definition by Last, who defines the HWE as

> A phenomenon observed initially in studies of occupational diseases: workers usually exhibit lower overall death rates than the general population, because the severely ill and chronically disabled are ordinarily excluded from employment.
>
> *(Last 1995)*

Thus, the HWE has long been considered as a source of selection bias (Fox & Collier 1976; Li & Sung 1999). It reflects that (1) an individual must be relatively healthy in order to be considered employable, (2) mortality and morbidity rates within the work force are usually lower than in the general population and (3) the health status of workers may be even better in "vigorous occupations" compared with those "of an easier character" (Li & Sung 1999). One important consequence of the HWE is that occupational hazards may be underestimated or even overlooked.

All occupations are more or less exposed to the selection out of unhealthy individuals. The proportion of unhealthy persons who must leave a workplace due to health issues, however, varies according to the physical and mental demands of any given occupation. Employees with reduced work ability may leave the workforce and become disability pensioned, while others may be channelled into occupations with lower demands. The term *unhealthy worker effect* (UWE) is used to denote the opposite of HWE, namely, the selection out and channelling of unhealthy persons into occupations with lower demands (Gamperiene 2008):

> A phenomenon in which workers in jobs with low-entry demands or requirements exhibit high morbidity rates partly because of selection of unhealthy persons into employment.

In this way, "unhealthy workers" recruited into lower demand jobs may 'bring with them' occupational exposure from previous jobs (Gamperiene 2008). Thus, these occupations may show higher morbidity rates than expected. They may also gain a bad reputation that is not necessarily deserved. One important consequence of the UWE is that occupational hazards may be overestimated.

Jobs with lower entrance demands are often "low status, low pay" jobs. The cleaning profession, for example, exhibits several characteristics of such a lower demand job. Specifically, cleaning represents an easy entryway to the workforce, with minimal educational and language requirements, flexible hours and the possibility of part-time employment.

Box 14.2 Sissel

Sissel, a Norwegian woman, started working at her father's small fish-processing firm at the age of 16. Her main work task is manual fish filleting, a task that does not require formal skills, only on-the-job training. Being dependent on her monthly earnings, she never finished secondary education. Her job was physically demanding but represented stable and safe employment. She married and has two children. When she was 36, all local fish-related industry, including her father's firm, shut down after vital parts of the fishery infrastructure were relocated within the region. That also meant that she, with her current skill set, was left without any local alternative employers. Her best employment option was a position as a cleaner in a nearby primary school, a job that did not require formal education.

After working as a cleaner for 5 years, Sissel developed a chronic inflammation in her shoulder and back. Her treatment took most of a year, during which she was on sick leave. Before returning to work, her employer, together with the health service, re-organised her duties to ease the physical strain on her shoulder and back and provided her with more ergonomic cleaning tools. However, after a few months back at work, even with working reduced hours, she suffered a serious relapse. At the age of 42, her doctor told her that she could no longer perform a physically demanding job. It seemed, he said, that her options were either to find employment that was less physically demanding, get a formal education or apply for a disability pension. Over the course of the next year, together with specialists from the Labour and Welfare Administration office, Sissel investigated the possibility of jobs that were less physically demanding. However, they all required different forms of formal education. She joined a restart programme for secondary education for adults, but failed. At 43, she applied for, and was granted, a permanent disability pension from the Norwegian government.

Firms in the cleaning business, to which people with less education or health issues have been able to turn, are making efforts to better their reputation. Through adopting modern work models, diversifying their range of services and becoming increasingly professionalised, they attempt to minimise the high turnover and health problems that have been associated with cleaning. Increasingly, cleaning jobs are full-time and day-time jobs, which means that the working hours are less flexible. Cleaning firms strive to employ younger individuals with more resources, more (vocational) education and better language skills. From the perspective of the firms, higher job-entry demands lead to a better reputation, in turn attracting more educated workers, considered a desirable outcome for the firms. In other words, these developments, which on one side elevate the status of cleaning for a living, also reduce employment options for workers with fewer skills. Both for the people in question and for society as a whole, these developments can be considered problematic, because they contribute to a less inclusive labour market.

Technology is changing our jobs faster than ever. Skill requirements in working life are increasing, because harnessing technology has the effect of rationalising and eliminating unskilled jobs. Such changes affect all sectors and occupations, but at this stage, "low threshold, low skills" and "manual labour" jobs are especially exposed to such elimination. Therefore, demand for employees with fewer skills and less formal education slumps. This trend is illustrated by the increasing theoretical education requirements for employment, even in "unskilled" occupations. Workplaces that traditionally have been open to workers with fewer resources, either mental or physical, may disappear. For some, such workplaces may represent the primary or, in some cases, the only opportunity to join the workforce.

Lack of education is a significant predictor for later exclusion from the workforce (Alvarez-Jimenez et al. 2012). In 2014, the Organisation for Economic Co-operation and Development (OECD) published a report revealing that 28% of students in Norwegian upper-secondary education did not complete in the standard time or did not complete at all. This is a higher proportion than the average in Europe, which for the same year was 13% (OECD 2014). There is a correlation between mental disorders and school absenteeism.

> **Box 14.3 Anne**
>
> Anne is Sissel's daughter. At the age of 13, she developed social anxiety. She resisted going to school, saying it was hard to breathe there. She received counselling from a community psychological service but also developed a habit of self-medication using alcohol and, eventually, drugs like amphetamine and ecstasy. She had few friends. The ones she had also use drugs. School was difficult; although she was a clever pupil, it was increasingly hard for her to perform school tasks in a classroom. At 17, she was formally diagnosed with Social Anxiety Disorder. Due to treatment, she had long periods of absence.
>
> At the age of 18, the anxiety was so pronounced that she stopped attending school at all. At this point, she had a part-time job at a local petrol station, performing tasks such as cleaning and restocking goods. It provided her with pocket money, but this did not amount to anything she could live on, and her family had limited means to support her. As she was a drop-out from secondary school, there were no full-time jobs available for her locally. At this point, her anxiety was so severe that it effectively precluded her from using public transport and thus from applying for jobs further away.
>
> In a collaboration between Anne's doctor, the Labour and Welfare Administration office, the local social service and a local private firm that specialises in such testing, Anne went through a year of work capability assessment, after which her functional, vocational and medical status was reviewed. Taken along with the fact that there were no local employment options for unskilled workers like her, the outcome was that she was granted a disability pension at the age of 19.

In the Nordic as well as other high-income countries, an upsetting trend can be observed: An increasing number of young people seem unable to work or attend education. Compared to just 10 years ago, there are twice as many young Norwegian disability pensioners today. Finding some young people in such a disability scheme is natural, given that the statistics also include persons with congenital illnesses or impairments of a severity that makes work participation unlikely, no matter the level of accommodation. The challenge does not lie here. In about 60% of cases where people under the age of 30 are disability pensioned, it is related to being diagnosed with various mental and behavioural disorders.

Difficulties in entering the labour market can be related to health problems obtained in working life or to health problems before entrance to working life. Generally speaking, these two mechanisms apply to two different groups: the first to adults with work experience, the second to young persons who have never worked due to reduced health or social challenges. Clearly, the average age in the first group will be significantly higher, and the second group's health issues cannot in the same way be ascribed to work. Nevertheless, they have a common challenge, namely limited possibilities to get job in a labour market with a dwindling amount of jobs for "unskilled" workers. These groups do not have the same opportunity to "catch the train" called "innovation and globalisation of the labour market", as do those groups with better health and education status. These exclusionary mechanisms create structural as well as social problems in a "normal model" designed for (nearly) full employment, where society is structured around work. As larger groups are cut off from work, not only will they lead lives blemished with poor economy, health issues and shorter life expectancy but they will also contribute to increasing imbalances in the systems, a poorer "social economy". As the working of these mechanisms should not be seen as being caused solely by factors related to the individuals themselves, neither should the responsibility for compensating for them. Alternative solutions, where society accept social costs for those who no longer are necessary in the current scheme of organisation of labour, should be considered. This is not a matter of reversing the development of the knowledge society but rather of building in a wider variety of options as a way to resolve the current contradiction between the call for *inclusion*, which aims to include and retain people in the labour market; and the growing trend of raising the *requirements for entering* the labour market, even in forms of work that traditionally have been "low threshold, low skills" jobs. Thus, the *unhealthy youth effect* (UYE) can help explain why "school losers" become a select group of young people who begin their adulthood with the brutal reality of being redundant before they ever enter the workforce. It is easy to think that the most important instrument is likely to get more young people to complete high school and higher education and move on to professional life. However, what should those who do not want or cannot take a master's degree or doctorate do? Another way to put the question is: How can we attain a labour market that is more inclusive, more tolerant of diversity?

Building a wider variety of options into the knowledge society, creating a more inclusive work life, may require turning a critical eye to the parameters of what constitutes a "job", which at present are fairly standardised. The goal may to create more variation in how a job may be and still be considered a job. For one, a person's existing work tasks may be modified in order to help employees who experience a reduction in work ability remain in the workforce. More radically, one may create "niche jobs", that is, jobs designed to match a particular skill level; or execute "job carving": extracting parts of existing jobs to make up sets of tasks that match a particular skill level (Borghouts-van de Pas & Freese 2017; Sainsbury, Coleman-Fountain & Trezzini 2017). This requires that managers need to be well-informed regarding employees', or potential employees', health status, work capacity and limitations. In turn, this means that achieving inclusion may require building a level of mutual trust between manager and employee.

The call for inclusion: Building down disabling barriers in organisations

Article 27 in the UN Convention on the Rights of Persons with Disabilities reaffirms the right of persons with disabilities to work on an equal basis with others, including "the opportunity to gain a living by work freely chosen or accepted in a labour market and work environment that is open, inclusive and accessible to persons with disabilities" (UN 2006). At present, most forms of disability correlate with significant labour market disadvantage. Globally, persons with disabilities

> experience significantly lower employment rates and much higher rates of unemployment than persons without disabilities. This is due to many factors, including lack of access to education and vocational rehabilitation and training, lack of access to financial resources, disincentives created by disability benefits, the inaccessibility of the workplace, and employers' perceptions of disability and disabled people.
> *(WHO 2011, p. 250)*

This employment gap has proved to be persistent, despite decades of policy initiatives and interventions. Interventions have largely focused on the "supply side", that is, aiming to enhance the employability of the individuals themselves, for example by increasing their "motivation, abilities and job search behaviour" (Borghouts-van de Pas & Freese 2017, p. 2). Some policy initiatives have focused on the "demand side", such as anti-discrimination legislation, quota systems and financial incentives and support to employers. However, the persistence of the employment gap suggests it is time to intensify efforts on the "demand side". After reviewing European public policies regarding persons with disabilities, a team of researchers concluded that:

> While it is important that practices aimed at increasing the employability of people are maintained and improved, the DISCIT project has shown that only by refocusing our attention on employers and the demand for labour can we expect to make the necessary progress towards closing the employment gap and achieving equality in the labour market for persons with disabilities.
> *(Sainsbury, Coleman-Fountain & Trezzini 2017, p. 112)*

Obviously, employers have a gatekeeper function. Recent reviews of research suggest that employers with previous experience of hiring individuals with disabilities are more positive about such hiring; that personal knowledge, for example, through knowing or being related to persons with disabilities, seems to help; and that larger companies are more disposed to hire persons with disabilities. One review of research identifies a positive trend whereby

> employers are increasingly recognising that the costs associated with hiring individuals with disabilities (e.g., insurance and accommodations) are reasonable and negotiable. Many accommodations incur no or minimal costs. Employers indicated a willingness to accommodate workers with disabilities to gain more benefits than having to repeatedly hire and train new workers due to high turnover rates by workers without disabilities.
> *(Ju, Roberts & Zhang 2013, p. 121)*

Other research reviews report how employers describe benefits of having employees with disabilities, such as increases in profitability, workforce diversity, retaining quality employees and avoiding costs associated with hiring and training new employees (Vornholt, Uitdewilligen & Nijhuis 2013).

Traditionally, interventions have largely aimed at helping individuals with disabilities to access existing types of jobs. Regarding persons with physical or sensory disabilities, this may first and foremost be a matter of (a) enhancing their skills to the point that the job requires, (b) overcoming any reservations that the potential employer might have and (c) making sure the workplace and work processes in themselves are accessible. How that is achieved will largely depend on the type of impairment; for instance, when it comes to a wheelchair user, the first consideration might be physical access. In the case of employees with severe visual or hearing impairments, securing access to information and communication processes in the organisation might loom larger.

However, such accommodations do not suffice for the growing group of people who are unable to meet the current, and rising, educational and skill requirements of existing jobs. Among these we find the "unhealthy workers" but also persons with disabilities. The latter group includes persons with "physical, mental, intellectual or sensory impairments" (UN 2006, article 1). The United Nations states that

> disability results from the interaction between persons with impairments and attitudinal and environmental barriers that hinders their full and effective participation in society on an equal basis with others,
>
> *(UN 2006, e)*

This modifies the more traditional view that ascribes any hindrances to participation to the impairment alone. The convention shifts the focus from solely looking at individuals to looking at their interaction with barriers that arise from features of the physical and social contexts they attempt to manoeuvre. In addition to the traditional focus on enhancing the skills of potential employees, this offers a rich second dimension along which to work: changing those features of the work environment that represent barriers for these particular individuals, that is, building down barriers. One fundamental barrier is the largely taken-for-granted parameters and perceptions of what constitutes a "job" in the "normal model" of work. Thus, recent suggestions for changing the "demand side" stress the importance of creating new types of jobs in ordinary workplaces, for example, as mentioned, through "niche job" creation or "job carving".

Box 14.4 Trygve

Trygve, a young man with Down Syndrome and an intellectual disability, has worked in a grocery store for many years. He likes his job, he says. He has a limited set of tasks: he empties the bottle deposit machine, restocks beer and soda to shelves, makes coffee and compacts cardboard. In the last year, he has also started restocking paper products.

> The store manager, who mentors Trygve, describes how he needs more support and follow-up than other employees. On those rare occasions where he starts a new task, she describes that he needs very simple, specific instructions and close follow-up. He needs to be "walked through" many repetitions of performing the task before he gradually can start doing it on his own. Also, she has learned that he cannot be rushed. He needs to work at his own speed and, if left alone, works patiently and hard.
>
> People with intellectual disability are a group with a huge variability in levels of impairment, resources and capacity. But a core characteristic that appears in a varying degree within the group is significant limitations in "reasoning, problem solving, planning, abstract thinking, judgement, academic learning, and learning from experience" (APA 2013, p. 33). Thus, Trygve's need for simple instructions, many repetitions and a limited set of simple, repetitive tasks reflects his intellectual impairment. Because he needs assistance when events occur that require improvisation and judgement, on his shifts, another employee is always asked to keep an eye out for him. When not learning a new task, he works alone.

Creating "niche jobs" and "job carving" is not a matter of making up tasks but of "reshuffling" existing ones: Work tasks, or parts of tasks, may be "repackaged" into jobs that match the specific skills of a particular employee. One may also design types of jobs that roughly match the strengths and limitations associated with a particular type of condition. An example of the latter is when Specialisterne (2017), which operates in numerous locations around the world, can "harness the special characteristics and talents of people with autism and use them as a competitive advantage" as "business consultants on tasks such as software testing, programming and data entry for the public and private sectors". Another example is the Norwegian Helt Med! ("All in!") project, where public and private-sector businesses receive help from an non-governmental organisation (NGO) to design jobs with task sets and levels of support that are considered suitable for people with an intellectual disability.

Another "tried-and-trusted" staple of support-to-work methods is establishing a system for extra support and follow-up by assigning internal mentors and collaborating with external "job coaches". Inclusive employers describe such support systems as essential:

> Coaching during integration is of the utmost importance and is stressed by every inclusive employer in our study. The employee needs at least one internal mentor to attend to possible start-up problems. External job coaching is also essential.
>
> (Borghouts-van de Pas & Freese 2017, p. 19)

Depending on the employee, such extra support and follow-up may be provided just in the initial phases, but it may also be required more long term, or, in the case of many employees with an intellectual disability or mental illness, permanently. Such systems may also provide support to the employer, and in some cases, to colleagues. Not least, they can play an important role in the hiring process:

> Employers described the benefits of being able to interact with employment support specialists ['job coaches'] during the hiring process including having a place to turn to when they have disability related questions, uncertainty about legislative requirements, and challenges related to accommodation.
>
> *(Gewurtz, Langan & Shand 2016, p. 142)*

After reviewing research into creating jobs for people with intellectual disabilities in ordinary workplaces, Lövgren, Markström and Sauer (2017, p. 26) reported that some critical factors seem to be "analysis of conditions to facilitate good matches" (between job requirements and skills), as well as "systematic, individualised design of support". Seino, Takezawa, Nomoto and Boeltzig-Brown (2017, p. 352) identify two additional factors: "constructing a support system (both inside and outside the workplace, and building trust so it is easy to ask for advice)" and "accumulating knowledge for support".

Box 14.5 Frank

A man with an intellectual disability, Frank works in the central kitchen of a large nursing home. His job is a result of "job carving": Parts of existing jobs were extracted to make up a set of tasks matching his skill level. He has a fixed set of tasks with some common qualities: They are practical, do not require much in the way of abstract thinking or judgement and are repetitive in that they need doing every day in about the same way.

The nursing home's many wards each have a small peripheral kitchen. One of Frank's tasks is to fill orders from the wards for different food products, both dry goods and fresh. Every evening, the staff on each ward fills out an order form specifying what they need the next day. Each morning, Frank fills their order from the storage rooms, piling the goods neatly on steel carts, each marked with the ward number.

When Frank's job was created, the external job coach assisted the nursing home in identifying how their ordinary routines needed to be modified in order to enable Frank to do his tasks. One modification was that storage areas for food needed to be arranged in a more logical and orderly manner, with a defined, clearly marked place for each product. This modification, which enabled Frank to fill the orders, also turned out to be helpful for the rest of the kitchen staff, as well as for the people delivering the goods. Another modification was that when filling out the order sheets, ward staff needed to use numbers. They could not simply "x" a box; if the order was for a single item, they needed to write "1". Also, the order forms needed to be written in uppercase letters, and when ordering items not printed on the form, staff needed to use all uppercase letters rather than mixing uppercase and lowercase. That co-workers should adhere to these simple modifications in their routines was decided by the kitchen manager and nursing home management, discussed with all ward managers, who in turn discussed it with their staff on the wards. The modification did not meet with any resistance, especially when explained in the context of Frank's employment and needs. In all, the staff were very positive to his inclusion. In the kitchen he was well liked. The work culture was informal, with continual displays of humour and good-natured joking, and Frank not only fitted into this culture but also added to it, and the kitchen staff embraced him. They also defended his needs, as when order forms from some wards were chronically filled out with "x"s where there should have been "1"s and mixed uppercase and lowercase letters, so Frank was unable to read them. After several polite reminders, where apologetic ward staff lamented about how hard these things were to remember, one of the kitchen assistants took it on himself to remedy this. From then, each time an order sheet was improperly filled out, he called the staff on that ward, insisting they come down and fill it out properly; otherwise they would not be receiving any goods that day. In a very short time, all order sheets were filled perfectly.

Another employee with an intellectual disability in the same nursing home was not so lucky. One of his tasks was to clear the table in some wards after resident had had lunch, and to fill the dishwasher. However, the ward staff found it hard to leave the tables without clearing them, and therefore on a daily basis this employee found himself unable to do his job, which is important to him, and he became upset and frustrated. And in this matter, there are no similarly simple, effective ways to remedy the staff's forgetfulness; the forgetful ones can continue to transgress without any tangible consequences.

It is time to bring together the elements of the discussion of inclusion. Regarding the case of Trygve (Box 14.4), what does "accumulating knowledge for support" mean here? As will be the case with many employees with an intellectual disability, the manager needs to adapt her way of providing instructions and follow-up to his cognitive capacity for processing information; if he is to understand, she needs to learn to speak in ways that enable him to understand. She needs to adapt her language, and it is primarily through his responses she will know when the adaptations are sufficient. She also needs to learn to let him work at his own speed and not attempt to rush him. This illustrates that in many cases, it is not only employees who need to learn skills in order to be included; managers may also need to learn skills in order to include. Trygve's case is an example of an inclusion process that primarily involves collaboration between an employee and management, not requiring any further involvement internally or externally. It illustrates the "prototypical" case in which an employee with issues and a manager (or human resources [HR] department) agree on a set of accommodations. In many cases this will suffice. Yet, when it comes to Trygve, his co-workers need to learn to respect his tasks, that is, not to do them. They also need to learn not to ask him to do other tasks, tasks they may see as trivial but that he has not been trained to do. Another aspect worth considering is that on one hand, the present accommodations enable him to work there, and he expresses satisfaction. On the other hand, he is rather isolated in the work environment and seems to be doing the same tasks year after year. A weakness with such "simple inclusion" schemes is that managers may not have the knowledge and skills necessary to mobilise and develop the full range of these employees' resources and potential. This is part of what collaborating with external job coaches (or other specialist services, depending on the specific issues) may offer. If Trygve were to be more fully included in work processes and collaborate more with co-workers, they might also need to learn more about how to communicate in ways that level the field: that enable him to understand, respond and be understood. A job coach may help them learn this. As they learn, they are accumulating knowledge, and by acting on this knowledge, they are chipping away at a disabling barrier, promoting participation. Without such help, they may not get very far. As Lövgren, Markström and Sauer (2017) note, colleagues simply being willing to support may be insufficient; for the support to be adequate, they need certain skills. Becerra, Montanero and Lucero (2016) found that spontaneous verbal help to workers with an intellectual disability from co-workers without training in providing such help was only marginally more effective than no help at all.

In the case of Frank (Box 14.5), the story illustrates, in a simple way, how building down barriers may require negotiating and legitimising new organisational practices. In order for him to do his tasks, co-workers need to modify their daily routines. Even if the changes are small, they may need to be co-ordinated and backed up by management, who must also explain why the changes are necessary; they need to be able to inform co-workers about Frank's intellectual impairment. This illustrates one of Borghouts-van de Pas and Freese's (2017, p. 19) points: "With regard to integration in the team, it is essential to give honest information about the skills, abilities and knowledge of the candidate". Frank's story also illustrates the value of create alliances in the work force, a sense that the inclusion is a group effort, which may be easier when employees work alongside co-workers and their tasks interweave. Lastly, it illustrates how ingrained "ingrained habits" are; even with the best of will, it may not be easy for co-workers to adjust their routines. It may take concerted and concentrated organisational effort, framed in the context of equality, social justice and human rights, and it may not happen even then if co-workers do not have the added motivation of avoiding unwanted, but good-natured, consequences, as the kitchen assistant helpfully provided in Frank's case.

If we go back to the case of Anne (Box 14.3), she struggles with mental illness and a labour market that has no jobs she is qualified for. Some of the research findings that Delman, Kovich, Burke and Martone (2017) highlight in their report on "demand side" strategies to employ people with serious mental illness is that the most frequent accommodations are flexible scheduling, "enhanced" training and supervision and modified job duties, and that direct costs associated with such accommodations are often nominal. After a review of research on factors that impact job tenure for people with mental illness, Williams et al. (2016, p. 80) note that the main supportive factors seem to be related to (1) the workers' experience of doing the job (e.g. experiencing that tasks are rewarding, accommodations available, feeling competent in tasks), (2) having natural supports in the workplace (e.g. experiencing supervisors and co-workers as supportive, work culture as accepting) and (3) that the workers themselves had strategies for integrating work, recovery and wellness (e.g. for managing symptoms at work, dealing with stressors and viewing work as shifting the focus away from illness) and external support (e.g. family, friends, peer support, vocational and/or mental health staff) to help them deal with work-related challenges. Therefore, it is not farfetched that Anne can work, if local businesses are willing to engage in some "job carving" and simple accommodations and make sure that the workplace culture is sufficiently supportive. The latter may require some "accumulating knowledge" for support; for example, educating co-workers on mental illness, creating realistic expectations, correcting misconceptions and later trying out and evaluating types of accommodations in an "epistemological alliance" with the employee and perhaps also co-workers.

Regarding the case of Sissel (Box 14.2), many of the same considerations apply. This does not mean that she can be compared to people with an intellectual disability or mental illness but that she may benefit from some degree of the same principles of inclusion of which these other groups need large degrees. A worker with chronic health issues might certainly benefit from an employer having extensive experience with "job carving", learning alongside employees what types and levels of accommodation work best and facilitating work processes where employees work together but each at their own optimal speed.

Matching job requirements with potential employees' skills, not the other way around, as the "normal model" is prone to do, shifts job parameters to effectively make whole new groups of people employable. In themselves, these principles are not new; 'job carving' has been a staple in support-to-work methods for decades. The innovation would be to use them on a much larger scale, as a standard form of human relations management with people with chronic health issues or disabilities (Borghouts-van de Pas & Freese 2017). As such, they may be equally applicable to existing employees who have experienced a reduction in work capacity, for example, older workers as an alternative to early retirement. In their systematic review of how to promote work participation in older workers, Steenstra et al. (2017, p. 98) found that the most effective interventions were "multi-component"; all included work modifications related to hours, ergonomics or duties, and then utilised various combinations of other components such as "job focused vocational rehabilitation: worker education/training", "a return to work plan" and "case management and communication between workplace and healthcare provider".

These examples of barriers and accommodations show how disabling barriers, in many cases, spring from social practices that are so entrenched that the knowledge they build can be understood as "doxa": knowledge so taken for granted that it is largely accepted as "a self-evident and natural order which goes without saying and therefore goes unquestioned" (Bourdieu 1977, p. 166). His point was that such "naturalisation" not only makes it hard to imagine alternative ways of ordering social practices, but that it also disposes actors to see these ways of ordering as the only possible, or sensible, ways.

This suggests that in building down disabling barriers in workplaces, there may be a qualitative difference between accommodations that aim to change the built environment, which seldom require co-workers to change their routines, and those that aim to change social practices that contribute to socially constituted barriers. The latter may require examining and discussing practices that usually are not discussed because they build on knowledge that normally "goes without saying and therefore goes unquestioned". This points to the need to establish arenas where such examinations and discussions can take place and to facilitate the process in ways that enable constructive exploration in an atmosphere of mutual respect. This may be essential, not least because changing social practices always will have an element of negotiation, where the outcome hinges on the extent to which the involved actors are willing, or even able, to change their practices.

The discussion illustrates how creating more inclusive organisations gives rise to new managerial and organisational challenges, creating the need to change new collaborative structures in ways that stretch the "normal model". It also illustrates the essential role *knowledge* will have in inclusive organisations. This strongly suggests that organisations wishing to become more inclusive organisations must become more reflective organisations; in fact, they must become *learning* organisations.

Box 14.6 Scandic hotels are creating jobs for people with intellectual disabilities

The Scandic hotel chain runs 230 hotels in seven countries, with 15,000 employees and a total of 44,000 rooms. In February 2017, Scandic, in collaboration with the Helt Med! ["All in!"] project, advertised eight positions for persons with an intellectual disability at two hotels in Bergen, Norway, as a small-scale pilot venture. The requirements were that applicants have intellectual disability, a permanent disability pension and an enthusiasm for working in a hotel. They would be assigned simplified task sets related to kitchen, restaurant and conference activities, as well as janitor services. They would each be assigned an internal mentor. Along with their mentor, they would receive monthly support and follow-up from an external job coach. Those who passed a four-week practice period would be hired on normal work contracts, with one important exception: With the blessing of the Norwegian Confederation of Trade Unions (LO), they would be paid 20% of the wage rate as determined in ordinary collective bargaining agreement processes. The condition for this blessing was that these employees did not supplant other, "ordinary" employees; they were only to be assigned tasks that otherwise would not have been done, so their contributions enabled the hotels to add an extra touch to their services. According to the agreement with Helt Med! the hotels do not receive any external financial compensation for creating these jobs; the only contribution from the Labour and Welfare Administration is that of paying for the support and follow-up from an external job coach.

This particular arrangement highlights some fundamental dilemmas in such job creation, at least within the current "normal model" of work:

1. If the employees' work capacity does not enable them to do an "ordinary job", employers are left with the choice of either paying these employees less, making them vulnerable to criticism for contributing to "social dumping"; or paying these employees an ordinary wage for work that produces less economic value. The last option may require a level of idealism that many employers may not be willing, or able, to fulfil. From this dilemma springs Scandic's requirement that applicants must have a permanent disability pension. In countries with a less developed welfare system, paying employees with reduced work capacity a reduced wage might require that their families or other external parties contribute to their daily subsistence, if they are not to be relegated to poverty even if employed to their full capacity.
2. When it comes to the matter of the employees only being assigned tasks that otherwise would not be done, a dilemma is that over time, when these tasks have been done for a while, they actually *are* being done and may enter the realm of what is expected from the hotels as a part of the normal service. At that point, one may expect a larger discussion about whether reserving these tasks for a specific type of employee who is being paid less actually does constitute social dumping, as well as a closer scrutiny of the grounds for upholding such reservation. Sorting jobs by medical diagnosis may prove not only a difficult exercise but also a slippery slope.
3. A third dilemma is concerned with who pays for the external support and follow-up. In Scandic's venture, part of the arrangement is that the Labour and Welfare Administration pays for this. But this is a strictly temporary and local arrangement for this specific venture. This administration has other, more expensive ways of creating jobs for people with disabilities in ordinary private and public-sector businesses, but, because they are so expensive, the number of jobs that can be created is pitifully limited. This illustrates how administration systems in themselves may function for some groups as barriers to participation in society, simply by being bureaucratic systems that do not adapt easily to changes in their environment, to new ideologies or to new opportunities.

So far, Scandic's venture is proving a success. Thirty applicants were interviewed and screened by the Helt Med! team. Eight were recommended for a four-week practice period at "their" hotel. After this period, six were hired. Six months on, all parties are happy with the arrangement, which also has generated much positive attention and media publicity in Norway. Plans are now in motion to upscale to a national level and create similar jobs in other Scandic hotels.

Redefining work?

This chapter illustrates the challenges of expanding the "normal model" of work in order to accommodate those who today are excluded from ordinary work. The idea is that work is the norm, and that full employment will benefit society. These challenges coincide with other changes indicating that the "normal model" is under threat. Many of the chapters in this book indicate that we are entering a new industrial era. It may be that we need to redefine the concept of work. Guy Standing's 2010 book *Work after Globalization: Building Occupational Citizenship* engages in such a debate. He questions the distinction between work and labour, building part of his argument on Hannah Arendt's terms *vita activa* and *vita contemplativa*, and her distinction between labour, work and activity.

In terms of the concept of work, it may turn out we have been living in a historical parenthesis, a period where "work" largely has been taken to be synonymous with "paid employment". The cab driver, though self-employed, obviously also works, as does the business owner or executive, albeit being an employer. For decades, feminist scholars have been pointing out that reducing work to "paid employment" is to make invisible forms of labour in other arenas, which, albeit "unpaid", not fitting the parameters of a "job" and lacking an 'employer', nonetheless should count as work. But even taking private-sphere "unpaid labour" and public-sphere "paid employment" into account, this still leaves substantial amounts of productive activity unaccounted for, such as various forms of voluntary work (Taylor 2004), as well as the "private and informal work" that maintaining a personal "employability" increasingly may require (Smith 2010).

Thus, a labour market that aspires to optimise equality and inclusion as well as business opportunity may need to be a differentiated labour market, in the sense of offering a variety of work conditions in order to accommodate the fact that workers differ, have different needs and wishes and thrive under different conditions. Such differentiation may transpire between different segments of a labour market, meaning that a variety of different work conditions with differing support levels are dispersed in the labour market. It may also transpire within a business or organisation, meaning that a variety of different work conditions with differing support levels are present inside a single organisation. In the latter case, this may also contribute to more lifespan-friendly work environments. This way, a labour market with greater differentiation in types of jobs and work conditions might also contribute to a more pluralistic, liberal and democratic society. This already represents a noticeable step away from the "normal model". However, coping with the future of work may require redefining work in even more radical ways, ways that bring work closer to the new reality and create less divides in society. What is the solution?

> **Box 14.7 The Kodak moment of work**
>
> ***The disruptiveness of economic change:***
>
> The normal model of work might collapse.
>
> ***The knowledge one failed to use:***
>
> The reason for its collapse might be that we burden the model with new intentions at the same time as the underlying support for this model is crumbling.
>
> ***Ability to adjust to future changes:***
>
> There are some hard choices ahead. It is difficult to see how the model can be more effective and efficient and at the same time more inclusive. One can retain the normal model, but then some of the ambitions in today's work life may have to be abandoned.
>
> ***The opportunity in the changes:***
>
> If the normal model in which everybody is at work with a paid, fixed, long-term contract is not to be sustainable in the future, we need to redefine work. We should consider rethinking the assumptions in the model. Work is more than labour. The definitions of work and the boundaries of work and non-work can be redefined. Work can be defined as contributing to social value.

This book does not purport to predict the future. A better strategy in the face of disruptive change may be to formulate explicit and robust understandings of what specific values we will attempt to steer by, come what may. If we were to pick one promising development that could hold the key to defusing some of the built-up tension in the present conundrum of work and welfare and ease the way forward, we would look to the idea of implementing Universal Basic Income (UBI): This offers all citizens a non-conditional flat-rate payment, with income earned above that taxed progressively, replacing the current welfare system. Forms of UBI are being piloted in Finland, Italy and Canada; are being considered in Scotland; and have been successfully piloted in economies of the global south, such as India and Namibia (Lacey 2017). Reed and Lansley (2016, p. 8) claim that a such a solution would "offer much greater financial independence and freedom of choice for individuals between work and leisure, education and caring while recognising the huge value of unpaid and voluntary work". It is radical. Yet, one of the dangers of the moment is not being radical.

> While a UBI may still seem utopian to many opponents, sometimes the long-term risks of radical changes are lower than the risks associated with a continuation of the existing system. Holding on to obsolete concepts for too long provokes not only social and political pressures as a consequence of increasing

polarisation, but it basically endangers the understanding and acceptance of the concept of solidarity, especially among the younger generation. Like the social market economy, the UBI reconciles economic efficiency and social security. It is radical, but also just. It is liberal and contemporary. That is why it offers the best social-political prerequisite for "prosperity for all" in the 21st century.

(Straubhaar 2017, p. 74)

Broadly speaking, our discussion points at three strategies:

- Strategy 0: Continue as before. This means "more of the same", basically resigning to the forces at large.
- Strategy 1: Work for change at an actor level. Increase social awareness "heart by heart", "mind by mind", think globally, work locally. The danger is that the total impact that may be achieved will be insufficient, particularly in regard to depth.
- Strategy 2: Look at present system configurations. Do they correspond to what we want? Consider system changes based on collective values and collective solutions. This may include some hard choices about the "normal model". But whether the answer is to continue broadening it or narrow it down: any model of work, to be sustainable, should enable any person with capacity to create value, i.e. everyone, to earn their daily bread.

CONCLUSION

*Hans Christian Garmann Johnsen,
Halvor Holtskog and Richard Ennals*

The challenge

The discussion in this book had three intentions: (a) to address the changes that we see, that are likely to come and that will influence society, business and work; (b) to discuss different ways of building knowledge about social and economic change; and (c) to discuss the special role of social science in providing valid knowledge for the future. We argued in the introduction that our approach to these issues would be practical and organisational, methodological and philosophical. Questions we have tried to discuss include:

- How can we balance technological change and meaningful work?
- How can we promote pluralism in organisational thinking, create human-centred systems and acknowledge the importance of local learning processes?
- How can we redefine work and understand the impact on how we conceptualise things – the importance of a comprehensive discourse at the workplace?
- What innovation creates institutional instability and how will multinational companies challenge local resilience?
- How can we redefine innovation policy and help leadership to redefine its generic core and business to rethink its role in the economy?
- How is sustainability related to how we think, acknowledging the limits to rationality and the need for a more comprehensive way of thinking?
- How well is the social and political order handling the challenges we face today?
- How can we analyse and change the social and political order and what is the role of social science?
- What is a sustainable political and social order?

Current innovation discourses in national debates, as well as in the European Union (EU) and international organisations, have provided arguments for increased globalisation and market-driven development. They assume that the past is a reliable guide to the future. However, this discourse has been insufficient in its handling of the comprehensiveness and inter-relatedness of social and economic change. Those with a focus on technology may have neglected basic human issues; those who focus on sustainability often neglect social and political organisation, to mention some. This incompleteness has seriously harmed the cause of developing a sustainable and prosperous future for the world population. It is therefore incomplete in relation to "coping with the future". The conventional argument for this is the following:

- Changes are more severe and rapid than the innovation paradigm presupposes. Changes are not isolated products, processes and services; innovative changes also affect the institutional landscape nationally and internationally.
- New challenges related to a sustainable future are not addressed sufficiently in the current innovation paradigm. The technological optimism often observed tends to ignore the fact that comprehensive change also has social, political and institutional aspects. Observers can be based in disciplinary or sectoral silos.

- We face a serious knowledge problem: The amount of information in society has never been greater and more accessible. Still, our processing of information into knowledge is far more complicated that simple linear thinking would assume.

We cannot know all the answers to as-yet-unasked questions about the future. Despite that, we need to be able to cope with the future. We have tried to present a framework for discussing this and have given some input into understanding the structures, forces and tendencies we need to consider. One of the main methodological strategies we have used is to see current development from a historical perspective.

Past, present and future

Throughout this book, we have subscribed to a story about the development of industrial society, where it is argued that we are at present in the third phase of industrialisation and probably entering a new, fourth phase. Are we facing systemic change? By *systemic change*, we refer to the interconnectedness of change. The argument is not that one factor only defines change, but that when change happens, it influences a complete set of factors. What we believe our society needs to consider and agree on are some of the priorities related to values. We have referred to enlightenment ideals. We have argued that they are conflicting. However, they are still trying to understand a human society based on respect for individuals and the individual freedom to speak, work and engage in society under a system of rule of law. Conflicting ideas exist on how to retain these values under systemic change. To this discussion, we have pointed at several things, such as how organisations act responsibly, how leaders exercise judgement, how the political system gives meaningful arenas for individuals to participate, how work is organised to include most people and how we think about Humanism, to mention some. However, we acknowledge that we are part of the problem under study, and we hope to be part of the answer. Philosophers have interpreted the world. We also need to try to change the world, and in so doing, come to a deeper understanding.

This book project has been a collaborative voyage of discovery, as we have developed arguments and arguments which derive from the research and experience of the contributors and editors. The material has been written, shared, cleaned, sculpted, massaged and polished. As with a diamond, new light has been cast on many facets of an imagined future in which we hope to play our individual and collective parts.

Rethinking assumptions for society, business and work

The background for our discussion has been the argument that we are facing a new stage in industrial development that is marked by a combination of two main issues: digitalisation and sustainability. Are we now facing a new era, due both to the technological shift towards digital technology and because of the pressure to find more sustainable solutions? In the contemporary debate, the question is what the implications will be for society, business and work. We argue that if we are facing a change, such a systemic change has a more comprehensive impact than just changing our technology or organisations. Our fourteen chapters cover many topics that might be affected. It is not an exhaustive list. Other issues could be added and other arguments applied. The main contribution of our discussion might be to point out the integrated nature of systemic change, which allows us to consider the larger picture that is at stake in such a systemic change.

Our answers have been presented in the different chapters, using the "Kodak Moment" as a metaphor, in order to highlight the challenges we are facing. The different chapters provide insightful overviews of political and economic contexts, the role of organisations, knowledge in multinational corporations, leadership, the changing nature of technology, recent approaches to innovation and regional development, the nature of work, meeting human needs and an active perspective on learning, with a focus on empowering young people to be part of creating the future.

Our contributors are international in perspective but typically Nordic by background. Their work perhaps reflects the calm rationalism and search for consensus and equity that characterise the Norwegian model. On this basis, a multiple-author text can speak with almost a single voice. In short, we have presented the following arguments:

> **Box C.1 Rethinking assumptions**
>
> In Chapter 1, "Coping with politics: From post-nationalism to re-nationalism": *criticism of the assumption* that there is a choice between nationalism and internationalism/universalism; and *rethinking the assumption* that we need to find solutions that balance localism, nationalism and internationalism.
>
> In Chapter 2, "Coping with structural change: Understanding framework conditions": *criticism of the assumption* that there are changes that work the same way in all societies; and *rethinking the assumption* in the sense that one has to acknowledge that structures differ in time, and that changes over time will look differently in different contexts.
>
> In Chapter 3, "Coping with globalisation: Local knowledge and MNCs": *criticism of the assumptions* that globalisation is a threat to the local, but the local can rely on its unique competencies; and *rethinking the assumption* in the sense that local strategies need to acknowledge global forces and develop more comprehensive responses to global challenges.
>
> In Chapter 4, "Coping with the economic policy: Innovation policy in times of disruption": *criticism of the assumptions* that economic policy is something one can just decide and implement and thereby modify and be ahead of the market; and *rethinking the assumptions* in terms of acknowledging that

economic policy historically has had an ideological basis, and in more disruptive markets, it cannot pretend to be ahead of disruption.

In Chapter 5, "Coping with ways of knowing: A pluralist perspective on knowledge": *criticism of the assumption* that knowledge is one thing and that ideas like fact-based policy build on a wrong understanding of knowledge; *rethinking the assumption* in terms of acknowledging that knowledge is a plural phenomenon that gives meaning in a social context and thereby is dependent on democratic dialogue

In Chapter 6, "Coping with decisions: First I imagine, then I know": *criticism of the assumption* that we can form rational knowledge about the future; *rethinking the assumptions* in terms of acknowledging that the future is dependent on our ability to anticipate and imagine and thereby see different realities and their consequences.

In Chapter 7, "Coping with sustainability: The need for non-instrumental thinking": *criticism of the assumption* of instrumental thinking; *rethinking the assumptions* that are the basis of our thinking, acknowledging how it is embedded in our social context and thereby considering reality beyond this context.

In Chapter 8, "Coping with methodology: Validity and knowledge about the future": *criticism of assumptions* that social science can provide facts and true knowledge for making decisions that can guide us into the future; *rethinking the assumptions* in terms of acknowledging that social science is a way of producing knowledge and that it is socially embedded, thereby acknowledging the limits to social science knowledge development.

In Chapter 9, "Coping with technology: A future of robots?" *criticism of assumptions* that technology is something independent of social reality that social reality has to comply with; *rethinking the assumptions* in terms of a more interactive approach to technology, acknowledging that it is a social product.

In Chapter 10, "Coping with Humanism: A Posthuman future?" *criticism of the assumptions* that Transhumanism and Posthumanism are a threat to human existence; *rethinking the assumptions* by acknowledging that they help us become aware of the need to redefine and restate human values and Humanism under new technological conditions.

In Chapter 11, "Coping with social learning: Social and economic change through engagement": *criticism of the assumption* that social change can happen from above; *rethinking the assumptions* on local engagement and dialogue, acknowledging that they are important in promoting social change.

In Chapter 12, "Coping with organisations: Socio-technical, dialogical and beyond": *criticism of the assumption* that there is a divide in between technologically driven and human-driven thinking in organisations, and that human thinking should modify the technological and functional aspects of organisations; *rethinking the assumptions* in terms of acknowledging the need to close that divide and think of organisations as social phenomena with a role and responsibility in society.

> In Chapter 13, "Coping with leadership: The role of judgement": *criticism of the assumptions* that leaders are commanders of some sort; *rethinking the assumptions* on leadership where leaders have to see themselves as part of a social dialogue.
>
> In Chapter 14, "Coping with work: Redefining relations between work life and society": *criticism of the assumption* that the normal model of everybody at work will be sustainable in the future; *rethinking the assumptions* about work, that work is more than labour. The definitions of work and boundaries of work and non-work have to be redefined. Work has to be defined as contributing to social value.

The core of the argument in this book, written by social scientists, is how social science can provide valid insight into issues about the future. Thus, even though we have pointed out practical and organisational issues that we find relevant in the current situation in Western societies, the more fundamental issues we are concerned with relate to how social science can help us cope with the future. These are both philosophical and methodological challenges. As we argued in the introduction, there are many examples of scholarly work that have made excellent analysis of their own time or of history but still have not been able to foresee the future. We therefore rule out the idea that social science can predict the future. Indeed, our work on the Brexit "Kodak Moment" has shown this to be the case. However, what we can do is to make sense of the knowledge that we have and argue for reasonable actions today that can have a long-term positive impact.

Research projects and publications are actions and may provoke responses. We should value knowledge that is based on experience and is presented following reflection. Researchers need to recognise that they can be significant actors. Their engagement is an important asset. How can they work together, deploying their resources of knowledge to create collaborative advantage? Our book reflects that insight. We have tried to cope with that challenge and hope to assist our readers in coping with the future. The future, and the questions that we ask about the future, will continue to change.

Our main methodology has been to have a reflective perspective on the kind of knowledge that social science can offer in understanding the future on that basis of the past and the present. In doing so, we have focused on identifying some of the underlying structures that are forming the society we live in. Understanding these, we argue, can help us understand future changes. Some social scientists have, understandably, felt helpless in face of the challenge of the unknown future, which they see as determined by factors that are beyond their control. It has been easier for them to outline conventional wisdom, which falls short of addressing our challenge, and to fall back on tradition. Often there could not be a single linear account, but chaotic access can also bring relief. In summary, social science is an expression of our individual and collective humanity in a changing world. We argue that it is our responsibility to go beyond merely describing that world, of which we are part. We are also participants in shaping the process of change.

REFERENCES

Ainger, A., Kaura, R., & Ennals, R. (1995). *Business success through human centred systems*. London: Springer.

Alvarez-Jimenez, M., Gleeson, J. F., Henry, L. P., Harrigan, S. M., Harris, M. G., Killackey, E. & McGorry, P. D. (2012). Road to full recovery: Longitudinal relationship between symptomatic remission and psychosocial recovery in first-episode psychosis over 7.5 years. *Psychological Medicine, 42*(3), 595–606.

Alvunger, D. & Nelson, B. (Eds.). (2014). *Journeys in search of the Baltic Sea Teacher – Cross-border collaboration and dialogues within the Cohab Project*. Report No. 24, 2014. Linnæus University Press.

Amin, A., & Cohendet, P. (2004). *Architectures of knowledge: Firms, capabilities, and communities*. Oxford: Oxford University Press.

Amin, A., & Roberts, J. (2008). The resurgence of community in economic thought and practice. In A. Amin & J. Roberts (Eds.), *Community, economic creativity, and organization* (pp. 11–34). New York, NY: Oxford University Press.

Andersen, J. G. (2011). From the edge of the abyss to bonanza – and beyond. Danish economy and economic policies 1980–2011. In L. Mjøset (Ed.), The Nordic varieties of capitalism. *Comparative Social Research*, vol. *28*. Bingley: Emerald.

APA (2013). *Diagnostic and statistical manual of mental disorders*, 5th revision. Arlington: American Psychiatric Association.

Appelbaum, B. (2017, February 23). The jobs Americans do. *New York Times Magazine*. Retrieved from: https://www.nytimes.com/2017/02/23/magazine/the-new-working-class.html

Argyris, C. (1957). The individual and organization: Some problems of mutual adjustment. *Administrative Science Quarterly*, 1–24.

Argyris, C., & Schön, D. A. (1974). *Theory in practice: Increasing professional effectiveness*. Jossey-Bass.

Argyris, C., & Schön, D. A. (1978). *Organizational learning: A theory of action perspective*. Reading, MA: Addison-Wesley.

Asimov, I. (1950). Runaround. In I. Asimov (Ed.), *I, Robot*. New York: Bantam Dell.

Audretsch, D., & Feldman, M. (1996). R&D spillovers and the geography of innovation and production. *The American Economy Review, 86*(3), 630–640.

Austin, J. (1962). *How to do things with words*. Oxford: Clarendon Press.
Avolio, B. J., & Gardner, W. L. (2005). Authentic leadership development: Getting to the root of positive forms of leadership. *The Leadership Quarterly, 16*(3), 315–338.
Banerjee, S. B. (2003). Who sustains whose development? Sustainable development and the reinvention of nature. *Organization Studies, 24*(1), 143–180.
Barney, J. (1991). Firm resources and sustained competitive advantage. *Journal of Management, 17*(1), 99–120.
Barr, M. S. (2003). *Envisioning the future: Science fiction and the next millennium*. Wesleyan University Press.
Barrett, D. (2006). *Leadership communication*. New York, NY: McGraw-Hill.
Bass, B. M., Avolio, B. J., & Atwater, L. E. (1996). The transformational and transactional leadership of men and women. *Applied Psychology: An International Review, 45*, 5–34.
Becerra, M.-T., Montanero, M., & Lucero, M. (2016). Graphic support resources for workers with intellectual disability engaged in office tasks: A comparison with verbal instructions from a work mate. *Disability and Rehabilitation, 15*, 1–9.
Belasco, W. (2000). Future notes: The meal-in-a-pill. *Food and Foodways, 8*(4), 253–271. doi:1 0.1080/07409710.2000.9962093.
Bell, D. (1979). *The coming of the post-industrial society*. New York, NY: Basic Books. (Original work published 1973.)
Benjamin, W. (2008). *The work of art in the age of its technological reproducibility and other writings on media*. In M. W. Jennings, B. Doherty, & T. Y. Levin (Eds.), London: Belknap Press of Harvard University Press.
Berg, O. (2008). Fra Unionsoppløsning til «nasjonsoppløsning». Modernisering versus nasjonsbygging. Tidsskrift for samfunnsforskning. *Universitetsforlaget, 49*(1), 107–121.
Berger, P. L. (2014). *The many altars of modernity: Towards a paradigm for religion in a pluralist age*. Boston, MA: De Gruyter.
Beveridge, W. (1942). *Social insurance and allied services*. British Library. BL. Retrieved 8 July 2014.
Beverungen, A., Dunne, S., & Hoedemaekers, C. (2013). The financialisation of business ethics. *Business Ethics: A European Review, 22*(1), 105–117.
Bilal, E. (1977). *La ville qui n'existait pas*. Paris: Dargaud.
Bloch, M. (1993). *Feudal society 1. The growth of the ties of dependence*. London: Routledge. (Original work published 1939.)
Bloom, A. (1991). *The Republic of Plato*. New York, NY: Basic Books.
Böhm, S., Bharucha, Z. P., & Pretty, J. (Eds.) (2015). *Ecocultures: Blueprints for sustainable communities*. (1st ed.). London: Routledge.
Bolland, B. (2010). O Dimiourgos os Skinothetis [The Designer as Director]. In A. Kawa & E. Sampanikou (Eds.), *Thea apo psila. Fantasia kai Afigisi sta Comics* [*View from above. Imagination and narrative in comics*] (pp. 18–24) (In Greek). Athens: Ilivaton.
Borghouts-van de Pas, I. & Freese, C. (2017). Inclusive HRM and employment security for disabled people: An interdisciplinary approach. *E-Journal of International and Comparative Labour Studies, 6*(1), 1–25.
Bourdieu, P. (1977). *Outline of a theory of practice*. Cambridge: Cambridge University Press.
Bourdieu, P. (2011). The forms of capital. In I. Szeman & T. Kaposy (Eds.), *Cultural theory: An anthology* (pp. 81–93). Madden, MA: Wiley-Blackwell.
Brödner, P. (1990). *The shape of future technology: The anthropocentric alternative*. London: Springer.
Brooking, A. (1999). *Corporate memory: Strategies for knowledge management*. Thompson Business Press.
Brulin G., & Svensson L. (2012). *Managing sustainable development programmes: A learning approach to change*. Farnham: Gower.

Brynjolfsson, E., McAfee, A. (2011). *Race against the machine: How the digital revolution is accelerating innovation, driving productivity, and irreversibly transforming employment and the economy*. Lexington, MA: Digital Frontier Press.

Brynjolfsson, E., & McAfee, A. (2014). *The second machine age: Work, progress, and prosperity in a time of brilliant technologies*. New York, NY: W. W. Norton & Company.

Burgess, R. F. (1975). *Ships beneath the sea: A history of subs and submersibles*. New York, NY: McGraw-Hill.

Burns, T., & Stalker, G. M. (1981). *The management of innovation*. London: Tavistock.

Calás, M. B. (1993). Deconstructing charismatic leadership: Re-reading Weber from the darker side. *The Leadership Quarterly, 4*(3–4), 305–328.

Carayannis, E. G., Campbell, D. F. J., & Rehman, S. S. (2016). Mode 3 knowledge production: Systems and systems theory, clusters and networks. *Journal of Innovation and Entrepreneurship, 5*(1), 5–17.

Cellan-Jones, R. (2014). Stephen Hawking warns artificial intelligence could end mankind. Retrieved from http://www.bbc.com/news/technology-30290540.

Cetina, K. K. (1999). *Epistemic cultures: How the sciences make knowledge*. MA: Harvard University Press.

Chelini, C., & Riva, S. (2013). On the relationships between Friedrich Hayek and Jean Piaget: A new paradigm for cognitive and evolutionary economists. In R. Frantz & R. Leeson (Eds.), *Hayek and behavioral economics* (pp. 127–148). London: Palgrave Macmillan UK.

Christensen, T., & Laegreid, P. (2001). New public management: The effects of contractualism and devolution on political control. *Public Management Review, 3*(1), 73–94.

Christin, P. & Billal, E. (2000). *Le Sarcophage*. Paris: Dargaud.

Coase, R. (1937). The nature of the firm. *Economica, 4*(16), 386–405.

Cohen, B, & Winn, M. I. (2007). Market imperfections, opportunity and sustainable entrepreneurship. *Journal of Business Venturing, 22*(1), 29–49.

Coleman, J. S. (1988). Social capital in the creation of human capital. *American Journal of Sociology*, S95–S120.

Collinson, D. (2011). Critical leadership studies. In D. Collinson, A. Bryman, K. Grint, B. Jackson, & M. Uhl Bien (Eds.), *Handbook of leadership studies*, (pp. 179–192). London: Sage.

Cooke, P. (2002). *Knowledge economies: Clusters, learning and cooperative advantage*. London: Routledge.

Cooley, M. (1987). *Architect or bee?* London: Chatto and Windus.

Cooper, J. M. (Ed.) (1997). *Plato: Complete works*. Indianapolis, IN: Hackett.

Corbett, J. M., Rasmussen, L. B., & Rauner F. (1991). *Crossing the border: The social and engineering design of computer integrated manufacturing systems*. London: Springer.

Creed, B. (1995). Horror and the carnivalesque. The body-monstrous. In L. Deveraux & R. Hillman (Eds.), *Fields of vision. Essays on film studies, visual anthropology and photography* (pp. 127–159). Berkeley: University of California Press.

Cue, A. (2015). Volkswagen's diesel emission scandal "Dieselgate". doi:http://dx.doi.org/10.1787/9789264013100-en.

Cummins, D. D. (2012). *Good thinking: seven powerful ideas that influence the way we think*. Cambridge: Cambridge University Press.

Day, D. V. (2001). Leadership development: A review in context. *The Leadership Quarterly, 11*(4), 581–613.

Delman, J., Kovich, L., Burke, S., & Martone, K. (2017). The promise of demand side employer-based strategies to increase employment rates for people living with serious mental illnesses. *Psychiatric Rehabilitation Journal, 40*(2), 179–182.

Demirdöğen, Ü. D. (2010). The roots of research in (political) persuasion: Ethos, pathos, logos and the Yale studies of persuasive communications. *International Journal of Social Inquiry*, *3*(1), 189–201.

Descartes, R. (1996). *Discourse on the method: And, meditations on first philosophy*. New Haven: Yale University Press.

Di Giovanna, J. (2009). Dr Manhattan, I presume? In M. D. White (Ed.), *Watchmen and philosophy: A Rorschach test* (pp. 103–114 [109]). New Jersey, NJ: John Wiley and Sons, Inc.

Docherty, P., Kira, M., & Shani, A. R. (Eds.). (2008). *Creating sustainable work systems: Developing social sustainability*. London: Routledge.

Drath, R., & Horch, A. (2014). Industrie 4.0: Hit or hype? [industry forum]. *IEEE Industrial Electronics Magazine*, *8*(2), 56–58.

Dreyfus, H. & Dreyfus, S. (1986). *Mind over machine: The power of human intuition and expertise in the era of the computer*. New York, NY: Free Press.

Drücker, P. F. (1988). The coming of the new organization. *Harvard Business Review*. *66*(1), 45.

Drücker, P. F. (1994). The age of social transformation. *Atlantic Monthly*, *274*(5), 53–58.

Druillet, P. (2000). *Chaos*. Paris: Guy Delcourt Productions.

Durkheim, E. (2014). *The division of labor in society*. New York, NY: Simon and Schuster. (Original work published 1893.)

Earl, M. J. (2000). Evolving the e-business. *Business Strategy Review*, *11*(2), 33–38.

Edler, J., & Fagerberg, J. (2017). Innovation policy: What, why and how. *Oxford Review of Economic Policy*, *33*(1), 2–23.

IEA (2017). Tracking clean energy progress 2017. Retrieved from https://www.iea.org/publications/freepublications/publication/TrackingCleanEnergyProgress2017.pdf

Eikeland, O. (2007). From epistemology to gnoseology – Understanding the knowledge claims of action research. *Management Research News*, *30*(5), 344–358.

Eikeland, O. (2006). Phronesis, Aristotle, and action research. *International Journal of Action Research*, *2*(1), 5–53.

Eikeland, O. (2008). *The ways of Aristotle – Aristotelian phronesis, Aristotelian philosophy of dialogue, and action research*. Bern: Verlag Peter Lang.

Ekman, M., Gustavsen, B., Asheim, B., & Pålshaugen, O. (Eds.). (2011). *Learning regional innovation: Scandinavian models*. Basingstoke: Palgrave Macmillan.

Elkington, J. (1997). *Cannibals with forks: The triple bottom line of 21st century business*. New York, NY: Capstone/John Wiley.

Elster, J. (2009). *Reason and rationality*. Princeton, NJ: Princeton University Press.

Emery, F. E., & Trist, E. L. (1960). Socio-technical systems. In C. W. Churchman & M. Verhulst (Eds.), *Management Science and Techniques*, Vol. 2 (pp. 83–97). Oxford: Pergamon Press.

Emery F., & Thorsrud E. (1976). *Democracy at work: The report of the Norwegian industrial democracy program*. Leiden: Martinus Nijhoff.

Ennals, R. (1986). *Star Wars: A question of initiative*. Chichester: Wiley.

Ennals, R., & Gustavsen B. (1999). *Work organisation and Europe as a development coalition*. Amsterdam: Benjamins.

Ennals, R. (2014). Development coalitions. In D. Coghlan & M. Brydon-Miller (Eds.), *Sage encyclopaedia of action research* (pp. 250–252). London: Sage.

Ennals, R., Göranzon, B., Nelson, B., & Alvunger, D. (2016). Dialogue, skill and tacit knowledge: Practical knowledge and corporate responsibility. In A. Habisch & R. Schmidpeter (Eds.), *Cultural roots of sustainable management: Practical wisdom and corporate social responsibility*. Switzerland: Springer.

Erixon, L. (2011). Under the influence of traumatic events, new ideas, economic experts and the ITC revolution – The economic policy and macroeconomic performance of

Sweden. In L. Mjøset, (Ed.), *The Nordic varieties of capitalism. Comparative social research*, Vol. 28. Bingley: Emerald.

Etzkowitz, H., & Leydesdorff, L. (2000). The dynamics of innovation: From national systems and "mode 2" to a triple helix of university–industry–government relations. *Research Policy, 29*, 109–23.

EU (1997). *Green paper: Partnership for a new organisation of work.* Brussels: European Commission.

EU (2017). *White paper on the future of Europe.* Brussels: European Commission.

Fagerberg, J., Mowery, D., & Verspagen, B. (2009). *Innovation, path dependency, and policy: The Norwegian case.* New York, NY: Oxford University Press.

Faulk, R. (2015). *The next big thing: A History of the boom-or-bust moments that shaped the modern world.* Zest.

Federal Ministry of Labour and Social Affairs. (2015). *Re-imagining work. Green paper: Work 4.0.* Berlin: Directorate-General for Basic Issues of the Social State, the Working World and the Social Market Economy.

Feldman, M. (1994). The university and economic development: The case of Johns Hopkins University and Baltimore. *Economic Development Quarterly, 8*(1), 67–77

Fellmann, S., Iversen, M., Sjögren, H., & Thue, L. (2008) *Creating Nordic capitalism: The business history of a competitive periphery.* Basingstoke: Palgrave Macmillan.

Feyerabend, P. (1975). *Against method: Outline of an anarchistic theory of knowledge.* Minneapolis, MN: University of Minnesota Press.

Florida, R. (1995). Toward the learning region. *Futures, 27*(5), 527–536.

Florida, R. (2002). *The rise of the creative class: And how it's transforming work, leisure, community and everyday life.* New York: Basic Books.

Foley, R. (1987). *The theory of epistemic rationality.* Cambridge: Harvard University Press.

Foray, D. (2015). *Smart specialization: Opportunities and challenges for regional innovation policy.* London: Routledge.

Foray, D., & Lundvall, B. (1998). The knowledge-based economy: From the economics of knowledge to the learning economy. *The Economic Impact of Knowledge*, 115–121.

Ford, M. (2015). *Rise of the robots: Technology and the threat of a jobless future.* New York, NY: Basic Books.

Foucault, M. (1965). *Madness and civilization.* (R. Howard, Trans.). New York, NY: Random House. (Original work published 1961.)

Fox, A. J., & Collier, P. F. (1976). Low mortality rates in industrial cohort studies due to selection of work and survival in the industry. *British Journal of Preventive & Social Medicine, 30*(4), 225–30.

Freeman, C. (1987). *Technology and economic performance: Lessons from Japan.* London: Pinter.

Freire, P. (2000). *Pedagogy of the oppressed.* London: Bloomsbury Publishing.

Freyssenet, M., Mair, A., Shimizu, K., & Volpato, G. (1998). *One best way? Trajectories and industrial models of the world's automobile producers.* Oxford: Oxford University Press.

Friedman, M. (1970, September 13). The social responsibility of business is to increase its profits. *The New York Times Magazine*, pp. 32–33, 122–124, 126.

Friedman, T. (2005). *The world is flat: A brief history of the globalized world in the 21st century.* London: Allen Lane.

Fukuyama, F. (2011). *The origins of political order.* London: Profile Books.

Fuller, S. (2002). *Knowledge management foundations.* Vermont: KMCI Press Butterworth-Heinemann.

Gadamer, H.-G. (2010). *Truth and method.* London: Continuum. (Original work published 1975.)

Gamperiene, M. (2008). Health and work environment among women in unskilled occupations (PhD Dissertation). Faculty of Medicine, University of Oslo.

Gastil, J. (1994) A definition and illustration of democratic leadership. *Human Relations*, 47(8), 953–975.

Gemmill, G., & Oakley, J. (1992). Leadership: An alienating social myth? *Human Relations*, 45(2), 113–129.

Gertler, M. S. (2004). *Manufacturing culture: The institutional geography of industrial practice.* Oxford: Oxford University Press.

Gewurtz, R. E., Langan, S., & Shand, D. (2016). Hiring people with disabilities: A scoping review. *Work*, 54, 135–148.

Gigerenzer, G. (2010). *Rationality for mortals: How people cope with uncertainty.* Oxford: Oxford University Press.

Gilbert, R. J., & Newbery, D. M. G. (1982). Preemptive patenting and the persistence of monopoly. *The American Economic Review*, 73(3), 514–526.

Gini, A. (1997). Moral leadership and business ethics. *Journal of Leadership Studies*, 4(4), 64–81.

Glaser, J. (2005). Technology roadmapping. *Clean Technologies and Environmental Policy*, 7(2), 75–77. doi:10.1007/s10098-004-0263-x.

Göranzon, B., Hammarén, M., & Ennals R. (Eds.). (2006). *Dialogue, skill and tacit knowledge.* Chichester: Wiley.

Granovetter, M. S. (1973). The strength of weak ties. *American Journal of Sociology*, 8(6), 1360–1380.

Granovetter, M. S. (1985). Economic action and social structure: the problem of embeddedness. *American Journal of Sociology*, 91(3), 481–510.

Grant, R. M. (1996). Prospering in dynamically competitive environments: Organizational capability as knowledge integration. *Organization Science* 7(4), 375–387.

Grint, K. (2005) Problems, problems, problems: The social construction of "leadership". *Human Relations*, 58(11), 1467–1494.

GTAI. (2016). *Germany Trade & Invest, Industrie 4.0 – Smart manufacturing for the future* (pp. 1–40). Berlin: Germany Trade & Invest.

Gustavsen B., Nyhan B., & Ennals R. (Eds.). (2007). *Learning together for local innovation: Promoting learning regions.* Luxembourg: Cedefop.

Gustavsen, B. (1992). *Dialogue and development: Theory of communication, action research and the restructuring of working life.* Assen/Maastricht: Van Gorcum.

Guttmann, L. (1950). The basis for scalogram analysis. In S. Stouffer (Ed.), *Measurement and prediction*, Vol. 4. New Jersey: John Wiley and Sons.

Habermas, J. (1964). *Theory and practice.* London: Heinemann.

Habermas, J. (1984). *The theory of communicative action.* London: Polity Press.

Habermas, J. (1991). *Strukturwandel der Öffentlichkeit. Untersuchungen zu einer Kategorie der bürgerlichen Gesellschaft* [The structural transformation of the public sphere: An inquiry into a category of bourgeois society]. Massachusetts: MIT press. (Original work published 1962.)

Habermas, J. (1971). *Erkenntnis und interesse* [Knowledge and human interests]. Chicago: Beacon Press.

Habermas, J. (2001). *The postnational constellation.* Cambridge: MIT Press.

Hall, P. A., & Soskice, D. (2011). *Varieties of capitalism: The institutional foundations of comparative advantages.* Oxford: Oxford University Press.

Hancké, B., Rhodes, M., & Thatcher, M. (2007). *Beyond varieties of capitalism: Conflict, contradictions, and complementarities in the European economy.* Oxford: Oxford University Press.

Hawkins, A. J. (2017). Watch this all-electric 'flying car' take its first test flight in Germany. Retrieved from: https://www.theverge.com/2017/4/20/15369850/lilium-jet-flying-car-first-flight-vtol-aviation-munich

Hayek, F. A. (1937). Economics and knowledge. *Economica*, 4(13), 33–54.
Hayek, F. A. (1945). The use of knowledge in society. *The American Economic Review*, 35(4), 519–530.
Hayek, F.A. (1967). Kinds of rationalism. In F. A. Hayek, (Ed.), *Studies in philosophy, politics and economics*(pp. 82–95). London: Routledge & Kegan Paul.
Hegel, G. F. W. (1835). *Vorlesungen über die Ästhetik*, I. Berlin: H. J. Hotho.
Heidegger, M. (1962). *Being and time*. (J. Macquarrie & E. Robinson, Trans.). New York, NY: Harper Row.
Heidegger, M. (1977). *The question concerning technology, and other essays*. New York, NY: Garland Pub.
Heidegger, M. (2002) *Heidegger: Off the beaten track*. Cambridge: Cambridge University Press.
Helliwell, J., Layard, R., & Sachs, J. (2017). *World happiness report 2017*. New York, NY: Sustainable Development Solutions Network.
Hirschman, A. O. (1976). *The passion and the interest. Political arguments for capitalism before its triumph*. Princeton, NJ: Princeton University Press.
Hood, C. (1995). The "New Public Management" in the 1980s: Variations on a theme. *Accounting, Organizations and Society*, 20(2–3), 93–109.
Horkheimer, M., Adorno, T. W., & Noeri, G. (Trans.). (2002). *Dialectic of enlightenment*. Stanford University Press.
How, J. (2000). *2000AD* and Hollywood: The special relationship between a British comic and American film. In A. Magnussen & H.-C. Christiansen, (Eds.), *Comics and culture: Analytical and theoretical approaches to comics* (pp. 225–241). Copenhagen: Museum Tusculanum Press/University of Copenhagen.
Howard, J. [Wagner, J.], Smith, R. et al. (2009), Judge Dredd. The judge child, Parts 1–5. In R. Hal (Ed.), *The best of Judge Dredd* (pp. 87–120). London: Prion Books. Also, the complete story in J. Oliver (Ed.) (2006), *Judge Dredd. The complete case files 04*. Oxford: Rebellion.
Huws, U., Spencer, N. H., & Joyce, S. (2016). Crowd Work in Europe. Preliminary results from a survey in the UK, Sweden, Germany, Austria and the Netherlands. Federation for Progressive Studies. Retrieved from http://www.feps-europe.eu/assets/39aad271-85ff-457c-8b23-b30d82bb808f/crowd-work-in-europe-draft-report-last-versionpdf.pdf
ILO (2016). 105th Session, 2016, *Report VI: Advancing social justice: Reviewing the impact of the ILO Declaration on Social Justice for a Fair Globalization*. Genève: The International Labour Conference.
Jackson, T. (2016). *Prosperity without growth: Foundations for the economy of tomorrow* (2nd ed.). London: Routledge.
Jacobs, J. (1985). *Cities and the wealth of nations*. New York, NY: Random House.
Jenkin, M. (2016). Written out of the story: The robots capable of making the news. Retrieved from https://www.theguardian.com/small-business-network/2016/jul/22/written-out-of-story-robots-capable-making-the-news
Hatch, M. J., & Schultz, M. (1997). Relations between organizational culture, identity and image. *European Journal of Marketing*, 31(5/6), 356–365.
Jodorowsky, A., & Gimenez, J. (1992). *La Caste des Méta-Barons* [The Metabarons Cast], *1: Othon le Trisaieul* [Othon, the Great-Great-Grandfather]. Genève: Les Humanoïdes Associées S.A.
Johnsen, H. C. G. (2014). *The new natural resource: Knowledge development, society and economics*. Ashgate Publishing, Ltd.
Johnsen, H. C. G., & Ennals, R. (Eds.). (2012). *Creating collaborative advantage: Innovation and knowledge creation in regional economies*. Farnham: Gower.

Johnsen, H. C. G., Torjesen, S., & Ennals, R. (Eds.). (2015). *Higher education in a sustainable society: A case for mutual competence building*. Switzerland: Springer.

Johnsen, H. C. G., Hauge, E., Magnussen, M-L., & Ennals, R. (Eds.). (2016). *Applied social science research in a regional knowledge system: Balancing validity, meaning and convenience*. London: Routledge.

Ju, S., Roberts, E., & Zhang, D. (2013). Employer attitudes toward workers with disabilities: A review of research in the past decade. *Journal of Vocational Rehabilitation*, 38, 113–123.

Kalberg, S. (1980). Max Weber's types of rationality: Cornerstones for the analysis of rationalization processes in history. *American Journal of Sociology*, 85(5), 1145–1179.

Kant, I. (2003). What is enlightenment? In H. S. Reiss, (Ed.). *Kant: Political writings* (L. Beck, Trans.). Cambridge: Cambridge University Press. (Original work published 1783.)

Kant, I. (2001). Critique of pure reason. In I. Kant (Ed.), *The basic writings of Kant*. New York, NY: The Modern Library. (Original work published 1781.)

Kant, I. (2001). Critique of Practical Reason. In I. Kant (Ed.), *The basic writings of Kant*. New York: The Modern Library. (Original work published 1788.)

Kawa, A. (2000). What if apocalypse never happens: Evolutionary narratives in contemporary comics. In A. Magnussen & H.-C. Christiansen (Eds.), *Comics and culture. Analytical and theoretical approaches to comics* (pp. 209–224). Copenhagen: Museum Tusculanum Press/ University of Copenhagen.

Keeping, J. (2009). Superheroes and supermen: Finding Nietzsche's *übermensch* in Watchmen. In M. D. White (Ed.), *Watchmen and philosophy. A Rorschach test*, (pp. 47–60 [55–58]). New Jersey: John Wiley and Sons.

Kesting, P., & Ulhøi, J. P. (2010). Employee-driven innovation: Extending the license to foster innovation. *Management Decisions*, 48(1), 65–84.

Khurana, R. (2007). *From higher aims to hired hands: The social transformation of American business schools and the unfulfilled promise of management as a profession*. New York, NY: Princeton University Press.

Kotter, J. P. (1996). *Leading change*. MA: Harvard Business Press.

Kotter, J. P. (2008). *Force for change: How leadership differs from management*. New York, NY: Simon and Schuster.

Kritikos, P. (2017). *Comics' worlds of the fantastic visualization and ideological representations in fantasy comics* (PhD Thesis). Mytilini 2017 (in Greek – English abstract).

Krugman, Paul. (1991). Increasing returns and economic geography. *Journal of Political Economy*, 99(3), 483–499.

Kuhn, T. S. (1970/2000). *The structure of scientific revolutions*. Chicago: Chicago University Press. (Original work published 1962.)

Laasch, O., & Conaway, R. (2014). *Principles of responsible management: Glocal sustainability, responsibility, and ethics*. Nelson Education.

Lacey, A. (2017). Universal basic income as development solution? *Global Social Policy*, 17(1), 93–97.

Lakatos, I., & Musgrave, A. (Eds). (1970). *Criticism and the growth of knowledge*. Cambridge: Cambridge University Press.

Larrea, M. & Karlsen, J., (2016). *Territorial development and action research: Innovation through dialogue*. London: Routledge.

Last, J. M. (1995). *Dictionary of epidemiology* (3rd ed.). Oxford: Oxford University Press.

Ledford, H. (2016). CRISPR: Gene editing is just the beginning. Retrieved from: http:// www.nature.com/news/crispr-gene-editing-is-just-the-beginning-1.19510

Levison, A. B. (1974). *Knowledge and society: An introduction to the philosophy of the social sciences*. Indianapolis, IN: Pegasus.

Li, C. Y., & Sung, F. C. (1999). A review of the healthy worker effect in occupational epidemiology. *Occupational Medicine, 49*(4), 225–229.

Lieberman, M. B., & Montgomery, D. B. (1988). First-mover advantages. *Strategic Management Journal, 9*(S1), 41–58.

Loftis, R. J. (2009). Means, ends and the critique of pure superheroes. In M. D. White (Ed.), *Watchmen and philosophy. A Rorschach test* (pp. 63–77 [65]). New Jersey: John Wiley and Sons, Inc.

Lord, R. G., Brown, D. J., Harvey, J. L., & Hall, R. J. (2001). Contextual constraints on prototype generation and their multilevel consequences for leadership perceptions. *The Leadership Quarterly, 12*(3), 311–338.

Lövgren, V., Markström, U., & Sauer, L. (2017). Towards employment: What research says about support-to-work in relation to psychiatric and intellectual disabilities. *Journal of Social Work in Disability & Rehabilitation, 16*(1), 14–37.

Luhmann, N. (1981). Organisation und Entscheidung. In *Soziologische Aufklärung 3* (pp. 335–389). VS Verlag für Sozialwissenschaften. Heidelberg: Springer.

Hatch, M. J., & Schultz, M. (1997). Relations between organizational culture, identity and image. *European Journal of Marketing, 31*(5/6) 356–365.

McCabe, A. C., Ingram, R., & Dato-On, M. C. (2006). The business of ethics and gender. *Journal of Business Ethics, 64*(2), 101–116.

McGregor, D. (1960). *The human side of enterprise.* New York, NY: McGraw Hill.

March, J. (1991). Exploration and exploitation in organizational learning. *Organization Science, 2*(1), 71–87.

March, J. G., & Simon, H. A. (1993). *Organizations* (2nd ed.). Hoboken: Wiley.

Marshall, A. (1920). *Principles of economics* (8th ed.). London: Macmillan and Co., Ltd. (Original work published 1890.)

Martin, R. (2002). *Financialization of daily life.* Philadelphia: Temple University Press.

Marx, K., & Engels, F. (2002). *The communist manifesto.* London: Penguin. (Original work published 1848.)

Mastorakis, A. (2010). To Epos ton Metavaronon: Treis vasikoi aksones tis diigisis kai I dynamiki tous [The Metabarons epic: Three basic directions of narrative and its dynamics]. In A. Kawa & E. Sampanikou (Eds.), *Thea apo psila. Fantasia kai Afigisi sta Comics* [*View from above. Imagination and narrative in comics*]. 18–24 (In Greek). Athens: Ilivaton.

Mavrikios, D., Papakostas, N., Mourtzis, D., & Chryssolouris, G. (2011). On industrial learning and training for the factories of the future: A conceptual, cognitive and technology framework. *Journal of Intelligent Manufacturing.* doi 10.1007/s10845-011-0590-9.

May, M. E. (2007). *The elegant solution: Toyota's formula for mastering innovation.* New York, NY: Free Press.

Meadows, D. H., Meadows D. L., Randers, J., & Behrens W. W. III. (1972). *The limits to growth.* New York, NY: Universe Books.

Mintzberg, H. (1979). *The structuring of organization: A synthesis of the research.* Englewood: Prentice-Hall.

Mjøset, L., & Cappelen, Å. (2011). The integration of the Norwegian oil economy into the world economy. In Mjøset, L. (Ed.), *The Nordic varieties of capitalism. Comparative social research,* Vol. 28. Bingley: Emerald.

Moebius, & Jodorowsky, A. (1981). *L'Incal noir,* Genève: Les Humanoïdes Associées S.A. [Also in this series: 2. *L'Incal Lumière,* 1982. 3. *Ce qui est en bas,* 1983. 4. *Ce qui est en haut,* 1984. 5. *La cinquième essence, première partie: Galaxie qui songe,* 1988. 6. *La cinquième essence, deuxième partie: La planète difool,* 1988].

Molinsky, E. (2017). Imaginary worlds. New York 2140. https://www.imaginaryworldspodcast.org/new-york-2140.html

Moore, A. & Bolland, B., et al. (1988). *Batman. The killing joke.* New York, NY: DC Comics.

Moore, A., & Gibbons, D. (1987). *Watchmen*. London: Titan Books. (Original work published in single magazine form as *WATCHMEN 1–12*, DC Comics, 1986–1987.)

Morgan, J., & Liker, J. K. (2006). *The Toyota product development system: Integrating people, process and technology*. New York, NY: Productivity Press.

Morgan, M. S. (2012). *The world in the model: How economists work and think*. New York, NY: Cambridge University Press.

Morvan, J.-D., & Buchet, Ph. (1998). Sillage. Paris: Delcourt Production.

Naess, A. (1999). *Økologi, samfunn og livsstil*. Oslo: Bokklubbens kulturbibliotek.

Nahapiet, J., & Ghoshal, S. (1998). Social capital, intellectual capital, and the organizational advantage. *Academy of Management Review, 23*(2), 242–266.

Neck, C. P., & Manz, C. C. (2010). *Mastering self-leadership: Empowering yourself for personal excellence*. London: Pearson.

Nelson, R., & Winter, S. (1982). *An evolutionary theory of economic change*. Cambridge, MA: Harvard University Press.

Nietzsche, F. W. (2000). *The birth of tragedy*. Oxford: Oxford University Press.

Nonaka, I., & Takeuchi, H. (1995). *The knowledge creating company: How Japanese companies create the dynamics of innovation*. New York, NY: Oxford University Press.

Nordhaus, W. D. (2013). *The climate casino: Risk, uncertainty, and economics for a warming world*. New Haven: Yale University Press.

North, D. C. (1990). *Institutions, institutional change, and economic performance*. New York, NY: Cambridge University Press.

North, D. C. (1994). Economic performance through time. *American Economic Review, 84*(3), 359–368.

Nowotny, H., Scott, P., & Gibbons, M. (2001). *Re-thinking science: Knowledge and the public in an age of uncertainty*. Cambridge: Polity Press.

Nowotny, H., Scott, P., & Gibbons, M. (2003). Mode 2 revisited: The new production of knowledge. *Minerva, 41*, 179–194.

Nuttall, A. (2009). Rorschach: When telling the truth is wrong. In M. D. White (Ed.), *Watchmen and philosophy. A Rorschach test* (pp. 91-99 [96]). New Jersey: John Wiley and Sons, Inc.

Tingley, K. (2017, February 23). Learning to love our robot co-workers. *New York Times Magazine*. Retrieved from: https://www.nytimes.com/2017/02/23/magazine/learning-to-love-our-robot-co-workers.html

OECD (1996). *The knowledge economy*. Paris: OCDE/GD(96)102.

OECD (1997). *National innovation systems*. Paris: OECD Publishing.

OECD (2008). *OECD Reviews of Innovation Policy: Norway Official Norwegian Reports (2015)*. Productivity – Underpinning growth and welfare. Retrieved from http://produktivitetskommisjonen.no/

OECD (2014). *Education at a glance 2014: OECD Indicators*. Paris: OECD Publishing. Retrieved from http://www.oecd.org/edu/education-at-a-glance-19991487.htm

OECD (2017). *OECD reviews of innovation policy: Norway 2017*. Paris: OECD Publishing.

OECD/Eurostat (2005). *Oslo manual: Guidelines for collecting and interpreting innovation data*. (3rd Ed.), Paris: OECD Publishing. doi: http://dx.doi.org/10.1787/9789264013100-en.

Ogle, W. (1885). Supplement to the 45th Annual Report of the Registrar General of Births, Deaths, and Marriages, in England.

Ólafsson, S. (2011). Icelandic capitalism – From statism to neoliberalism and financial collapse. In Mjøset, L. (Ed.) *The Nordic varieties of capitalism* (Comparative Social Research, Vol. 28. (pp. 1–51). Bingley: Emerald.

Orsato, R. J. (2006). Competitive environmental strategies: When does it pay to be green? *California Management Review, 48*(2), 127–143.

Painter-Morland, M., and Ten Bos, R. (2016). Should environmental concern pay off? A Heideggerian perspective. *Organization Studies* 37(4): 547–564.

Papamichalopoulos, C. (2000). *O Giaponas* [The Japanese]. Athens: Futura (In Greek).

Papamichalopoulos, C. (2008). *O Giaponas. Deuteronomion* [The Japanese. Deuteronomion]. Enati Diastasi, Mytilini (In Greek).

Papastephanou, M. (2010). Aristotle, the action researcher. *Journal of Philosophy of Education*, 44(4), 589–595.

Partanen, A. (2016). *The Nordic theory of everything: In search of a better life*. New York, NY: Harper.

Patel, N. V. (2015). The creepy collective behavior of Boston Dynamics' new robot dog. Retrieved from https://www.wired.com/2015/02/creepy-collective-behavior-boston-dynamics-new-robot-dog/

Pellitteri, M. (2011). Alan Moore, *Watchmen* and some notes on the ideology of superhero comics. In *Studies in Comics (STIC)*, 2(1), 81–91. Bristol: Intellect Journals /Intellect Ltd.

Perez, C. (2002). *Technological revolutions and financial capital: The dynamics of bubbles and golden ages*. Cheltenham: Edward Elgar.

Pesce, M. (2017). Autonomous cars are about to do to transport what the internet did to information. Retrieved from https://www.theregister.co.uk/2017/02/27/autonomous_cars_2040/

Piore, M. J., & Sabel, C. F. (1984). *The second industrial divide: Possibilities for prosperity*. New York, NY: Basic Books.

Plato (1996). *The collected dialogues*. Princeton, NJ: Princeton University Press.

Polanyi, M. (1964). *Science, faith and society*. Chicago, IL: University of Chicago Press.

Polanyi, K. (2001). *The great transformation*. Boston, MA: Beacon Press. (Original work published 1944.)

Polanyi, M. (2009). *The tacit dimension*. Chicago, IL: University of Chicago Press.

Popper, K. R. (1979). *Truth, rationality and the growth of scientific knowledge*. Frankfurt: Vittorio Klostermann.

Porter, M. E. (1990). *The competitive advantage of nations*. New York, NY: The Free Press.

Porter, M. E., & Kramer, M. R. (2011). The big idea: Creating shared value, rethinking capitalism. *Harvard Business Review*, January–February.

Putnam, R. (1993). *Making democracy work: Civic traditions in modern Italy*. New Jersey: Princeton University Press.

Putnam, R. D. (2000). Bowling alone: America's declining social capital. In L. Crothers & C. Lockhart (Eds.), *Culture and politics* (pp. 223–234). New York, NY: Springer.

Putnam, R. D. (2016). *Our kids: The American Dream in crisis*. New York, NY: Simon and Schuster.

Reason, P., & Bradbury, H. (2006). *Handbook of action research: The concise paperback edition*. London: Sage.

Reed, H. & Lansley, S. (2016). *Universal Basic Income: An idea whose time has come?* London: Compass Impact Hub Islington.

Reeve, J. (2009). *Understanding motivation and emotion*. (5th ed.). New Jersey: John Wiley & Sons.

Reinganum, J. F. (1983). Uncertain innovation and the persistence of monopoly. *The American Economic Review*, 73(4), 741–748.

Ricketts, C. (2010, May 27). Tesla paid $42M for NUMMI but doesn't have deal to build cars with Toyota. *Venture Beat*. Retrieved from https://venturebeat.com/2010/05/27/tesla-paid-42m-for-nummi-but-doesnt-have-deal-to-build-cars-with-toyota/

Ritsos, Y., 1982. *You can touch the moisture*. Ta Chartina [Papermade], Kedros, 99 (In Greek).

Robichaud, C. (2008). The joker's wild: Can we hold the clown prince morally responsible? In M. D. White & R. Arp (Eds.), *Batman and philosophy: The Dark Knight of the soul* (pp. 70–81). New Jersey: John Wiley and Sons, Inc.

Robichaud, C. (2009). The Superman exists and he's American. Morality in the face of absolute power. In M. D. White (Ed.), *Watchmen and philosophy. A Rorschach test*, (5–17 [10–13]). New Jersey: John Wiley and Sons, Inc.

Robinson, K. S. (2017). *New York 2140*. London: Orbit.

Rockström, J., Steffen, W., & Kevin Noone. (2009). A safe operating space for humanity. *Nature, 461*(7263), 472–475.

Rodrigues, M. J. (2002). *The new knowledge economy in Europe: A strategy for international competitiveness and social cohesion*. Cheltenham: Edward Elgar.

Rodríguez-Pose, A. (2013). Do institutions matter for regional development? *Regional Studies, 47*(7), 1034–1047.

Rokkan, S. (1967). Geography, religion and social class: Cross-cutting cleavages in Norwegian politics. In S. M. Lipset & S. Rokkan (Eds.). *Party systems and voter alignments*, (pp. 367–444). New York, NY: The Free Press.

Rosenbrock, H. (1989). *Designing human-centred technology: A cross-disciplinary project in computer-aided manufacturing*. London: Springer.

Ryle, G. (2009). *The concept of mind*. London: Routledge.

Sachtouris M. 2000. *Ta Synnefa* [The Clouds], *Poems 1945–1971*, Kedros 93 (In Greek).

Sainsbury, R., Coleman-Fountain, E., & Trezzini, B. (2017). How to enhance Active Citizenship for persons with disabilities in Europe through labour market participation. European and national perspectives. In R. Halvorsen, B. Hvinden, J. Bickenbach, D. Ferri, & A. M. G Rodriguez (Eds.), *The changing disability policy system. Active Citizenship and disability in Europe*, Vol. 1. (pp. 90–107). London: Routledge.

Sampanikou, E. (2004), Enki Bilal, Sarcofagos. Ena Mouseio tou Mellontos [Enki Bilal, Sarcofagus. A Museum of the Future]. In S. Dascalopoulou, et al. (Eds), Mouseio, Epikoinonia kai Nees Texnologies [Museum, Communication and New Technologies]. Proceedings of the First International Conference on Museology – Mytilini 31/05 – 02/06 2002, University of the Aegean – Department of Cultural Technology and Communication, Mytilini, 193-216 [In Greek].

Sampanikou, E. (Ed.). (2017). *Audiovisual posthumanism*. Newcastle: Cambridge Scholars Press.

Sampanikou, E. D. (2001). Science fiction in the world of contemporary visual arts: The European science fiction comics culture. In D. Pastourmatzi (Ed.), *Biotechnological and medical themes in science fiction*, (pp. 438–473). Thessaloniki: University Studio Press.

Sartre, J.-P. (1969). *Being and nothingness*. London: Routledge.

Sartre, J.-P. (2004). *The imaginary*. London: Routledge.

Scase, R. (1977). *Social democracy in capitalist society: Working class politics in Britain and Sweden*. London: Croom Helm.

Schaffer, J., Schleich, H., Reis, A. D. C., & Fernandes, T. C. (2008). *Handling product variety and its effects in automotive production*. Paper presented at the POMS 19th Annual Conference, La Jolla, California, U.S. http://www.labnexo.com/wp-content/uploads/2013/08/pdf-n%C2%BA75-Handling-product-variety-and-its-effects-in-automotive-production.-2008.pdf

Schein, E. H. (1985). *Organizational culture and leadership*. San Francisco, CA: Jossey-Bass.

Schneider, M. R., & Paunescu, M. (2012). Changing varieties of capitalism and revealed comparative advantages from 1990 to 2005: A test of the Hall and Soskice claims. *Socio-Economic Review, 10*(4), 731–53.

Schön, D. A. (1983). *The reflective practitioner: How professionals think in action* (Vol. 5126). New York, NY: Basic Books.

Schumpeter, J. (1976). *Capitalism, socialism and democracy*. London: George Allen & Unwin Ltd. (Original work published 1942.)

Schumpeter, J. (2008). *Theorie der wirtschaftlichen Entwicklung* (transl. 1934, The theory of economic development: An inquiry into profits, capital, credit, interest and the business cycle). London: Transaction Publishers. (Original work published 1911.)

Searle J. (1979). *Speech acts*. Cambridge: Cambridge University Press.

Seino, K., Takezawa, T., Nomoto, A., & Boeltzig-Brown, H. (2017). The diversity management for employment of the persons with disabilities: Evidence of vocational rehabilitation in the United States and Japan. In B. Christiansen & H. C. Chandan (Eds.), *Handbook of research on human factors in contemporary workforce development*, (pp. 333–356). Hershey: IGI Global.

Sejersted, F. (2005). *Sosialdemokratiets tidsalder. Norge og Sverige i det 20 århundre*. Oslo: Pax forlag.

Selznick, P. (2011). *Leadership in administration: A sociological interpretation*. New Orleans: Quid Pro Books.

Serpieri, P.-E. (1986). *Morbus Gravis*. Paris: Dargaud Editeur.

Shotter, J. (2006). Dialogue, depth and life inside responsive orders: From external observation to participatory understanding. In B. Göranzon, M. Hammarén, & R. Ennals (Eds.), *Dialogue, skill and tacit knowledge*. Chichester: Wiley.

Simon, H. A. (1980). *From substantive to procedural rationality: Method and appraisal in economics* (pp. 129–148). Cambridge University Press.

Sinclair, A. (1998). *Doing leadership differently: Gender, power and sexuality in a changing business culture*. Carlton South: Melbourne University Press.

Śliwa, M., Spoelstra, S., Sørensen, B. M., & Land, C. (2013). Profaning the sacred in leadership studies: A reading of Murakami's 'A Wild Sheep Chase'. *Organization, 20*(6), 860–880.

Smith, A. (1976). *A theory of moral sentiments*. Indianapolis, IN: Liberty Press. (Original work published 1759.)

Smith, A. (1976). *An inquiry into the nature and causes of the wealth of nations*. Oxford: Oxford University Press. (Original work published 1776.)

Smith, V. (2010). Review article: Enhancing employability: Human, cultural, and social capital in an era of turbulent unpredictability. *Human Relations, 63*(2), 279–303.

Smith, V. L. (2003). Constructivist and ecological rationality in economics. *American Economic Review, 93*(3), 465–508.

Smyth, E. J. (2000). *Jules Verne: Narratives of modernity*. Liverpool: Liverpool University Press.

Sorgner, S. (2011). Zarathustra 2.0 and beyond. Further remarks on the complex relationship Between Nietzsche and transhumanism. *The Agonist, 4*(2), 1–46. Retrieved from http://www.nietzschecircle.com/AGONIST/2011_08/stefan_sorger.html

Southerland, S. A., Sinatra, G. M., & Matthews, M. R. (2001). Belief, knowledge, and science education. *Educational Psychology Review, 13*(4), 325–351.

Specialisterne (2017). Welcome to Specialisterne. Retrieved from: http://specialisterne.com/

Specter, M. (2017, January 2). Rewriting the code of life. *The New Yorker*. Retrieved from http://www.newyorker.com/magazine/2017/01/02/rewriting-the-code-of-life

Spence, M. (1981). The learning curve and competition. *Bell Journal of Economics, 12*(1), 49–70.

Spreitzer, G. M. (1995). Psychological empowerment in the workplace: Dimensions, measurement, and validation. *Academy of Management Journal, 38*(5), 1442–1465.

Standing, G. (2010). *Work after globalization. Building occupational citizenship*. Cheltenham and Northhampton: Edward Elgar Publishing.

Steenstra, I., Cullen, K., Irvin, E., Van Eerd, D., & IWH Older Worker Research team. (2017). A systematic review of interventions to promote work participation in older workers. *Journal of Safety Research, 60*, 93–102.

Stein, M. (2013). When does narcissistic leadership become problematic? Dick Fuld at Lehman Brothers. *Journal of Management Inquiry, 22*(3), 282–293.

Stewart, I., & Davey, J. (2012). *Seventeen equations that changed the world*. London: Profile Books.

Stilgoe, J., Owen, R., & Macnaghten, P. (2013). Developing a framework for responsible innovation. *Research Policy*, *42*(9), 1568–1580.

Straubhaar, T. (2017). On the economics of a universal basic income. *Intereconomics*, *52*(2), 74–80.

Swedberg, R. (2014). *The art of social theory*. Princeton University Press.

Taleb, N. N. (2009). *The black swan*. Random House.

Tangian, A. (2007). European flexicurity: Concepts, methodology and policies. *European Review of Labour and Research*, *13*(4), 551–573.

Taylor, F. W. (1911). *Principles of scientific management*. New York, NY: Harper & Brothers.

Taylor, R. F. (2004). Extending conceptual boundaries: Work, voluntary work and employment. *Work, Employment and Society*, *18*(1), 29–49.

Teece, D., Pisano, G., & Shuen, A. (1997). Dynamic capabilities and strategic management. *Strategic Management Journal*, *18*(7), 509–533.

The Economist (2010, August 7). Leviathan Inc. The state goes back into business. London: The Economist Newspaper Limited.

The Economist (2013, February 2). The Nordic countries are reinventing their model of capitalism. London: The Economist Newspaper Limited.

Thue, L. (2008). Norway: A resource-based and democratic capitalism. In S. Fellman, M. J. Iversen, H. Sjögren, & L. Thue (Eds.), *Creating Nordic capitalism*. Basingstoke: Palgrave.

Todd, E. (1987). *The causes of progress. Culture, authority and change*. Oxford: Basil Blackwell.

Todd, E. (1990). *L'Invention de l'Europe*. Paris: Seuil.

Tödtling, F., & Trippl, M. (2005). One size fits all?: Towards a differentiated regional innovation policy approach. *Research Policy*, 3(8), 1203–1219.

Torjesen, S., Rodvelt, M., & Landmark, K. (2015). Agder as mutual competence builders. In Johnsen et al. 2015.

Toulmin, S., & Gustavsen, B. (Eds.). (1996). *Beyond theory: Changing organisations through participation*. Amsterdam: Benjamins.

Toulmin, S. (1958). *The uses of argument*. Cambridge: Cambridge University Press.

Toulmin, S. (2001). *Return to reason*. Cambridge, MA: Harvard University Press.

Trist, E., and Bamforth, W. (1951). Some social and psychological consequences of the long wall method of coal-getting. *Human Relations*, *4*, 3–38.

Tuncel, Y. (Ed.) (2017), *Nietzsche and transhumanism: Precursor or enemy?* New Castle: Cambridge Scholars Press.

Tversky, A., & Kahneman, D. (1974). Judgment under uncertainty: Heuristics and biases. *Science*, *185*(4157), 1124–1131.

UN (1948). Universal Declaration of Human Rights, adopted by the United Nations General Assembly in Paris in 1948.

UN (2006). *Convention on the rights of persons with disabilities (CRPD)*. Retrieved from https://www.un.org/development/desa/disabilities/convention-on-the-rights-of-persons-with-disabilities.html

Unwin, T. (2000). The fiction of science, or the science of fiction. In E. J. Smyth (Ed.), *Jules Verne: Narratives of modernity*. Liverpool University Press.

US Government (2013). The White House Office of the Press Secretary For Immediate Release. January 21, 2013. Inaugural Address by President Barack Obama

US Government (2016). *Preparing for the future of artificial intelligence*. Washington: Executive Office of the President National Science and Technology Council Committee on Technology.

Valereto, D. K. (2011), Philosophy in the fairground: Thoughts on madness and madness in thought in *The Killing Joke. Studies in Comics (STIC)*, *2*(1), s /Intellect Ltd, 69–80.

van den Bergh, J. C. J. M. (2008). Optimal diversity: Increasing returns versus recombinant innovation. *Journal of Economic Behavior & Organization*, *68*(3–4), 565–580. doi:https://doi.org/10.1016/j.jebo.2008.09.003.

Vartiainen, J. (2011). The Finnish model of economic and social policy – From Cold War primitive accumulation to generational conflicts? In L. Mjøset, (Ed.). *The Nordic varieties of capitalism. Comparative social research*, Vol. *28*. Bingley: Emerald.

Vernon, R. (1979). The product cycle hypothesis in a new international environment. *Oxford Bulletin of Economics and Statistics*, *41*(4), 255–267.

Vornholt, K., Uitdewilligen, S. and Nijhuis, F. J. N. (2013). Factors affecting the acceptance of people with disabilities at work: A literature review. *Journal of Occupational Rehabilitation*, *23*, 463–475.

Wagner, J., Bolland, B., & McMahon, M. (2002). *Judge Dredd. The day the law died.* London: Titan Books in association with 2000 AD.

Wagner, J., Grant, A., & Bolland, B., et al. (2005). *Judge Dredd. Dredd VS death*. Oxford: Rebellion/2000 AD. (Original work published 1978.)

Weber, M. (1947). *The theory of social and economic organization*. New York, NY: Oxford University Press.

Weber, M. (1978). *Economy and society*. Vols. *1 and 2*. Berkeley, CA: University of California Press. (Original work published 1920.)

Whitehead A. N. (1967). *Science and the modern world*. New York, NY: The Free Press.

Whitehead, A. N. (2010). *Process and reality*. New York, NY: Simon and Schuster.

WHO (2011). *World report on disability*. Geneva: World Health Organization.

Wicken, O. (2005). Diverse regional industrialisation: Norway during the first half of the 20th century. In K. Bruland (Ed.), *Essays on industrialisation in France, Norway and Spain* (pp. 59–80). Oslo: Unipub.

Williams, A. E., Fossey, E., Corbière, M., Paluch, T., & Harvey, C. (2016). Work participation for people with severe mental illnesses: An integrative review of factors impacting job tenure. *Australian Occupational Therapy Journal*, *63*(2), 65–85.

Williamson, O. E. (1981). The economics of organization: The transaction cost approach. *The American Journal of Sociology*, *87*(3), 548–577.

Wilson, D. S., & Kirman, A. (2016). *Complexity and evolution: Toward a new synthesis for economics*. The MIT Press.

Winch, P. (1985). *The idea of a social science and its relation to philosophy*. London: Routledge and Keegan Paul. (Original work published 1958.)

Wind, E. (1986). *Techni kai Anarchia* [Art and Anarchy]. Athens: Nefeli. (Greek transl.)

Wire, B. (2011, February 15). Tesla Motors reports fourth quarter and full year 2010 results. TheStreet. Retrieved from https://www.thestreet.com/story/11009706/3/tesla-motors-reports-fourth-quarter-and-full-year-2010-results.html

Wittgenstein, L. (1953). *Philosophical investigations*. Oxford: Blackwell.

Wolsk, D. (Ed.) (1975). *Experience centred curriculum*. Paris: UNESCO.

World Economic Forum (2016). *The global competitiveness report 2016–2017*. Switzerland.

Yukl, G., & Mahsud, R. (2010). Why flexible and adaptive leadership is essential. *Consulting Psychology Journal: Practice and Research*, *62*(2), 81–93.

Zaccaro, S. J., & Klimoski, R. J. (2002). *The nature of organizational leadership: Understanding the performance imperatives confronting today's leaders* (Vol. *12*). New Jersey: John Wiley & Sons.

AUTHOR INDEX

Amin, A. 52, 62, 265
Argyris, C. 207, 26
Aristotle 88, 89, 91, 92, 97, 101, 217
Asimov, I. 108, 109, 265
Atwood, M. 112
Austin, J. 209, 265

Barney, J. 56, 61, 266
Belasco, W. 108, 109, 266
Bell, D. 9, 266
Berger, P. 27, 266
Beveridge, W. 73, 237, 266
Bloch, M. 25, 26, 266
Bloom, A. 219, 220, 266
Bourdieu, P. 129, 140, 253, 266
Bradbury, H. 218, 220
Bradbury, R. 108
Brödner, P. 210, 266
Burns, T. 204, 212, 266

Christensen, T. 75, 26
Coleman, J. S. 140, 267
Cooke, P. 56, 267
Cooley, M. 209, 210, 267
Corbett, J. M. 210, 267

Descartes, R. 23, 96, 101, 118, 131, 132, 133, 167, 267
Drath, R. 37, 268
Dreyfus, H. & Dreyfus S. 204, 268
Drücker, P. 222, 223, 227, 231, 268
Durkheim, E. 144, 236, 268

Earl, M. 154, 268
Edler, J. 70, 72, 268
Eikeland, O. 88, 89, 90, 218, 268
Einstein, A. 115
Elster, J. 102, 268
Emery, F. 46, 268
Engels, F. 202, 273
Erixon, L. 44, 268

Fagerberg, J. 70, 72, 73, 268
Faulk, R. 108, 109, 269
Feyerabend, P. 88, 129, 269
Florida, R. 9, 55, 56, 237, 269
Foley, R. 101, 269
Ford, M. 2, 3, 9, 269
Freeman, C. 36, 269
Freire, P. 228, 269
Friedman, M. 208, 215, 269
Friedman, T. 52, 269
Fukuyama, F. 24, 27, 35, 269

Gadamer, H.-G. 134, 269
Gibbons, M. 52, 163, 274
Grant, R. M. 56, 270
Gustavsen, B. 188, 193, 211, 221, 270
Guttmann, I. 154, 270
Göranzon, B. 195, 270

Habermas, J. 10, 22, 28, 29, 31, 33, 96, 97, 102, 128, 129, 130, 167, 210, 211, 270
Hall, P. 41, 42, 270
Hawkins, A. J. 109, 270

Author index

Hayek, F. A. 95, 96, 131, 132, 270
Hegel, G. F. W. 24, 130, 270
Heidegger, M. 115, 118, 119, 121, 123, 124, 125, 167, 270, 271
Hirschman, A. O. 26, 271
Hood, C. 75, 271
Horkheimer, M. 170, 271
Hume, D. 92, 131, 132, 169
Huws, U. 240, 271

Jackson, T. 120, 121, 271
Jacobs, J. 41, 271
Johnsen, H. C. G. 134, 136, 188, 198, 206, 231, 271

Kalberg, S. 103, 271
Kant, I. 23, 29, 97, 102, 132, 133, 215, 271, 272
Karlsen, J. 134, 138, 142, 272
Keynes, J. M. 72, 73
Kotter, J. P. 219, 227, 228, 272
Krugman, P. 41, 55, 272
Kuhn, T. 128, 129, 209, 272

Lakatos, I. 129, 272
Larrea, M. 134, 138, 142, 272
Luhmann, N. 212, 273

McGregor, D. 203, 208
Marshall, A. 54, 273
Marx, K. 202, 273
Mintzberg, H. 207, 273
Moore, A. 275
Morgan, M. S. 111, 273

Naess, A. 115, 122, 123, 124, 125, 273
Nahapiet, J. 140, 273
Nietzsche, F. W. 167, 169, 170, 274
Nonaka, I. 52, 274
North, D. C. 35, 274
Nowotny, H. 52, 163, 274

Obama, B. 30, 31
Orwell, G. 112

Partanen, A. 35, 274
Perez, C. 37, 38, 274
Piore, M. J. 41, 275

Plato 88, 89, 97, 101, 132, 169, 219
Polanyi, K. 2, 3, 8, 9, 66, 139, 275
Polanyi, M. 10, 275
Popper, K. 90, 92, 129, 130, 275
Porter, M. 21, 41, 55, 59, 61, 208, 275
Putnam, R. 139, 140, 193, 275

Rasmussen, L. B. 210, 275
Rauner, F. 210, 275
Reason, P. 218, 220, 275
Rokkan, S. 42, 275
Rosenbrock, H. 209, 210, 275
Ryle, G. 138, 139, 276

Sabel, C. F. 41, 275
Sartre, J.-P. 104, 105, 276
Schön, D. 207, 225, 226, 227, 230, 231, 276
Schumpeter, J. 5, 6, 7, 8, 9, 276
Scott, P. 56, 163, 274
Searle, J. 209, 276
Simon, H. 102, 276
Smith, A. 204, 216, 277
Soskice, D. 41, 42
Stalker, G. M. 204, 212, 266
Swedberg, R. 231, 277

Takeuchi, H. 52, 274
Taleb, N. 113, 277
Tangian, A. 44, 277
Taylor, F. W. 204, 207, 277
Teece, D. 56, 277
Todd, E. 26, 40, 42, 277
Tödtling, F. 75, 278
Torjesen, S. 117, 278
Toulmin, S. 10, 129, 209, 278
Trippl, M. 75, 278
Trist, E. 208, 278
Trump, D. 8, 112
Tversky, A. 102, 278

Verne, J. 100, 104, 107, 108
Vernon, R. 56, 278

Weber, M. 102, 103, 204, 207, 217, 220, 278
Whitehead, A. N. 2, 8, 9, 88, 278
Wicken, O. 41, 43, 279
Winch, P. 129, 279
Wittgenstein, L. 92, 209, 279

SUBJECT INDEX

action research 92, 209, 224, 232
Agder 8, 53, 54, 57, 80
agglomeration 41, 54
Anne 244, 251
Apple 7, 153
apprenticeship 236
artificial intelligence 70, 109, 110
automation 37, 60, 154, 161, 206
autonomy 48, 204, 208, 219

banks 18, 43, 162
Belgium 32
belief 10
biotechnology 75, 78
The Black Incal 174
Brexit 18, 263
business schools 215, 216

California 158
Canada 60, 64, 65, 256
capabilities 62
capitalism 5, 8, 9, 37, 55, 56, 73
care 121, 122
car industry 43, 59, 63, 100, 155, 156, 158, 160, 163, 237
Cashhan 182
Catalonia 20
change 3
chaos 10
China 7, 24, 43, 109, 162
Chrysler 157
The City that Never Existed 177
class conflict 9

climate change 59, 116
cluster 36, 53, 55, 59, 60, 61, 67, 80, 81, 120, 163
collaboration 47, 83
collaborative advantage 192, 263
Collateralised Debt Obligations 215
collective knowing 139, 140, 142
comics 168
common sense 12
communitarian 23, 25
communities of practice 62, 68
competence 54, 59, 140
competition 5, 48, 164
competitive advantage 38, 53, 54, 59, 66, 75
complexity 19
constitutional democracy 25, 29
consumerism 8
continuous improvement 153
co-operation 63, 80
co-ordinated market economy 41, 42
co-ordination 74, 77
Corporate Social Responsibility 211, 257
creative class 9
creative destruction 5, 6
creativity 43, 104
cultural practices 35
cultural situatedness 10

data 91, 92, 229
decision making 6, 29, 77, 100, 102, 108, 111, 159
deduction 88, 89, 91, 96, 132
deliberative democracy 23, 25

Subject index

democracy 2, 23, 32, 35, 43, 79, 206, 210, 255
democratic dialogue 142
demographic change 12, 40
Denmark 20, 26, 27, 42, 43, 44, 45, 162
Detroit 60, 237
Deuteronomium 180
dialectic 24, 131, 132
dialogue 31, 89, 96, 142, 143, 165, 188, 190, 197, 199, 201, 203, 206, 210, 221
Dialogue Seminar Method 190, 195
Dialogue Seminars 189, 190, 191
diesel 222
digitalisation 37, 70, 81, 152, 153, 159
Digital Norway 80
disability 235, 243, 244, 245, 246, 247, 248
disruption 1, 2, 4, 5, 13, 32, 69, 70, 79, 82, 98, 112, 155, 164, 184, 199, 213, 233, 256
diversification 71, 77, 81
diversity 39, 40, 48, 156, 229
Druuna 173
dualism 167

Eastman Kodak 4
ecology 103, 115, 123
e-commerce 154, 155
ecosophy 122, 123
education 40, 74, 75
electric cars 99, 157, 222
embeddedness 66, 89, 97, 188
employee driven innovation 46, 47
employment 71
engagement 62, 187, 197
engineering 58
Enlightenment 2, 3, 7, 26, 30, 102
entrepreneurial discovery processes 77, 78
entrepreneurship 5, 36, 59, 202
environment 8, 18, 53, 118
epistemology 4, 90, 97, 128, 132, 133, 145
equilibrium 10
Ericsson 43
Estonia 76
ethics 90, 118, 222, 223
ethos 218, 223
Euromanga 168, 176
European Commission 21, 22
European Union 20, 21, 28, 31, 32, 43, 76, 77, 78, 163, 194, 209, 243
experience 64
Eyde 53

falsification 92
financial crash 215
financialisation 215

Finland 20, 26, 28, 42, 43, 44, 256
fisheries 42, 43, 75
flexibility 47, 57, 116, 156, 157, 159, 215
flexicurity 44
Ford 6, 19, 100, 157
foreign direct investment (FDI) 46, 74
forest and wood 192, 197
France 100, 205
Frank 249, 250, 251
Fukushima 6
functionalism 130

General Motors 60, 65, 66, 157, 158, 237
genetic engineering 109, 110
geography 55
Germany 109, 158, 163, 222, 239, 240
globalisation 2, 3, 7, 9, 12, 39, 49, 51, 52, 53, 54, 56, 59, 61, 66, 72, 229, 245
governance 56, 77, 139
grammar 92, 93, 94
Greece 19
Greenland 20
growth 116, 117

Hanseatic League 20
healthy worker effect 241
healthy workplaces 47
hermeneutics 133, 134
Horizon 2020 163
Houston 57
Human-Centred 12, 206, 209, 210
Humanism 23, 166, 169
human rights 2, 21, 30
Hungary 26

Iceland 20, 28, 44
ICT (information and communication technology) 75, 153
IKEA 193
ILO (International Labour Conference) 238, 239, 240
imagination 99, 101, 104, 105, 106, 110, 111, 113
improvement 54
inclusion 212, 213, 245, 248, 249, 250, 253
induction 10, 89, 92, 132
industrialisation 3, 8, 9, 45
Industry 4.0 38, 154, 155, 159, 160, 161, 235, 237
inequality 3, 12, 40, 42
innovation 5, 6, 12, 21, 35, 36, 43, 48, 53, 57, 72, 156, 157, 212
innovation policy 69, 70, 72, 75, 78, 79, 82, 259

instability 12
institutional stability 49
instrumentalisation 118
instrumental thinking 114, 116, 117, 119, 123
instruments 95
integration 7, 11, 29
intervention 91
iPhone 7, 151, 153
Ireland 20
Italy 19, 32, 41, 256

The Japanese 178
Judaea 19
Judge Dredd 172

Kalmar 189, 190
Kalmar Union 20, 27
The Killing Joke 171, 172
knowledge creation 64, 143
knowledge diffusion 53, 134, 138
knowledge economy 75, 79, 81
knowledge management 52, 53
knowledge sharing 53, 58, 64
knowledge society 88, 98, 213, 245
knowledge system 146
knowledge transfer 52, 53, 63, 65, 97, 205
Kodak moment 4, 5, 10, 12, 13, 32, 43, 49, 82, 98, 112, 124, 146, 164, 184, 193, 199, 213, 216, 233, 256, 263
Kongsberg 80
Kristiansand 57, 63, 64

leadership 61, 116, 145, 214–30
League of Nations 21
Lean 75, 223–6
learning 62, 63, 145
Lego 43
liberal market capitalism 41
libertarian 23, 25
life cycle 56
Linnaeus University 188, 189, 191, 193, 196, 197, 201
local knowledge 51, 52, 54, 63

manufacturing 48, 55, 63, 155, 158, 205
market 6, 12, 23, 37, 70, 71, 74, 164, 259
mass production 3, 5, 8, 37, 158, 160, 202, 237
mathematical logic 2
mental illness 251, 252
Mercedes 157
Metabarons 175
methodology 11, 77, 79, 126, 127, 143, 146

Mexico 65
migration 12, 18, 40
model 12
modernisation 2, 38, 70, 72
modernism 22, 30, 91
modernity 22, 24, 26, 27, 33, 35, 48
monopolistic competition 41
multicultural society 40
multinational companies 51, 52, 53, 56, 59, 61, 62, 66, 67, 68
myths 10

nationalism 26, 28, 30, 31
nation state 18, 20, 22
NATO (North Atlantic Treaty Organisation) 28
network 36, 54, 55, 56, 57, 59, 80, 140, 152, 161, 163, 196, 203
New Public Management 75, 199
Nissan 19
Nokia 43
Nordic Model 28, 32, 35, 38, 42, 43, 221
normative 92, 117, 122, 125
Norway 8, 18, 20, 26, 27, 28, 41, 42, 43, 44, 45, 46, 47, 57, 64, 65, 70, 72, 73, 74, 79, 81, 100, 120, 157, 162, 203, 204, 206, 213, 243
Norwegian General Agreement 45
nuclear power 6, 107, 117

observation 91
occupational health and safety 241
OECD (Organisation for Economic Co-operation and Development) 36, 75, 76, 81, 189, 190, 243
oil and gas 42, 43, 46, 57, 71, 75, 81, 204
ontology 132, 133
optimism 2, 120, 125, 259
organisational learning 62, 199
organisations 149, 201, 202

paradigms 128
participation 42, 46, 56, 134, 203
phenomenology 133
philosophy 11, 121, 127
philosophy of social science 127
photography 4
planning 73, 95, 196
pluralism 87, 88, 92, 98, 146, 259
Poland 26, 58, 76
policy 71, 162
politics 17, 22, 23, 50, 76
Porsche 157
positivism 88, 127, 204

post-capitalist 237
Posthumanism 166, 167, 182
postmodernism 22, 88, 91
post-nationalism 3, 17, 18
post-positivism 128
practical knowledge 223
practice 56, 92, 93, 213
precarity 48, 235
prediction 12, 103, 108, 142
process industry 53
product 72
productivity 2, 76, 79
progress 2
proximity 63

Quadruple Helix 197, 198
quality 155, 199
Quality Circles 204
rationality 6, 10, 30, 95, 96, 98, 100, 101, 102, 112, 219

Raufoss 59, 60, 61, 80
reason 96
reconstruction 2, 3, 8
reflection 54, 97, 107, 190, 223, 232
region 21, 31, 71, 139
regional development 41, 59, 77, 189, 190, 209
regional innovation policy 75
regional innovation system 36, 55, 75, 77, 79, 83
regulation 38, 45, 47, 73, 74
relevance 98
Renaissance 25, 26, 122
re-nationalism 3, 17
renewable energy 116, 117
republican 23
research and development 57, 60, 63, 71, 74, 75, 80, 155, 162
resilience 42, 43
responsibility 140
restructuring 57
re-thinking assumptions 261, 262, 263
robotics 2, 48, 70, 109, 110, 151, 162
Rome 21
rules 94
Russia 20, 43

Saab 43
The Sarcophagus 178
Scandic hotels 253–5
Scandinavia 19, 20, 28
science fiction 100, 104, 110
Scotland 20, 32
security 251

shared value 211
Silicon Valley 71, 164
Sissel 242, 243, 252
skill 55, 88, 159, 197, 212, 224, 235, 243
Skill and Technology 189, 193, 194, 199, 209
Småland 189, 193
small and medium sized business 73, 193
social capital 36, 139, 140
social cohesion 40
social construction 9, 143
social dumping 48
social inclusion 235, 236
social knowledge 89, 96
social learning 187, 188
social media 8
social science 2, 3, 9, 10, 88, 127, 128, 146, 259, 263
society 47
socio-technical systems 201, 208
Spain 20, 32
specialisation 70, 76, 77, 78, 83
stability 10
strategy 19, 56, 67, 68, 75, 153, 155, 162
structural change 34
Student Circles 193, 194, 198
Student Union 191, 192, 194, 197, 198
sustainability 2, 6, 7, 9, 12, 78, 114, 115, 116, 124, 213, 259
sustainable development 44, 53, 192
sustainable regional development 188, 189, 192, 194, 200
Sweden 20, 26, 27, 42, 44, 45, 47, 72, 73, 74, 188, 189, 205, 209
systemic change 3, 6, 8, 260
systems thinking 144

tacit knowing 11, 58, 61, 62, 63, 65, 190, 198, 199, 210, 221, 227
tacit knowledge 88, 139, 190, 197, 212
technology 149, 151, 152
technology change 12, 35, 153, 165
technology push 75
territorial development 138, 140
Tesla 6, 100, 112, 120, 157
time 101, 229, 230
Total Quality Management 204
Toyota 19, 153, 157
trade unions 18, 41
transformation 3, 4, 8, 46, 81, 104, 118, 188
Transhumanism 167, 169, 182
tripartism 44, 46, 47

Triple Helix 197
trust 43, 48, 56, 120
truth 138, 141
Trygve 247, 248, 250, 251
Turkey 26

Uber 112
UK 18, 163
uncertainty 12, 18, 188
understanding 11, 91, 94, 102, 116, 134, 211, 213, 232
unemployment 47
unhealthy worker effect 236, 241, 242
unhealthy youth effect 245
United Nations 21
Universal Basic Income 256, 257
universalism 28, 30, 48, 89
university 19, 71
unpredictability 10, 12
urbanisation 2, 8, 40

USA 30, 31, 35, 57, 58, 60, 71, 109, 110, 222, 239

validity 98, 126, 127, 143, 219
value chain 161
varieties of capitalism 41, 42, 71
Vienna 19, 20
Vocational Teacher Education 188, 195, 196, 200
Vocational Teacher Network 195
Volvo 43

Watchmen 171, 172
welfare 2, 3, 5, 42, 46, 235
well-being 42, 115
Westphalia 19
work 12, 46, 146, 149, 234
WTO (World Trade Organisation) 52

zero hours 235